Are You the Problem Solver?
Or the Problem?

In the high-pressure, high-stakes world of enterprise technology, you're either the problem solver—or you're the problem. When the network goes down, when a schedule-buster bug can't be found, when your personal machine crashes, when a whole department of new workstations must be configured before tomorrow, *time* is the enemy. Even if you have the skill to get the job done, if you can't get it done *fast*, you'd better step aside and let someone else take over.

We created the Coriolis *Black Book* series to give you a weapon in this War Against Time. Our goal is to gather essential technical facts and techniques on the title topic into single, focused volumes, and make those facts easy to find when you most need them. (And if you need additional focus, we also publish the Coriolis *Little Black Book* series, in which more compact volumes zoom in on significant technical niche topics, like the Windows 98 Registry.)

Every Coriolis Black Book is highly structured and focused on its topic, so you won't be furiously flipping past pages and pages of irrelevant material. Every fact and solution we publish is designed to be located quickly, with minimal searching.

Each chapter begins with an in-depth technical discussion of the topic at hand. After the technical discussion are the solutions, which tell you step-by-step how to handle even the ugliest technical problems.

We've put a lot of thought into making this format work—but we won't know for sure how well it works until you let us know. Please write to us and tells us whether the Black Book formula delivers: **blackbookinfo@coriolis.com**.

If you're reading this, you're probably on the firing line and need to return to the battle. Good luck—with this book in your hand, time is now on your side!

Jeff Duntemann
Editorial Director
Coriolis Group Books

Keith Weiskamp
Publisher
Coriolis Group Books

ACTIVE SERVER PAGES

Black Book

Al Williams, Kim Barber,
and Paul Newkirk

Publisher
Keith Weiskamp

Acquisitions
Stephanie Wall

Marketing Specialist
Jody Kent

Project Editor
Mariann Hansen Barsolo

Production Coordinator
Wendy Littley

Cover Design
Anthony Stock

Layout Design
April Nielsen

CD-ROM Development
Robert Clarfield

Active Server Pages Black Book

Limits of Liability and Disclaimer of Warranty

The author and publisher of this book have used their best efforts in preparing the book and the programs contained in it. These efforts include the development, research, and testing of the theories and programs to determine their effectiveness. The author and publisher make no warranty of any kind, expressed or implied, with regard to these programs or the documentation contained in this book.

The author and publisher shall not be liable in the event of incidental or consequential damages in connection with, or arising out of, the furnishing, performance, or use of the programs, associated instructions, and/or claims of productivity gains.

Trademarks

Trademarked names appear throughout this book. Rather than list the names and entities that own the trademarks or insert a trademark symbol with each mention of the trademarked name, the publisher states that it is using the names for editorial purposes only and to the benefit of the trademark owner, with no intention of infringing upon that trademark.

The Coriolis Group, Inc.
An International Thomson Publishing Company
14455 N. Hayden Road, Suite 220
Scottsdale, Arizona 85260
602.483.0192
FAX 602.483.0193
http://www.coriolis.com

Library of Congress Cataloging-In-Publication Data
Williams, Al, 1963-
    Active Server Pages black book /by Al Williams, Kim Barber, and Paul Newkirk.
        p. cm.
    Includes index.
    ISBN 1-57610-247-5
    1. Active server pages   2. Web sites – Design. I. Barber, Kim,
1953-   , II. Newkirk, Paul.   III.Title
TK5105.8885.A26W56   1998
005.2'76--dc21   98-23300
                                                                                                           CIP

Printed in the United States of America
10 9 8 7 6 5 4 3 2

an International Thomson Publishing company

Albany, NY • Belmont, CA • Bonn • Boston • Cincinnati • Detroit • Johannesburg • London
Madrid • Melbourne • Mexico City • New York • Paris • Singapore • Tokyo • Toronto • Washington

About The Authors

Al Williams

Al Williams is the author of many programming books including *MFC Black Book*, *Developing ActiveX Web Controls*, and *Developing ActiveX Controls with VB5* (all from Coriolis). He also writes regular columns for *Visual Developer Magazine* and *Web Techniques*. A long-time consultant, Al has worked on everything from tiny embedded systems for the Department of Defense, to mainframe computers supporting the International Space Station. Al's Web sites have won several awards, including the itmWeb Five Star Selection award. In addition to writing and consulting, Al teaches seminars all around the country and frequently speaks at conferences such as Software Development and Web Development.

Kim Barber

Kim Barber is a senior network engineer for CompuServe and an accomplished instructor and programmer. He is a graduate of Hawaii Pacific University and has written and taught several courses on programming, Web development, and the Internet. Additionally, he spent 20 years as an Intelligence Analyst in the U.S. Army. Kim is currently a Project Manager at CompuServe Interactive Services Inc. in Columbus, Ohio.

Paul Newkirk

Paul Newkirk is a project and process manager for CompuServe Network Services' Network Product Engineering group and an experienced technical trainer. He has eleven years' experience in the computing and telecommunications industries. In the nine years of his first career, he documented systems and network software for companies including CompuServe and AT&T/Bell Labs. When the Internet became the Web, he noticed it looked a lot like TROFF and NROFF, and he jumped right in. His Unix and networking background paved the way for building numerous sites and teaching others how to do the same. Paul built on this expertise and leveraged it in a second career as a technical trainer and then training supervisor. He has taught HTML; coordinated the design and delivery of courses, such as an in-house, five-day course called Web Camp (designed to bring legacy programmers to the Web); and vendor-supplied courses on Java and ActiveX.

Acknowledgments

You'd think three authors would be plenty of people to write a book. Nope. Like a movie, there are plenty of people who contribute to a book like this, even though there are only a few names on the cover. If you ever watch the credits at the end of a movie, they stretch on and on and on. Everyone is there, even the carpenter's girlfriend's hairstylist, I think.

Well, this page is the closest thing we get to rolling the credits. Since it comes in the front of the book instead of the back, we can't list every single person. It's like the Academy Awards—take too much time, and you'll find the band playing, and they cut off your microphone. Still, there are some people we'd like to especially thank.

All three of us would like to thank all the Coriolis people who worked on the book, including Mariann Barsolo, Wendy Littley, Robert Clarfield, Anthony Stock, and April Nielsen. Thanks also to copyeditor Bruce Owens, proofreader Mary Millhollon, and typesetter Deb Shenenberg. They make us look good, and we appreciate it.

Special thanks go to Bob Kaehms and Mike Floyd at Web Techniques for their permission to adapt the ASP Top 10 Tips for this book.

Since this book was a team effort, there are a few people each of us would like to thank individually.

I would like to acknowledge the help of my co-authors, Al Williams and Kim Barber. I'm also indebted to Al Cline for letting me use his computing resources when I unexpectedly ended up in need. I'd especially like to thank Al Williams for asking me to do this book with him and helping so much along the way.

—Paul Newkirk

I would like to thank Al for giving me the opportunity to work with him on this book. I would also like to thank Paul who is always a source for good ideas and humor. And last, but very important, I would like to thank my family for their patience and understanding.

—Kim Barber

Thanks to Kim and Paul for letting me drag them into my special brand of madness. Of course, I'm always grateful to my family for putting up with yet more deadlines. I also want to say thanks to the families of my three sisters-in-law: Shirley Ransom, Betty Turner, and Wanda Hicks for not giving me a hard time when I was writing much of this book while visiting them in Henderson, Kentucky.

—*Al Williams*

Table Of Contents

Introduction

Only a few inventions in history have held as much revolutionary potential as the World Wide Web. Oddly enough, nearly all these inventions have involved communications. In the Middle Ages, for example, books were rare and jealously guarded. The effort required to copy a book by hand was extraordinary. Most people couldn't read and didn't care to because books were so scarce. The idea of a public library where practically anyone could check out a book for free was ridiculous.

About 1450, Johannes Gutenberg devised a system for printing with movable type (a new idea in Europe but not in China). In almost no time, the printing press spread across Europe. Soon, books were plentiful and affordable, fostering enormous changes in politics, religion, education, and economics. (Too bad Gutenberg didn't make enough money out of it to pay his bills, however.) Only a few other inventions have had such a widespread and long-lasting effect.

The television was another world-shaping invention. Educator, babysitter, and entertainer, television is a major part of modern life and has changed the way we look at the world.

Of course, both of these inventions have carried a price. For every Shakespearean play there are hundreds of comic books. For every "Sesame Street" there is a "Beavis and Butthead." The printing press and television have often been vehicles for spreading propaganda. Certainly, television has the potential for making us better informed, but clearly it has also reduced the effectiveness of political elections—there is no free lunch.

The parallels to the Web are astonishing. Imagine if, in 1450, everyone had their own printing press (and a means to distribute their books, which is at least as important). Imagine if, in the 1960s, everyone had their own TV station. That's the promise of the Web. That's also the problem with the Web.

Sure, it's fun to imagine all the great things you can do on the Web: educate, inform, and entertain. But the Web also provides an easily accessible worldwide outlet for hate groups and other unsavory types.

Even those with good intentions can spread misinformation on the Web. When you read something in a book or see something on TV, it may be wrong, but it had to fool a lot of people to get in that book or on television. On the Web, people can say anything they want.

I have often said that the Web reminds me of what would happen if you blew up the Library of Congress. You would be surrounded by fragments of information in no discernible order, some fact and some fiction, and have no way to tell them apart.

As a Web designer, you are creating some of these fragments. How can you make your fragments more compelling than the rest?

The best way to make your fragment stand out is to make it demand attention. Make it active. Better still, make it interactive. That's exactly what this book is about. By using scripting on both the client and the server, you can build powerful interactive Web pages that will help your site stand above the all the others. This can help you both attract visitors and increase repeat ones.

Of course, the possibility also exists that the Web is nothing more than a fad. Many people said the same thing about television. The truth is, TV wasn't a fad, but it did evolve into something quite different from what most people expected. That will probably be true of the Web as well. The Web that your children will use will be very different from the Web you use today. The future of the Web is interactive, and active pages are the first step in making that future a reality.

Why This Book Is For You

The three of us sat down to discuss writing this book out of frustration. All of us have been involved, in one way or another, in teaching Web development (as well as actually doing it). The frustration was that we saw no books that really captured the subject matter we were teaching. So we decided to write one.

What does this mean to you? It means that, in this book, you'll find a snapshot of Web development as it exists today. Practical examples show you how today's sites run and how you can get the same results easily and quickly with commonly used tools.

If you want to develop exciting, interactive Web pages, you need to understand this technology, and this book is all about helping you achieve that understanding. Even if your job is to simply design or manage (but not create) a Web site, you should understand what these new technologies make possible. This book will help you there as well.

The Road Less Traveled

Don't you find it annoying to buy clothes that are one-size-fits-all? It might be more honest to call them "one size fits no one." Books are a lot like that, too. It's tempting to tell you that each word in this book is a priceless gem that you should read carefully. But the truth is that different people need different information from a book.

No one path is the correct one to take through this book. You can pick and choose chapters on the basis of your interests and skill level. For example, if you already are an HTML wizard, you probably won't want to read Chapter 2 (and might not read Chapter 3). If you have little or no experience developing Web pages, you'll probably want to read each chapter carefully.

Because this book is part of the Black Book series, you'll find that most chapters conclude with a Practical Guide. This section encapsulates the main ideas of the chapter in a cookbook-like format. These sections will be useful as a reference when you start working on your own projects. You might also find it helpful to skim the Practical Guide to decide whether you want to read the entire chapter. If you find that you know most of the information in the Practical Guide, you can probably skip the corresponding chapter and move to the next one.

With that in mind, here are some suggestions:

If you are interested in:	Read chapters:
Java	4, 6, 7, 14
VBScript	4, 5, 7, 14
Server-side scripting	9, 10, 11, 13
HTML	2, 3

(continued)

If you are interested in:	Read chapters:
Dynamic HTML	8
Developing custom objects	13, 14
Case studies	12

If you are new to HTML (the language you use to write Web pages), you'll want to carefully read and absorb chapters 2 and 3.

What Do I Need?

To work with some of the examples in this book, you need only an appropriate Web browser. Microsoft's Internet Explorer 4.0 supports all the features (including dynamic HTML). However, many of the examples will work with version 3.0. The Java examples will also work with Netscape Navigator. If you have the appropriate plug-ins, you can also run VBScript and ActiveX controls with Navigator.

Many of the examples in this book, however, require you to run a Web server. This can be as simple as Microsoft's Personal Web Server (PWS) or as complex as the full version of Microsoft's Internet Information Server. A few of the examples that require a server will probably run on any other server. However, because PWS is free and can run right on your own computer, this shouldn't pose a problem.

Chapters 13 and 14 discuss writing your own objects (which is an advanced topic). For these chapters, you'll need either Visual Basic 5 or Visual J++, depending on which objects you're interested in. The examples that show the Microsoft Personalizatin System (MPS) require Microsoft Site Server or a version of IIS that supports MPS.

Get On With It

So why are you still here? Read Chapter 1, then go back to the table above and jump right in. The future is waiting for you to create it.

The World Wide Why

The Web is incurring some fundamental changes, and you need Web scripting—particularly with Active Server Pages—to stay on top of them.

Paul Newkirk

Notes…

Chapter 1

This chapter provides an overview of the growth of the Web and describes why everyone who wants to be a player (whether as programmer, graphic designer, or Web wizard) will have to master Web scripting and active content. This is an insider's view not only of the history of the Web but also of the transitions in the industry, the latest and most significant of which is active Web content. Scripting, in its various forms, will help you meet and exceed the rapidly expanding expectations of Web surfers. If you already know the history, how Web scripting fits into the future, and why you want active content, skip ahead to the chapters that will help you become an expert in this pivotal technology. Of course, even seasoned veterans might get some new insights into the Web and Web scripting from this chapter.

There are many ways you can script a Web page. As you might guess, this book focuses on Active Server Pages (ASP). Currently ASP works with Microsoft's Internet Information Server (IIS), but it is possible that other Web servers may soon support it. Although this book is mostly about ASP, you'll find you have to do some scripting on the user's computer to get the job done. Therefore, you'll also find a great deal of information about client-side scripting in JavaScript and VBScript. Armed with these tools (and a good understanding of HTML), you'll be ready to conquer the Web.

Even Grandma Has A URL

By now, it is a foregone conclusion that the Web is here to stay, and everyone wants to be on it. Grandparents are getting email addresses, every other commercial in any medium (radio, TV, print) contains a reference to a Web page, and most "talking head" announcers have gotten past sounding ill-informed when giving a URL ("That's at HTTP..., say, wait a minute folks, what is the rest of this stuff?"). I was in San Diego for a convention, and my waitress, after finding out I was a professional geek, started telling me about the multimedia system for which she had just plunked down two grand. She had a vague idea what the numbers were (one number we figured out was the amount of RAM she had) but no idea what they meant (yet she happily spent a large chunk of change to get there). Friends and neighbors who used to have no interest are now keenly signing up, and some have used whatever tools they can find to create rudimentary Web pages.

Days Of Change

For those of us who have been in the industry for some time, these are heady and exciting times. Not only has the consumer base and popular recognition changed and exponentially expanded, but, as anyone who remembers surfing the Net using only tools such as FTP, Telnet, or RN will tell you, the Net is changing, and it is doing so at a more fundamental level. That change is what this book is about.

From Democracy To "Corpocracy"

When *the Net* became *the Web*, there was something excitingly democratic about it. All of a sudden, you didn't have to wear suspenders and tie-dyed shirts and grunt over a command-line interface to play on the Net. It was graphical, and all that command-line stuff was hidden behind the scenes (for the most part). Perhaps even more democratic than that, the standard currency of the Web—HTML—was just a text markup language that almost anyone could understand, so almost anyone could have a Web page. Even more enjoyable was that the playing field was now level. Billy Bob's page on exciting facts about minnow gills was just as big, spiffy, and accessible as the pages of companies with 200,000 employees.

This is exactly the problem with the Web today. There is almost too much of a good thing. A Web site put out by a one-woman part-time business has the potential to look every bit as good as one put out by a Fortune 10 corporation. There is so much content on the Web that visitors tend to hop from one site to another as they surf, never lingering for long at any one place.

How can you make your site stand out? How can you attract and retain visitors? How can you make visitors want to return and become repeat visitors? Just having a Web site isn't enough anymore. Having great content helps, but nothing sells steak better than the sizzle. Today's successful sites must look good, provide interaction, and capture the interest of people who are accustomed to watching million-dollar special effects on a big-screen home theater.

As the big companies (and the big company wannabes) start pouring money into their Web sites, they find they have to make their sites bigger and better to compete, and this raises the bar for everyone searching for cost-effective ways to make their sites just a little bit better.

Upward And Onward From Plain HTML

Now that the first-generation Web is stabilizing, we are on the cusp of the next stage of the Web's evolutionary development: Web scripting and active content. HTML is fine for static pages if all you want to do is to put up documents and pictures—a magazine or book, if you will—on your computer screen (with very nice linking capabilities). However, with regrets to Billy Bob's minnow page and all its wonderful friends, the big boys are here now, and they are using programming to make Web pages not only stand out but also leap ahead by fully exploiting the competitive possibilities of the medium.

Just like a command-line interface to the Net looked ancient compared to the Net using Mosaic's browser, plain HTML pages are beginning to look as archaic next to the jazzed-up sites using active content and scripting. As Microsoft belatedly noticed the Web (and hurriedly made up for it), the technical battleground has moved from the PC-based environment to the Web-based environment. If you are a Web wizard (which can span a lot of definitions, depending on who you ask), a programmer, or someone who wants to join in the fun, Web scripting is the main tool you will need to master to stay ahead.

Web And Net Changes

One of the charming things about the early Internet was all those sites where volunteers put up things such as guitar chord progressions in ASCII for every song known to humanity. (How they found the time to put those things up is amazing.) As the Net became the Internet, most of those long-tenured and popular sites were shut down one by one as people from the real world began to pay attention and perceive a need to stake out and defend turf there (such as attorneys representing recording music copyright holders). The latest similar change is the wholesale migration to the Net by programmers, graphic designers, database specialists, "marketroids," and any other mainstream corporate specialists.

From the first time I used a browser (early Mosaic), I was told how you could include sound and video. It was a cool idea, but no one at that time had anything more than a speaker good for a few beeps every now and then. Now people have sound cards, speakers, and AVI players (and you don't have to be an expert in setting up MIME types to use them). Also, people from the visual and musical worlds are jumping in to add their expertise with bouncy buttons, sounds, and visual effects that sometimes make you think the fake, amazing, and overly simple "computer" representations in Hollywood films aren't as far-fetched as you thought.

After all, what good is looking at simple text pages when you have a multithousand-dollar computer on your desk? What good is the medium if you can't push the potential of your PC and the limitations of the networks to the extent that they (and your imagination) let you?

Two Pivotal Questions

Ultimately, most professionals should ask two questions about the World Wide Web, even if only for curiosity: (1) How much of the future Web is going to have some kind of subscription basis for use, and what will the model for that system be? and (2) What kind of tools and development environment will software developers, hackers, Web wizards, and graphic designers use to take us warp speed into the future?

The first question is very difficult to answer now. It is clear that the advertising revenue of some sites is currently insufficient to support their Web presence. Already, some sites featuring material ranging from X-rated subjects to national news now place virtual bouncers at their doors to collect entry fees. It is unclear whether the advertising model will improve enough to support the costs of all who want to provide Web sites or if the number of sites charging fees will continue to increase. The current advertising model can support smaller sites with fewer employees, but it cannot cover the salaries, vacations, bonuses, 401(k) plans, office rent, and Fourth of July parties for the entire staff of a New York Times or ABC. Until it can, some larger-site managers will have to decide whether to charge access fees, take a loss, or reduce content. But it is hard to tell what the eventual model will be—advertising with access to larger revenue streams or more pay-as-you-go sites.

The second question is a lot easier to answer. With strict programming on one end of the spectrum (in languages such as C, C++, Pascal, and COBOL) and HTML on the other, a vibrant new middle ground is expanding rapidly in both directions like never before. That middle ground is scripting. Although you can use traditional languages for scripting, newer scripting languages are evolving that drive toward both ends, becoming more powerful and easier to use at the same time.

Scripting: The New Currency Of The Web

The currency of programmers, Web wizards, and graphic artists is now Web scripting. Although scripting has always been used to add that little extra bit of functionality to the Web (often CGI scripts using PERL), the new wave is something much more exciting. It encompasses new languages, new tools, and ever-increasing new capabilities within the browsers, servers, and languages themselves.

Plain HTML Ignores And Excludes The Web's Potential

If the Web remained just a method to display text (as it would with just HTML), with only a few odd programming gadgets (such as counters and so on) thrown in for good measure, the Web would probably exclude at least two-thirds of its potential. There are only so many publishers and companies that want to make documents available. The real power of the Web is (and will continue to be) when you hook it up to databases and create custom applications that let you do any kind of business you want.

The ability to search through databases for information on the Web adds another layer of people who have valid business reasons to be on the Web (people who have data, not just documents, for sale). The ability to alter those databases adds two more large layers (traditional retail businesses and industries that depend on exchanging information electronically, whether internally or externally). For example, on one hand, you will have every merchant doing business on the Web, on the other, you will have corporations with large, diverse sales forces using Web browsers to get leads, log sales, and fill out customer orders (instead of using proprietary systems). "So, you want to order $20,000 worth of pharmaceuticals? Let me enter your order on our Web page, get confirmation we have it in stock, and get you the shipping date."

Then, there is that unknown element for businesses new to the Web—they either will enhance their profit margin by exploiting the potential of the Web in new ways, or they will create profit centers by satisfying the demands created in this new arena.

Web Scripting Is The Answer

Web scripting is the medium that will let you meet all these current and future needs. Simply stated, you must become a master of Web scripting to solve today's and tomorrow's problems, to push the envelope, and to stay competitive (or even kick some tail). The sooner you do it, the better for you and your company.

This book, of course, covers ASP scripting. Is this the only answer? No. But it may be the best answer available today. ASP runs with Internet Information Server (IIS) and Personal Web Server (PWS). Microsoft gives both of these products away. That means you can easily get started using ASP with no investment. Although it is free, ASP is fairly robust and scalable. You can write an example on your laptop computer and deploy it on a giant NT Web server with little difficulty.

Once you get used to writing active pages, you won't ever be satisfied with ordinary, static Web pages again. More importantly, your users are already dissatisfied with them. In academia, the battle cry is "Publish or perish!" On the new Web, it might well be "Interact or perish!"

Where Do You Jump In?

Even if you take the time to learn what all the acronyms and tools and funny "product groups" are (for example., what does ActiveX contain—a product, a language, a frame of mind?), how do you pick which ones to master? Should you master them all? Perhaps most important, where do you get solid real-world examples that you can use today?

The truth is, if you sat down and took the time to learn Java, Visual Basic, VBScript, JavaScript, JScript, OLE, COM, CGI, ActiveX, Server Side Includes, ISAPI, DHTML, PERL, and so on one by one, even in 21-day increments you would be left foolishly in the dust. The technology would pass you by, and you wouldn't have time for anything else.

So, how do you understand and keep track of it all? How do you quickly pick and choose between the languages, technologies, and tools while making informed decisions? How do you find out about the tips, tricks, techniques, and gotchas without trudging through it and finding out the hard way, firsthand? How do you get *the edge* without having to read every white paper and read-me file in existence? Trust me, even in white papers and help files, there are a lot of times when little, hidden, apparently harmless notes are really camouflaged warnings or notices. The world would be a much simpler place if companies just used a more clearly and explicitly stated "this feature doesn't work very well" with a follow-up enumeration of the places where the feature will bite you. It's not as if we won't find out anyway.

Start With An Expert Who Has Done It Before

One of my favorite technical questions I have been asked is, How do you learn X-Windows? If you have a Unix background, the answer is like a lot of things in Unix (and life): It's a little complex. First, go borrow someone else's profile or environment configuration file. Second, you figure out what each of the pieces is doing.

Finally, you start modifying the ones you understand and try to make them do what you want them to do (once you have a feel for it). If you are lucky, you ask a patient guy next door to answer your tough questions when you get stuck. Strange as it may seem, the Internet and, by extension, the Web have strong roots in Unix and the Unix mentality. The best (fastest and sometimes only) way of learning has been to start poking around and asking the guy next door some questions—that is, unless a couple of the guys next door happened to sift through all the documentation, paid all the dues and hard knocks firsthand, organized the resultant information, and put it all together in a handy book.

Fortunately, that is what you have in this book. So many things in the computer business are best learned by "osmosis." You soak it up from someone who has already driven up the learning curve. In this book, you'll see the examples that capture what we have learned about this technology.

What HMTL Gave Us

HTML gave us text, graphics, links, movies, sound, colors, tables, and even forms (although to do anything with forms you had to do some scripting). HTML is based on 30-year-old technology (GML and then SGML), and even with pretty colors and backgrounds and table layouts, "straight" HTML pales in comparison to the effect and power of scripted pages. After all, a scripted page is just HTML with something extra.

What HMTL With Early Scripting Gave Us

Early scripting (for example, CGI) gave us:

- Image maps

- Forms to collect data and submit that data to the server

- Counters

- Rough access to databases

- Some custom applications

Although these are certainly good things, it is difficult to do everything using the unwieldy programs and PERL scripts you usually use with CGI, which is a lot like Tinkertoys. Some people have built working computers that can play tic-tac-toe with nothing but Tinkertoys. However, you don't want to do that. It is too much work for the average person.

What You Get With Modern Scripting

CGI and other early scripting gave us ways to broaden the horizon of the Web, but the current tools give vastly different capabilities:

- Buttons that change when you pass over them

- Pages that know who you are and remember things about you

- Pages that respond to your actions by dynamically changing

- Pages that are dynamically generated to reflect, for example, changing information

- Easier access to databases

- "Libraries" of predefined objects that make your life easier

- Predefined objects that do not require you to learn all the underlying technology

- More modern development environments

- Special sound and video effects (going to a movie instead of a magazine stand)

- The ability to easily create "applications" for the Web with program flow and logic

This book contains examples, such as a restaurant reservation page and the infamous Elvis sighting page, which has been used in training classes all over the country. These show not only how two-dimensional the HTML-based Web looks next to the Active content-based Web, but also all the important points for using the same technology to meet your own needs. If plain HTML is like 1950s black-and-white TV, Active content is circa 1990s home theatre with surround sound.

Languages You Can Learn For Scripting

You can essentially use any language for Web scripting (PERL, C, C++, FORTRAN, and so on) as long as you know how to hide it in a control or otherwise integrate it with the browser or server. However, modern script languages that are built in to the browser and server (such as VBScript and JavaScript) are better integrated and much easier to use.

This book uses primarily VBScript and JavaScript in its examples: VBScript because it is an easy-to-use scripting language and JavaScript (not JScript) because it is universally recognizable. On the server side, the examples use Microsoft's ASP scripting, usually with VBScript (although ASP will support JScript). These tools are all easily accessible and widely used to create exciting, dynamic Web sites.

Choices You Have To Make (Client, Server, Browser, Language)

When you decide to do scripting, you will need to make decisions regarding the scripting language, whether you want your script to run on the client or the server, and so on. Most of these decisions have the potential to cut off certain segments of your audience. For example, if you choose to do client-side scripting using VBScript, you have shut out a large number of people, because Netscape Navigator doesn't do VBScript without an add-in. This book will help you make the best decisions.

What Do You Have To Learn?

Scripting isn't for grandma—at least not most people's grandmas. You have to learn HTML and HTML forms. A solid understanding of advanced HTML is useful. You can also use Dynamic HTML in many cases. You have to understand what procedures, arrays, objects, data types, and operators are. You have to learn the choices you need to make to get your job done for your audience. This book is the best place to start learning.

Gratuitous Roswell Rumor

You will no doubt notice that this chapter spared the obligatory, normal, chronological and acronym-filled history of the Internet/Web. If you want one, search the Net (they usually go like this: ARPA, DARPA, Urbana Champaign, CERN, boom!). Instead, I decided to include a gratuitous rumor about some history I made up. In my version, the whole thing was stolen from an alien ship recovered at Roswell, N.M., by the U.S. Air Force. For grins, tell some friends. Act serious. Silly rumor-mongering can certainly be more fun than recanting the real history (yet again). As an example, explain to Web newbies, with a straight face, "Yeah, the TCP/IP protocol and distributed network topology really came from some books found by the Air Force on an alien ship in New Mexico." Maybe someday the rumor will even get back to me ("Son, it is true that the Internet is really alien technology") or will be reported in the tabloids.

If nothing else, have some fun with Web scripting and this book. The challenges and opportunities in this new and quickly changing environment are exciting, fun, and certainly never dull.

Chapter 2

HTML In Review

Before you leap into ASP and other scripting techniques, it pays to have a solid grounding in HTML.

Al Williams

Notes…

Chapter 2

Have you ever dealt with someone who doesn't speak your language but has one of those little books that supply common phrases in your language and theirs? Very frustrating, isn't it? Of course, those with the book usually have no idea how to pronounce what they want to say, and the book's phrases often aren't exactly what they want to say anyway.

The British comedy troupe Monty Python has a hilarious sketch about a man with a phrase book that was purposely wrong. Instead of asking a store clerk for matches (or something), he exclaims, "I will not buy this record, it is scratched!" Eventually, the conversation deteriorates to the point that the man is arrested, and the publisher of the book winds up on trial for deliberately misprinting the book.

This sketch reminds me of computers. Each program has its own unique file format. In the old days, it was especially frustrating to try to interchange data. I once worked for a firm that was completely sold on WordPerfect (version 3 or 4). Too bad I was a firmly entrenched WordStar user (back from CP/M days, even). There was no end to the frustrations that caused. Sure, WordPerfect had a phrase book for WordStar (well, a conversion filter), and WordStar came with a program that could export and import WordPerfect, but somehow those never worked exactly right. Too bad you couldn't put those software publishers on trial.

Interchanging across platforms is even worse. Even if the same program is on a PC and a Mac, good luck trading data between them. This is a central issue with the Web. The Web consists of many different kinds of computers: Unix workstations, minicomputers, PCs, Macs, Power PCs, and there is probably even a Commodore 64 out there somewhere. How can you trade anything other than plain text between all these machines?

HTML (Hypertext Markup Language) is the *lingua franca* of the Web. Web content, ranging from the simplest personal home page to a state-of-the-art virtual reality extravaganza, uses HTML to define the appearance of the page. All Web browsers are supposed to understand HTML. Also, HTML is forgiving so that if someone sends you something you don't understand, you can just skip it and hope for the best. This allows older browsers to display some content even if the document is for newer browsers.

Of course, HTML by itself isn't powerful enough to build virtual reality venues, but it is powerful enough to contain objects (such as ActiveX objects or Java applets) that can do anything you can dream up.

There have been entire books written on how to create HTML, but this chapter shows you enough HTML to get started and try a few things. You can use this chapter as a reference or to refresh your understanding of some of the finer points. More advanced topics appear in the next chapter, and you'll find dynamic HTML in Chapter 8.

Of course, there are many tools that create HTML for you without much effort on your part. Still, if you want to do anything out of the ordinary, you'll need to know HTML, so you might as well dig right in and get started. Even the best tools won't do everything you need. Also, it isn't unusual to have to tweak automatically generated HTML to get the results you want.

By the way, HTML started as a subset of SGML (Standard Generalized Markup Language), which was designed to transfer documents between systems. If you know SGML, you might find that you practically know HTML already.

The Basic Structure

HTML files are really just ASCII text files. By convention, they use the .HTML extension unless DOS is involved, in which case the .HTM extension is the standard.

Ordinary text in an HTML file appears as ordinary text in the produced document. What could be easier? The magic comes into play when you add tags to produce special formatting. Most tags come in pairs so that they affect the text between them. For example, to indicate boldface, you use the **<B>** and **</B>** tags:

```
<B>This is bold text</B> This is not!
```

The starting tag has no slash, but the ending one does. In a few special cases, you can omit the ending tag, but usually you need it. For example, the preceding line needs the **</B>** tag so that the remaining text is not in bold. By the way, tags are not case sensitive. You could just as well use **** and **** in the preceding example.

Some tags take parameters that appear *inside* the angle brackets. Others are required by the HTML specification but not required by common browsers. Like most other things involving computers, HTML is subject to some interpretation.

An HTML Document

An HTML document has several standard elements. Some of these elements are optional in some cases, but all of them are available if you want to use them. Here is the structure of a correctly formatted HTML document:

```
<!DOCTYPE HTML PUBLIC "-//W3C//DTD HTML 3.2//EN">
<HTML>
<!-- A comment - these can go anywhere-->
<HEAD>
<!-- Header information (e.g., the page title)-->
</HEAD>
<BODY>
<!-- Main text, consisting of headings, paragraphs, and images-->
</BODY>
</HTML>
```

The first line is technically a comment and is frequently left off. If it is present, it informs newer browsers about which version of HTML the document uses (3.2 in this case).

Notice that the entire visible content appears between the **<HTML>** and **</HTML>** tags. Although this is officially correct, most browsers display any file with an .HTM or .HTML extension as HTML, even if it doesn't contain these tags.

The first portion of the HTML document appears between the **<HEAD>** tags. This is for special information pertaining to the entire document. You can use the **<TITLE>** tag in the **<HEAD>** section, for example, to set a title for your page. Keep it 64 characters or fewer if you expect it to be visible in its entirety.

Another tag that can appear in the **<HEAD>** section is the **<BASE>** tag. This tag has no closing tag; it appears by itself. You can use it to specify the address of the page. This is helpful if someone copies your page (such as to a local machine). If someone tries to follow a link and the browser can't find it, it will search relative to the address specified in the **<BASE>** tag. Any time you need to specify a URL in a tag, you use the **HREF** parameter, as in:

```
<BASE HREF=http://www.coriolis.com/made_up.html>
```

It isn't strictly necessary, but some pages place an **<ADDRESS>** tag pair after the **</BODY>** tag. The intent of this tag is to place information about the page's authorship, revision date, and so on at the bottom of the page. When you see a line at the bottom of the page that reads:

```
Last modified: April 1, 1998. Send comments to webmaster@coriolis.com
```

that text is probably inside a pair of **<ADDRESS>** tags.

You can enter special characters by using an ampersand (&). This is especially important for the less than (<), greater than (>), and ampersand (&) characters, because these have special meaning to the browser. It is also important for currency and other non-ASCII characters that you may not be able to easily enter from the keyboard. You can use a letter name followed by a semicolon. For example, **<** is the less than (<) character, and **>** the greater than (>) character. Alternately, you can use the sequence **&#nnn;** where **nnn** is a decimal character code from the ISO Latin-1 character set. Table 2.1 shows a list of common character names. Character names, by the way, are one place where HTML is case-sensitive.

Table 2.1 Common character names.

Name	Character
<	Less than (<)
>	Greater than (>)
&	Ampersand (&)
©	Copyright (©)
** **	Nonbreaking space
"	Quotation mark (")
®	Registered trademark (®)
­	Soft hyphen

Inside The Body (With Apologies To Asimov)

Within the body of the document, the browser wraps all normal words into one long paragraph—unless you tell it otherwise. This makes sense because you can't know how wide the user's screen is. It would be a bad idea, but you could put one word on each line of your HTML source, and the browser would take care of wrapping it into a paragraph.

When you want to start a new paragraph, use the **<P>** tag. Technically, you use this tag to start a paragraph and the **</P>** tag to end it. However, very few people actually use the **</P>** tag because it is optional.

Sometimes, you will want a line break inside the same paragraph. For this, you use the **
** tag to start a new line. This tag has no corresponding ending tag. For example, to format an address, you might write:

```
Coriolis Group Books<BR>
14455 North Hayden Road #220<BR>
Scottsdale, AZ 85260<BR>
```

You can format text in a variety of ways. The best way is to use a logical formatting attribute. You tell the browser what you want to do, and it figures out how to represent that format. For example, if you tell the browser you want strong emphasis (using the **<STRONG>** tag), it will probably render the text in boldface. Table 2.2 shows the common logical attributes and common ways that browsers render them. Notice

Table 2.2 Common logical attributes.

Tag	Name	Use	Often rendered as ...
<CITE>	Citation	References to books	Italic
<CODE>	Code	Source code	Monospace
<DFN>	Definition	Definition of a word	Italic
<EM>	Emphasis	Special emphasis	Italic
<KBD>	Keyboard	Text the user should type	Bold/monospace
<SAMP>	Sample	Sample output	Monospace
<STRONG>	Strong	Strong emphasis	Bold
<VAR>	Variable	Placeholder text	Italic

that the browser may elect to show different items in different colors or to use a user-defined style, so don't count on the appearance of these items to be consistent. Naturally, all these tags have a corresponding closing tag.

Sometimes, you will want more control over the appearance of your text. For this, you use the physical attribute tags shown in Table 2.3. These allow you to specify exactly how the text should look, if the browser is capable of producing the effect you desire.

You can nest attributes. For example, if you wanted bold underlined text, you might use:

```
Try <B><U>ActiveX</U></B>
```

Be sure to place the closing tags in the reverse order of the starting tags. Otherwise, some browsers may get confused. Again, you can't be sure the browser will respect your wishes. A text-based browser on Unix, for example, might not be able to show bold text (or it may elect to put it in reverse video). It is hard to know exactly what each browser might do.

In addition to normal paragraphs, HTML can create paragraphs in six different styles for headings. You may use these as headings for different sections of the document. Actually, you may use them for anything you like. You may also use them in any order, or you don't have to use them at all. The tags are **<H1>** through **<H6>** (and, of course, the usual closing tags).

You might often want to place lines between sections of your documents. Printers (that is, people who print things, not computer printers) call these lines *rules*. HTML allows you to use the **<HR>** tag (by itself) to insert a horizontal rule in the text. This is better than drawing a line with ASCII characters (or even a graphic) because you don't know how wide the user's screen is.

Table 2.3 Physical attributes.

Tag	Name	Description
<B>	Bold	Heavy-face text
<I>	Italic	Italic typeface
<U>	Underline	Line drawn beneath text
<TT>	Teletype	Monospace text

In addition to the header styles, HTML also provides the **<BLOCKQUOTE>** and **<PRE>** paragraph tags. The **<BLOCKQUOTE>** style sets off text in some way (usually by using indentation and italics). The **<PRE>** style implies that the text is preformatted. The browser does *not* wrap text in a **<PRE>**-style paragraph but shows it exactly as it is in the HTML file. This is useful for source code. Usually, a **<PRE>** paragraph appears in monospace type. You can specify the width of the text in characters by using the **WIDTH** parameter to the **<PRE>** tag. Don't forget the closing tags **</BLOCKQUOTE>** and **</PRE>**.

Images And Objects

Of course, the big selling point of the Web is graphics. The **<IMG>** tag is the ordinary way to insert a graphic in your document. However, the **<OBJECT>** tag will also insert graphics (among other things). But, because the **<OBJECT>** tag is new, most pages still use the **<IMG>** tag for simple graphics. Many browsers don't support **<OBJECT>** yet, and those that do may not support it completely.

Each **<IMG>** tag requires an **SRC** parameter to name the file that contains the image. This file name can be a full-blown URL or just a file name if the file is in the same location as the Web page (or its base address). Because some browsers don't show graphics (or users will turn graphics off), it is a good idea to also specify the **ALT** parameter, which specifies showing some text in case the image does not display. Here's a typical image statement:

```
<IMG SRC="PIX1.GIF" ALT="The first picture">
```

Normally, an image acts like a single character in your text. If you don't want things to appear after your image, you'll need a **
** or **<P>** tag following it. You can also control the alignment of text around the image by using the **ALIGN** parameter. This parameter can take one of three values: **TOP**, **BOTTOM**, or **MIDDLE**. If you don't use an **ALIGN** parameter in your **<IMG>** tag, the text will line up with the bottom of the image.

Of course, you could also insert the same image with:

```
<OBJECT DATA="PIX1.GIF">
</OBJECT>
```

The **<OBJECT>** tag is more flexible because it can insert typed data (like a GIF file) or an object. Table 2.4 shows a summary of parameters the **<OBJECT>** tag accepts.

Table 2.4 Object tag parameters.

Parameter	Description
ALIGN	Alignment properties
BORDER	Size of border (0 = no border)
CODEBASE	Location to download object from
CODETYPE	Type of object
DATA	Data to use with object (object may be implied by type)
DECLARE	Don't create object until referenced
HEIGHT	Height of object
HSPACE	Horizontal space around object
ID	Name of object
NAME	Name used in forms
SHAPES	Use client-side image map to create anchors
STANDBY	Message to display while loading
TYPE	Type of data (if not implied by file extension)
USEMAP	Use an image map to create anchors
VSPACE	Vertical space around object
WIDTH	Width of object

The **WIDTH** and **HEIGHT** parameters allow you to specify the desired size (which need not match the actual size). This allows you to scale up a small image (which transfers faster). You can specify sizes in pixels or in the units found in Table 2.5. For example, to make an image two inches square, you would specify "2in" in both parameters.

It is recommended that you supply the **WIDTH** and **HEIGHT** of all images. This allows the browser to correctly lay out the page the right away. If you don't supply a size, the browser reserves a very small place for the graphic and then recomposes the page when it actually loads the picture. This causes the page to jump around and is very distracting to users.

Table 2.5 Unit suffixes.

Suffix	Description
%	Percentage of display area
pt	Point (72 points per inch)
pi	Picas (6 picas per inch)
in	Inches
cm	Centimeters

Lists

HTML supports several types of lists. These are similar to paragraph styles. The most common types of lists use the **<LI>** tag to denote the beginning of a list element. To create a numbered list, use the **<OL>** (ordered list) tag. For example:

```
<OL>
<LI> Item 1 </LI>
<LI> Item 2 </LI>
</OL>
```

This produces what you see in Figure 2.1.

If you prefer a bulleted list, use the **<UL>** (unnumbered list) tag (see Figure 2.2). You can also get a more compact list with some browsers by using **<MENU>** or **<DIR>**.

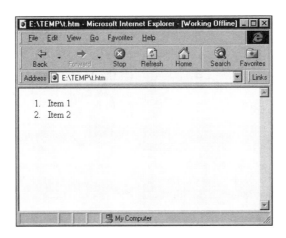

Figure 2.1

A numbered list.

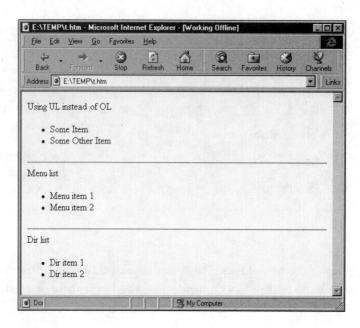

Figure 2.2

Some unnumbered lists.

Items in a menu list should not exceed one line of text. The **<DIR>** list items shouldn't exceed 20 characters so that the browser can form columns, if it has that capability.

There is another kind of list that HTML supports—the description list. This type of list uses text instead of a bullet and may be used for lexicons or encyclopedia-style entries. The **<DL>** tag starts the list. You begin each text "bullet" with the **<DT>** tag. After the text, place a **<DD>** tag (not a **</DT>** tag). Then follow with the text that goes with that pseudo-bullet. There is no **</DD>** tag; just start another **<DT>** entry or end with **</DL>**. Some browsers will attempt to place short text bullets on the same line as the other text if you specify the **COMPACT** parameter to the **<DL>** tag.

For example, suppose you have the following HTML:

```
<DL>
<DT>Megatarts<DD>Stratagem spelled backwards
<DT>Yoodoo<DD>Popular person in songs ("no one can love me like yoodoo")
<DT>Neutron bomb<DD>Bomb that
kills people, while leaving property intact (see also, mortgage)
</DL>
```

This would create a display like the one in Figure 2.3.

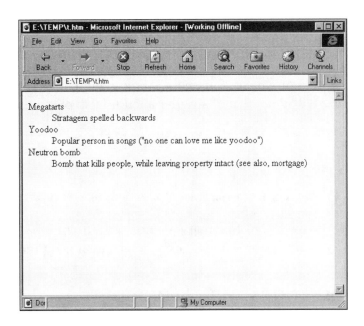

Figure 2.3

A definition list.

Hyperlinks

The *H* in HTML stands for hypertext, and the Web wouldn't be the same without links, would it? Each link has two parts: a presentation part (text or graphics) and an invisible part (the *anchor* that specifies where to go).

The **<A>** tag inserts anchors. The presentation portion can be any mix of text or graphics you like. This allows you to create very sophisticated links, because you can use any text or HTML commands you like in the presentation. Here is a simple link:

```
To continue click
<A HREF="http://www.coriolis.com/nextpage.htm">here</A>
```

When you click the word *here*, the browser jumps to the correct URL. Of course, many people think it is amateurish to create a link that says "click here," but this is just an example. Usually, the browser will show the link word underlined (and possibly in a special color). Of course, you can also use graphics as the presentation portion:

```
<A HREF="http://www.coriolis.com/p1.htm"><IMG SRC="clickme.gif"></A>
```

You can also use anchors to name a spot in your document. For example:

```
<A NAME="Summary">My Conclusions</A>
```

This line creates an anchor named "Summary." You can jump to it by using a number (#) character in the **HREF** portion of another anchor tag. For example:

```
<A HREF="#Summary">Jump directly to summary</A>
```

or

```
<A HREF="http://www.coriolis.com/report.html#Summary">See summary</A>
```

The first example jumps to the Summary anchor on the same page. The second example jumps to a new page and finds the Summary anchor on that page.

Image Maps, Forms, And More

There is much more to HTML. For example, you can divide a single graphic into multiple anchors or use a background graphic. You can use tables and multiple windows (frames). You can create forms and process them on your server. You can also add sounds, scrolling marquees, and—well, you get the idea.

With each new browser release comes new HTML features. One of the best ways to get information about HTML is from the Web itself. Technical specifications, tutorials, and even software are available to help you create HTML. For the latest specifications for HTML, check out **www.w3.org**. After all, what better place to find information about the Web than on the Web?

Practical Guide To

HTML

- Creating An HTML File
- The Parts Of An HTML Document
- Inserting Special Characters
- Controlling Spacing
- Starting A New Paragraph
- Formatting Text
- Adding A Horizontal Line Or Rule
- Inserting An Image
- Scaling Graphics
- Creating A Numbered List
- Creating An Unnumbered List
- Creating A Description List
- Linking To Another Page
- Defining An Anchor
- Linking To An Anchor

Creating An HTML File

Many choices exist today for editing HTML files. Many Web authors who do a lot of low-level HTML simply use Notepad. However, most people will want a slightly higher-level interface. Microsoft makes several HTML editors, including Visual InterDev (aimed at low-level HTML authors) and FrontPage. FrontPage allows you to work with a page as it will look when it is done or to work directly with HTML. Internet Explorer 4 also includes FrontPage Express, a stripped-down version of FrontPage.

Several other tools are also available from other vendors. HoTMetaL Pro (from SoftQuad) and HotDog (from Sausage Software) are just two of these. In addition, many other products can now generate HTML, even though that is not their primary function. For example, many word processors can now work with Web pages directly.

The Parts Of An HTML Document

Although most browsers aren't very picky, there is a particular format that HTML documents should follow. The first line defines the HTML version employed and the language. It should look like this:

```
<!DOCTYPE HTML PUBLIC "-//W3C//DTD HTML 3.2//EN">
```

Next, there is an **<HTML>** tag. Everything that appears between this tag and the corresponding **</HTML>** tag constitutes the document. The **<HEAD>** tag is usually the first section after the **<HTML>** section. This area of the file contains information about the document (such as the title and the base URL).

The main portion of the HTML file lies between the **<BODY>** and **</BODY>** tags. This is where ordinary text, hyperlinks, graphics, and so on appear.

Inserting Special Characters

Because HTML interprets many characters in a special way, there must be an escape mechanism to allow you to insert any character without it having any special meaning. For example, suppose you want to compose a line that looks like this:

```
Is 10<20?
```

The problem is that the browser will assume the "<" character is the start of a tag. Here, it is just a less-than sign. To solve this problem, you need to use an escape sequence (in this case, **<**) to stand in for the special character. You can find a list of common escape sequences in Table 2.1 (although many others are available).

You can also use a special escape sequence to specify a character by its decimal character code. For example, an uppercase A is code 65, so you could write:

A

This is the same as placing an uppercase A in your HTML document. Of course, there isn't much reason to do this for an A, but there are characters you might wish to specify this way.

Controlling Spacing

Sometimes, you will just *have* to have a real space. HTML usually consumes multiple white space into a single space, but what if you really want a legitimate space? One answer is to use the special escape sequence ** **.

Another way to control spacing is to enclose your text in one of the tags that doesn't reformat your text (such as **<PRE>** or **<PLAINTEXT>**). Of course, this also changes the appearance of that text, which may not be desirable.

Starting A New Paragraph

Because the browser consumes white space, your document will wind up as one long line of text, wrapping at the margins. Of course, you really want to break things into paragraphs. Usually, you do this by means of a paragraph tag (usually **<P>**). If you want to break the line but not start a new paragraph, use **
**. The distinction is usually subtle, but situations will arise in which it is important to break a line without starting a new paragraph.

Other paragraph tags exist that have different styles. For example, the **<H1>** tag starts a first-level head.

Formatting Text

There are two approaches you can take to formatting text. The first is to decide what kind of text you are formatting and ask the browser to do something appropriate. The second approach is to simply ask the browser for a specific type of formatting.

Table 2.2 shows the tags you can use to define a type of text. The browser then formats the text in some way that it thinks is appropriate. Of course, you can never know exactly what the browser will do.

Table 2.3 shows the physical formats you can request. You use these tags when you want absolute control over the appearance. However, some browsers may not be able to render these formats, in which case the text just appears normal. Of course, modern browsers on graphical operating systems like Windows display these as requested. The problems arise with browsers limited to text-only displays.

Adding A Horizontal Line Or Rule

Among people who design pages, there is fierce debate over rules (horizontal lines that break up sections of text). Many respected print designers think that you should never use rules. Others think that rules are acceptable on the Web. You can decide for yourself. However, if you want to create a rule, simply use the **<HR>** tag. This tag sets a thin line across the entire width of the page.

A nice effect is to make the line smaller than the page and center it. You can do this with the following code (assuming you want the rule to be 80 percent of the page width):

```
<CENTER>
<HR WIDTH=80%>
</CENTER>
```

You can also use a graphic for a rule (see the next section), but, again, you won't know how wide the browser's screen is. You must either set a particular size or scale the graphic. Scaling often ruins the graphic's appearance (it depends on the graphic). If you decide to set a certain size, you can at least center the graphic so it will look acceptable on larger screens.

Inserting An Image

You can insert an image using the **<IMG>** tag. You can also use the **<OBJECT>** tag, but because all browsers don't support it, you are better off using **<IMG>** for images. You must use **<OBJECT>** for certain things (such as ActiveX controls) but not for images.

The **<IMG>** tag is very simple. You supply a file name (or a URL) with the **SRC** parameter. You can optionally provide the height, width, and some text to associate with the graphic.

Although these parameters are optional, you should include them. Browsers that can't show graphics (or that have graphics turned off) will display the text (specified with the **ALT** parameter). You should also provide the size of the graphic so the browser doesn't have to lay out the page several times as it loads graphics.

Here is a typical image in an HTML file:

```
<IMG SRC="ourlogo.gif" WIDTH=200 HEIGHT=200 ALT="Our Logo">
```

Because the **SRC** parameter is a simple name, the browser will request it from the same place the document resides. However, you could just as easily put a whole or partial URL to use a graphic from anywhere on the Web.

Scaling Graphics

The size you provide to the **<IMG>** tag need not match the actual size of the graphic. If it doesn't, the browser scales the image to match the selected size. This can be useful if you want to use a graphic as a rule, for example.

Suppose you create a graphic 20 pixels high by 1 pixel wide that has a variety of shades of red in it. You could transform this into a nice-looking rule with this HTML:

```
<IMG SRC="redrule.gif" HEIGHT=20 WIDTH=100% ALT="Section Break">
```

There are other reasons you might want to scale a graphic. For example, you might load a large image but display it only as a thumbnail. Of course, the large image will still load more slowly than a real thumbnail, but then the image will be completely in the browser's cache, making subsequent display faster.

Creating A Numbered List

To create a numbered list (like the one in Figure 2.1), simply begin with the **<OL>** tag. Surround each list item with **<LI>** and **</LI>**, and end the list with **</OL>**.

Creating An Unnumbered List

To create an unnumbered list (like the one in Figure 2.2), simply begin with the **<UL>** tag. Surround each list item with **<LI>** and **</LI>**, and end the list with **</UL>**. You can also use **<MENU>** or **<DIR>** instead of **<UL>**, which may display somewhat differently on certain browsers.

Creating A Description List

A description list is a handy way to show definitions of words, as in a glossary (see Figure 2.3). These are simple to create using the **<DL>** tag. Place a **<DT>** tag in front of the word you want to define and a **<DD>** tag ahead of the definition.

Linking To Another Page

When you want to put a hyperlink in your page to another URL, use the **<A>** tag. This tag defines where the link goes. Whatever text or graphic you put between the **<A>** and **</A>** tags is what the user clicks on to travel to the new page.

Use the **HREF** argument to specify the URL you want to jump to when the user clicks the link. For example:

```
<A HREF="http://www.coriolis.com">Coriolis Web Site</A>
```

Defining An Anchor

You can define a particular spot in your document by using the **<A>** tag in conjunction with the **NAME** parameter. Hyperlink anchors can refer to the named anchors to select a portion of your document. Here's an example:

```
<A NAME="Summary">My Conclusions</A>
```

Linking To An Anchor

You can link to named anchors in the current page or link to an anchor on a different page. Suppose you have a page that has information for three years: 1997, 1998, and 1999. You might have your document look like this:

```
Navigation:<BR>
<A HREF="#YR1997">1997</A> <A HREF="#YR1998">1998</A>
<A HREF="#YR1999">1999</A><BR>
<!--begin 1997 data -->
<A NAME="YR1997"></A>
<H1>1997</H1>
. . .
<!--begin 1998 data -->
<A NAME="YR1998"></A>
<H1>1998</H1>
. . .
<!--begin 1999 data -->
<A NAME="YR1999"></A>
<H1>1999</H1>
```

You can also link to one of these anchors from outside the document. Suppose the data is the file YEARDATA.HTM. From another document, you could write:

```
<A HREF="http://www.al-williams.com/YEARDATA.HTM#YR1999">
View 1999 Projections
</A>
```

Advanced HTML

*Knowing advanced HTML tags
and tricks will lead you to
Web scripting.*

Paul Newkirk

Notes...

Chapter 3

If you read Chapter 2 or are familiar with the information it contains, you should know that basic HTML is little more than a system for formatting text for display by a browser. From that chapter, you will now leap to the core of using more-advanced HTML tags as well as some tricks that are still the bread and butter of most of the Web. From here, you will leap to the new core—Web scripting.

Almost anyone with some computer background has worked with something that looked and worked like HTML. If you have experience in Unix, you used NROFF or TROFF. You might be familiar with SGML, of which HTML is a subset. What is modestly different are the specific tags used, and that takes only a little bit of learning. What is exceptionally different are the new tag attributes and techniques that allow you to operate in and take advantage of the graphically aware, interactive, Internet-connected environment, rather than formatting for print.

Using Arguments With Tags

Most HTML tags let you use arguments to further expand their capabilities. For example, from the simple **<HR>** tag, you can create **<HR SIZE=4 WIDTH=70% ALIGN= LEFT NOSHADE>**. In paired tags, such as the **<H1>...</H1>** tags, arguments are enclosed in the first of the paired tags. For example, **<H1 ALIGN=CENTER>My Heading</H1>** shows how attributes are included in the first of a tag pair.

As you try to do more with HTML, you'll notice that most of the fun, control-type stuff happens within the argument area of the tags. Although an exhaustive list of tags and arguments is not included in this book, you can find one online in a variety of places, including **www.w3.org/TR/REC-htm32** or **www.microsoft.com/workshop/ author/newhtml/default.htm**. Refer to this chapter's Practical Guide for examples of how to perform specific tasks.

If you want to do something in HTML with a tag, an argument likely exists that will let you do it. As tags and HTML specifications evolve rapidly, you have to read the latest news about them practically every day to keep up with them all. However, the newer tags and arguments continue to make your life easier and your pages more fun. For example, when specifying colors, you once had to find the hex RGB (Red, Green, Blue) value for the color (described later in this chapter). Now, you can use an argument such as **COLOR=RED** inside the **<FONT>** tag (instead of **COLOR="#FF0000"**).

Making Your Pages Prettier (Bargain Shopper Overview)

Almost anything is more attractive than plain text on a Web page. There are some fundamental tricks you can use to make Web pages more stylish that even the most graphically challenged Web apprentice can understand.

Changing Page Backgrounds

Backgrounds were one of the first features to add pizzazz to Web pages. Backgrounds began as gray, then parchment colored, then pebbles in a stream, and so on. Everyone was well-versed in using ASCII menus, so these new backgrounds looked amazing. You can still use these techniques (in the **<BODY>** tag), which are described in this chapter's Practical Guide, but use them with caution. Most professional or large corporate sites shy away from funny backgrounds, and with good reason. For one, they often make text more difficult to read. For another, some browsers let you override the backgrounds and colors of a page. This can create problems, for example, if you used a black, star-field background with white text and users decide to override all backgrounds to make them white on their browsers (leaving white text on a white background).

Microsoft Internet Explorer 4 does not allow you to override the backgrounds, whereas Netscape Navigator 4 still does. The final word is that backgrounds are an easy way to make your page look nice with very little effort, but use them with knowledge of their limitations and pitfalls. Of course, you can still get into trouble with the star field and Internet Explorer if the user changes the text to black.

Using Fancier Bullets, Rule Lines, And Buttons

You have seen how to make bulleted lists (using **<UL>**), rule lines (**<HR>**), and images (**<IMG SRC="file.gif">**). It is fairly easy to combine these for some nice effects, and you can make your own or find thousands of free samples on the Web.

Plain old bullets are fine for paper, but for the Web, you can use marbles, smiley faces, or pretty much anything. Just throw away your unordered list set of tags, and use the **<IMG SRC>** tag, text or links, and breaks to get some fancy-looking buttons.

For fancier rule lines, throw away the **<HR>** tag, and use the **<IMG SRC>** tag. As with buttons, you can create your own rule line images or get some of the thousands available on the Web. You can discard your plain old rule lines and find ones with marble textures, wild colors, and even movement (if your graphic is an animated GIF file).

It does not take much to extrapolate from using graphics as bullets to set off a text list or a bunch of links to figuring out how to effectively use the graphics themselves as links (or buttons). You can make your own button graphics using tools that almost every computer has natively (such as Microsoft Paint), use inexpensive shareware (such as LView), or use an Internet search engine using the words *icons* and *buttons*. See this chapter's Practical Guide for more details.

One major caveat for these tricks: Use graphics over text when possible (a picture paints a thousand words), but avoid using gratuitous or incomprehensible graphics. For example, I once found a great button of a dog with tread marks from a car across its sprawled body. I was amused by its "roadkill on the information superhighway" meaning but decided it was both gratuitous and unintuitive (what sensible thing would *that* link to without words to explain it?), so it did not make the cut.

 If you are looking for more exciting examples of making Web pages more attractive, read the following sections. It is sometimes hard to distinguish between techniques that make navigation easier and ones that just make the pages prettier. For that reason, you'll find features such as image maps, which make pages more eye-appealing but are used mostly for navigation, in the next section. An ardent disclaimer: This is a book about programming. Some of the techniques here (frames, for example) are considered bad by Web design professionals. You'll have to make up your own mind about that. I'm just showing you how HTML works; I'm not passing judgment.

Improving Navigation, Ease Of Use, And Layout

Making pages prettier goes hand in hand with making them easier to use. There is a fine line between making pages more attractive and making them more navigable, and, in doing one, you often step back and forth across that line and do the other. For that reason, I'm squeezing all these topic overviews in this one area.

The curse of the Web medium is that you must work with only one page at a time. A gift of the Web is that you can use hypertext links to leave that one page and go to a large number of places and do a large number of things. With print media, such as books, magazines, and manuals, you have some control of the path your users will take. You also have a few helpers, such as indexes, tables of contents, and page and chapter numbers. Regardless of the path users choose to read your book or selected parts thereof, you hope they will always know which book they are in and roughly where they are in relation to the rest of the book.

Within the Web medium, you have a few more obligations:

- Maintaining site continuity in a medium where page numbers and beginnings and ends can have no meaning whatsoever

- Ruthlessly judging every potential tenant on your pages' real estate for economy, clarity, and effect, because it's very easy to zip off to another Web page (click!) if this one does not let you find what you want

- Meeting or exceeding the expectations of surfers whose expectations span not only a variety of historical media but also the ever-changing developments in this new one

To maintain continuity, carry a map with you onto each page of your site. At its simplest, your map could be a group of hypertext links repeated at the bottom of every page on the site. No matter where you are, you can use these links to navigate back to the top of the site or the top of certain sections.

From this humble beginning, you can go many places. You can use images as hypertext links instead of just textual links. Better yet, you can arrange the images so they look like a nice row or column of buttons. You can create image maps that act as navigational tools. Image maps divide one graphic into multiple clickable regions. With creativity, you can make an image that represents in pictures or text the topography of your site and repeat that image map on all your pages as a navigational aid.

For example, you can create an architect's view of a mall where you click on each store to navigate. A simpler approach is to create a textual, hierarchical view of a site with colored lines drawn between the top and the current pages, the other sites being either unlined or having lines of a different color. A more button-ish use of image maps is to create the effect of a series of buttons or menu items where the button for the page you are on is set off in some way.

Tables, forms, and frames are another matter entirely. All these can be used to help manage navigation at a site, although with tables and frames, it is usually also within the context of managing a more complex layout than plainer HTML pages. Forms are usually used for collecting and submitting data, but they can also be used for navigation (although we're now crossing over into scripting). For example, you can use selection lists in a form (and other list elements for that matter) to help provide a concise area for selecting links on a site. Selection lists give you the functionality of a pull-down menu on a Web page, which means that, by having little in the way of an original real estate outlay, you can provide a lot more hidden punch and still stay on the same, single page.

For layout, the preeminent tools are tables and frames. In their simplest form, tables allow you to organize sets of data on a page (using the **<TABLE>** tag). For example, putting lists or categories of links into a table makes for a nice arrangement on a Web page (better than a bunch of unending left-justified text). Also, many sites use tables without borders to create newspaper-style layouts. You can use tables within tables within tables (and so on) to provide finely detailed page layouts. Just remember that the more complex you get, the more you need to leave yourself a healthy dose of comments to help you remember which table contains which part of the page.

What about frames? Well, for as many people there are who hate them, there seems to be as many who use them religiously. I think tables offer a cleaner-looking approach. However, frames are uniquely suited to catalog-type sites, where you want to keep some kind of navigational menu on the screen and where, from clicks on the navigational area, you have only one target window change (again and again and again).

Finally, style sheets are a method to exert complete control in laying out a page. Style sheets can cascade. That is, when the designer specifies a style sheet, there may be other sheets (some provided by the user) that override those styles.

A very stylish page with lots of effects and tricks can be very difficult to create by hand. For example, if you want all level-one heads (**<H1>**) to look a certain way, why can't you simply specify that in a list and have all the files on your site read it in from that one site? Then, if you want to change the appearance of your site, you can make the change in one place. This is exactly how style sheets work.

Putting Your Page To Work

To conclude an introduction to an HTML class I teach, I often make this assertion: Placing documents and pictures on the Web is all good and fine, but if the Web is ever going to be any good to businesses other than publishers, you are going to have to be able to hook up Web pages to other things, like databases.

Therein lies the essence of a whole range of businesses that might otherwise get very little value out of having a Web presence. If you can collect or provide data, you are in a whole new exciting realm, beyond using just pages for reading.

Love it or hate it, HTML has been a great provider (and, as in the Unix world, if you want something, it always seems like someone has made it available to you). For example, if you want to quote the code of Hammurabi in HTML, you do not have to change the text's font, size, and so on in the paragraph tag to set it off—the **<BLOCKQUOTE>** tag is already there.

The same is true with forms. HTML forms give you a prepackaged way to create forms and enter data—the foundation of business interactions—that you will want to shoot off across the Web to some application. Do you want prize-seeking suckers to fill out personal information pages on themselves so that you can inundate them with junk mail? Do it with a form. Do you want to sell anything? Let them fill out a form that indicates their name, size, mailing address, and so on. Do you want to pay your taxes, sign up for life insurance, make a bank deposit, or get your driver's license renewed? Fill out some forms.

Now, however, the forms are not paper—they are on the Web. A limitation is that forms can do practically nothing by themselves, so they need to be hooked up to a helper or gateway application or a script that can do something with the information entered on the forms. In the early days, these helper applications were usually PERL programs known as CGI scripts. Today, they are more often ActiveX or Java Scripts.

Like all other HTML, you will find the tags and attributes for forms used in conjunction with all the other HTML and non-HTML tools. Many Web scripts use forms as the front end for gathering input. You can find an example of using forms in this chapter's Practical Guide.

Inside HTTP

HTTP is the networking protocol that makes Web pages work. It is really quite simple. The client (usually the browser) sends a request. The request may contain data (like form data), and it will contain request headers. These headers provide information about the browser and its current state. For example, the browser may tell the server what kind of files it will accept.

The server returns a response. You hope this response contains data (the Web page). It also contains headers that inform the browser of certain things (for example, the kind of data the response represents).

Headers can hold all kinds of information. For example, a browser might ask the server to send the document only if it has been modified after a certain date. The browser also sends the user-agent string by way of the header, which is how the server can identify which browser and operating system is in use.

If you want to see the action firsthand, fire up a Telnet client (Windows comes with one). Connect to a Web server, but instead of using the standard Telnet port, use port 80. When you connect, you probably won't see anything. Then, if you connect to AltaVista, for example, type:

```
GET http://www.altavista.digital.com/ HTTP/1.0
```

Then, press Enter and Control+J (line feed). Depending on how your system is set up, you may not see what you typed. However, you will see the Web page's raw HTML appear on your Telnet screen. If you can scroll back, you'll see that the first few lines are the response headers that were sent to you.

Client Pull

Sometimes, it is useful to have a page update after a certain amount of time. You might want to show something that changes frequently (for example, a stock quote). You might also display a message that redirects the user to another page automatically. Although you could use redirection on the server, you wouldn't get to display a message.

Client pull is the way to accomplish these tasks. Actually, client pull is a special HTTP header (**REFRESH**) that informs the browser (the client) that it should reload in a certain number of seconds. You can ask the browser to load a different page or simply reload the current page. Like all headers, you use the **<META>** tag to insert it. To find more about headers and HTTP, you might start at **rs.internic.net/cgi-bin/ 15min/mkmodule.cgi/http/sld01.html**. InterNIC provides a nice series of "15-Minute" training materials on Web terminology, protocols, history, and so on that are a very digestible and easily accessible start to learning more about the Web.

Frames

If there is a more controversial HTML feature than frames, I don't know what it is. Frames allow you to split the browser's windows into portions and display different data in each piece independently. This allows you to create very convenient interfaces. For example, Figure 3.1 shows a frame that keeps a menu visible at the top of the screen at all times. Other sites use similar ideas to create permanent navigation bars on one side of the screen (see Figure 3.2).

However, frames have a downside, mainly that they chew up screen space. Your framed Web site might look great on your 1,024x768-pixel screen, but it might not look as good at 640x480. Also, some browsers don't support frames at all.

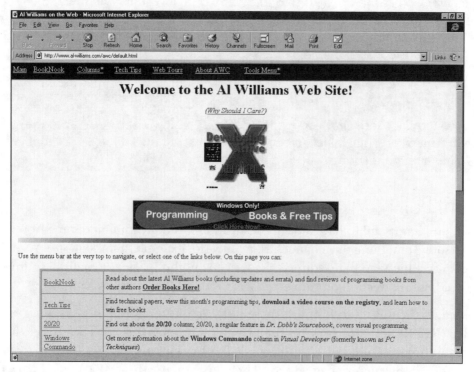

Figure 3.1

A menu bar.

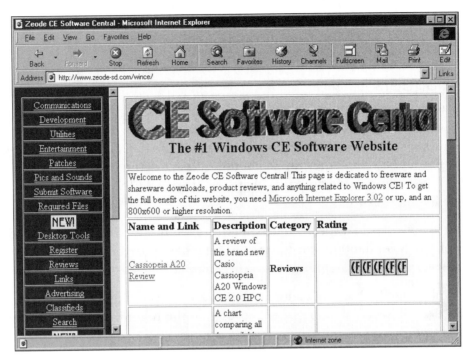

Figure 3.2

A navigation pane.

Another problem with frames is that some browsers treat them differently. Suppose you do a search on AltaVista and end up viewing the site shown in Figure 3.1. You click on Book Nook, read a bit, and push the Back button. What happens? The answer depends on your browser. Internet Explorer will take you back to the page in Figure 3.1. Netscape returns you to AltaVista (you would have to right-click and select Back in Frame to go to the first page).

The last major complaint with frames is bookmarking. When you bookmark a framed page, the bookmark always returns to the initial page, regardless of the particular frames that are visible when you create the bookmark (you'll see why shortly). Some designers see this as an advantage, because it forces users to enter the site at the front door.

In the end, only you (and perhaps your users) can decide whether frames are right for your site. But you still should know how to make them if you want to use them. If you simply hate frames, you might consider skipping this section.

The document that displays frames doesn't contain any HTML pages itself. It merely defines the frames. The HTML comes from other documents. You define a set of frames with the **<FRAMESET>** tag and individual frames with the **<FRAME>** tag. You'll find examples in this chapter's Practical Guide.

Style Sheets

For the ultimate control in page layout, you can use *cascading style sheets* (CSS), sometimes simply called *style sheets*. This powerful new standard lets you control the appearance and position of everything in your document. Of course, most browsers don't support CSS yet (or they support it poorly, as does Internet Explorer 3). However, it is possible to develop pages that look great in CSS-capable browsers and passable in other browsers.

You can apply styles to a specific element (for example, a paragraph) or to all elements of one type. In other words, you can set a particular paragraph to use green text, or you can set all paragraphs to use green text.

You can also specify classes of elements. For example, you might mark certain paragraphs "urgent." You could arrange it so that all the urgent paragraphs appear in bold red type.

The cascading part of CSS occurs when your commands conflict with one another. For example, you mark a paragraph as urgent, but you also directly specify that that paragraph should appear in green. Because the direct command is more specific, it wins. The browser will display the text in green (although it will use the other styles that were afforded urgent paragraphs, if any). Details on CSS are discussed in this chapter's Practical Guide.

Practical Guide To

Using Advanced HTML In Web Pages

- Using Graphics For Bullets And Rule Lines
- Changing Backgrounds And Colors
- Good Places To Look For Web Graphics
- Using Mailto To Receive Email
- Using Meta For Search Engines
- Using Client Pull
- Using Image Maps
- Using Forms
- Using Tables For Page Layout
- Creating Frame Sets
- Using Style Sheets To Affect A Particular Element

Thus far, this chapter has provided the context and background of using HTML. To get to the heart of HTML, we'll now look at illustrations of the tasks most commonly used in building HTML pages. You can use these illustrations to create and modify your own pages and as a key to understanding how other sites work. Remember also that viewing the sources of other pages is a great way to learn.

Using Graphics For Bullets And Rule Lines

Listing 3.1 (see also Figure 3.3) shows the use of standard HTML techniques to create bullets and rule lines. Listing 3.2 (see also Figure 3.4) shows the use of graphics to do the

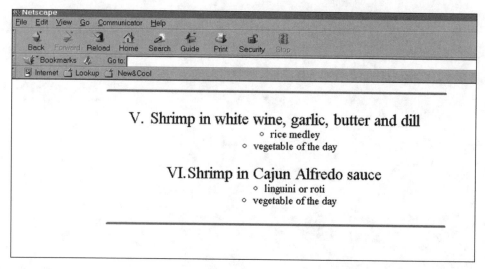

Figure 3.3

The nested menu list.

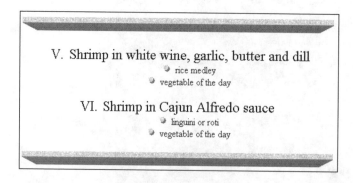

Figure 3.4

An example using graphics as bullets to add pizzazz.

same. In both, note also the use of a nested list and some list arguments. The list arguments **TYPE=I** and **START=5** for the ordered list give you large roman numerals and start the list counting at 5. Also, note that the indents on the nested list have no effect on the indents on the Web page's list. They are indented automatically on the Web page for readability.

Listing 3.1   A nested, nongraphical menu.

```
<CENTER>
<HR SIZE=4 WIDTH=65% NOSHADE>
<OL TYPE=I START=5>
<FONT SIZE=5><LI>Shrimp in white wine, garlic, butter and dill</FONT>
<UL>
<LI>rice medley
<LI>vegetable of the day
<P>
</UL>
<FONT SIZE=5><LI>Shrimp in Cajun Alfredo sauce</FONT>
<UL>
<LI>linguini or roti
<LI>vegetable of the day
<P>
</UL>
</OL>
<HR SIZE=4 WIDTH=65% NOSHADE>
</CENTER>
```

Notice that whereas some tags have an **ALIGN=** attribute, others do not. Therefore, you must improvise with the **<CENTER>** tag to center the list. Note the font change outside the list item tags. If you place the tag on the other side of the list item tag, the roman numerals will appear small. Note also that you use paragraph tags for spacing instead of **
** (break) tags. Try the same code with break tags and see whether your browser does what you expect.

This is not a bad example, as it is better than just text, but look at Listing 3.2. It creates some unique buttons and rule lines using simple tools to add some pizzazz. Remember that you can find thousands of buttons and rule lines on the Web.

Listing 3.2   Add pizzazz to pages by using graphics as buttons or bullets.

```
<CENTER>
<IMG SRC="RULE1.GIF">
<OL TYPE=I START=5>
<FONT SIZE=5><LI>Shrimp in white wine, garlic, butter and dill</FONT>
<BR>
<IMG SRC="BALL1.GIF">
rice medley <BR>
```

```
<IMG SRC="BALL1.GIF">
vegetable of the day
<P>
<FONT SIZE=5><LI>Shrimp in Cajun Alfredo sauce</FONT>
<BR>
<IMG SRC="BALL1.GIF">
linguini or roti <BR>
<IMG SRC="BALL1.GIF">
vegetable of the day
<P>
</OL>
<IMG SRC="RULE1.GIF">
</CENTER>
```

Note the difference in look. The first example did not look bad originally, but it looks awful next to the second one.

 There are many ways to create simple graphics using tools that you already have or that are nearly free. You don't have to buy a $600 program. Believe it or not, my favorite nearly free tools are Word and LView. Most people already have Word. You can use its drawing capabilities to create graphics and move them around on the page (easier than in Paint because the images are clickable objects that can be dragged). Then, you can capture the window with LView, crop it, use the dropper to make the background transparent (so you don't have a rectangular box around an image), and save it in GIF 89a format. It is quick and easy, although there are many other drawing and capture program combinations you can use.

 ## Changing Backgrounds And Colors

Although gray is the default color for backgrounds, you can use the following techniques for other backgrounds. You can use a graphic (for example, a GIF, JPEG, or BMP file), set the background to a color, or even do a trick that gives you a colored bar or pattern down the side of the page (maybe to put navigation tools on). The action happens inside the body tag. Before we get started, let's quickly discuss how to find the hex values for colors.

Cheap Trick For Finding Hex Color Values

You have probably seen tags such as **<COLOR="#FF8000">**. If you are a hex gearhead, you know exactly what that means. If you aren't, this quick discussion is for you.

The number in the tag is the hexadecimal representation of the RGB (Red, Green, Blue) values for a color. To find these colors (assuming you're a Windows user), open Paint (an often useless program that comes with the operating system) under Start|Programs|Accessories (you can also use the Run menu and type "MSPAINT" or type "MSPAINT" in a DOS window). Click on Options|Edit|Colors, and then click on Define Custom Colors. In the lower-right corner of Paint's screen, you will see Red, Green, and Blue. After you pick a color (by clicking on one), the RGB decimal values for that color will appear. For example, if you click on that sort of yellowish, greenish-brown color, you'll see the RGB values change (to 128, 128, 0). To convert those to hex, open Calculator, select the Scientific view, enter a number, and change the radio button setting from Dec to Hex to convert. In this case, we find that 128 decimal is 80 hex and that 0 decimal is 0 hex. So, if you want to use that color in HTML, you can use **<COLOR="#808000">**. Because there are two values for each, just fill in an extra zero for the zero value.

Note that you can now use actual color names, such as **<COLOR="RED">**, but it is unclear how different browsers will handle that (as opposed to the specific hex value). Stay tuned—maybe striped avocado mousse will become one of the standard colors you can specify by name (in addition to red). More than likely, if the browser cannot handle the color, it will try to fake it in some way.

Using A Graphic As A Background
Inside the body tag, enter **<BODY BACKGROUND="file.gif">**, where "**file.gif**" (or .JPG, .BMP, and so on) is the name of the graphic you want to use as a background.

Using A Color As A Background
Inside the body tag, enter **<BODY BGCOLOR="#808000">**, where "**#808000**" is the hex value of the color you want.

Using The Bar-On-The-Side-Of-The-Page Trick
It's quick, it's easy, it's useful, and it takes almost no bandwidth whatsoever. What is it? You've seen it all over the Internet. Take a very small, colored line (say, light blue or gray, about the width of a paper clip laid flat), and extend that line with a white, transparent, or parchment-colored line farther than any browser on any huge monitor could ever display. Use this as your background. Browsers automatically repeat this very small image down the page, and, for very little bandwidth, you get a nice tool to divide your page.

Suppose you have this **<BODY>** statement:

```
<BODY BACKGROUND="file.gif">
```

Figure 3.5 shows what the GIF looks like by itself. Figure 3.6 shows the result. Notice that the page is now divided nicely for text and navigation buttons. To take advantage of this, you can use tables without borders to place the items on your page on the right part of the background.

 ## Good Places To Look For Web Graphics

The Web is full of pages that have graphics you can use for bullets, lines, icons, and backgrounds. Here are a few of my favorites:

- **www.enders-realm.com/rg**

Figure 3.5

The border GIF.

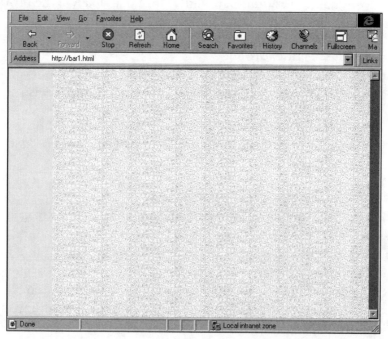

Figure 3.6

The border GIF on a page.

- **www.clark.net/pub/evins/Icons**

- **www.iconbazaar.com**

- **aplusart.simplenet.com/aplusart/index.html**

Because any of these links could be dead by the time you read this, you might also check out Yahoo's list of Web graphics at **www.yahoo.com/Computers_and_Internet/ Internet/World_Wide_Web/Page_Design_and_Layout/Graphics**. Be sure to read and follow any conditions that the site places on using its graphics.

 ## Using Mailto To Receive Email

A nice feature of the major browsers is the ability to click on a link and automatically pop open an email program (usually without having to set MIME types and so on like you once had to). It's a nice way to let users send you feedback. At the bottom of your pages, consider adding:

```
<A HREF="mailto:bs@bscompany.com">Bill Smithers</A>
```

When users click on Bill's name, their browsers should pop open an email program with Bill's email address already tucked into the To field.

 ## Using Meta For Search Engines

The **<META>** tag can help boost your image with search engines. Have you ever noticed how most search engine displays read like a hackneyed chop list of words? They use their own criteria for automatically pulling out a descriptive "paragraph" from your site. You can help most search engines by using the **<META>** tag. Inside the **<HEAD>** tags, consider using:

```
<META NAME="Keywords"  CONTENT="clacker store,
dangerous amusements, clackers">
<META NAME="Description"  CONTENT="Remember
those two plastic balls on a string back in the '70s that kids smacked
together and were rumored to kill kids who used them near their temples?
Bill's clacker page has them for sale, in 454 colors!">
```

For help on these tags, a neat site is **vancouver-webpages.com/Vwbot/mk-metas.html**, which will generate them for you and point you to documentation.

Using Client Pull

The **<META>** tag can also implement client pull, whereby you inform the Web browser to reload after a certain number of seconds. Be careful, though. People are easily annoyed with this feature, but in some cases (for example, when your Web site moves), it is indispensable. It is also great when you want to update live data.

Suppose that you want to reload a page every 30 seconds. You can put the following statement in the **<HEAD>** section of the page:

```
<META HTTP-EQUIV="REFRESH" CONTENT=30>
```

What if you want the page to go somewhere else? The syntax is straightforward but odd looking:

```
<META HTTP-EQUIV="REFRESH" CONTENT="5;URL=http://www.newplace.com">
```

This isn't a typo; the quotes go before **5** and after **.com**. The meaning here is that the content of the **<REFRESH>** header is literally "**5;URL=http://www.newplace.com**".

By the way, some old browsers don't support this tag, so it's a good idea to put an equivalent link on the page, such as:

```
<P>We've moved</P>
<P>If your browser doesn't go to our new site, use this link:
<A HREF="http://www.newplace.com">http://www.newplace.com</A></P>
```

Using Image Maps

Image maps take a graphic and define multiple regions on the graphic as hypertext links. Because image maps are easier to do than they are to explain, I will provide only a brief explanation and then get into the "doing" part. Once you do it and see how it works, the process explains itself.

There are two types of image maps, and each operates on the same principles but has different implementations. The first is server-side image mapping, and the second is client-side image mapping. Each lets you take an image and map out areas on the image as clickable regions. Once a region is clicked on, some action occurs, usually a hypertext link to another page or to a picture.

Server-Side Image Maps

Server-side image mapping, so called because all the work is done by a gateway application residing on the server, requires these four things to work:

- A graphic

- A Web page with the correct set of image map tags

- A Web site with a gateway application (such as imagemap.dll, usually in the cgi-bin directory)

- A separate map file (which maps out the graphic by providing coordinates and the corresponding actions to be taken when a region is clicked on)

You know what a graphic is (any image will do). The correct tags in a Web page look like this:

```
<A HREF="http://www.server.com/cgi-bin/imagemap/mapdir/file1.map">
  <IMG SRC="file1.gif" ISMAP></A>
```

This is a confusing line, but here is a quick explanation: The first part you know—the anchor tag. This is followed by a URL, a link to a graphic, and then a closing anchor tag. What's different here is the **ISMAP** part of the **IMG** tag, which is a flag that says this line is different—that it's an image map. The URL is also different. If the browser were thinking out loud as it processed this line, it might say:

- Oh, this is a hyperlink.

- Plop file1.gif on the page as a picture.

- I see **ISMAP**, so this picture is an image map.

- When the user clicks, I'll send the coordinates to a gateway application on the server.

Here's what a server-side image map file looks like:

```
#This is an image map for Darlene's Big Hair Salon
recthttp://www.hair.com     0,0 35,48
circle       http://www.nails.com     66, 24 85,40
poly         /pics/customers.htm      99,45 140,2 144,55
default      http://www.hair.com
```

Note a couple of things here. Unlike the rest of HTML, comments in map files are preceded by a number symbol (#). Comments in map files help remind you where links are going, so use them liberally. You can see the types of regions you can define (I neglected to include *point,* which is also valid).

From left to right, you're defining a region, a destination, and Cartesian coordinates that define the region. The destination can be to either a local file on the server or a full URL on another server. For coordinates, a point is the easiest to define (you just need one x and one y coordinate), although a point is probably the most useless (unless you're playing a game in which you drag your mouse around on the page until you find the secret link). It takes two coordinates to define a rectangle or a circle, and with a polygon, you can define as many as you want. This gives you the best chance to be most accurate and detailed because all the areas within the collection of x and y coordinates become hot. The default takes care of clicks that occur on undefined areas of the map. It is considered good practice to set the default to reload the same page. This usually causes clicks to be more accurate.

Client-Side Image Maps

Client-side image maps are a horse of another color (or shade at least). To do client-side image maps, you need:

- A graphic

- A Web page with the correct set of image map tags and mapped coordinates on the same page

- A Web browser that supports client-side image mapping

Again, you know what a graphic is (any image will do). The correct tags and mapped coordinates in a Web page look like this:

```
<IMG BORDER=0 SRC="/graphics/zippo.gif" USEMAP="#mapfile1">
<MAP NAME="mapfile1">
<AREA SHAPE="RECT" COORDS="7,5,168,139" HREF="http://www.wacky.com" >
<AREA SHAPE="RECT" COORDS="171,4,426,137" HREF="http://www.zany.com">
<AREA SHAPE="RECT" COORDS="430,5,612,141" HREF="http://www.wow.com">
</MAP>
```

Notice a few things going on here. The first line is an **IMG** tag with a few extras. The first extra is **BORDER=0**. This turns off the default blue border around image maps, which is a good idea because they look rather stupid. (A few years ago, when no one knew that you could click on images, the blue border helped the feeble-minded among us by saying, "Pssst, hey, you—this thing is clickable!" Nowadays, you assume that almost anything is clickable, so the blue border looks lame.) The next extra simply specifies where the graphic file is. The last part of this line is like the **ISMAP** argument, except for client side you write **USEMAP** and then give internal directions on where to find the map in the same document (instead of in a different file). In this case, the browser will look in the file for a map with the same name (for example, MAPFILE1). Note that the names must be exact matches. Also note that case matters because you could have several **USEMAP**s and maps in one document, and the browser has to be able to connect the right ones.

You don't need a gateway application because the browser does the work here. The downside is that the browser has to support client-side image maps (and not all of them do). Therefore, server-side maps are more general because they work with any browser. Note that the layout of client-side maps is also different, with quotes and all (although, to be honest, more HTML-like).

Comments On Client Vs. Server Map Files

When it comes to client-side and server-side map files, the advantages of one are almost the disadvantages of the other, and vice versa (see Table 3.1).

Table 3.1 Advantages and disadvantages of client and server map files.

Advantages Of Server-Side Map Files

They work with all browsers.

Map files remain hidden from surfers.

Advantages Of Client-Side Map Files

They have reduced bandwidth and increased speed (mapping is done on the client without repeated trips back to the server to resolve clicks).

It's easier to maintain a single file.

They're portable, so it doesn't matter which server or platform is being used.

Disadvantages Of Server-Side Map Files

You must have a gateway application (like imagemap.dll).

To port to another server, you have to find an appropriate gateway application for each new server.

They're slower if the network is slow.

You must maintain more files.

Some server sites don't provide for gateway applications.

Disadvantages Of Client-Side Map Files

They work with only some browsers.

Your map file is viewable.

Getting Map Coordinates

There are a number of ways to get map coordinates. For me, the easiest way is by hand, using nearly free tools that almost everyone has access to. Paint, a program that most people would admit has very limited usefulness as a graphics tool, nevertheless does the trick here. "But," some of the wise grasshoppers say, "Paint, evil incarnate that it is, does not read GIFs (for some unfathomable or sinister reason)." Yes, that is true. So, open up your graphic with your Web browser, right-click on it with your mouse, and choose the Save As option to save it as a BMP file. No, you don't have to use it as a BMP—simply use the BMP to map the coordinates in Paint.

Once you've opened the file in Paint, you'll notice that as you drag your mouse across it, coordinates appear in the lower right-hand corner of the screen. Let's say you're trying to map the ABC checkboxes in Figure 3.7.

Put your mouse over the top-left corner of the A box, and you have two coordinates. Put it on the lower-right corner of the A box, and you have two more (enough to define a rectangle). Repeat the process for B and C, and you can now define three regions. At this point, you don't have to worry if it's not exact. Most people will click somewhere around the letter, and that area is not hard to define.

Are there easier ways? Yes. There are programs that do this for free, but they take almost as much time to learn as the pencil-and-paper way shown here. You can find several sites on the Web that will help you calculate image maps (for example, **tns-www.lcs.mit.edu/cgi-bin/mapmaker** and **zenith.berkeley.edu/~seidel/ ClrHlpr/imagemap.html**). There is also a site that will convert your server-side maps to client-side format: **www.popco.com/popco/convertmaps.html**.

Using Forms

HTML forms give you a way to allow users to input text; make choices from checkboxes, radio buttons, and selection lists; and submit the data to an application to process it. Although HTML forms give you a nice predefined way of putting up

Figure 3.7

An image for you to map.

boxes and so on to collect data, they are useless without some application to process the form. Listing 3.3 provides a sample form to give you an idea.

Listing 3.3   A sample form.

```
<FORM METHOD=POST ACTION="/cgi-bin/foo.exe">
<H3>Newsletter Subscription Order Form</H3>

<FORM METHOD=POST ACTION="/cgi-bin/foo.exe">
<H3>Gourmet Dining Club Membership Form</H3>

<PRE>
<B>Membership Options:</B>

        <INPUT TYPE="radio" NAME="MembershipType" CHECKED
            VALUE=1> 1 Year Prestige Membership ($29.99)
        <INPUT TYPE="radio" NAME="MembershipType"
            VALUE=2> 2 Years Prestige Membership ($49.99)
        <INPUT TYPE="radio" NAME="MembershipType"
            VALUE=3> 1 Year Ambassador Membership ($39.99)
        <INPUT TYPE="radio" NAME="MembershipType"
            VALUE=4> 2 Years Ambassador Membership ($59.99)

        <INPUT TYPE="checkbox" NAME="SendBroch"
            VALUE="Yes"> Please send me more information on
            the different valuable membership options.

<B>Your Mailing Address:</B>

        Name:<INPUT NAME="FirstName" size=16> <INPUT NAME="LastName" size=27>
     Address:<INPUT NAME="Address1" size=43>
            <INPUT NAME="Address2" size=43>
        City:<INPUT NAME="City" size=15> State:<INPUT NAME="State" size=2>
Zip:<input NAME="PostalCode" size=10>
     Country:<INPUT NAME="Country" size=20>

<B>Your Credit Card Information:</B>

        Type:<SELECT NAME="CardType">
          <OPTION SELECTED>Visa
          <OPTION>MasterCard
          <OPTION>Discover
        </SELECT> Name:<INPUT NAME="CardName" size=25>
      Number:<INPUT NAME="CardNumber" SIZE=20>
     Expires:<INPUT NAME="CardExpDate" SIZE=7>

        <INPUT Type="submit" Value="   Send   "> <INPUT Type="reset"
                                                Value="Clear Form">
</PRE>
</FORM>
```

The first line is the beginning form tag. The first argument specifies that the name/value pairs of the form will be passed (posted) to the application by way of stdin. Action specifies the URL of the application that will process the data, where foo.exe stands for any program.

Next, notice the preformatted text tags around this form. These may seem crude, but such tags are one way to get the form to line up on the page. (Notice also, if you are trying to use this example, that the breaks made to fit the 80-character limit of code examples in this book may cause your output to appear slightly different.)

The next thing to notice is a bunch of tags that say **INPUT** followed by arguments. The **INPUT** element is used for single-line text entry boxes, radio buttons, and checkboxes and two predefined buttons (**SUBMIT** and **RESET**). Notice that type is specified in each case except for text entries (**TYPE="TEXT"**) because text is the default. You might also notice that the size of the submit and reset buttons is determined by the size of the text within. If you want the buttons to be the same size, you can pad the **Value** arguments with spaces. Figure 3.8 shows the resulting form.

Other tags you might see are the **TEXTAREA** element for entering in multiple lines of text (not in this example) and the **SELECT** element for selection and scrolling lists.

In later parts of this book, you will see how scripts, applets, and controls are used with these same, predefined form tags.

Using Tables For Page Layout

If you have experimented with simple HTML, you have no doubt been frustrated by the tendency of every piece of text or graphic to not go exactly where you want it to go. If you don't have a tool, complex layout (for example, multicolumns) can seem difficult. Tables to the rescue!

You can use tables without borders to set up a layout for your Web page and then use tables within tables to define the layout even more. Listing 3.4 offers a simple two-column example (you can see the page in Figure 3.9).

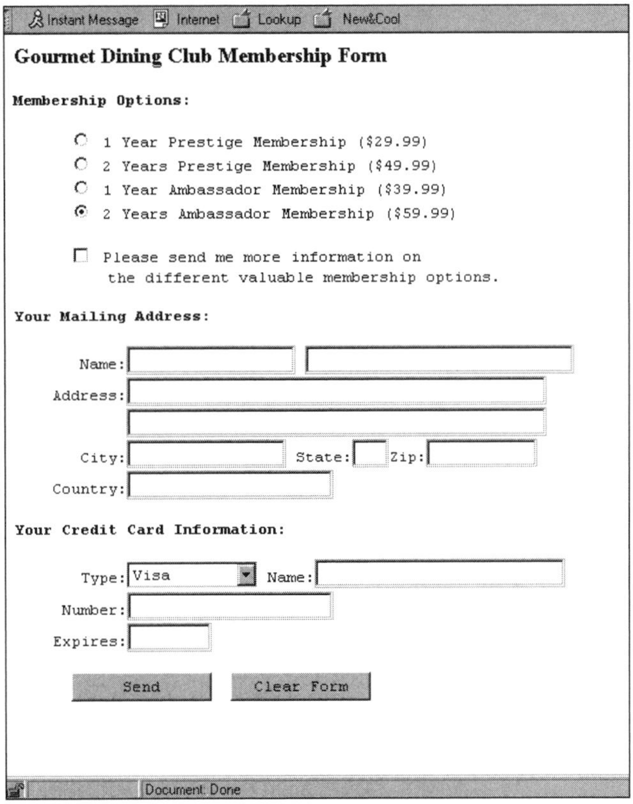

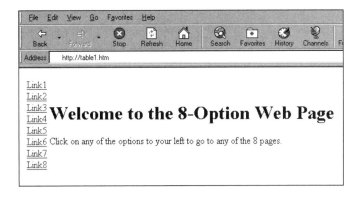

Figure 3.8

What the form looks like.

Figure 3.9

What a two-column table looks like.

Listing 3.4 A two-column layout.

```
<TABLE BORDER=0>
<TD>
<!--This is the left cell of the table, the left column of the two.-->
<A HREF="http://www.linkone.htm">Link1</A><BR>
<A HREF="http://www.linktwo.htm">Link2</A><BR>
<A HREF="http://www.linkthree.htm">Link3</A><BR>
<A HREF="http://www.linkfour.htm">Link4</A><BR>
<A HREF="http://www.linkfive.htm">Link5</A><BR>
<A HREF="http://www.linksix.htm">Link6</A><BR>
<A HREF="http://www.linkseven.htm">Link7</A><BR>
<A HREF="http://www.linkeight.htm">Link8</A>
<TD>
<!--This is the right cell of the table, the right column of the two.-->
<H1>Welcome to the 8-Option Web Page</H1>
<P>
Click on any of the options to your left to go to any of the 8 pages.
</TABLE>
```

Although this is a rather simple example, you can see where it's going. Let's say that you use the same table template on all eight pages but you change the text in the second cell for each page. Then, to make it more visually different, you put a long line down the side of the page, as described earlier (using the **<BODY>** tag). This way, all the navigational items on each page appear on a colored bar.

To add a little more flair, make another table in the second cell of each page, such as:

```
<TABLE BORDER=0>
<TD>
<!--This is the top of the page, for banners and graphics.-->
Fancy banner stuff and graphics
<TR>
<TD>
<!--This is the bottom of the page, for most of the text.-->
Lots of text and more text…
    .
    .
</TABLE>
```

The complete package would give you a menu bar down one side, a large page display area to the right with a newspaper-size header on top (if that's the size of the stuff you stuck in there), and a larger text display area on the bottom. A newspaper-style layout gives you greater control over your pages. Unless you specify otherwise, tables automatically size to their contents.

Creating Frame Sets

The HTML document that creates a framed page (a frame set) doesn't contain any of the actual display data. Instead, it simply defines the size and shape of each frame. The initial content of each frame comes from separate URLs. Hyperlinks (or scripts) can change the contents of each frame later. In fact, a link in one frame can change the contents of another frame (which is what allows the menu in Figure 3.1 to work).

Here is a simple frame set:

```
<HTML>
<HEAD>
<TITLE>A simple example</TITLE>
</HEAD>
<FRAMESET ROWS="35,*">
<FRAME NORESIZE SCROLLING=NO NAME=MENU MARGINHEIGHT=0 MARGINWIDTH=0
  FRAMEBORDER=0 FRAMESPACING=0 SRC="menu.htm">
<FRAME NAME=BODY MARGINHEIGHT=0 MARGINWIDTH=0 FRAMEBORDER=0
  FRAMESPACING=0 SRC="main.htm">
</FRAMESET>
</HTML>
```

This is a simple example, but it works. By setting options in the **<FRAMESET>** and **<FRAME>** tags, you can get different effects. Notice that each frame has a name. This makes it easy to work with the frame in other hyperlinks and scripts. The **MENU** frame is 35 pixels high, and the user can't resize it (**NORESIZE**). It also has no margins or border. The actual content of the frame is in MENU.HTM.

Notice that the **<FRAMESET>** and related tags don't go in the **<BODY>** section. Some browsers will allow you to put a frame set inside a **<BODY>** tag, but others won't. Besides, you can't really have a body with a frame set anyway, so why bother?

Here is another simple example:

```
<HTML>
<HEAD>
<TITLE>Another example</TITLE>
</HEAD>
<FRAMESET ROWS="50%,50%">
<FRAME NAME=TOP SRC="frame1.htm">
<FRAME NAME=BOTTOM  SRC="frame2.htm">
</FRAMESET>
</HTML>
```

This example splits the screen in two, leaving one portion along the top and one along the bottom. If you wanted three areas, you would simply add another argument to the **ROWS** parameter. You can use **COLS** instead of **ROWS** to split the screen vertically instead of horizontally.

You can set the size of the rows and columns using any of the conventional measurement units. Often, percentage is useful (as in the preceding example). If you have a graphic or a menu, you might prefer to use pixels (the default). Another useful measurement is the asterisk (*), which tells the browser to allocate all remaining space to the frame. For example, if you want a 30-pixel-high graphic at the top and bottom of the screen, you write:

```
<FRAMESET ROWS="30,*,30">
```

Nesting Frames

Sometimes, you might want to subdivide a frame into another frame (for an example, see Figure 3.2). You can do this by nesting frame sets. Usually, you'll do this in one file (although you can use a frame set file as the content for a frame). Frames that you nest inside another frame inherit many of the outer frame's properties. For example, if the outer frame doesn't have a border and you don't specify the border width in the inner frame, the inner frame won't have a border either.

Here is the HTML that creates the layout in Figure 3.2:

```
<HTML>
<HEAD>
<TITLE>Example</TITLE>
</HEAD>
<FRAMESET ROWS="50%,50%">
<FRAME NAME=TOPFRAME SRC="top.htm">
  <FRAMESET COLS="50%,50%">
  <FRAME NAME=LEFTFRAME SRC="left.htm">
  <FRAME NAME=RIGHTFRAME SRC="right.htm">
  </FRAMESET>
</FRAMESET>
</HTML>
```

Changing Frame Contents

Changing the content of a frame is easy to do with a hyperlink. Simply specify the name of the frame using a **TARGET** argument, as in:

```
<A HREF="left2.htm" TARGET=LEFTFRAME>
```

If you don't use the **TARGET** argument, the link replaces the document in the current frame as you would expect. There are several twists on this. First, in the **<BASE>** tag (part of the **<HEAD>** section), you can specify a default target to use if a link in that document doesn't explicitly name a target. This is useful when you have a menu bar that almost always links to another frame. Here is a simple navigation bar that sits to the right of a frame named **PAGE** and lets the user change pages:

```
<HTML>
<HEAD>
<BASE TARGET=PAGE>
</HEAD>
<BODY>
<A HREF="p1.htm">Page 1</A><BR>
<A HREF="p2.htm">Page 2</A><BR>
<A HREF="p3.htm">Page 3</A><BR>
</BODY>
</HTML>
```

Another problem arises when you want to wipe out the entire set of frames and load the new document in its own window. Of course, the new document may supply its own frame set, or it may be a simple document. You can do this by using the predefined target name **_top**. You can use **_blank** instead to open a completely new browser window with the new document. You can replace your parent frame set with the **_parent** target. The final predefined target name is **_self**. This is useful when you are using **BASE** to set a default target but you want a link to act like it normally would. Instead of naming the current frame explicitly, you can simply use **_self**.

Floating Frames
Internet Explorer (but not Netscape Navigator) supports a different type of frame called a *floating frame.* This is simply a window that can appear at any place containing HTML (a feature reminiscent of Microsoft Word Help files). Unlike a regular frame, a floating frame can appear anywhere in your document. This makes it ideal for displaying things (for example, advertisements) that you want to change without disturbing your document.

For example, imagine that you want to display a news file in a scrolling window:

```
<HTML>
<BODY>
<P>Welcome to the WizzBang Web Site!</P>
```

```
Today's news:
<CENTER>
   <IFRAME HEIGHT=50 WIDTH=200 SRC="NEWS.HTM">
   <A HREF="news.htm">View the News</A></IFRAME>
</CENTER>

</BODY>
</HTML>
```

Notice that there is a hypertext link (**<A HREF="NEWS.HTM">**) between **<IFRAME>** and **</IFRAME>**. This causes browsers that don't understand **<IFRAME>** to display the link instead of the floating frame. Browsers that understand the **<IFRAME>** tag will ignore such things between the two **IFRAME** tags.

Dealing With Nonframe Browsers

This brings up a good question: How do you handle browsers that don't support frames in general? Some Windows CE Web browsers don't handle frames, and neither do text-based browsers.

The answer is to use the **<NOFRAMES>** tag inside the frame set. Frame-aware browsers will skip everything between **<NOFRAMES>** and **</NOFRAMES>**. Other browsers will ignore the tags themselves and process the items between them.

What do you put in the **<NOFRAMES>** section? That's a difficult question. If you use frames as an auxiliary navigation aid, you might put a link to your main page here along with a message explaining that the site will look different without frames. If you just can't live without frames, you can explain that too. Some sites maintain completely separate sets of pages for browsers that don't handle frames (certainly enough of an argument for some people to stay away from frames entirely).

 ## Using Style Sheets To Affect A Particular Element

Any element, such as **<B>** or **<H1>**, can accept a **STYLE** parameter (see Table 3.1) to affect the element. For example, suppose you want a link to a help file. You might write:

```
<A STYLE="cursor:help" HREF="help.htm">Help!</A>
```

This will cause the hyperlink to display a help cursor (that is, an arrow with a question mark).

The advantage of this method is that it specifically overrides any other styles in effect. However, it is also a problem to maintain, because your styles are scattered about each element. If you have multiple elements you want to apply the same style to, you'll have a lot of ugly repetition.

Using *<SPAN>* And *<DIV>*

Sometimes, you will want to affect more than one element with the same style. That's what the **<SPAN>** and **<DIV>** tags are for. You can use these, along with a style parameter, to group parts of your document together. The **<SPAN>** tag affects all the text from where it occurs to the **</SPAN>** tag but doesn't affect text flow. The **<DIV>** tag affects everything from the tag to the corresponding **</DIV>** tag and places the affected text in its own paragraph.

For example, consider this HTML fragment:

```
<P>I am on one line and not green!
<DIV STYLE="color:green">I'm green on my own line!<BR>
I'm green too
</DIV>
```

The text, "I'm green on my own line!" will indeed appear on a separate line. In a way, the **<DIV>** tag acts like a paragraph tag. If you use **<SPAN>** instead, the text simply flows as it would have flowed had no style tags been used.

Naming A Style Sheet Element

To prevent confusion when using styles, you can name an element. This allows you to embed the style information in the **<HEAD>** section of the document, where it is easy to find and change. For example, suppose you have a special offer you want to call attention to. You might write:

```
<HEAD>
<STYLE>
<!--
#Special { color:salmon; font-size:33pt; }
-->
</STYLE>
</HEAD>
<BODY>
<P ID=Special>A Special Offer</P>
```

The comments are for the benefit of browsers that don't understand style information. This will cause them to skip the style data. The ID must begin with the number sign (#), but you don't use it when you reference the ID (as in the **<P>** tag). There is nothing to stop you from having more than one element with the same ID, but, usually, you think of an ID as referring to some particular element. If you want to have a group of elements with the same style, use a class (see "Using One Style For Multiple Elements").

Applying A Style To An Element Type

You can use the same syntax you use for a style ID to set the style for a particular type of element. Suppose you want all bold text to be in red. You could write:

```
<STYLE>
<!--
B { color:red; }
-->
</STYLE>
```

Now, all the bold elements will be in red. You can also override a particular bold item:

```
<B STYLE="color:black;">
```

Style Classes

If you want to group a bunch of elements together, you can assign them to a class. This is similar to an ID except that you usually think of a class as having more than one item. For example:

```
<STYLE>
<!--
.JanuaryItems { color:salmon;}
.FebruaryItems { color:blue;}
-->
</STYLE>
<BODY>
<H1 CLASS=JanuaryItems>January Specials</H1>
<H1 CLASS=FebruaryItems>February Specials</H1>
```

Again, notice that the class name must start with a period but that you don't use the period when you reference the class.

Using One Style For Multiple Elements

If you want to apply the same style to multiple elements, list the elements and separate them with commas. For example, to make first- and second-level heads blue, you would write:

```
<STYLE>
<!--
H1, H2 { color:blue;}
-->
</STYLE>
```

Nested Styles

You can nest styles when you define them by listing them with a space between them. Nesting means that the element will have a certain style only when it appears within another element. For example:

```
<STYLE>
<!--
H1 B { color:red;  }
H2 B { color:yellow; }
B { color:orange; }
-->
</STYLE>
</HEAD>
<BODY>
<H1>What is <B>HTML</B></H1>
<H2>An Introduction to the <B>Web</B></H2>
<P>Here is some <B>bold</B> text.</P>
```

Now, bold items that appear in **<H1>** tags are red, bold items in **<H2>** tags are yellow, and ordinary bold items are orange.

Using External Style Sheets

The biggest problem so far with style sheets is that they are integrated into your document. Wouldn't it be nice if you could have a single style sheet apply to all the pages in your site? Of course, you could do this with server-side includes, but some servers don't offer that. It would be better if the style sheets themselves could take care of the problem.

There are two answers. First, you can link the style sheet to the document by using the **<LINK>** tag in the header of your document. In this case, the contents of the style sheet are all the lines you would have normally put between the **<STYLE>** and **</STYLE>** tags (except for the comment lines). Don't include the comments, and don't include the **<STYLE>** tags. If your style sheet were named MYSTYLE.CSS, you would put a **<LINK>** tag like this in each document:

```
<LINK REL=stylesheet HREF="MYSTYLE.CSS" TYPE=text/css>
```

Another option is to use the **@import:** style. You put this as the first line in a style block or style sheet. For example:

```
<STYLE>
<!--
@import:url(dept.css);
H1 { font-size=44pt;}
```

```
-->
</STYLE>
```

The styles you set will have priority over imported styles as long as you import them before making any other definitions.

Resolving Style Sheet Conflicts

In general, if you specify more than one style for an element, the most specific style will take precedence. For example, suppose you have this line:

```
<H1 CLASS=BigHeader STYLE="font-size:33pt;">
```

If the **BigHeader** class defines a font size, it won't be used (for this header at least). The 33-point directive takes priority. However, the browser will observe the other attributes for the **BigHeader** class (color perhaps).

If you really want to be sure that a style takes hold, you can suffix it with **!important**, and some browsers will respect it. For example, suppose you want to make sure that a certain style text is always red, no matter what. You can write:

```
{color:red!important; }
```

Available Styles

For your reference, Table 3.2 shows many of the styles you can use in a style sheet. Of course, these are subject to change, and not all browsers support everything in the same way, so beware. You can find a lot of information about style sheets at **www.w3.org/Style/css**.

Table 3.2 Selected styles for cascading style sheets.

Style	Description	Typical Values	Applies To	Inherited During Cascading?	Notes
@font-face	Specifies downloadable font		All	Yes	Allows you to specify a font and where to download the font
background	Combines all background attributes		All	Yes	
background-attachment	Used to create watermarks	Scroll, fixed	All	No	

(continued)

Table 3.2 Selected styles for cascading style sheets (continued).

Style	Description	Typical Values	Applies To	Inherited During Cascading?	Notes
background-color	Background color	Black, white, transparent	All	Yes	
background-image	Background image	bkgnd.gif	All	No	
background-position	Positions background	Top, center, none, right	Block-level elements	No	
background-repeat	Controls tiling of background	Repeat, repeat-x, repeat-y, no-repeat	All	No	
border-style	Border style	None, solid, double, grove, ridge, inset, outset	Block-level elements	No	
color	Element color	Red, blue, orange	All	Yes	
cursor	Sets cursor shape	Auto, crosshair, default, hand, move, text, wait, help	All	Yes	
font	Completely specifies font	Bold 12pt Times	All	Yes	Combines other font styles together in one
font-family	The font name	MS Sans Serif	All	Yes	Separate alternative font names with commas
font-size	Type size	12pt, large, larger	All	Yes	Can specify size as percentage, absolute, or relative size
font-style	Style	Italic, normal	All	Yes	
font-variant	Indicates regular or small-cap face	Normal, small caps	All	Yes	

(continued)

Table 3.2 Selected styles for cascading style sheets *(continued)*.

Style	Description	Typical Values	Applies To	Inherited During Cascading?	Notes
font-weight	Bold	Normal, bold	All	Yes	
letter-spacing	Spacing of letters	Normal, 2pt	All	Yes	
line-height	Line spacing	Normal, 5pt, 10%	All	Yes	
margin	Sets unified margin	5px, 2pt, auto	Block-level elements	No	
margin-bottom	Bottom margin	5px, 2pt, auto	Block-level elements	No	
margin-left	Left margin	5px, 2pt, auto	Block-level elements	No	
margin-right	Right margin	5px, 2pt, auto	Block-level elements	No	
margin-top	Top margin	5px, 2pt, auto	Block-level elements	No	
text-align	Alignment	Left, right, center, justify	Block-level elements	Yes	
text-decoration	Text effects	None, underline, line-through	All	Yes	
text-indent	Indentation	10px, 2pt, 5%	All	Yes	
text-transform	Shifts case	Capitalize, uppercase, lowercase, none	All	Yes	
vertical-align	Sub- and superscripting	Sub, super	Inline elements	No	

This chapter is certainly not an exhaustive reference on HTML. Plenty of such references are available in other books and on the Web. This is more of a cookbook that allows you to cut and paste items of interest into your own Web pages.

Before you tackle scripting, the major focus of this book, you really do need to understand forms and form processing because nearly all server-side scripts work with forms in some way. Style sheets are important if you are interested in dynamic HTML (see Chapter 8).

Using ActiveX Controls And Java Applets

I want to insert some scripts, and I want to do it NOW! If that describes you, this chapter is a good place to start. It describes the basics of using the script tag, ActiveX controls, and Java applets.

Paul Newkirk

Notes…

Chapter

4

Remember learning to ride a bike (or teaching a child to ride one)? At first, it seemed impossibly difficult, especially as someone, maybe your dad, pushed you to warp speed, then let go with only the words "now ride" separating you from imminent bodily harm. Then, something clicked. Suddenly, it was easy, and you were off tooling around the neighborhood. After the "click," you never even thought about doing it—it was second nature.

You'll find the same is true of working with Java applets and ActiveX controls. At first, you might think it's impossibly difficult. But with a little practice, you won't even notice you're using them. It will seem like just some more HTML.

The method for inserting scripts into a Web page is fairly easy and straightforward (there are three tags you can choose from). However, for useful examples, you have to understand the sometimes-hairy scripts or corresponding HTML.

You also have to understand what some of the terminology means. New technologies usually aren't planned. They evolve from existing technology, like a ball rolling downhill gathering mud. That's why we have terms like *controls* and *applets*. I have to admit, *applet* is kind of cute. But what does it mean? Presumably, it means a small application, right? But isn't that what a script is? If you say, "No, a script is smaller," that doesn't make sense, because I've seen some fairly large scripts and some fairly small applets. The same goes for controls. When is something, say, a VBScript, and when is it an ActiveX control?

In the first part of this chapter, I'll try to quickly clear up some of these terminology issues and, in the Practical Guide, I'll describe how to insert scripts, controls, and applets into your Web pages.

Getting Started

In the beginning, there was HTML, and it was good. Then, we wanted something more, and scripting was invented—often CGI scripting, which ran on the server and lived in the special cgi-bin directory. However, depending on who you ask, *scripting* as a term can cover nearly everything, from the wide range of tasks you can accomplish in the cgi-bin directory, to what you do between the **<SCRIPT>** tags, to ActiveX controls and Java applets. So, where do you draw the line between these things? After all, the applications (or scripts) that run in the cgi-bin directory (such as imagemap.dll) are scripts that are embedded right into a Web page within the **<SCRIPT>** and **</SCRIPT>** tag pairs. Between those tag pairs, you might use JavaScript or VBScript to add functionality to your Web page. For example, you can use scripting to add flow control operations, like checking to see which browser your client is using and displaying appropriate results. Instead of using the predefined Submit and Clear buttons of HTML forms for passing information to your script, you can access the HTML form controls (radio buttons, checkboxes, buttons, and so on) from a script within the script tags. In addition, depending on your browser and the scripting language you're using, you can get a lot of functionality from a very small amount of scripting using predefined classes and functions that are easy to use.

To most people, *applets* refers to Java or JavaScript applications that run on a Web page. Most Web authors use the **<APPLET>** and **</APPLET>** tag pairs to include a Java applet. However, with the advent of HTML 4, **<APPLET>** and **</APPLET>** have been deprecated in favor of the **<OBJECT>** and **</OBJECT>** tag pairs. *Deprecated* means that the **<APPLET>** tag is still available (so older pages will work) but that the **<OBJECT>** tag is preferable for new pages. Of course, if you want to make sure your pages still work with older browsers, you'll want to stick with **<APPLET>**.

Unlike a script between the **<SCRIPT>** tags, applets are actually object-oriented applications, and you must have the appropriate files (mostly class files) to use them. You should also know about all the properties, arguments, and parameters associated with the applet to be able to use it. You do not have to be a Java programmer to use a Java applet in your Web page, but you will need to tinker a bit to figure out how to make it work and how to modify its parameters. Of course, for most of us, that's half the fun of the Web—opening up each new technology that comes out and tinkering under the hood to see how it works.

Are you still wondering why it is called an *applet?* An applet is a small Java program that runs as a guest on another machine (in this case, the Web surfer's machine). The applet depends on the host program (the surfer's browser) to create its main window. The host might also impose security restrictions on the applet. A full Java application, on the other hand, creates its own window and usually has no security restrictions. Of course, applications don't work with Web browsers and other programs (although it is possible to write programs that can serve as an applet or an application, depending on the situation).

While Sun Microsystems has been pushing Java, Microsoft has developed ActiveX to provide many functions, including adding controls to Web pages. Like Java applets, ActiveX controls can be described as object-oriented applications or just plain old objects. If you're familiar with object-oriented technologies, that description is plenty. If you're not, look at the sidebar "What's An Object?"

What's An Object?

With all the talk about objects, it's useful to have a clear definition of what an object is. For the purposes of this book, an *object* is a self-contained piece of code. All you care about is what the object does, not how it does it.

For example, you might have an ActiveX object that displays a phone book and offers to dial a number for you. That's all you need to know about the object. If the object reads entries from a file on the server, fine. Tomorrow, someone could change the object to read entries from an Oracle database. So what? You don't care how it does its job, only how it interfaces. That's the power of object-oriented programming: You deal with functionality, not specific implementation details.

As a quick analogy, let's use an elevator. As long as it meets the requirements (such as getting safely from floor to floor in a reasonable amount of time), most people don't care how it does it. It could use cables and counterweights, hydraulics, or, in the future, maybe some kind of antigravity device. As long as you understand the interfaces, you can use it. You don't have to understand how it does its job or even care if last week it used cables and counterweights and this week hydraulics.

How is this possible? Each object supports a set of properties, methods, and events. These three items (sometimes called the *public interface*) don't change. As long as the object supports the same properties, methods, and events, you don't care how it works.

A property is like a variable. You can usually read the variable or set it. The object might change its behavior, depending on the variable's value. For example, a phone book might have a font property that you set, and the phone book then appears in that font. It also might have a read-only property to show the current phone number so that the Web page could manipulate it.

Methods are like function calls that affect the object. The phone book might support a method named **Sort** to sort the listing by, for example, a certain key. However, a good designer likely will provide a **Sort** property instead. You set the property with the key field, and the object obeys. However, either method works. Methods can also return values to your scripts.

Events are functions in your code that the object calls when something interesting happens. The phone book might have an event that fires when someone double-clicks an entry. You then could write an event handler to do something when that occurs. Another event might indicate a network failure. You don't have to handle events, but they are there if you need them. You'll find out exactly how to handle events later in this book.

One of the big differences between controls and applets is that only Internet Explorer supports ActiveX controls directly, whereas both Internet Explorer and Netscape Navigator support Java applets. Of course, this could change. Also, Navigator can support some ActiveX controls by using a special plug-in (available at **www.ncompasslabs.com/framed/product.htm** for a $21, 10-day demo).

You'll find more about all the pieces and parts of applets and controls in the later chapters of this book. In the rest of this chapter, I'll give some of the basic do's and don'ts and provide a few examples. When you read about scripting, you'll find how to take full advantage of objects.

Why Use Objects?

You might wonder why you would use objects at all. The answer depends on your perspective. From a Web designer's point of view, objects allow you to take advantage of someone else's hard work and do things that would normally be difficult or impossible to do with straight HTML. In addition, you don't have to understand how objects work, just how the interfaces to the objects work.

From a programming or maintenance perspective, objects can be much cleaner and easier to maintain. For example, if a new object comes out, you should be able to simply plug it in where the old one was without caring what kind of changes have gone on under the hood. This is a distinct advantage and time-saver. Of course, this assumes that the public interface of the object remains the same (as it should). A couple examples illustrate these points. Suppose you want a Web page that examines the user's hard drive, finds an existing copy of your product, checks the version number, and offers appropriate updates. You really can't do that with ordinary HTML, but you can do it with existing and available objects, making use of other people's work to enhance your pages.

Reconsider the phone book analogy used in the What's An Object? sidebar. Imagine you have a phone book object that looks up numbers and offers to dial them for you. Yesterday it looked up numbers from a flat file on a remote server. Today a new version gives us an SQL database. The changes underneath should not be an issue, as long as you get your phone numbers using the same interface.

One of these examples brings up an interesting point—security. Some users don't want you poking around their hard drives. What will stop you from erasing, reading, or modifying files? How about reading passwords or other sensitive information? And in case you didn't catch it, these are programs that can run on your user's machine, sometimes without them even knowing about it. Sound like an invitation for a virus or something else spooky, sneaky, or malevolent? Read the next section for more information.

Security

Security is a vast unknown for many people who cruise the Net. Even some experienced and practicing Web wizards tend to treat the security issue as a question they don't want to know the answer to, preferring to assume it is safe and spend their time wandering the Web instead of worrying. Safety on the Web is a lot like traveling by plane. Sure, there is some risk involved in flying. However, it would be a shame to never fly just because you were afraid of being one of the few people who experience a crash. On the other hand, you don't want to board a rickety old plane with no seat belts.

There is a lot to know about security, so you should at least understand the common assumptions on Web security. If you are seriously worried about security, and maybe you should be, you have some serious reading to do. It is a complex and changing topic.

The Many Faces Of Security

Because you can look at the issue of security from many different angles (that is, as Web surfer, Web designer, server maintainer, intranet manager, or application builder) and get many different slants (from Microsoft, Sun, and Netscape), it's hard to know where to start describing it. So, let's start quickly at the bottom and work our way up to our topic—applets and controls.

In general, and at the lowest level, most savvy people are not very concerned with the security of straight HTML files because they have been surfing the Net for a while and probably have not been burned by them.

In fact, few security issues exist with straight HTML files. For the most part, you are simply downloading text files that cannot execute. Your browser simply interprets them.

After straight HTML, another worry might be graphics files, which, when you view them, are temporarily downloaded and stored on your machine. This reloads pages you just visited more quickly, because your browser simply fetches a copy from your local cache instead of fetching it all over again from the server. But graphics files are really not a security issue. These files do not execute. Your browser or graphics program interprets them.

What about *cookies*? Cookies are a way of storing state information (such as your preferred background color). For example, if you go to a site regularly, the site won't annoy you with the same welcome message every time. However, the server can't store anything in your cookie that it doesn't already know. When cookies first came out, there was a lot of discussion about their security. After all, some machine was writing things to your hard drive without asking you. Again, like text and graphics, cookies are generally not a security threat unless someone evilly tries to drop a 50GB cookie on your machine.

Next, some people might have wondered about those cgi-bin applications that were described earlier. After all, you click on something, and an application does some work for you. For the Web surfer, there is little threat from applications that run in the cgi-bin directory, principally because that directory resides and executes on the server, not on your machine. It might be a cause of concern for some server administrators, but that's another issue. For information on IIS security, see Appendix B.

The real security issues we want to talk about concern the topics of this book, namely, scripts, applets, and controls. And here is where the "religious war" begins.

Script Security

Regardless of where you go to find out about security, after you put all the hype aside and read between the lines, you'll notice that there is no such thing as security on today's Web. Currently, however, there are a couple different ways of dealing with security threats, some of which are even combined. And, as of this writing, the boundaries of the different camps are shifting.

One approach is to limit your applications. For example, the promoters of VBScript say that all the things in Visual Basic that were potentially dangerous in a Web environment are absent in VBScript. The promoters of Java and most of its iterations place a big emphasis on the Java Virtual Machine (VM), which lets the applications run but does not let them access any dangerous parts of the system. It also does some internal checks on the applets before deciding they are safe to run. In addition, the Java language is much safer than most, providing built-in checks and prohibitions (no pointers, for example), leading to a more secure model.

However, not only do these approaches fail to make your applications 100 percent secure, but, by definition, they also limit your applications. For example, most Java VMs won't let you access files on the local computer, so don't try to write a Java program that scans the user's hard disk for a program that it will automatically update. You simply can't do it because the user's VM won't let you (in most cases).

Microsoft, with its ActiveX controls, seems to want to go another way. ActiveX doesn't circumscribe its ability to create applications that take advantage of the entire native platform. Instead, it uses a trust-and-verify mechanism. You (a software developer) obtain a certificate from a "trusted" source that lets users know that you are really who you say you are. The certificate also ensures the user that the code is the same as it was when you shipped it. If you want to write a program that formats the user's hard disk, go ahead, as long as the user trusts you. Perhaps you'll be legally liable, because the user can prove it was your code. Perhaps not. The courts are unreliable when it comes to computer technology.

Authenticode, which is what Microsoft calls this technology, is a little bit hokey for several reasons, and I hope and expect that someone will come up with a better method. "Why?" you might ask. First, the signatures look stupid. As a human, I'm supposed to be able to make a safety determination based on something that looks like a sweepstakes coupon? If my Pentium 300 and the server's Pentium 300 can't use all their processing power to check the security, why should I, Joe User, know any better? Second, it's clunky. I don't want to see these things or make determinations, and I know my mom won't. As a solution for the Web elite, it might be fine, but, as a solution for the masses, it's idiotic. Most people want to surf the Web like they watch television, not spend half their time playing "avoid the virus roulette" by paying attention to these signed and unsigned controls. To see how people can use Internet Explorer to make even more of a mess out of the issue, see the next section, "Browser Security."

Another hole in this process is that you can still get malicious controls that have been signed and that meet all the security requirements. If that happens, so the supporters say, at least you have the address of whom to sue (probably the company that built it and verified it while unknowingly employing a sociopathic virus maker). This after-the-fact security might be comforting if you have the budget to hire lawyers and can survive the havoc that might be caused, but, for the rest of us, it is less than even a token comfort.

Of course, another problem is that the agencies that parcel out certificates have a great deal of power. If they decide to charge $50,000 a year for a certificate, will you be able to get one? So far, certificates are reasonably easy to obtain, but Authenticode puts the issuing trust agencies in the driver's seat.

That being said, if you want to create ActiveX controls that fit somewhere in the security model currently in fashion (which most people will, despite my gripes), you need to know how to package them, how to sign them, and how to get them onto your user's machine. Java, on the other hand, is more intrinsically secure (as described earlier) and less obtrusive and demanding of your attention. Yes, you can sign Java applets to make them annoying too, but, on the whole, Java is treated as more safe "as is." However, this might change, because efforts are under way to allow Java more access to the user's system. Why? Because then Java can go after that added functionality outside its traditional environment (like that enjoyed by ActiveX applications running on Windows machines).

What does this mean? Certainly it means that as Java reaches out for added performance, functionality, or both, it will likely compromise its inherent security.

Browser Security

Another issue is browser security. Internet Explorer lets users set security levels (low, medium, and high). You would hope that most users set their security levels on medium, but if you depend on a control being downloaded for your page to work, you should take into account the effect that browser security might have on the delivery of your applications. If the user is using high security and your control is not signed, the browser will simply refuse to load it. Even on medium security, the user might not allow your control to load.

A Note On OS/Web Server Security

If you are running a Web server, you should understand file system security, operating system security, and Web server security. They allow you to limit many potential threats to security simply by turning off directory browsing access and permissions to certain directories and files. With IIS, you can easily work with the server's security settings from the IIS administration console.

Security Wrap-Up

The current Internet security model comes down to limiting applications, using some trust mechanism, or some combination of both. The more I think of it, the trust mechanism employed by Microsoft reminds me of domain administration for an NT network. You set your browsers to certain trust levels, you get your controls from trusted places inside your trusted regions first, and you can X-out untrustworthy sites, all of which has to be managed. Yikes! Currently, security with Java relies on the way it was designed. This presents much less trouble in the security sense, although you might pay the cost of functionality or performance. You make the choice, and, together, we can hope for the arrival of a better, universal model.

And for those who don't really want to worry about security, you can somewhat reasonably assume that the world and the Net will do some safeguarding and policing for you. But I suggest you be more cautious about downloading applications to your machine from sites you have no reason to trust.

Downloading

The first thing to note about downloading ActiveX controls and Java applets is that, generally speaking, ActiveX controls download once and thereafter execute very fast, whereas Java applets may be re-downloaded every time you use them. When downloading, your user's browser might (or might not) be set to warn them and ask permission for the download. If the browser is set to warn them, and they decide not to download, you need to make certain that your page has a backup plan.

The only time ActiveX controls have to be re-downloaded to a user's machine is when a new version comes out. You can account for that in the **CODE** attribute of the **<OBJECT>** tag. For example, you can use the following attribute in your **<OBJECT>** tag:

```
CODE=http://www.smittys.com/foo.ocx#Version=2
```

If the user's machine doesn't have the control or it has an earlier version, this will download the newer control.

One other point should be brought up about downloading controls and applets: The controls and applets you create are usually much more detailed than just one file. The most common way to get around this is with *container* files, like those described in the following section.

JARs, INFs, And CABs

More often than not, controls and applets are made up of more than one file. As such, inviting surfers to your site to download a collection of files and then to figure out how to tell their browsers what to do with them could be problematic. If you're running a server and adding controls and applets to your Web pages, it's no big deal because the details are handled by the server, and average users and their browsers need not be concerned with how the applets or controls work or where the files go. For example, when I grabbed a Java clock (in this chapter's Practical Guide) and put it on my server, the collection of class and graphics files came in a zip file. I unzipped it onto my server, referenced it correctly, and it worked.

However, if you are trying to drop, for example, an ActiveX control or a complex Java applet—made up of multiple class files—onto users' machines, you must look at the container files (JARs, CABs, and INFs), which let you combine multiple files potentially in a compressed format. That way, when you point at a control or an applet, you have to point at only one file, not several.

JARs stand for Java archive files, *CABs* for cabinets (a method used historically by Microsoft for distributing multiple compressed files), and *INFs* for information files. Usually, INF files are included as one of the files inside a CAB file to tell the browser how to install and uncompress the rest of the CAB file. You can also download an INF file directly to manipulate multiple CAB files.

The INF file can select different CABs for different platforms. It also can notify the browser of the current version of an ActiveX control so the browser can decide whether it needs to download.

A couple of notes. You can sign (in the checksum security sense) both JARs and CABs. CABs can be used for Java and ActiveX. In fact, one way of speeding up downloads of Java applets is to use CABs because of the built-in compression (although some browsers can download Java zip files too).

Once you learn the techniques for creating controls and applets in the rest of this book, you'll need to take some time to explore these containers and how you can use them to deliver the multiple files of your controls and applets.

Performance

There are two machine-performance issues between ActiveX controls and Java applets: run-time performance and downloading performance, most of which were touched on in the previous sections. The downloading issue is that, if an ActiveX control has not been downloaded, the process for downloading it may seem slow, especially with the security checks involved. However, once a control has been downloaded, it never has to be downloaded again (unless a newer model comes out). Thus, once an ActiveX control has been downloaded, it can be very fast compared to a Java applet, which usually has to be re-downloaded every time you use it. In addition, Java applets, because they are safer and more restricted than ActiveX, usually run much slower. Many browsers interpret Java, slowing it down further. A few browsers compile Java on the fly, taking some extra time up front but perhaps speeding things up if the Java code executes repeatedly (like an animation).

Consider two other elements of the performance picture—perception and cross-platform performance. If you refuse to download ActiveX controls because you fear them or can't use them because of your browser, Java applets will always perform better. If you are creating controls or applets for multiple platforms, you need only create it once with Java, which is not the case with ActiveX (which forces you to re-create for each different platform).

Know HTML

Finally, before we continue, it is important that you understand the basic HTML form tags and basic scripting used with Java applets and ActiveX controls. In many cases, you'll mix HTML forms with controls or applets and throw in a bit of script to polish it off. If you feel you need some extra help in HTML forms (radio buttons, checkboxes, and so on) or basic scripting, be sure to review Chapters 2 and 3.

Practical Guide To

ActiveX Controls And Java Applets

- Inserting ActiveX Controls Into Your Web Pages
- Finding Applets And ActiveX Controls

Inserting ActiveX Controls Into Your Web Pages

Following is a simple example of adding an Active X control to a Web page using the **<OBJECT>** tag. Once again, it requires that you view it either with Internet Explorer or using Netscape with an appropriate add-on.

There are a lot of Active X controls you can use. For this example (mostly because it was short and simple to show), I chose the marquee control. (Note that this is not the **<MARQUEE>** tag, but an ActiveX control) To use this control, you need to manage and modify three files on your server. The first file looks something like this:

```
<TITLE>Active X Marquee Control</TITLE>
</HEAD>
<BODY>
<OBJECT
    ALIGN=CENTER
    CLASSID="clsid:1a4da620-6217-11cf-be62-0080c72edd2d"
    WIDTH=248 HEIGHT=90 BORDER=0 HSPACE=0
    ID=marquee>
<PARAM NAME="ScrollStyleX" VALUE="Circular">
<PARAM NAME="ScrollStyleY" VALUE="Circular">
<PARAM NAME="szURL" VALUE="temp.html">
<PARAM NAME="ScrollDelay" VALUE=60>
<PARAM NAME="LoopsX" VALUE=-1>
<PARAM NAME="LoopsY" VALUE=-1>
<PARAM NAME="ScrollPixelsX" VALUE=0>
<PARAM NAME="ScrollPixelsY" VALUE=-3>
<PARAM NAME="DrawImmediately" VALUE=0>
<PARAM NAME="Whitespace" VALUE=0>
<PARAM NAME="PageFlippingOn" VALUE=0>
<PARAM NAME="Zoom" VALUE=100>
<PARAM NAME="WidthOfPage" VALUE=100>
</OBJECT>
</BODY>
</HTML>
```

The long string that begins with **clsid** uniquely identifies the marquee control. If you want to use a different ActiveX control, you'll need to use its ID. Of course, parameters will differ for other controls.

You'll name the file file.htm (or whatever) and view it from your browser. You should also note the temp.html file in the eleventh line of the preceding file. That's the second file you need. It contains the text (or whatever) that will be scrolled across the marquee. It might look like this:

```
<TABLE BORDER=0>
 <TR>
   <TD WIDTH=100 HEIGHT=60 ALIGN=CENTER VALIGN=CENTER>
     <SPAN STYLE="font: 8pt/10pt Arial; color: blue; font-weight: bold">
     Brought to you by
     <BR>

       <img src="billsfh.gif">
   </TD>
 </TR>
</TABLE>
```

This file is saved as described (as temp.html). The last file you need is the billsfh.gif file, which is an image. If you save all three files in a directory on your server, you can try out your first ActiveX control. See what it looks like in Figure 4.1.

It's hard to show a scrolling applet in a static book, but you get the idea. You could use this control to insert text or a series of graphics and have a nice rolling banner of nearly any size (it doesn't have to be this size). And if you are an enterprising sort, you can find somebody to pay you for it, generating revenue from a rotating, graphical ad on your Web page (one which took you very little work to implement).

As you can see, then, inserting an ActiveX control is not that hard! However, you can make it even easier if you use some special tools.

Tools For Inserting ActiveX Controls

Although it isn't very hard to insert an ActiveX control, it can be cumbersome. Several tools can help you with this task. On the low end, you can use the ActiveX Control

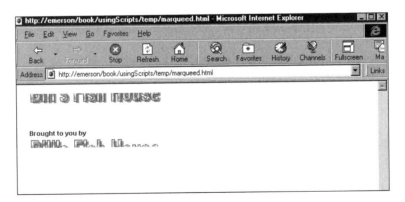

Figure 4.1

The ActiveX control in action.

Pad. It's free, it's functional, but it's not the hottest thing Microsoft is pushing. One step up is a new product that comes with Internet Explorer 4 (full install) called FrontPage Express (formerly called FrontPad). Another step up is Microsoft's full version of FrontPage. At the time of this writing, it retailed for about $100, but its HTML editor alone would probably be worth that much money to a lot of users. On the higher end and more for programmers is Microsoft's Visual InterDev, which provides the same style of development environment used in Visual C++ and Visual J++.

Inserting Java Applets Into Your Web Pages

The following is a simple example of adding a Java applet to a Web page using the **<OBJECT>** tag. Unlike the ActiveX control, a Java applet doesn't require that you view it either with Netscape Navigator with the plug-in or Internet Explorer.

There are many Java applets you can use. In fact, when looking for examples of Java applets and ActiveX control applets, I seemed to find many more Java applets more easily. Time will only tell whether that remains the same.

For this example, I decided to fetch a freeware clock and show how to include it. (Thanks to Bill Giel for his freeware clock.) To use this applet, you need to install all the class and other associated files. It comes on the companion CD as a zipped file called bills_clock.zip. After you unzip it, you'll find seven files:

```
06/17/96   08:59p              10,644  billsClock.class
06/17/96   08:59p              19,455  billsClock.java
06/17/96   08:59p                 921  clockHand.class
06/17/96   08:59p                 926  hmHand.class
06/17/96   08:59p                 640  hms.class
01/19/96   04:51p                 146  java.gif
06/17/96   08:59p                 756  sweepHand.class
```

You don't even have to know what these files do. Simply stick them all in the right directory, and create a Web page that looks like this:

```
<HTML>
<HEAD>
<TITLE>Including a Clock</TITLE>
</HEAD>
<BODY>

     <applet code="billsClock.class" width=100 height=100 ALIGN=MIDDLE>
         <param name=BGCOLOR value="000000">
         <param name=FACECOLOR value="FFFFFF">
         <param name=SWEEPCOLOR value="FF0000">
         <param name=MINUTECOLOR value="008080">
```

```
<param name=HOURCOLOR value="000080">
<param name=TEXTCOLOR value="000000">
<param name=CASECOLOR value="000080">
<param name=TRIMCOLOR value="C0C0C0">
<param name=LOGOIMAGEURL value="java.gif">
<param name=LOCALONLY value=1>
</applet>
</BODY>
</HTML>
```

You can see the result in Figure 4.2. If you want, you can change some of the colors and the size. This nice looking clock complements any Web page.

Finding Applets And ActiveX Controls

What is the best way to add controls and applets to your Web pages? Using someone else's, of course. As you might imagine, creating these takes some work, and the more work that goes into them, the less *free* they usually are. As you look for controls and applets, you'll notice that people are trying to (and even succeeding at) making a business out of building these applications. Further, you'll notice a definite division between the control and applet camps.

You'll find a lot more applets than controls using normal search engines. And, at the risk of starting a flame war, by and large the Java sites (for me at least) had more of a traditional and open Internet feel to them. On the other hand, to find controls, you're better off starting at Microsoft's Web site and going from there. Because of

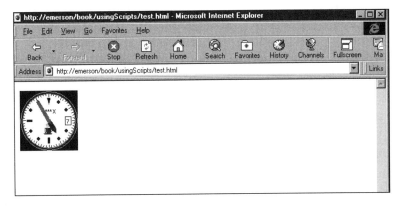

Figure 4.2

The Web clock.

that, again at the risk of starting a flame war, the control sites have a slight Microsoft feel to them. Which one of those is more attractive to you is your choice. The following are some links for each.

ActiveX Control Links

- CNet's ActiveX site is at **www.activex.com**.

- Add-ons for Microsoft-centric world are available at **www.xtras.com**.

Java Applet Links

- News, applets, and information on Java applets are available at **javaboutique.internet.com**.

- Find more applets at at **www.km-cd.com/black_coffee**.

- Even more applets at at **www.oasis.leo.org/java**.

Links For ActiveX Controls And Java Applets

- The Techweb magazine and store is at **www.techweb.com/tools/developers**.

- News, controls, and applets are available at **www.activex.partbank.com**.

- For information, controls, and applets, go to **www.windx.com**. However, be careful at this site, as I accessed it using Netscape 3, and it automatically took me to **www.devx.com/home/devxhome.asp**. While I was there, I managed to blow the browser up three times in as many minutes. Despite that, it still seems to have some good information.

- Information, links, and applets (Java by name but also ActiveX) are available at **www.jars.com**.

- Reference, news, shopping, and more are available at **www.developer.com/directories/pages/dir.java.html**.

Other Resources

You can also go to the Microsoft, Sun, and Netscape sites.

Finally, if you want really great controls and applets, read the rest of this book and you can make your own. You might also enjoy *Creating ActiveX Controls with Visual Basic 5* or *Developing ActiveX Web Controls* (the latter uses Visual C++).

Adding Client-Side VBScript

Web pages are no longer limited to static content. With this frequently familiar and easy-to-learn language, you can incorporate application logic into your Web pages.

Kim Barber

Notes...

Chapter 5

VBScript is a scripting language that allows you to write programs that are embedded in HTML documents. With VBScript, you can create rich, dynamic, interactive Web content. Because VBScript is interpreted, the host environment must have the correct software to execute the code. In the case of client-side script (the focus of this chapter), the Web browser must be aware of VBScript. Microsoft Internet Explorer has this ability built in, but many browsers require a plug-in to interpret VBScript. With server-side script, the server processes the code (server-side scripting is discussed in Chapter 9).

VBScript provides the capability to incorporate application-like behavior in your Web pages. Many tasks that once required processing on the server can be done on the client. This reduces both the number of "trips" to the server and the workload placed on the server. For example, a single Web page can request user input, perform calculations or some other processing, and output the results. Using the CGI approach would require two HTML pages and a CGI script or executable on the server to perform the same task.

The ability to perform calculations on the client is a relatively small but powerful aspect of client-side scripting. For example, client-side VBScript can be used to process HTML forms and perform data validation. This ensures that form data is complete and correct prior to submitting the data to the server. Your script code can respond to user actions, such as clicking an HTML button control, by executing blocks of code you define. Your code can interact with HTML elements. For example, you can set the values of text controls and the radio button and checkbox settings. VBScript can control the appearance and behavior of ActiveX controls and Java applets by setting properties and calling methods. If all this isn't enough, VBScript can interact with the browser itself.

This chapter discusses the details of VBScript language and how VBScript is embedded in HTML documents. Examples will show you how VBScript interacts with HTML forms and intrinsic HTML controls, how to attach script to events, and how to control ActiveX controls and Java applets. Basic script debugging using the Microsoft Script Debugger is also discussed.

What Is VBScript?

VBScript, a subset of Visual Basic for Applications, was developed by Microsoft to add scripting capability to Web pages. Portability is a primary consideration, so Microsoft omitted platform-specific features to make VBScript portable. Therefore, features such as Dynamic Data Exchange, Clipboard, and many advanced features are not available in VBScript. If you have programmed in Visual Basic, you know that it uses a main forms window to contain your program. This, too, is absent from VBScript. Instead, VBScript programs run as part of the Web browser (or other host).

VBScript has very limited I/O capabilities. This limitation results primarily from security concerns. VBScript does not have access to resources, such as the printer and disk I/O, on the client computer. In this chapter, you'll see that client-side VBScript provides only a few intrinsic functions to get user input and to display output to the user.

Show Me The Code

Before going any further, let's take a look at a very simple example of client-side VBScript. Many books on programming contain the very familiar "Hello World" example. There is an unwritten rule that any text on programming must contain this example. Although I can't validate this rumor, I've heard that this is a primary consideration in selecting textbooks for computer science departments in universities. Well, just to make sure I'm not violating any implied laws, Listing 5.1 shows the classic "Hello World" example.

Listing 5.1 A client-side VBScript "Hello World" program.

```
<HTML>
<HEAD>
<TITLE>Hello World</TITLE>
<SCRIPT LANGUAGE=VBScript>
<!--
```

```
      MsgBox "Hello World"
-->
</SCRIPT>
</HEAD>
<BODY>
</BODY>
</HTML>
```

As you can see, Listing 5.1 is a fairly typical HTML file. VBScript is embedded in the HTML with the **<SCRIPT>** tag, which is used to include client-side script in HTML documents. This tag is paired, meaning it requires the **</SCRIPT>** ending tag, and the script code is placed within this tag pair. Like many HTML tags, the **<SCRIPT>** tag has attributes that allow modifying the tag's behavior. Because browsers can support many different languages, the **LANGUAGE** attribute is used to specify the scripting language. SRC is another useful attribute. You can use SRC to specify the URL of a file that contains the script source code. This is convenient if you use the same script in several files. Also, an HTML document can contain multiple scripts in different languages (see Chapter 6, which discusses JavaScript).

The VBScript **MsgBox** function displays the output. Figure 5.1 shows how this page is displayed in Internet Explorer 4. In this example, the function takes the string "Hello World" as an argument and displays it. It also provides an OK button for the user to press to continue. The **MsgBox** function can take other arguments to specify both the buttons to include and the caption displayed at the top of the box.

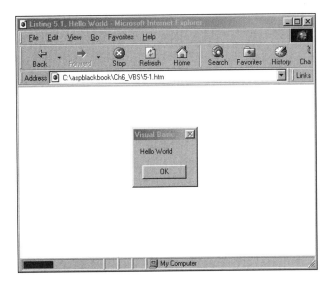

Figure 5.1

The "Hello World" program in Internet Explorer 4.

Although this chapter covers much of the VBScript language details, a complete and current VBScript reference is available at **www.microsoft.com/vbscript**. You'll also find a quick reference in this chapter's Practical Guide.

Also notice the use of the HTML comment tags: **<!--** and **-->**. It's a very good idea to place script code within comment tags because some browsers don't support client-side scripting. Browsers that don't support scripting ignore script placed within comment tags. A browser that doesn't understand script will simply display the code as text and confuse the user.

You can place VBScript code anywhere in an HTML document, although normally it's placed in the **HEAD** section. The exception to this general rule is when you need to include inline script in the **BODY** section. This is commonly done to respond to events, such as a button click, or when you want script to generate HTML. The thing to remember is that code must be defined before it is referenced. (Later in this chapter, you'll learn about VBScript procedures, which are blocks of code that other parts of the script can call.) The script code that defines a procedure must be placed in the HTML document before it is called.

The browser processes VBScript code as the page is loaded. Code that isn't part of a procedure or inline event-driven code is executed immediately.

Advantages Of Client-Side VBScript

There are many ways you can add logic to a Web page. However, there are some distinct advantages to client-side scripting:

- *Processing on the client*—Processing can be performed on the client, thereby reducing the number of trips to the server and the workload placed on the server. This also improves the user's experience, as the Web pages are more responsive.

- *Interactive*—You can create pages that involve the user by requesting information and displaying responses using functions provided by VBScript. Web pages can also respond to user actions, such as clicking a button or selecting or changing a form element.

- *Access to ActiveX controls and Java applets*—Client-side script can control the appearance and behavior of ActiveX controls and Java applets. This allows you to add a very high level of richness and functionality to Web pages.

- *Access to the browser*—Client-side script can interact with the browser itself and with the document contained within the browser (discussed in Chapter 7).

Disadvantages Of Client-Side Scripting

Like most things, especially in programming, there are often disadvantages to consider as well as advantages. Two of the more significant disadvantages of client-side scripting are:

- *Browser dependency*—Client-side script is useful only if the user's browser supports it. Microsoft's Internet Explorer is the only browser currently supporting VBScript without a plug-in. Netscape supports JavaScript, and Internet Explorer supports Microsoft's implementation: JScript. (JavaScript and JScript are discussed in Chapter 6.)

- *Source viewable on client*—Just like HTML, client-side script code can be viewed on the client. As a result, you're sharing your hard work and intellectual property with the world.

The Nuts And Bolts Of VBScript

The next section of this chapter focuses on the details of VBScript. If you are new to this language, this section will give you the information you need to begin writing client-side programs. If you are already familiar with VBScript, you might want to study some examples in this chapter's Practical Guide.

VBScript Comments

Many of the examples in this chapter use comments that you likely will use in your script. VBScript comments may be entered anywhere in the script and are ignored by the VBScript interpreter. There are two methods for inserting comments: the **Rem** keyword and the apostrophe ('). The **Rem** keyword is typically used at the beginning of a line:

```
Rem Comments are ignored by the interpreter
```

Rem may also follow a program statement but must be separated from the statement with a colon (:):

```
Dim intCounter          : Rem Declaring a variable
```

At least one space character must be placed between **Rem** and the comment.

You can also use an apostrophe at the beginning of a line or on the same line as a program statement:

```
Dim intCounter          'Declaring a variable
```

Keep in mind that, although the interpreter ignores comments, client-side script comments are part of the document the browser downloads. Therefore, a lot of comments can affect performance by increasing download and formatting time. Also, because the document source can be viewed on the client, your users can read your comments.

Data Types

Many programming languages, including Visual Basic, support multiple data types, such as integer, string, floating-point, Boolean, and so on. However, VBScript has only one data type—the *variant*. The variant data type can contain different types of data, depending on how it is used. The different data types represented by the variant are referred to as *subtypes*. Table 5.1 shows the various subtypes, and Table 5.2 shows the conversion subtypes you will encounter.

Table 5.1 VBScript variant subtypes.

Subtype	Meaning
Boolean	TRUE or FALSE
Byte	Integer in the range from 0 through 255
Currency	Numeric value in the range from -922,337,203,685,477.5808 through 922,337,203,685,477.5808
Date (Time)	Number representing a date from January 1, 100, through December 31, 9999
Double	Double-precision floating-point number in the range from -1.79769313486232E308 through -4.94065645841247E-324 for negative values; 4.94065645841247E-324 through 1.79769313486232E308 for positive values
Empty	Uninitialized; VBScript interprets this value as either 0 (zero) for numeric expressions or a zero-length string for string expressions

(continued)

Table 5.1 VBScript variant subtypes (continued).

Subtype	Meaning
Error	Error number
Integer	Integer in the range from -32,768 through 32,767
Long	Integer in the range from -2,147,483,648 through 2,147,483,647
Null	Intentionally contains no valid data
Object	An object
Single	Single-precision floating-point number in the range from -3.402823E38 through -1.401298E-45 for negative values; 1.401298E-45 through 3.402823E38 for positive values
String	A variable-length string up to about 2 billion characters in length

Table 5.2 VBScript conversion functions.

Function	Returns Subtype
Asc(string)	Integer ANSI character code of the first letter in the string
CBool(expression)	Boolean
CByte(expression)	Byte
CCur(expression)	Currency
CDate(date)	Date
CDbl(expression)	Double
Chr(charcode)	String
CInt(expression)	Integer
CLng(expression)	Long
CSng(expression)	Single
CStr(expression)	String
Hex(number)	String
Oct(number)	String

Usually, any kind of data can be stored in a variant and will work as it should for the type of data it contains. If a numeric value is stored in a variant, VBScript assumes that it is a number and handles it accordingly. A string value placed in a variant is treated as a string.

VBScript will automatically perform subtype conversions when necessary. Suppose you store a numeric value in a variant and want to use it as a string. VBScript will convert the numeric value in memory and perform the specified operation. Listing 5.2 shows a couple of examples of automatic type conversion.

Listing 5.2 Automatic data type conversion.

```
<SCRIPT LANGUAGE=VBScript>
<!--
    MsgBox "25" + 75
    MsgBox "25" & 75
-->
</SCRIPT>
```

The first statement outputs the numeric value 100. Because arithmetic is being performed with the + operator (operators are discussed later), VBScript temporarily converts the string "25" to a number and then performs the arithmetic operation.

The second statement performs string concatenation with the & operator. In this case, VBScript converts the integer 75 to a string value and appends it to the string "25". The **MsgBox** function then outputs the string value 2575.

What would result from the following?

```
MsgBox "VBScript" + 75
```

VBScript will generate a "type-mismatch" error because the string "VBScript" can't be converted to a numeric value.

However, sometimes it is necessary to explicitly convert a variant from one subtype to another. VBScript provides several conversion functions to perform this task. For example, a variant contains a string value representing a date, "January 1, 1998". You need to increment this date by two weeks to display a due date for your library Web application. This could be done using the **CDate** conversion function as follows:

```
MsgBox CDate("January 1, 1998") + 14
```

However, a better way to do this is to use one of VBScript's date functions. VBScript date functions are described in this chapter's Practical Guide.

Variables

It's good to know that VBScript uses the variant data type to contain a wide variety of data, but how is this data referenced in script? Data items are referenced by storing them in variables. A variable is simply a location in memory that has been given a name and whose contents can be changed. Assigning a name to a memory location creates a variable. You determine a meaningful name for the variable, and VBScript takes care of the details of associating the name with a memory location. Data is then placed in the variable and subsequently accessed through the variable name.

Let's revisit the "Hello World" program. This time, the greeting is stored in a variable. Listing 5.3 shows the revised program.

Listing 5.3 A revised "Hello World" program.
```
<SCRIPT LANGUAGE=VBScript>
<!--
     strGreeting = "Hello World"
     MsgBox strGreeting
-->
</SCRIPT>
```

The first statement declares the variable **strGreeting** and assigns a string value to it. The assignment operator (=) is used to assign values to variables. The **MsgBox** function then outputs the contents of the variable.

Declaring Variables

Variables can be declared either *implicitly* or *explicitly*. Variables are declared implicitly by simply using them, as in Listing 5.3. Variables are declared explicitly by using the **Dim** statement. The following statement explicitly declares the **strGreeting** variable:

```
Dim strGreeting
```

Notice that, unlike Visual Basic, no type information is included here because all variables are of type **Variant**. Multiple variables can be explicitly declared in the same statement by separating the variable names with a comma:

```
Dim strGreeting, strName
```

It is a very good idea to declare variables explicitly. Implicit declaration can cause problems. For example, if a variable name is misspelled, VBScript will think it is a different variable. This can easily produce unexpected results in your program. You can force explicit variable declaration in your program by including the **Option Explicit** statement in the script. If you include this statement and later try to implicitly declare a variable, VBScript will generate a "Variable is undefined" error message. **Option Explicit** should be included as the first statement inside the **<SCRIPT>** body, as shown in Listing 5.4. Also, the **Option Explicit** statement affects only variable declarations within the same **<SCRIPT>** body. If the HTML document contains multiple scripts, each script must include the **Option Explicit** statement to force explicit variable declaration within each script.

Listing 5.4   Using the Option Explicit statement.

```
<SCRIPT LANGUAGE=VBScript>
<!--
    Option Explicit
    Dim strGreeting

    strGreeting = "Good morning"     ' this is okay
    strName = "Mr. Phelps"           ' implicit declaration not allowed
-->
</SCRIPT>
```

Naming Variables

VBScript has a few rules that apply to variable names:

- Names must begin with an alphabetic character.

- Names can't contain periods, spaces, and some special characters, such as #, ~, /.

- Names can't be longer than 255 characters.

- Names must be unique in the scope in which they are declared (scope is discussed in the next section).

- Reserved words (for example, **if**, **option**, **for**, **dim**, and so on) can't be used as variable names.

In addition to these rules are some other considerations in naming variables. VBScript is not case sensitive, as some languages are. Therefore, **LastName** and **lastname** are equivalent. Variable names should be descriptive of the value they contain or of their use. This makes the code easier to read when you come back to it in six months or when someone else must maintain the code. Variable names such as **i** and **fn** are certainly more cryptic than, say, **Count** and **FileName**.

It is also a good idea to adopt some sort of naming convention. This not only improves the readability of your code but also adds consistency. Programmers often use mixed cases, such as **EmployeeID** and **CalculatePayment**, when assigning names. Prefixing the variable name to indicate the subtype it contains is also a good practice. Table 5.3 shows some of the more common subtype prefixes.

Variable Scope

Scope refers to where a variable is available for use within a script. The two levels of scope in VBScript are *script level* and *procedure level*.

A variable has script-level scope when it is declared outside of any procedures. A script-level variable can be used anywhere in the script after the variable is declared and is useful for maintaining information that is required throughout the script. Script-level variables are similar to *global* variables in other languages, such as C. It is good practice to declare script-level variables at the top of the script.

Variables declared within a procedure have procedure-level scope and are available only within the procedure. Procedure-level variables are also known as *local* variables.

The variable-naming rule that names must be unique in the scope in which they are declared means that you can use the same variable name at both the script and the procedure level (although, this is a bad idea, because it can be very confusing). Also, a given variable name can be used in multiple procedures (a common occurrence). Listing 5.5 shows the use of script- and procedure-level variables. Don't worry about the details of procedures right now, as they are discussed later in this chapter.

Table 5.3   Common subtype prefixes.

Prefix	Subtype
dbl	Double
err	Error
int	Integer
lng	Long
obj	Object
str	String

Listing 5.5   Script-level and procedure-level variables.

```
<SCRIPT LANGUAGE=VBScript>
<!--
Option Explicit
Dim VarA                          ' script-level variables
Dim VarB

VarA = 5
VarB = 10

Sub SomeProcedure()
    Dim VarA                      ' procedure-level variable

    VarA = 15
    VarB = 20
End Sub

SomeProcedure()                   ' call the procedure

MsgBox VarA                       ' still equals 5
MsgBox VarB                       ' now equals 20

-->
</SCRIPT>
```

Private And *Public*

Script-level variables are public by default, which means that they are available in all scripts in all currently loaded documents. However, VBScript provides two replacements for the **Dim** statement that allow you to change the default. The **Private** statement creates variables that are available only in the script that declares them. **Public** is used to explicitly declare variables that are available to all scripts (the same as using **Dim**). You can use only **Private** and **Public** at the script level.

Listings 5.6, 5.7, and 5.8 show the use of **Private** and **Public**. Listing 5.6 defines a document that contains two frames. Document 5-7.htm is displayed in the left frame and document 5-8.htm in the right frame. Document 5-7.htm declares three variables: **VarA** is a public variable by default, **VarB** is declared public explicitly, and **VarC** is declared private. Listing 5.8 attempts to display the variables, which are defined in the document displayed in **left_frame** and referenced through the **Window** object (discussed in Chapter 7). For example, the statement **top.left_frame.VarA** refers to **VarA** in the left-hand frame. The public variables are visible to the script in **right_frame**, but the private variable is not. The last statement in Listing 5.8 produces an error message because **VarC** is not visible.

Listing 5.6   Creating HTML frames.

```
<HTML>
<HEAD>
<TITLE>Listing 5.6</TITLE>
</HEAD>
<FRAMESET COLS="50%, 50%">
    <FRAME SRC="5-7.htm" NAME="left_frame">
    <FRAME SRC="5-8.htm" NAME="right_frame">
</FRAMESET>
<BODY>
</BODY>
</HTML>
```

Listing 5.7   Declaring and initializing public and private variables.

```
<HTML>
<HEAD>
<TITLE>Listing 5.7</TITLE>
<SCRIPT LANGUAGE=VBScript>
<!--
Option Explicit
Dim VarA
Public VarB
Private VarC

    VarA = "Default Public VarA"
    VarB = "Public VarB"
    VarC = "Private VarC"
-->
</SCRIPT>
</HEAD>
<BODY>
</BODY>
</HTML>
```

Listing 5.8   Accessing variables in another document.

```
<HTML>
<HEAD>
<TITLE>Listing 5.8</TITLE>
<SCRIPT LANGUAGE=VBScript>
<!--
    MsgBox top.left_frame.VarA
    MsgBox top.left_frame.VarB
    MsgBox top.left_frame.VarC
-->
</SCRIPT>
</HEAD>
<BODY>
</BODY>
</HTML>
```

Lifetime

The variable *lifetime* refers to the amount of time a variable exists. Script-level variables exist from the time they are declared until the script finishes running. Procedure-level variables exist from the time they are declared until the procedure is finished executing.

VBScript Variant Functions

VBScript provides several functions that return information about variants. Table 5.4 lists the available functions.

IsArray

The **IsArray** function is used to determine whether a variable is an array (arrays are discussed in the next section). The function returns a Boolean of **TRUE** if the variable is an array and **FALSE** if it isn't:

```
Dim intCount
document.write IsArray(intCount)               ' returns FALSE
```

IsDate

IsDate is used to determine whether VBScript can convert a variable or expression to a date. The variable or expression must be in the format of a valid date:

```
Dim DateDue
DateDue = "4/15/98"
document.write IsDate(DateDue)                  ' returns TRUE
```

Table 5.4   VBScript variant functions.

Function	Returns
IsArray()	Boolean indicating whether a variable is an array
IsDate()	Boolean indicating whether a variable can be converted to a date
IsEmpty()	Boolean indicating whether a variable has been initialized
IsNull()	Boolean indicating whether a variable is Null
IsNumeric()	Boolean indicating whether a variable can be evaluated as a number
IsObject()	Boolean indicating whether a variable references an OLE Automation object
TypeName()	String providing subtype information
VarType()	Value indicating the variant subtype

IsEmpty

IsEmpty returns **TRUE** if the variable is uninitialized or set to **Empty**. Variables are empty when you declare them or explicitly set them to **Empty**:

```
Dim DateDue
document.write IsEmpty(DateDue)          ' returns TRUE
DateDue = "4/15/98"
document.write IsEmpty(DateDue)          ' returns FALSE
DateDue = Empty
document.write IsEmpty(DateDue)          ' returns TRUE
```

IsNull

IsNull returns **TRUE** if the variable is set to a **Null** value. This isn't the same as **Empty**, which means that the variable hasn't been initialized. **Null** means that the variable contains no valid data. Variables must be set to **Null** explicitly:

```
Dim DateDue
document.write IsNull(DateDue)           ' returns FALSE
DateDue = Empty
document.write IsNull(DateDue)           ' returns FALSE
DateDue = Null
document.write IsNull(DateDue)           ' returns TRUE
```

IsNumeric

IsNumeric returns **TRUE** if the variable can be evaluated as a number. This function is frequently used to determine whether a user entered a valid number:

```
if not IsNumeric(Quantity) then
     MsgBox "Please re-enter Quantity"
end if
```

TypeName

TypeName returns a string that provides the name of the variant subtype contained in a variable. Table 5.5 contains the possible return values and their descriptions.

VarType

VarType returns a value that indicates the subtype of a variable. Table 5.6 contains the possible values returned and the VBScript constant names for each variable type value. Constants are variables, but their values cannot be changed. VBScript defines many constants. Their names always begin with **vb**. You'll see how to create user-defined constants later in this chapter.

Table 5.5 TypeName result strings.

Return	Description
Byte	Byte value
Integer	Integer value
Long	Long integer value
Single	Single-precision floating-point value
Double	Double-precision floating-point value
Decimal	Decimal value
Date	Date or time value
Currency	Currency value
String	String value
Boolean	Boolean value
Empty	Uninitialized
Null	Not valid data; variable set to Null
Error	Error
Object	Generic object
object type	Type name of an object
Unknown	Unknown object type
Nothing	Object variable; does not refer to an object

Table 5.6 VarType return values.

Value	Constant	Description
0	vbEmpty	Uninitialized
1	vbNull	Contains no valid data
2	vbInteger	Integer
3	vbLong	Long

(continued)

Table 5.6 **VarType** return values *(continued).*

Value	Constant	Description
4	vbSingle	Single-precision floating-point number
5	vbDouble	Double-precision floating-point number
6	vbCurrency	Currency
7	vbDate	Date
8	vbString	String
9	vbObject	Automation object
10	vbError	Error
11	vbBoolean	Boolean
12	vbVariant	Variant (used only with arrays of variants)
13	vbDataObject	Data-access object
17	vbByte	Byte
8192/8204	vbArray	Array (8192 added to type of array; see text)

The **VarType** function does not actually return 8192 for an array. VBScript supports only arrays of variants, so this function always returns 8204, which is equal to 8192 plus the value for the variant type. However, **VarType** will return the appropriate value for individual array elements.

Arrays

Unlike *scalar* variables, which can hold only one value, *array* variables can hold multiple values. These variables are useful for storing data items of related information.

You declare arrays with the **Dim** statement. This is just like scalars, except that array variables use parentheses following the variable name. The following statement declares an array variable, **arrFavoriteLinks**, that will store a collection of favorite hyperlinks:

```
Dim arrFavoriteLinks(9)
```

The value in parentheses specifies the number of items the array can store. The previous statement declares an array that can contain 10 items, or *array elements*. Why 10? Arrays in VBScript are *zero-based*, which means that the first element in the array is element zero (0). Therefore, the number of array elements the array can contain is the number in parentheses plus one. The element number is often referred to as the array *subscript* or *index*.

Individual elements in an array are referenced by specifying the element number in parentheses. Listing 5.9 assigns a value to the first element in our favorite-hyperlinks array and then displays the value stored there using the **MsgBox** statement.

Listing 5.9   Referencing array elements.
```
<SCRIPT LANGUAGE=VBScript>
<!--
Option Explicit
Dim arrFavoriteLinks(9)

    arrFavoriteLinks(0)  = "http://www.al-williams.com"
    MsgBox arrFavoriteLinks(0)

-->
</SCRIPT>
```

You may also specify the array subscript using a variable of subtype integer. This statement references an array element using a variable:

```
n = 0
arrFavoriteLinks(n) = http://www.al-williams.com
```

Arrays can contain only data items of the same type. Of course, VBScript has only the variant type, which can hold a variety of subtypes. This allows you to store strings, integers, doubles, and so on in the same array. Take a look at the following:

```
arrMenuItem(0) = "Large Pizza"
arrMenuItem(1) = 14.75
```

Now **arrMenuItem(0)** contains a string and **arrMenuItem(1)** a floating-point value.

Multidimensional Arrays

The array **arrFavoriteLinks(9)** is a *one-dimensional* array. *Multidimensional* arrays are arrays with more than one dimension. Suppose you want to store descriptive text with the URL. You do this by declaring the array as a two-dimensional array—conceptually, an array of rows and columns. A multidimensional array is declared like a one-dimensional array, with a size specifier for each dimension, separated by commas. VBScript allows arrays of up to 60 dimensions. However, arrays with more than three dimensions are seldom useful and always confusing.

The following statement declares a two-dimensional array of 10 rows and 2 columns:

```
Dim arrFavoriteLinks(9,1)
```

Values are assigned to the two-dimensional array as follows:

```
arrFavoriteLinks(0,0) = "http://www.al-williams.com"
arrFavoriteLinks(0,1) = "Al Williams Consulting"
```

In these statements, the URL is assigned to the first row and first column of the array. The text is stored in the first row, second column.

Listing 5.10 shows the use of a multidimensional array to output a list of favorite hyperlinks. All the previous examples used **MsgBox** for output. Although this works, it causes the output to appear in a pop-up dialog box. In many cases, you will want to write output into the HTML stream (you'll find additional information on HTML output in Chapter 7). The Scripting Object Model contains the **Document** object, which provides access to the document currently displayed in the browser. The **Document** object has many methods, including the **Write** method, which writes to the current document. This is just what you need to output your hyperlinks.

Listing 5.10 Using multidimensional arrays.

```
<SCRIPT LANGUAGE=VBScript>
<!--
Option Explicit
Dim arrFavoriteLinks(9,1)

    arrFavoriteLinks(0,0) = "http://www.al-williams.com"
    arrFavoriteLinks(0,1) = "Al Williams Consulting"
    arrFavoriteLinks(1,0) = "http://www.coriolis.com"
    arrFavoriteLinks(1,1) = "The Coriolis Group"
    arrFavoriteLinks(2,0) = "http://www.microsoft.com/vbscript/"
    arrFavoriteLinks(2,1) = "Microsoft's VBScript Site"

    document.write "<A HREF=" & arrFavoriteLinks(0,0) & ">"
    document.write arrFavoriteLinks(0,1) & "</A>"
    document.write "<BR>"

    document.write "<A HREF=" & arrFavoriteLinks(1,0) & ">"
    document.write arrFavoriteLinks(1,1) & "</A>"
    document.write "<BR>"

    document.write "<A HREF=" & arrFavoriteLinks(2,0) & ">"
    document.write arrFavoriteLinks(2,1) & "</A>"
-->
</SCRIPT>
```

Figure 5.2 shows the browser displaying the list. The script stores the URLs for the hyperlinks in the first column of the array and the text in the second column. Then the **document.write** outputs the hyperlink in HTML. This is an example of calling the **write** method of the **document** object. The **document.write** method outputs strings constructed of the HTML anchor element and the URLs contained within the array. The browser interprets the string and displays it as a hyperlink. Notice that the **document.write** method is also sending pure HTML in this example (notice the lines that write the **
** tag).

Dynamic Arrays

The **arrFavoriteLinks** array is a *fixed-size* array. Once you declare its size, that size doesn't change. You can resize *dynamic* arrays as necessary during script execution by increasing the size of the array to hold more data or decreasing it if space is no longer needed. You can also resize both one- and multidimensional dynamic arrays. However, there is a limitation when using multidimensional dynamic arrays, as you'll see shortly.

Use the **Dim** statement to declare both static and dynamic arrays. You can tell a dynamic array declaration from a fixed-size one because the size of a dynamic array

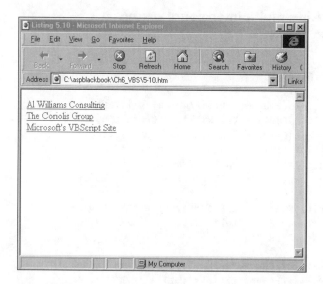

Figure 5.2

A multidimensional array of hyperlinks displayed in the browser.

isn't specified. Instead, the parentheses are empty. The following statement declares a dynamic array:

```
Dim arrFavoriteLinks()
```

Private and **Public** are also used to declare a dynamic array. The following statement declares a private dynamic array:

```
Private arrFavoriteLinks()
```

Dynamic arrays can also be declared with the **ReDim** statement, in which case an initial size must be specified as follows:

```
ReDim arrFavoriteLinks(9)
```

You can resize dynamic arrays using **ReDim** and specifying the new size in parentheses. Your program can make the array larger by specifying a larger number or smaller by specifying a smaller number. Be careful when resizing dynamic arrays as the array elements are initialized by default to subtype **Empty** when the array is resized. Sometimes you want this behavior. If you want the contents of the array to remain, include the **Preserve** keyword in the **ReDim** statement. The following statement resizes the array without losing the array contents:

```
ReDim Preserve arrFavoriteLinks(20)
```

This works well when you must increase the array size. However, when reducing the array size, you'll lose all the data that lies beyond the new array boundary.

You can resize multidimensional arrays as well. You can modify the size of each dimension as well as add and remove dimensions. The following statements declare a one-dimensional dynamic array and then resize the array to make it two-dimensional:

```
Dim arrFavoriteLinks()
ReDim arrFavoriteLinks(10)
...
ReDim arrFavoriteLinks(9,1)
```

One limitation you must remember when working with multidimensional dynamic arrays is that **Preserve** works only if the last dimension is being changed. If a dimension other than the last dimension is resized or you are adding or removing dimensions, **Preserve** cannot be used. In that case, VBScript discards all the array data.

VBScript Array Functions And Statements

VBScript provides several functions and statements that work with arrays. The VBScript array features are shown in Table 5.7.

The **Array** Function

Some languages allow you to initialize arrays during declaration. For example, the following C statement declares an array of integers and fills the first three locations with 1, 2, and 3:

```
int somevariable[ ] = {1,2,3};
```

VBScript can't do this directly. However, you can accomplish almost the same result using the **Array** function, which returns a variant containing an array:

```
Dim somevariable
somevariable = Array(1,2,3)
```

The variable **somevariable** is now a variant that contains an array of variants. You can access the individual array elements as usual.

The **Erase** Statement

The **Erase** statement reinitializes fixed-size arrays and releases dynamic array memory. The elements of a fixed-size array are still accessible after **Erase** but are set to their initial values of zero for numeric arrays, zero-length strings ("") for string arrays, and **nothing** for arrays of objects. Dynamic arrays must be declared again with **ReDim** before the array can be accessed:

```
Erase somevariable
```

Table 5.7   VBScript array functions and statements.

Keyword	Action
Array()	Returns a variant containing an array
Dim, ReDim	Declares variables; **ReDim** also resizes array variables
Erase	Reinitializes fixed-size arrays; frees memory used by dynamic arrays
IsArray()	Returns a Boolean indicating whether a variable is an array
LBound(), **UBound()**	Returns the lower and upper limits of an array dimension
Private, Public	Declares **Private** and **Public** variables

The *IsArray* Function

The **IsArray** function allows you to determine whether a variable is an array. The function returns a Boolean of **TRUE** if the variable is an array and **FALSE** if it isn't:

```
Dim c
document.write IsArray(c)        ' returns FALSE
c = Array(1,2,3)
document.write IsArray(c)        ' returns TRUE
```

The *LBound* And *UBound* Functions

The **LBound** function returns the lowest subscript of an array, which is always zero in VBScript (but not always in Visual Basic). The **UBound** function returns the highest subscript of the array. As an option, you can specify an array dimension in both functions:

```
Dim arrFavoriteLinks(9,1)
' returns upper bound for first dimension (9)
document.write UBound(arrFavoriteLinks)
' returns upper bound for second dimension (1)
document.write UBound(arrFavoriteLinks, 2)
```

Constants

Variables provide a way to store values that may change as the program executes. It's often convenient to store values that do not change. Suppose you are writing a program that makes many calculations using the value of pi (π), which is about 3.1415967. You could simply type this number wherever it is needed, but this would be no fun and full of errors for those of us who are typing challenged. Alternatively, you could assign it to a variable and use the variable throughout the program. This would be easier and less error prone, but it still has a disadvantage. Because it is a variable, its value can be changed, and if it is changed (by accident, of course), calculations using the variable will produce erroneous results.

You can use *constants* in expressions as if they were variables, but you can't change their values. Constants provide the convenience of referencing nonchanging values by name without the possibility of accidentally changing the values. Constants can also provide some level of self-documentation if meaningful names are used. You can declare a constant with the **Const** statement:

```
Const PI = 3.1415967
```

The standard naming rules that apply to variables also apply to constants. Variables, expressions with operators, intrinsic VBScript functions, and user-defined functions can't be used in constant declarations. Programmers commonly use all uppercase names to distinguish constants from variables.

By default, script-level constants are public and procedure-level constants private. You can declare script-level constants explicitly public or explicitly private:

```
Private Const PI = 3.1415967
```

VBScript defines many constants to specify colors, date and times, date formats, comparisons, and more. These constants are documented on the Microsoft VBScript Web site at **www.microsoft.com/scripting/vbscript/vbslang/vbstoc.htm**.

Operators

Operators form expressions that perform calculations, comparisons, and logical operations. VBScript has a complete set of operators that you will use extensively in all but the simplest programs. The three classifications of operators are arithmetic, comparison, and logical.

Arithmetic Operators

Arithmetic operators allow you to perform arithmetic on one or more variables. Table 5.8 contains the VBScript arithmetic operators.

Table 5.8   Arithmetic operators.

Operator	Operation	Description	Syntax
^	Exponentiation	Raises a number to the power of the exponent	c = a ^ b
*	Multiplication	Multiplies two numbers	c = a * b
/	Division	Divides two numbers and returns a floating-point value	c = a / b
\	Integer division	Divides two numbers and returns an integer	c = a \ b
Mod	Modulo arithmetic	Divides two numbers and returns only the remainder	c = a mod b

(continued)

Table 5.8 Arithmetic operators (continued).

Operator	Operation	Description	Syntax
+	Addition	Adds two expressions	c = a + b
-	Subtraction*	Finds the difference between two expressions	c = a - b
&	String concatenation	Joins two string expressions	c = a & b

* Also used for unary negation, that is, to change the sign of the value of an expression.

The string concatenation operator is not actually an arithmetic operator; rather, it fits with arithmetic operators in order of operator precedence. The addition operator can also be used to perform string concatenation, but its use for this is sometimes confusing when reading code and can lead to ambiguities. Consider this code:

```
s="10"
s1=s+9
```

Should **s1** equal 19? Or should it equal "109"? It isn't clear. You should always use **&** to join strings.

Comparison Operators

Comparison operators compare two expressions. The operators return **True**, **False**, or **Null** if either expression is a **Null** value. Comparison operators are listed in Table 5.9.

Table 5.9 Comparison operators.

Operator	Operation
=	Equality
<>	Inequality
<	Less than
>	Greater than
<=	Less than or equal to
>=	Greater than or equal to
Is	Object reference comparison (see text)

The **Is** operator does not compare two objects. Rather, it compares two object references to determine whether they both refer to the same object.

Logical Operators

Logical operators evaluate one or more logical expressions and return a **True** or a **False** result. These operators also perform a bitwise evaluation and return a numeric result if the two expressions are numeric values. Table 5.10 lists the logical operators.

Table 5.10   Logical operators.

Operator	Operation	Syntax	Expression1	Expression2	Result
Not	Logical negation	result = Not expression1	True		False
			False		True
			Null		Null
And	Logical conjunction	result = expression1 And expression2	True	True	True
			True	False	False
			True	Null	Null
			False	True	False
			False	False	False
			False	Null	False
			Null	True	Null
			Null	False	False
			Null	Null	Null
Or	Logical disjunction	result = expression1 Or expression2	True	True	True
			False	False	False
			True	Null	Null
			False	True	True

(continued)

Table 5.10 Logical operators (continued).

Operator	Operation	Syntax	Expression1	Expression2	Result
			False	False	False
			False	Null	Null
			Null	True	True
			Null	False	Null
			Null	Null	Null
Xor	Logical exclusion	result = expression1 Xor expression2	True	True	False
			True	False	True
			False	True	True
			False	False	False
Eqv	Logical equivalence	result = expression1 Eqv expression2	True	True	True
			True	False	False
			False	True	False
			False	False	True
Imp	Logical implication	result = expression1 Imp expression2	True	True	True
			True	False	False
			True	Null	Null
			False	True	True
			False	False	True
			False	Null	True
			Null	True	True
			Null	False	Null
			Null	Null	Null

Operator Precedence

VBScript frequently evaluates operators in an order different than they appear in your program. The *order of precedence* rules determine which operators have priority over other operators. First, arithmetic operators are evaluated, then comparison operators, and then logical operators. There is also an order of precedence within the arithmetic and logical categories. Comparison operators have equal precedence, so VBScript evaluates them from left to right.

The preceding tables list the arithmetic and logical operators in their order of precedence. Some of the arithmetic operators have equal precedence. Multiplication, division, and integer division have equal precedence, as do addition and subtraction. Operators with a high precedence are evaluated before lower-precedence operators. Operators with equal precedence are evaluated left to right. Because multiplication has higher precedence than addition, the expression

```
10+2*3
```

results in 16, not 36, just as it does in standard mathematics.

The standard order of precedence can be overridden by enclosing operations in parentheses. Operations in parentheses take precedence over those not in parentheses, and normal precedence is maintained within parentheses. Parentheses can be nested to further control the order of operation, and operations within the innermost parentheses are evaluated first.

The following statements illustrate how operator precedence is controlled using parentheses:

```
A = 1 * 2 + 6 / 3
A = 1 * (2 + 6) / 3
```

These statements produce different results. In the first example, the product of 1 * 2 is added to the result of 6 / 3, and yields 4. In the second example, the sum of 2 + 6 is multiplied by 1 and then divided by 3, and yields 2.667.

Controlling The Flow

You could write a very modest VBScript program using only the information you already have. However, robust applications require much more than the very basics of VBScript. Most programs make decisions and follow an execution path as a result of those decisions. These decisions frequently depend on the value of a variable or on other things, such as the setting of a radio button or other HTML control. VBScript comes equipped with a fairly complete package of conditional statements (discussed in the next section) that you use to add decision-making capability to programs. Conditional statements evaluate a condition and specify statements to execute on the basis of whether the condition is true or false.

Most applications also execute some lines of code repeatedly. If you need to initialize a 100-element array to a specific value using only the information covered so far, you would have a bit of work on your hands. You could use 100 assignment statements or use the **Array** function with a 100-element argument list, neither of which is desirable. VBScript provides looping statements that are used to execute lines of code a specific number of times or while a condition is true or false.

Conditional Statements

Conditional statements allow programs to make decisions and execute specific lines of code on the basis of the value of a condition. The ability to make decisions and act on them increases your program's "IQ." VBScript supports the following conditional statements:

- **If...Then**
- **If...Then...Else**
- **If...Then...ElseIf**
- **Select Case**

If...Then

The **If...Then** statement, by far the most common conditional statement, executes a statement or statements if a condition evaluates to true:

```
If condition Then
      statement(s) to execute
End If
```

If the condition evaluates to true, the block of statements between the **If...Then** statement and the **End If** statement is executed. The **End If** statement is used to mark the end of the code block. Program execution jumps to the first line of code following the **End If** statement if the condition is false. If only one statement is executed on a true condition, it can be written as follows:

```
If condition Then statement
```

Listing 5.11 shows the use of **If...Then**. In this example, a block of code is executed if the value of a variable is greater than or equal to $10,000.00.

Listing 5.11   The If...Then statement.

```
<SCRIPT LANGUAGE=VBScript>
<!--
Option Explicit
Dim Sales, Commission

    Commission = .05
    Sales = 12500.00  'in real life this would be a computed value
    If Sales >= 10000.00 Then
        Commission = .10
        MsgBox "You're doing well!"
    End If


-->
</SCRIPT>
```

 End If Versus **EndIf**

*If you are used to using Visual Basic, you may type **End If** as one word instead of two. This is permissible with Visual Basic because the VB editor automatically converts **EndIf** to **End If**. However, when writing script, you are usually using a regular text editor that does not do this conversion. Therefore, be sure to include the space between **End** and **If** so that your scripts will work properly.*

If...Then...Else

The **If...Then...Else** statement provides an alternative. One block of statements is executed if the condition is true, and another block is executed if the condition is false:

```
If condition Then
      statements(s) to execute if true
Else
      statement(s) to execute if false
End If
```

Listing 5.12 uses **If...Then...Else** to evaluate the **Sales** variable and displays an alternate message if **Sales** is less than an expected value.

Listing 5.12   The If...Then...Else statement.

```
<SCRIPT LANGUAGE=VBScript>
<!--
Option Explicit
Dim Sales, Commission
```

```
        Commission = .05
        Sales = 12500.00
        If Sales >= 10000.00 Then
            Commission = .10
            MsgBox "You're doing well!"
        Else
            MsgBox "You need to work harder."
        End If

-->
</SCRIPT>
```

If...Then...ElseIf

If...Then...ElseIf is used to evaluate several conditions:

```
If condition1 Then
        statements(s) to execute if condition1 is true
ElseIf condition2 Then
        statement(s) to execute if condition2 is true
ElseIf condition3 Then
        statement(s) to execute if condition3 is true
Else
        statement(s) to execute if none of the above is true
End If
```

Listing 5.13 uses **If...Then...ElseIf** to evaluate possible values of the variable **Sales** and sets the value for **Commission** on the basis of that value. The **Else** statement is used as a default if none of the conditions evaluate to true, which in this case occurs when the value of **Sales** is less than $1,000.00.

Listing 5.13   Using If...Then...ElseIf.

```
<SCRIPT LANGUAGE=VBScript>
<!--
Option Explicit
Dim Sales, Commission

    If Sales >= 10000 Then
        Commission = .20
    ElseIf Sales >= 5000 Then
        Commission = .15
    ElseIf Sales >= 1000 Then
        Commission = .10
    Else
        Commission = .05
    End If

-->
</SCRIPT>
```

Logical operators are often used in conditional statements to further define the evaluation. Listing 5.14 uses the **And** logical operator to determine whether **Sales** is within specific ranges.

Listing 5.14   Using logical operators in conditional statements.

```
<SCRIPT LANGUAGE=VBScript>
<!--
Option Explicit
Dim Sales, Commission

    If Sales < 1000 Then
        Commission = .05
    ElseIf Sales >= 1000 And Sales < 5000 Then
        Commission = .10
    ElseIf Sales >= 5000 And Sales < 10000 Then
        Commission = .15
    Else
        Commission = .20
    End If

-->
</SCRIPT>
```

Listing 5.14 gives the same result as 5.13 but also shows how logical operators are used to define possible conditions. However, in this example, Listing 5.13 is more efficient.

Select Case

The **Select Case** statement is used to execute one of many groups of statements depending on the value of an expression. **Case Else** is used to specify statements to execute if no match is found. Here is the syntax for **Select Case**:

```
Select Case expression
    Case condition1
        statement(s) to execute
    Case condition2
        statement(s) to execute
    . . .
    Case Else
        statement(s) to execute if no match
End Case
```

Listing 5.15 uses **Select Case** to evaluate the possible values of **Commission** and set the variable **Bonus** accordingly.

Listing 5.15   Using Select Case.

```
<SCRIPT LANGUAGE=VBScript>
<!--
Option Explicit
Dim Sales, Commission, Bonus

     Select Case Commission
     Case .05
          Bonus = 0
     Case .10
          Bonus = 500
     Case .15
          Bonus = 1000
     Case .20
          Bonus = 1500
     Case Else
          MsgBox "Invalid Commission Value"
     End Case

-->
</SCRIPT>
```

Looping

You can use *looping* statements to execute selected lines of code repeatedly. VBScript has looping statements that can repeat lines of code a specific number of times or while or until a condition is true. There are four loop statements in VBScript:

- **For...Next**

- **For Each...Next**

- **Do...Loop**

- **While...Wend**

For...Next

The **For...Next** loop executes a block of statements a specific number of times. A *counter* track out variable is used to control the number of times the loop is repeated, the value of which is increased or decreased automatically each time the loop is repeated.

The **For...Next** loop has the following syntax:

```
For counter_variable = start_value To end_value
     statement(s) to execute
Next
```

Visual Basic programmers know that the counter variable may be specified after **next** *and is typically done in nested* **for** *loops to improve code readability. This is not allowed in VBScript.*

The counter variable is an integer that you must declare explicitly if you specified **Option Explicit**. The starting and ending values are variables or literal expressions that specify the number of times the loop is repeated. The counter variable is automatically incremented by one each time the loop is executed, and the loop ends when the counter variable is equal to or greater than the ending value. The **Next** statement marks the end of the loop.

Listing 5.16 uses the **For...Next** loop to output an array of favorite hyperlinks.

Listing 5.16   Using the For...Next loop.

```
<SCRIPT LANGUAGE=VBScript>
<!--
Option Explicit
Dim arrFavoriteLinks(9, 1)
Dim intCounter

    For intCounter = 0 To 9
        document.write "<A HREF=" & arrFavoriteLinks(intCounter,0) & ">"
        document.write arrFavoriteLinks(intCounter,1) & "</A>"
        document.write "<BR>"
    Next

-->
</SCRIPT>
```

The **Step** keyword is used to specify an increment other than one. You can even specify a negative step value to decrement the counter. The following lines of code display the favorite-links array backward:

```
For intCounter = 9 To 0 Step -1
    document.write "<A HREF=" & arrFavoriteLinks(intCounter,0) & ">"
    document.write arrFavoriteLinks(intCounter,1) & "</A>"
    document.write "<BR>"
Next
```

The **Exit For** statement is used to exit the loop early:

```
For intCounter = 0 To 9
    if IsEmpty(arrFavoriteLinks(intCounter, 0)) Then Exit For
    document.write "<A HREF=" & arrFavoriteLinks(intCounter,0) & ">"
    document.write arrFavoriteLinks(intCounter,1) & "</A>"
    document.write "<BR>"
Next
```

This example uses the **IsEmpty** function to test array elements. If **IsEmpty** returns **TRUE**, then **Exit For** is executed and the loop exited.

For Each...Next

The **For Each...Next** loop executes a block of code for each element in an array or *collection*. A collection is an object that contains related objects, such as all the controls in an HTML form. **For Each...Next** is used as follows:

```
For Each item In array_or_collection
     statement(s) to execute
Next
```

Item is a variable that references each item in *array_or_collection*, which is the name of an array or collection. The statements within the loop are executed once for each item, and the loop terminates when there are no more items in the array or collection. The **Exit For** statement can be used to exit from the loop early.

Listing 5.17 uses **For Each...Next** to search for a string in the favorite-links array. The script uses the **InputBox** function to get a search string from the user. The **InputBox** function displays a dialog box and waits for the user to input text into a text box and click the OK button. It returns the contents of the text box to the script. The variable **arrItem** is used to reference each item in **arrFavoriteLinks**. As the loop repeats for each item, the program compares **arrItem** to **strSearchString**. If there is a match, the program sets the Boolean variable **blnFound** to **TRUE** and terminates the loop. **For Each...Next** doesn't automatically maintain a counter variable, so **intIndex** is used to keep track of the number of times the loop repeats. It's useful in this example to increment **intIndex** at the end of the loop because the variable is used later as an array subscript. Therefore, **intIndex** will equal the correct subscript if the routine finds the search string.

Listing 5.17   Using the For Each...Next loop.
```
<SCRIPT LANGUAGE=VBScript>
<!--
Option Explicit
Dim arrFavoriteLinks(9)
Dim strSearchString
Dim arrItem, intIndex
Dim blnFound

     arrFavoriteLinks(0) = "Al Williams Consulting"
     arrFavoriteLinks(1) = "The Coriolis Group"
     arrFavoriteLinks(2) = "Microsoft's VBScript Site"
```

```
    strSearchString = InputBox("Enter search string: ")

    For Each arrItem in arrFavoriteLinks
        If arrItem =  strSearchString Then
            blnFound = TRUE
            Exit For
        End If
        intIndex = intIndex + 1
    Next

    If blnFound Then
        MsgBox arrFavoriteLinks(intIndex)
    Else
        MsgBox "Search string not found."
    End If

-->
</SCRIPT>
```

Do...Loop

The **Do...Loop** repeats a block of statements while or until a condition is true. The **Do...Loop** uses two keywords: **While** and **Until**. **While** causes the loop to repeat while a condition is true, and **Until** causes the loop to repeat until a condition is true. In either case, the condition may be evaluated either at the beginning or at the end of the loop. The statements in the loop always execute at least once when the evaluation is made at the end. **Exit Do** is used to break out of the loop before the condition is met.

The **Do...Loop** is used with **While** as follows:

```
Do While condition_is_true        Do
    statement(s) to execute               statement(s) to execute
Loop                      Loop While condition_is_true
```

The **Do...Loop** is used with **Until** as follows:

```
Do Until condition_is_true        Do
    statement(s) to execute               statement(s) to execute
Loop                      Loop Until condition_is_true
```

Listing 5.18 demonstrates how to use the **Do...Loop** with the **Until** keyword to output the **arrFavoriteLinks** array.

Listing 5.18   Using the Do...Loop.
```
<SCRIPT LANGUAGE=VBScript>
<!--
Option Explicit
```

```
Dim arrFavoriteLinks(9, 1)
Dim intIndex

    arrFavoriteLinks(0,0) = "http://www.al-williams.com"
    arrFavoriteLinks(0,1) = "Al Williams Consulting"
    arrFavoriteLinks(1,0) = "http://www.coriolis.com"
    arrFavoriteLinks(1,1) = "The Coriolis Group"
    arrFavoriteLinks(2,0) = "http://www.microsoft.com/vbscript/"
    arrFavoriteLinks(2,1) = "Microsoft's VBScript Site"

    intIndex = 0
    Do Until IsEmpty(arrFavoriteLinks(intIndex, 0))
        document.write "<A HREF=" & arrFavoriteLinks(intIndex,0) & ">"
        document.write arrFavoriteLinks(intIndex,1) & "</A>"
        document.write "<BR>"
        intIndex = intIndex + 1
    Loop

-->
</SCRIPT>
```

While...Wend

The **While...Wend** loop is an old-fashioned way to write a loop that repeats while a condition is true. This loop is much like the **Do...Loop** (and you can replace it with one). The **While...Wend** loop's condition must be evaluated at the beginning of the loop:

```
While condition_is_true
    statement(s) to execute
Wend
```

VBScript Procedures

There are times when your program must perform certain tasks many times. Perhaps you are writing a program that calculates the distance between several pairs of geographic coordinates and displays the results graphically. Rather than entering the program statements each time the calculation and drawing are needed, you could place the necessary code in *procedures*. A procedure is a block of code that is called to perform a specific task. Each time the program needs to make the calculation, a call is made to the appropriate procedure.

VBScript supports two types of procedures: *subroutines* and *functions*. Subroutines perform a specific task but don't return a result. Functions also perform a specific task and do return a result. If you wanted to calculate the distance between two coordinates, you'd probably use a function because you want the procedure to return a result. Some procedures take *arguments*, or *parameters*, which are pieces of information that a procedure uses, such as the two geographic coordinates in the distance calculation function.

Most of your VBScript programs will include procedures to perform calculations, verify form data, build pages dynamically, and so on. You will also write procedures to respond to *events*. An event is an action that the system generates to inform your program that something interesting has happened. For example, a click event occurs when the user clicks on a button control. You can have your program respond to this event by writing an *event procedure*. The system will then call this procedure when the event occurs.

Subroutines

A subroutine is a procedure that performs an action but doesn't return a result. You can define a subroutine by embedding the necessary program statements between the **Sub** and **End Sub** statements. The **Sub** statement also assigns a name to the subroutine. Subroutine names follow the same naming rules as variables do.

The following subroutine displays a message:

```
Sub ShowMessage
    MsgBox "VBScript is fun!"
End Sub
```

This subroutine has the name **ShowMessage**. Like variables, procedures are **Public** by default but can be declared either **Public** or **Private**:

```
Private Sub ShowMessage
```

Subroutine names can optionally include empty parentheses:

```
Sub ShowMessage()
```

However, parentheses are required for subroutines that take arguments.

Subroutines can be called in a variety of ways, depending on whether they take arguments. Because **ShowMessage** doesn't take an argument, you can call it in any of the following ways:

```
ShowMessage            ' no arguments
ShowMessage()          ' empty argument list
Call ShowMessage    ' Call statement and no arguments
Call ShowMessage()  ' Call statement with empty argument list
```

You also have the option to use the **Call** statement, in which case you must enclose any arguments in parentheses.

Passing Arguments

You can define arguments for your subroutines by including an *argument list* in parentheses. The following redefines **ShowMessage** to take a single argument containing the message to display:

```
Sub ShowMessage(strMessage)
    MsgBox strMessage
End Sub
```

The argument **strMessage** is simply a variable that will contain the value passed to the subroutine. It has local scope (that is, it is visible only within **ShowMessage**). Now that **ShowMessage** has an argument, you can call it as follows:

```
ShowMessage "Hello"
ShowMessage("Hello")
Call ShowMessage("Hello")
```

You can define procedures that take multiple arguments by separating the arguments with a comma in the argument list. Listing 5.19 defines a subroutine that displays the array of favorite hyperlinks. The subroutine takes an array containing the hyperlinks and an integer containing the size of the array as arguments. Compare this to Listing 5.10, which does the same thing. Clearly, Listing 5.19 is more efficient to write because the output code appears only once. It will also be easier to change the format of the output or to add more items using Listing 5.19.

Listing 5.19 Using a subroutine with multiple arguments.

```
<SCRIPT LANGUAGE=VBScript>
<!--
Option Explicit
Dim arrFavoriteLinks(9, 1)

    arrFavoriteLinks(0,0) = "http://www.al-williams.com"
    arrFavoriteLinks(0,1) = "Al Williams Consulting"
    arrFavoriteLinks(1,0) = "http://www.coriolis.com"
    arrFavoriteLinks(1,1) = "The Coriolis Group"
    arrFavoriteLinks(2,0) = "http://www.microsoft.com/vbscript/"
    arrFavoriteLinks(2,1) = "Microsoft's VBScript Site"

    Sub ShowLinks(arrLinkArray, intCount)
    Dim intIndex
```

```
        for intIndex = 0 to intCount
            if IsEmpty(arrFavoriteLinks(intIndex,0)) Then Exit Sub
            document.write "<A HREF=" & arrLinkArray(intIndex,0) & ">"
            document.write arrLinkArray(intIndex,1) & "</A>"
            document.write "<BR>"
        Next
    End Sub

    Call ShowLinks (arrFavoriteLinks, UBound(arrFavoriteLinks))

-->
</SCRIPT>
```

Listing 5.19 also uses the **IsEmpty** function to check the contents of the array. If the array element is empty, a call is made to **Exit Sub** to immediately exit the subroutine. Use **Exit Sub** to prematurely end a subroutine and **Exit Function** to terminate a function.

Changing The Argument Value

VBScript allows your programs to pass variables to procedures *by value* or *by reference*. When a variable is passed by value, VBScript makes a private copy of the variable for the procedure. The procedure can change the value of the variable locally but not the value of the original variable.

If you need to change the value of a variable within a procedure, you must pass the variable by reference. When a variable is passed by reference, VBScript allows the procedure to alter the original variable. By default, VBScript passes arguments by value. You can explicitly use either method by using the **ByVal** and **ByRef** keywords.

Listing 5.20 contains two subroutines that calculate the square of a number. The program passes the number to the subroutine **SqByVal** by value. The value of the variable changes only locally, and the original value remains unchanged outside the subroutine. The program passes the number to the subroutine **SqByRef** by reference. Changes made to the variable are retained when the subroutine finishes executing.

Listing 5.20   Passing arguments by value and by reference.
```
<SCRIPT LANGUAGE=VBScript>
<!--
Option Explicit
Dim lngNumber

    Sub SqByVal(ByVal x)
        x = x * x
    End Sub
```

```
    Sub SqByRef(ByRef x)
        x = x * x
    End Sub

    lngNumber = 5
    Call SqByVal(lngNumber)
    MsgBox lngNumber                    ' lngNumber still equals 5

    Call SqByRef(lngNumber)
    MsgBox lngNumber                    ' lngNumber now equals 25

-->
</SCRIPT>
```

Functions

Functions are very similar to subroutines, but a function can return a value, whereas a subroutine can't. You define functions by using the **Function** and **End Function** statements:

```
Function Sq(x)
    function statement(s)
End Function
```

Functions return values by assigning a value to the function name within the function body. Listing 5.21 contains a function that returns the square of a number.

Listing 5.21   A VBScript function that squares a number.

```
<SCRIPT LANGUAGE=VBScript>
<!--
Option Explicit
Dim lngNumber
Dim lngResult

    lngNumber = 5

    Function Sq(x)
        Sq = x * x
    End Function

    lngResult = Sq(lngNumber)

-->
</SCRIPT>
```

Function calls normally appear in expressions:

```
MsgBox Sq(lngNumber)
```

You may also use a function on the right side of an assignment statement (see Listing 5.21).

Event Procedures

VBScript makes it easy to write procedures that respond to events, such as a button click, selecting a checkbox control, and changing a text box control. The ability to respond to events is very useful. For example, an event procedure can respond to a user clicking on the **Submit** button. Instead of forwarding the form data to the server right away, you can arrange for VBScript to call your event procedure to validate the form data and submit the data to the server only if it is correct. Also, an ActiveX control could generate an event that code can respond to. The Microsoft Timer control has a timer event that occurs when a specified timeout interval expires. An event procedure can respond to this event and perform an action, such as reloading the page.

You can define an event procedure as you would any other procedure. The only difference is that event procedures have special names. Event procedure names consist of the name of the control and the name of the event joined by the underscore character:

```
Sub ControlName_EventName
```

The HTML Button control has an **OnClick** event that occurs when the button is clicked. Assuming there is a button named **Calculate**, you can define a procedure to respond to the **OnClick** event as follows:

```
Sub Calculate_OnClick
    procedure statement(s)
End Sub
```

Listing 5.22 contains an event procedure that calculates the area of a rectangle. The user enters the length and width into a form, and the calculation is made when the **Calculate** button fires its **OnClick** event. In other words, the user presses the **Calculate** button to perform the computation.

Listing 5.22   A VBScript event procedure.

```
<HTML>
<HEAD>
```

```
<TITLE>Listing 5.22</TITLE>
<SCRIPT LANGUAGE=VBScript>
<!--
Option Explicit

    Sub Calculate_OnClick
        MsgBox "Area is " & area.length.value * area.width.value
    End Sub

-->
</SCRIPT>
</HEAD>
<BODY>

<FORM NAME="area">
Length:<INPUT TYPE=TEXT NAME="length"><BR>
Width:<INPUT TYPE=TEXT NAME="width"><BR>
<INPUT TYPE=BUTTON NAME="Calculate" VALUE="Calculate">
</FORM>

</BODY>
</HTML>
```

VBScript calls the event procedure **Calculate_OnClick** when the user clicks the **Calculate** button. You can access the values in the text box's **length** and **width** through their **value** properties. HTML controls are objects, so they have events, methods, and properties that you can use in a script (the intrinsic HTML controls and their events, methods, and properties are discussed later in this chapter). The controls **length** and **width** are members of the form **area**, which is why the code uses the notation **area.width.value** to access the width and **area.height.value** to access the height.

Using **<SCRIPT FOR>**

You can also attach code to a control by using the **FOR** attribute of the **<SCRIPT>** tag. The **FOR** attribute specifies the control the code is attached to:

```
<SCRIPT FOR="ControlName"...>
```

Specify which event the code handles with the **EVENT** attribute:

```
<SCRIPT FOR="ControlName" EVENT="EventName" LANGUAGE=VBScript>
```

Using this method, you could write the event procedure **Calculate_OnClick** as it appears in Listing 5.23.

Listing 5.23   Using the FOR and EVENT attributes.

```
<HTML>
<HEAD>
<TITLE>Listing 5.23</TITLE>
<SCRIPT FOR="Calculate" EVENT="OnClick" LANGUAGE="VBScript">
    MsgBox "Area is " & area.length.value * area.width.value
</SCRIPT>
</HEAD>
<BODY>

<FORM NAME="area">
Length:<INPUT TYPE=TEXT NAME="length"><BR>
Width:<INPUT TYPE=TEXT NAME="width"><BR>
<INPUT TYPE=BUTTON NAME="Calculate" VALUE="Calculate">
</FORM>

</BODY>
</HTML>
```

You don't use **Sub** and **End Sub** when using this method. Instead, there is a **<SCRIPT FOR...>** for each control and event that you want to handle. Listing 5.23 has the **<SCRIPT>** tag in the **HEAD** section. You will often see the **<SCRIPT>** tag used in the **BODY** section with the control the code is attached to:

```
<INPUT TYPE=BUTTON NAME="Calculate" VALUE="Calculate">
<SCRIPT FOR="Calculate" EVENT="OnClick" Language="VBScript">
    MsgBox "Area is " & length.value * width.value
</SCRIPT>
```

Notice that when using this method, you do not need to specify the form name.

Method Procedures

Method procedures are procedures belonging to objects. Many objects expose these procedures for use in applications. You saw examples of this when you used the **write** method of the **document** object to output HTML to the browser. You can call method procedures by specifying the object name and method name and joining these with a period:

```
object.method
document.write
```

Most HTML controls have methods you can call. The Button control has a **Click** that, when called, generates an **OnClick** event:

```
Calculate.Click
```

Many ActiveX controls and Java applets have methods. For example, the Microsoft Timer control has an **AboutBox** method that you can call to display information about the control.

VBScript Error Handling

Let's face it: Errors happen. The programmer's job is to anticipate errors and write code to prevent errors from crashing the program. You can use several strategies to prevent many runtime errors. You can add data validation routines to all sections of code where there is a possibility of an incorrect value causing an error (for example, a divide-by-zero error). Another strategy is to use VBScript's ability to instruct the interpreter not to halt when an error occurs.

Basic Data Validation

Data validation routines are frequently a large part of a program for a number of reasons, one of which is to prevent errors. Assume for a moment that you are writing a program that calculates loan payments. The user enters the annual interest rate and the number of payment periods. The program must divide the annual interest rate by the number of payments to calculate the interest rate per period. If the user enters a zero for the number of periods, a divide-by-zero error will result. To prevent this, the program needs to check the user's input to determine whether the period is zero. If it is, the user is prompted to reenter the number of periods. Listing 5.24 shows how you might write this validation code using VBScript.

Listing 5.24   Validating data to prevent a runtime error.

```
<SCRIPT LANGUAGE=VBScript>
<!--
Dim Rate
Dim PeriodicRate
Dim Periods

    Function ValidatePeriods
    ValidatePeriods = -1
        If Periods = 0 Then
            ValidatePeriods = 0
        End If
    End Function

    If Not ValidatePeriods Then
        MsgBox "Please reenter the number of periods.", vbExclamation
```

```
        Else
            PeriodicRate = Rate / Periods
        End If

-->
</SCRIPT>
```

Listing 5.24 uses a function, **ValidatePeriods**, to check the value entered by the user. If the user entered 0, **ValidatePeriods** returns 0; otherwise, it returns -1. If the function returns 0, the program displays a message box instructing the user to reenter the number of periods. Because this is an error condition, the program instructs the message box to use an exclamation icon.

VBScript Error Handling

VBScript provides the capability to prevent the program from crashing when a fatal error occurs. The **On Error Resume Next** statement tells the interpreter to ignore the error and continue executing on the next statement following the one in which the error occurred. Keep in mind that this doesn't handle the error; rather, it simply tells the program to salute and continue to march.

The following statements show the use of **On Error Resume Next**:

```
Rate = 18
Periods = 0
On error Resume Next
PeriodicRate = Rate / Periods
program execution resumes here
. . .
```

On Error Resume Next is automatically reset when you call another procedure. Therefore, you should include it in all routines that might be susceptible to errors.

The **Err** Object

The **Err** object contains information about runtime errors and, in combination with **On Error Resume Next**, offers a powerful way to handle errors. When an error occurs, the properties of the **Err** object are set to information that identifies the error as well as information that you can use to handle the error. Table 5.11 lists the **Err** object properties. You can find the **Err** object's methods in Table 5.12.

Table 5.11 Err object properties.

Property	Description
Description	Returns or sets a string describing the error
HelpContext	Context ID for a topic in a help file
HelpFile	Path to a help file
Number	Number specifying the error
Source	Name of the application or object that generated the error

Table 5.12 Err object methods.

Method	Description
Clear	Clears the setting of the **Err** object properties
Raise	Generates a runtime error

The **Raise** method is useful during debugging to test error-handling routines. It is also useful if you want to cause an error that will be visible to another part of the program. The **Raise** method uses the following syntax:

```
Err.Raise(number, source, description, helpfile, helpcontext)
```

Listing 5.25 uses the **On Error Resume Next** statement with the **Err** object to trap and handle an error.

Listing 5.25 Using On Error Resume Next with the Err object.
```
<SCRIPT LANGUAGE=VBScript>
<!--
Dim Rate
Dim PeriodicRate
Dim Periods

    Sub ErrorHandler(num, desc, src)
        MsgBox "Error: " & num & ": " & desc & " generated by " & src
    End Sub

    On Error Resume Next
    Rate = 18
```

```
        Periods = 0
        PeriodicRate = Rate / Periods
        If Err.number <> 0 Then
            Call ErrorHandler(Err.number, Err.description, Err.source)
        End If

-->
</SCRIPT>
```

After the division operation executes, the program examines the value of **Err.number**. If it is non-zero, there is an error, in which case the program calls a routine to handle the error. The subroutine **ErrorHandler** simply displays some of the properties of the **Err** object. A real program might use a much more sophisticated error-handling routine.

Microsoft's Script Wizard

If you use Microsoft's Visual InterDev (using the Source or the Layout Editor), FrontPage, or ActiveX Control Pad, you can use Microsoft's Script Wizard to help you develop client-side scripts. In a nutshell, the Script Wizard is a WYSIWYG tool for displaying events on a page, attaching actions to them, and magically generating the appropriate code (in VBScript or JScript). Of course, this doesn't always work, so the wizard provides an environment for tweaking the code by hand when you need help generating the magic script.

Wizard Or Wizard's Assistant?

There should be some commandments that companies must live by before they can glorify their software with appellations like "WYSIWYG" and "wizard." For WYSIWYG, the rule should be, *Thou shalt not have to spend too much time learning to use the tool to work with it.* For wizard, the main commandment should be, *Thou shalt not have to be a wizard to use the wizard.* Although a worthwhile tool, Microsoft's Script Wizard still slips on these two tests, especially the latter one.

As a perhaps unfair comparison, take PowerPoint's wizard. Anyone can use it to create professional-looking presentations with no knowledge of colors, graphics, backgrounds, or even insight into the theory of the logical ordering of presentations. In this case, "wizard" implies that you simply open it up and cannot help but fall down the right path.

Regardless of what some sources might try to claim, Microsoft's Script Wizard is not yet ready for any weekend HTML warrior who wants to use it to painlessly and flawlessly generate great effects with scripts. You have to understand a lot of details (events, objects, procedures, variables, controls, and so on) to get much use out of the tool. Of course, that's what this chapter is all about.

You also need to know how to find the wizard. You might think in Visual InterDev that you would just open up Tools I Options I Script Wizard or that there would be some kind of icon on the toolbar. (Hint: The right mouse button is your friend in Visual InterDev.) Fortunately, if you are using Control Pad or FrontPage, the wizard is easily accessible from the menu and toolbar.

That said, if you want to read all the documentation on the tool and if you're already a script wizard, the wizard can be helpful (but it's a wizard's *assistant*, not a wizard).

Where Do You Find It?

In the ActiveX Control Pad, it is easy to find the wizard by clicking on the scroll-like icon in the toolbar. You can also select Tools I Script Wizard from the menu. In FrontPage, you select Insert I Script. Visual InterDev hides the wizard. Once you have a file open, you can select View I Script Wizard. Also, as a surprise (although you might never know it), if you left-click an opened HTML document (in the HTML Source or Layout Editor window of Visual InterDev) and then right-click, you will find a shortcut to select Script Wizard.

Overview Of Working With The Script Wizard

In general, you will open the Script Wizard on an existing HTML file and see a three-paned window. This interface allows you to see and select the events associated with a page (in the Event pane), associate actions with the events with the click of a mouse (in the Action pane), and then view and manipulate the assigned actions (in the Script pane).

Choosing A Scripting Language

Before you begin, you should consider what scripting language you want to use: VBScript or JScript. By default in Visual InterDev and Control Pad, you will be using VBScript. To change that in Control Pad, select Tools I Options I Script, and then make your change. In Visual InterDev, select Tools I Options, and then click the HTML tab to select your option. Only in FrontPage Editor do you get the choice up front to select Insert I Script. Then you can select your choice before starting to use the wizard.

Note that the wizard lets you use only one language on a page, and if you open a page with VBScript or JScript already on it, that will be your choice of scripting language while you use the wizard on that page.

What Does It Look Like?

Figure 5.3 shows the three-paned window of the Script Wizard opened on a blank HTML file in Visual InterDev.

If you double-click on Window in the Event pane, it will expand to show you all the events associated with that page. For a blank page, this includes **onLoad**, **onParseComplete**, and **onUnload**. If you double-click on Window in the Action pane, you'll see all the available actions, objects, properties, and events.

Icon Map

If you aren't sure what the icons mean, refer to Table 5.13.

A Simple Example

As you can probably tell from the figures in Table 5.13, it is relatively simple to use the Script Wizard to create a page that automatically links to another page. Here are the steps:

1. Open a page in the HTML Editor of Visual InterDev.

2. Double-click on Window in the Event pane to display the events available for that page.

3. Click on the **onLoad** event.

4. Double-click on Go to Page in the Action pane.

5. Enter a URL, and click OK (this step assumes you are in List View; see the following if you are using Code View).

Table 5.13   Script Wizard icons.

Icon	Description
◇	An event that has not been scripted
◆	An event that has been scripted
⬆	An action
▤	A property
▩	An object
▢	The window object

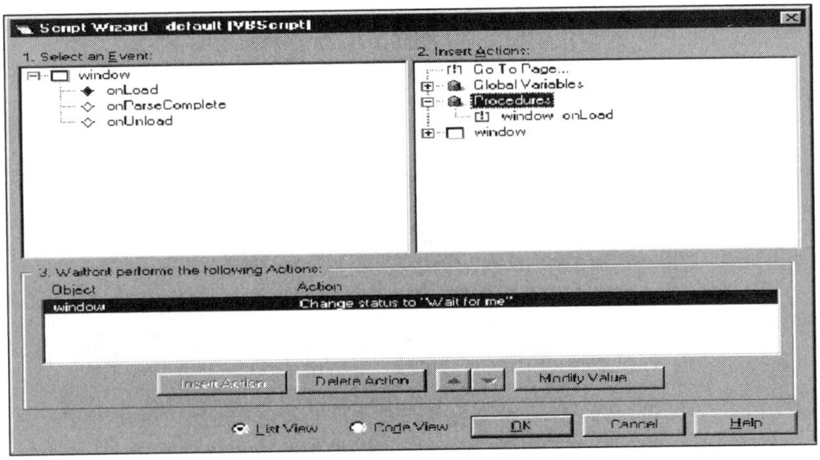

Figure 5.3

The Script Wizard.

If you are in List View, you will see Go to Page... "http://www.foo.com" page in the Script pane (assuming you entered http://www.foo.com as the URL). If you are in Code View (using VBScript) and you follow the same steps, you will see:

```
Sub window_onLoad()
Window.location.href = ""
```

Then you can simply type in the URL between the quotes. In any case, the resultant script generated by the wizard should look like this:

```
Sub window_onLoad()
Window.location.href = "http://www.foo.com"
```

Benefits

- If for nothing else, Script Wizard is a neat tool for displaying all events associated with a page and the available actions.

- It gives you the option of creating scripts in VBScript or JScript.

- You can use it as a tool to learn scripting (the hard way), letting it create scripts for you and then using the Code View option on the Script pane to see, learn, and then understand what you did.

- You can use it to create simple scripts as a starting point and then use the Script pane to modify and enhance.

- You can use it as a very handy wizard's assistant for complex scripting (if you already are a scripting wizard), associating objects, events, forms, applets, and controls with the click of the mouse.

Weaknesses

- Script Wizard is not very useful for scripting novices.

- You can have only one script language per page.

- If you're adding a new procedure or object to an existing HTML file that already has procedures, objects, or both, the Script Wizard does not check for duplicates (you have to check for duplicate names by hand). The Wizard does JScript, not JavaScript (for some that may be a weakness). You'll read more about JScript versus JavaScript in the next chapter.

Hints

- You can change the Script pane font, a nice feature that makes your environment more homey (left-click in Visual InterDev's Script Wizard Script pane, then right-click).

- Right-click at random. There seems to be a lot of things you can do with a right-click, and maybe you'll find something new.

Expectations

As has been the trend with Microsoft products lately, if Microsoft sticks with them, they develop into solid products. Just as you would not likely code an HTML table by hand after having used FrontPage's table generator, most people would choose to point and click to select events, associate actions with them, and generate code using the Script Wizard instead of pounding it out by hand.

Given that, this tool will probably stay around in some form and get better and easier to use, although it may be a while before the weekend HTML warrior can simply pick it up and run with no background in scripting. Of course, once you have absorbed the material in this chapter, you should have no difficulties with the wizard.

Summary

VBScript provides a substantial amount of scripting ability that can be put to use in writing robust, interesting, and functional Web pages. Other parts of this book discuss the use of VBScript on the client and server sides to interface with the browser and its components and to generate HTML. In the Practical Guide, you'll find examples of VBScript processing forms, performing data validation, and controlling ActiveX controls.

Practical Guide To

VBScript

- Using VBScript With HTML Forms
- Using VBScript With ActiveX Controls
- Debugging With The Microsoft Script Debugger
- VBScript Quick Reference Specifications

Most client-side VBScript programs work with forms, HTML controls, and objects. This section shows you how to write scripts that interact with forms and HTML controls and ActiveX controls. You'll also see how to use the Microsoft Script Debugger to debug client-side script and find a VBScript Quick Reference and an HTML Intrinsic Controls Reference.

Using VBScript With HTML Forms

The next several chapters of this book build on the Community Dining Club application. This Web site is for people who enjoy dining out. It offers the convenience of learning about participating restaurants and making reservations online. Listing 5.26 allows new club members to register and illustrates how VBScript works with the form's elements, performs basic data validation, and responds to control events.

Listing 5.26   Using VBScript with an HTML form.

```
<HTML>
<HEAD>
<TITLE>New Member Registration</TITLE>
<SCRIPT LANGUAGE="VBScript">
<!--
Sub cmdSubmit_OnClick()


    Dim TheForm
    Set TheForm = Document.RegistrationForm


    If Len(TheForm.firstname.Value) = 0 Then
        MsgBox "Please enter your first name.", vbOKOnly, "First Name"
        TheForm.firstname.Focus


    ElseIf Len(TheForm.lastname.Value) = 0 Then
        TheForm.lastname.value =
            InputBox ("Please enter your last name.", "Last Name")
        If Len(TheForm.lastname.Value) <> 0 Then TheForm.addr1.Focus
    ElseIf Len(TheForm.addr1.Value) = 0 Then
        MsgBox "Please enter your address.", vbOKOnly, "Address1"
        TheForm.lastname.Focus
    ElseIf Len(TheForm.city.Value) = 0 Then
        MsgBox "Please enter the city.", vbOKOnly, "City"
        TheForm.city.Focus


    ElseIf Len(TheForm.state.Value) <> 2 Then
        MsgBox "Please enter the 2-letter state abbreviation.", _
            vbOKOnly, "State"
```

```vbscript
        TheForm.state.Focus
        TheForm.state.Select

    ElseIf Len(TheForm.zip.Value) < 5 Then
        MsgBox "Please enter a valid ZIP code.", vbOKOnly, "ZIP Code"
        TheForm.zip.Focus
        TheForm.zip.Select
    ElseIf Len(TheForm.code.Value) <> 3 _
    Or Not IsNumeric(TheForm.code.Value) Then
        MsgBox "Please enter a valid area code.", vbOKOnly, "Area Code"
        TheForm.code.Focus
        TheForm.code.Select
    ElseIf Len(TheForm.phone.Value) <> 7 _
    Or Not IsNumeric(TheForm.phone.Value) Then
        MsgBox "Please enter a valid phone number.", vbOKOnly, "Phone Number"
        TheForm.phone.Focus
        TheForm.phone.Select

    ElseIf TheForm.cuisine.SelectedIndex = 0 Then
        MsgBox "Please let us know what your favorite cuisine is.", _
            vbOKOnly, "Cuisine"
        TheForm.cuisine.Focus

    End If
End Sub
-->
</SCRIPT>
</HEAD>
<BODY>
<H1 Align=Center>Community Dining Club</H1>
<H2 Align=Center>New Member Registration</H2>
<HR SIZE=5 WIDTH=90%>
<PRE>
<FORM NAME="RegistrationForm">
<B>First Name:      </B><INPUT TYPE=TEXT NAME="firstname">
<B>Last Name:       </B><INPUT TYPE=TEXT NAME="lastname">
<B>Address1:        </B><INPUT TYPE=TEXT NAME="addr1">
<B>Address2:        </B><INPUT TYPE=TEXT NAME="addr2">
<B>City:            </B><INPUT TYPE=TEXT NAME="city">
<B>State:           </B><INPUT TYPE=TEXT NAME="state" MAXLENGTH=2 SIZE=2>
<B>Zip:             </B><INPUT TYPE=TEXT NAME="zip" MAXLENGTH=10 SIZE=10>
<B>Area Code:</B>
<INPUT TYPE=TEXT NAME="code" MAXLENGTH=3 SIZE=3>
<B>Phone:</B>
<INPUT TYPE=TEXT NAME="phone" MAXLENGTH=7 SIZE=7>

<B>Preferred Cuisine: </B><SELECT NAME="cuisine" SIZE="1">
```

```
                    <OPTION VALUE="1">American
                    <OPTION VALUE="2">Chinese
                    <OPTION VALUE="3">French
                    <OPTION VALUE="4">German
                    <OPTION VALUE="5">Greek
                    <OPTION VALUE="6">Indian
                    <OPTION VALUE="7">Italian
                    <OPTION VALUE="8">Japanese
                    <OPTION VALUE="9">Other
                    </SELECT>
<INPUT TYPE=BUTTON NAME="cmdSubmit" VALUE="Submit">
 <INPUT TYPE="RESET" VALUE="Clear">
</PRE>
</FORM>
</BODY>
</HTML>
```

The document defines a form to collect user information in the **BODY** section. When the user clicks the Submit button, VBScript calls the event procedure **cmdSubmit_OnClick**. This procedure checks the form to ensure that the required data is available and in some cases valid.

First, **cmdSubmit_OnClick** declares the variable **TheForm**, then sets it to reference the form **RegistrationForm**. The **Document** object (discussed in Chapter 7) contains subobjects that correspond to each form in the document. You can access the form elements using a statement such as:

```
document.RegistrationForm.firstname.Value
```

However, assigning a variable to reference the form reduces typing and makes the code easier to read. Because **TheForm** references an object, you must use the **Set** statement to make the assignment.

The remainder of the procedure validates the input. The first test checks the length of **firstname**'s **Value** property. If it is equal to zero, the code displays a message box asking the user to enter his or her first name. Then the code calls the text box control's **Focus** method to place the cursor in the incorrect text box.

If there is nothing in **lastname**, the user can enter it in response to a prompt from the **InputBox** function. Although this is inconsistent with the rest of the script, it shows that HTML control properties are easy to change programmatically. Once the new name is in place, the code rechecks the **Value** property and moves the focus to the next control.

If the information entered for **state** is not two characters, the program asks the user to enter a two-character abbreviation. Then the program calls the text box control's **Select** method to highlight any text already there. This allows the user to easily overtype the incorrect information.

Finally, the code checks the **SelectedIndex** property of the selection control to determine whether the user selected a preferred cuisine. The **SelectedIndex** property is set to the value of the selected item or to zero if nothing is selected.

Using VBScript With ActiveX Controls

ActiveX control properties are set in HTML using the **<PARAM>** tag when the page is loaded. The property settings are otherwise static, unless the control itself is changing them. Properties, methods, and events exposed by ActiveX controls can be accessed using VBScript and can be used programmatically. Therefore, the control's behavior can be modified dynamically.

Listing 5.27 "spruces up" the Community Dining Club New Member Registration page with a spinning billboard. The script uses two controls that Microsoft supplies with Internet Explorer: **Label** and **Timer**. The **Label** control displays text. You can change the control's properties to set the font, angle, and other display characteristics. The **Label** control also has several events and one method, but you won't need them for this example. The user never sees the **Timer** control in the browser. The timer's only purpose is to fire a **Timer** event at a specified interval. Each time the script detects a **Timer** event, it spins the text by changing the label's properties. VBScript is the glue that connects these two controls. Through VBScript, the **Timer** control affects the characteristics of the **Label** control.

Listing 5.27 Controlling ActiveX controls with VBScript.

```
<HTML>
<HEAD>
<TITLE>New Member Registration</TITLE>
<SCRIPT LANGUAGE=VBScript>
    Dim Angle
    Dim Message, MsgNo

    Randomize
    Message = Array("Join Today!", "Fine Dining!", "Impress Friends!", _
                        "Save Money!", "Be Cool!")

    MsgNo = 0
    ColorNo = 1
    Angle = 0
```

```
Sub IeTimer_Timer
    IeLabel.Caption = Message(MsgNo)
    IeLabel.Angle = Angle
    Angle = Angle + 5
    If Angle > 360 Then
        Angle = 0
        MsgNo = MsgNo + 1
        If MsgNo > 4 Then MsgNo = 0
        ChangeColor
    End If
End Sub


Sub ChangeColor
    IeLabel.ForeColor = Rnd * 16777215
End Sub

Sub cmdSubmit_OnClick()
    Dim TheForm
    Set TheForm = Document.RegistrationForm

    If Len(TheForm.firstname.Value) = 0 Then
        MsgBox "Please enter your first name.", vbOKOnly, "First Name"
        TheForm.firstname.Focus
    ElseIf Len(TheForm.lastname.Value) = 0 Then
        TheForm.lastname.value =
        InputBox ("Please enter your last name.", "Last Name")
        If Len(TheForm.lastname.Value) <> 0 Then TheForm.addr1.Focus
    ElseIf Len(TheForm.addr1.Value) = 0 Then
        MsgBox "Please enter your address.", vbOKOnly, "Address1"
        TheForm.lastname.Focus
    ElseIf Len(TheForm.city.Value) = 0 Then
        MsgBox "Please enter the city.", vbOKOnly, "City"
        TheForm.city.Focus
    ElseIf Len(TheForm.state.Value) <> 2 Then
        MsgBox "Please enter the 2-letter state abbreviation.", _
            vbOKOnly, "State"
        TheForm.state.Focus
        TheForm.state.Select
    ElseIf Len(TheForm.zip.Value) < 5 Then
        MsgBox "Please enter a valid ZIP code.", _
        vbOKOnly, "ZIP Code"
        TheForm.zip.Focus
        TheForm.zip.Select
    ElseIf Len(TheForm.code.Value) <> 3 _
    Or Not IsNumeric(TheForm.code.Value) Then
        MsgBox "Please enter a valid area code.", vbOKOnly, "Area Code"
```

```
                   TheForm.code.Focus
                   TheForm.code.Select
              ElseIf Len(TheForm.phone.Value) <> 7 _
              Or Not IsNumeric(TheForm.phone.Value) Then
                   MsgBox "Please enter a valid phone number.", _
                   vbOKOnly, "Phone Number"
                   TheForm.phone.Focus
                   TheForm.phone.Select
              ElseIf TheForm.cuisine.SelectedIndex = 0 Then
                   MsgBox "Please let us know what your favorite cuisine is.", _
                    vbOKOnly, "Cuisine"
                   TheForm.cuisine.Focus
              End If
       End Sub
</SCRIPT>
</HEAD>
<BODY>

<H1 Align=Center>Community Dining Club</H1>
<H2 Align=Center>New Member Registration</H2>
<HR SIZE=5 WIDTH=90%>

<OBJECT ID="IeTimer" WIDTH=39 HEIGHT=39
 CLASSID="CLSID:59CCB4A0-727D-11CF-AC36-00AA00A47DD2">
     <PARAM NAME="Interval" VALUE="50">
</OBJECT>

<TABLE>
<TD>
<OBJECT ID="IeLabel" WIDTH=150 HEIGHT=150
 CLASSID="CLSID:99B42120-6EC7-11CF-A6C7-00AA00A47DD2">
     <PARAM NAME="Caption" VALUE=" ">
     <PARAM NAME="Angle" VALUE="0">
     <PARAM NAME="Alignment" VALUE="4">
     <PARAM NAME="Mode" VALUE="1">
     <PARAM NAME="FillStyle" VALUE="0">
     <PARAM NAME="ForeColor" VALUE="#000000">
     <PARAM NAME="BackColor" VALUE="#C0C0C0">
     <PARAM NAME="FontName" VALUE="Arial">
     <PARAM NAME="FontSize" VALUE="14">
     <PARAM NAME="FontItalic" VALUE="0">
     <PARAM NAME="FontBold" VALUE="1">
     <PARAM NAME="FontUnderline" VALUE="0">
     <PARAM NAME="FontStrikeout" VALUE="0">
```

```
    <PARAM NAME="TopPoints" VALUE="0">
    <PARAM NAME="BotPoints" VALUE="0">
</OBJECT>
</TD>
<TD>
<PRE>
<FORM NAME="RegistrationForm">
<B>First Name:      </B><INPUT TYPE=TEXT NAME="firstname">
<B>Last Name:       </B><INPUT TYPE=TEXT NAME="lastname">
<B>Address1:        </B><INPUT TYPE=TEXT NAME="addr1">
<B>Address2:        </B><INPUT TYPE=TEXT NAME="addr2">
<B>City:            </B><INPUT TYPE=TEXT NAME="city">
<B>State:           </B><INPUT TYPE=TEXT NAME="state" MAXLENGTH=2 SIZE=2>
<B>Zip:             </B><INPUT TYPE=TEXT NAME="zip" MAXLENGTH=10 SIZE=10>
<B>Area Code: </B>
<INPUT TYPE=TEXT NAME="code" MAXLENGTH=3 SIZE=3>
<B>Phone:</B>
 <INPUT TYPE=TEXT NAME="phone" MAXLENGTH=7 SIZE=7>

<B>Preferred Cuisine: </B><SELECT NAME="cuisine" SIZE="1">
                        <OPTION VALUE="1">American
                        <OPTION VALUE="2">Chinese
                        <OPTION VALUE="3">French
                        <OPTION VALUE="4">German
                        <OPTION VALUE="5">Greek
                        <OPTION VALUE="6">Indian
                        <OPTION VALUE="7">Italian
                        <OPTION VALUE="8">Japanese
                        <OPTION VALUE="9">Other
                        </SELECT>

<INPUT TYPE=BUTTON NAME="cmdSubmit" VALUE="Submit">
<INPUT TYPE="RESET" VALUE="Clear">
</PRE>
</FORM>
</TD>
</TABLE>

</BODY>
</HTML>
```

Figure 5.4 shows the page in Internet Explorer 4. The script first performs some initialization by seeding the random number generator with the **Randomize** statement. The random number generator is used in the **ChangeColor** subroutine to set the text color. The billboard will cycle through five messages that are stored in the **Message** array (which is initialized using the **Array** function).

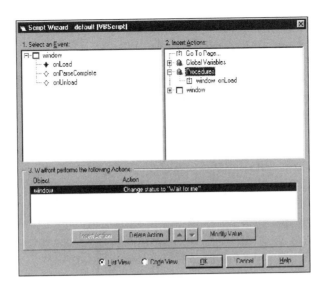

Figure 5.4

The New Member Registration page.

VBScript calls the event procedure **IeTimer_Timer** when the **Timer** control fires the **Timer** event. The procedure sets the **Label** control's **Caption** property from the **Message** array and sets the **Angle** property from a variable. The script increments the **Angle** variable and checks to see whether it is greater than 360 degrees. If it is, the code resets the angle to zero and increments **MsgNo** so that the next message will appear on the next **Timer** event. A call to **ChangeColor** then changes the text color. **ChangeColor** simply sets the **Label** control's **ForeColor** property to a random color.

The **Timer** control resides in the body of the HTML document. The **Interval** property specifies the time in milliseconds between calls to the **Timer** event. The document sets the **Interval** property to 50, which results in a rapidly spinning billboard.

The **Label** control and HTML form are inside a table so that the control appears next to the form. Notice that the **Label** control has several properties, but we need only the **Caption** and **ForeColor** properties.

Debugging With The Microsoft Script Debugger

Debugging code can be tedious and time-consuming. Until recently, client-side script debugging tools were very limited. To trace program flow, stop execution, and view variables (or properties), you had to use the **MsgBox** or **Alert** functions. Newer tools make the debugging task better, but the tools still are not as sophisticated as the ones found in other environments, such as VC++ or VB.

The Microsoft Script Debugger provides a greatly improved debugging experience. The debugger allows you to debug scripts while they are running in the browser. You can also do the following:

- View the source code
- Trace program execution
- View and change variables and properties
- View values of expressions and VBScript functions
- Set breakpoints
- Step into, out of, and over procedures
- Watch the call stack

The debugger has the following windows (see Figure 5.5):

- *Source Editor*—Allows you to view the source and set and clear breakpoints. The script is read-only, so you cannot edit the file. However, you can save the file with a different name, make the necessary changes, save it with the original name, and then reload it.

- *Running Documents*—Displays a list of documents that are available for debugging.

- *Command*—Allows you to enter commands and execute them immediately. You can view or set the values of variables and properties and view the values of expressions and VBScript functions.

- *Call Stack*—Displays the active procedure calls made by the program.

Starting The Debugger

You can start the debugger in the following ways:

- *Manually*—Open the debugger from the Windows Start menu as a standalone application.

- *From the browser*—Select Source from the View menu to debug scripts in the current document.

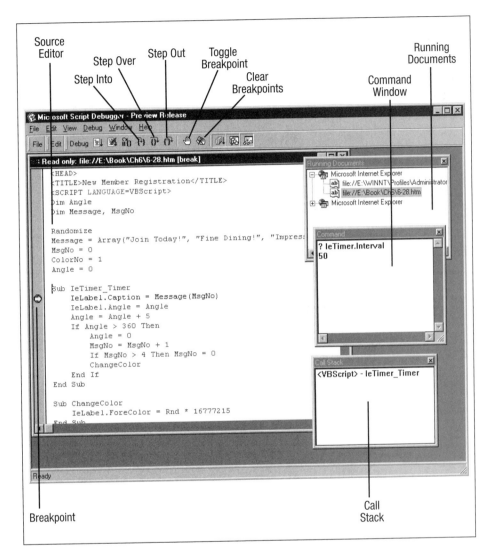

Figure 5.5

The Microsoft Script Debugger.

- *Automatically*—When a runtime error occurs, start the debugger by clicking on Yes when prompted.

- *Programmatically*—Insert the **Stop** command in the source to cause program execution to stop and run the debugger.

How To Set Breakpoints

A breakpoint is set or cleared by placing the cursor on the line of interest and selecting Toggle Breakpoint from the Debug menu. Alternately, you can press F9 or select the toggle breakpoint icon (a small hand) on the toolbar. All breakpoints can be cleared at the same time by selecting Clear All Breakpoints from the View menu, pressing Ctrl+Shift+F9, or selecting the Clear All Breakpoints icon (a hand with an X over it) on the toolbar. Figure 5.5 shows a breakpoint set on the first statement of the **IeTimer_Timer** subroutine.

How To Step Through Script

With execution halted on a breakpoint, you can step through the script one line at a time using the following choices:

- **Step Into**—Executes the next line of script. **Step Into** allows you to follow the script line by line. If the next line is a procedure call, execution halts at the first line of the procedure. **Step Into** is available from the Debug menu by pressing F8 and from the toolbar.

- **Step Over**—Steps over procedure calls. If the current line of code is a procedure call, the debugger executes the entire procedure. Execution halts at the line immediately following the procedure call. **Step Over** is available from the Debug menu by pressing Shift+F8 and from the toolbar.

- **Step Out**—Used when **Step Into** stepped into a procedure and you want to step out of it and proceed to the next line following the procedure call. You can think of this as an undo **Step Into** command.

How To Use The Command Window

You can use the Command window to view and change variables and properties while the script is running. The changes made immediately affect the running script.

To examine a variable or property, use the following syntax:

```
? IeTimer.Interval
```

The Command window displays the value of the **Interval** property when you press Enter.

To set a variable or property type, set the following syntax:

```
IeTimer.Interval = 25
```

In addition to changing variables and properties, you can call procedures. With the script halted, you could call the **ChangeColor** subroutine like this:

```
ChangeColor
```

This will cause the text color to change when you resume program execution.

 VBScript Quick Reference Specifications
These tables contain a quick reference to the features available in VBScript.

Array Handling Quick Reference

Keyword	Description	Syntax
Array	Returns a variant containing an array	x = Array(*argument list*)
Dim	Declares a variable and allocates memory	Dim x(*dimensions*)
Erase	Reinitializes fixed-size array and releases dynamic array memory	Erase x
IsArray	Returns a Boolean indicating whether a variable is an array	IsArray(x)
LBound	Returns the lower limit of an array dimension (always 0)	LBound(x[,*dimension*])
Private	Declares a private variable	Private x(*dimensions*)
Public	Declares a public variable	Public x(*dimensions*)
Redim	Declares a dynamic array and reallocates	Redim [Preserve] x(*dimensions*)memory
UBound	Returns the upper limit of an array dimension	UBound(s,[,*dimension*])

Assignment Operators Quick Reference

Keyword	Description	Syntax
=	Assigns the value of a literal or expression to a variable	x = 10
Set	Assigns an object reference to a variable	Set x = *object*

Comments Quick Reference

Keyword	Description	Syntax
'	Begins a comment	' *comment*
Rem	Begins a comment line	Rem *comment*

Constants And Literals Quick Reference

Keyword	Description	Syntax
Empty	Indicates an uninitialized variable	x = Empty
Nothing	Releases an object variable reference	Set x = Nothing
Null	Indicates a variable; contains no valid data	x = Null
True, False	Boolean values -1 and 0, respectively	x = True

Control Flow Quick Reference

Keyword	Description	Syntax
Do...Loop	Loops while or until a condition is True	Do While x < 10 *statements* Loop
		Do *statements* Loop While x < 10
		Do Until x = 10 *statements* Loop
		Do *statements* Loop Until x = 10
For...Next	Repeats a loop a specified number of times	For x = 1 to 10 *statements* Next
For Each...Next	Repeats statements for each element in an array or a collection	For Each x in y *statements* Next
If...Then...Else	Conditionally executes statements	If *true* then *statements* Else *statements* End If

(continued)

Control Flow Quick Reference (continued)

Keyword	Description	Syntax
Select Case	Executes one of several groups of statements	Select Case x Case value1 *statements* Case value2 *statements* ... End Case
While...Wend	Repeats a loop while a condition is true	While x < 10 *statements* Wend

Conversion Functions Quick Reference

Keyword	Description	Syntax
Abs	Returns the absolute value of a number	Abs(x)
Asc, AscB, AscW	Returns the ANSI character code of the first letter in a string	Asc("x")
Chr, Chrb, ChrW	Returns the character for the specified character code	Chr(65)
CBool	Returns a subtype Boolean	CBool(x)
CByte	Returns a subtype Byte	CByte(x)
CCur	Returns a subtype Currency	CCur(x)
CDbl	Returns a subtype Double	CDbl(x)
CInt	Returns a subtype Integer	CInt(x)
CLng	Returns a subtype Long	CLng(x)
CSng	Returns a subtype Single	CSng(x)
CStr	Returns a subtype String.	CStr(x)
DateSerial	Returns a subtype Date	DateSerial(*month, day, year*)
DateValue	Returns a subtype Date	DateValue(*date string*)

(continued)

Conversion Functions Quick Reference *(continued)*

Keyword	Description	Syntax
Fix	Returns the integer portion of a number	Fix(*number*)
Hex	Returns a string representing a hexadecimal value	Hex(*number*)
Int	Returns the integer portion of a number	Int(*number*)
Oct	Returns a string representing an octal value	Oct(*number*)
Round	Returns a number rounded to a specified number of decimal places	Round(*number* [,*numberofdecimalplaces*])
Sgn	Returns an integer indicating the sign of a number	Sgn(*number*)
TimeSerial	Returns a subtype Date containing the time	TimeSerial(*hour, minute, second*)
TimeValue	Returns a subtype Date containing the time	TimeValue(*time string*)

Date And Time Functions Quick Reference

Keyword	Description	Syntax
Date	Returns the system date	Date
DateAdd	Returns a date to which a time interval has been added	DateAdd(*interval, number, date*)
DateDiff	Returns the number if intervals between two dates	DateDiff(*interval, date1, date2* [,*firstdayofweek* [,*firstweekofyear*]])
DatePart	Returns the specified part of a date	DatePart(*interval, date* [,*firstdayofweek* [,*firstweekofyear*]])
DateSerial	Returns a subtype Date	DateSerial(*month, day, year*)
DateValue	Returns a subtype Date	DateValue(*date string*)

(continued)

Date And Time Functions Quick Reference *(continued)*

Keyword	Description	Syntax
Day	Returns a number representing the day of the month	Day(*date expression*)
Hour	Returns a number (0 through 23) representing the hour	Hour(*time expression*)
Minute	Returns a number (0 through 59) representing the minute	Minute(*time expression*)
Month	Returns a number representing the month	Month(*date expression*)
Now	Returns the current date and time	Now
Second	Returns a number (0 through 59) representing the second	Second(*time expression*)
Time	Returns a subtype Date containing the system time	Time
TimeSerial	Returns a subtype Date containing the time	TimeSerial(*hour, minute, second*)
TimeValue	Returns a subtype Date containing the time	TimeValue(*time string*)
Weekday	Returns a number representing the day of the week	Weekday(*date [,firstdayofweek]*)
Year	Returns a number representing the year	Year(*date expression*)

Declaration Statements Quick Reference

Keyword	Description	Syntax
Const	Declares a constant	Const PI = 3.14159
Dim	Declares a variable	Dim x
Function	Declares a function	[Private] [Public] Function *name[(arguments)]* *statements* End Function
Private	Declares a private variable	Private x

(continued)

Declaration Statements Quick Reference *(continued)*

Keyword	Description	Syntax
Public	Declares a public variable	Public x
ReDim	Declares a dynamic array variable	ReDim [Preserve] x(*dimensions*)
Sub	Declares a subroutine	[Private] [Public] Sub *name*[(*arguments*)]

Error Handling Quick Reference

Keyword	Description	Syntax
On Error	Enables error-handling routing	On Error Resume Next
Err	Object containing information about the last error	Err[.*property or method*]

Input And Output Functions Quick Reference

Keyword	Description	Syntax
InputBox	Displays a prompt and waits for input	InputBox(*prompt*[,*title*][,*default*][,*xpos*][,*ypos*][,*helpfile,context*])
LoadPicture	Returns a picture object	LoadPicture(*picture_name*)
MsgBox	Displays a message and waits for a button click	MsgBox(*prompt*[,*buttons*][,*title*][,*helpfile, context*])

Math Functions Quick Reference

Keyword	Description	Syntax
Atn	Returns the arctangent of a number	Atn(x)
Cos	Returns the cosine of an angle	Cos(x)

(continued)

Math Functions Quick Reference *(continued)*

Keyword	Description	Syntax
Exp	Returns a number raised to a power	Exp(x)
Log	Returns the logarithm of a number	Log(x)
Randomize	Initializes the random number generator	Randomize [*number*]
Rnd	Returns a random number less than 1	Rnd [[*number*]]
Sin	Returns the sine of an angle	Sin(x)
Sqr	Returns the square root of a number	Sqr(x)
Tan	Returns the tangent of an angle	Tan(x)

Operators Quick Reference

Keyword	Description	Syntax
+, -	Addition, subtraction	a + b, a - b
^	Exponentiation	a^b
Mod	Modulus arithmetic	a Mod b
*****	Multiplication	a * b
/	Division	a / b
****	Integer division	a \ b
-	Negation	- a
&	String concatenation	a & b
=	Equity	a = b
<>	Inequity	a <> b
<	Less than	a < b
<=	Less than or equal to	a <= b
>	Greater than	a > b

(continued)

Operators Quick Reference *(continued)*

Keyword	Description	Syntax
>=	Greater than or equal to	a >= b
Is	Object reference equivalence	obj1 Is obj2
And	Logical conjunction	a And b
Or	Logical disjunction	a Or b
Xor	Logical exclusion	a Xor b
Eqv	Logical equivalence	a Eqv b
Imp	Logical implication	a Imp b

Objects And Object Functions Quick Reference

Keyword	Description	Syntax
CreateObject	Returns a reference to an automation object	CreateObject(*objectclassname*)
Dictionary	Object that stores key/item pairs	Set *objvar* = CreateObject ("Scripting.Dictionary")
Err	Object containing information about the last error	Err[.*property or method*]
FileSystem Object	Object that provides access to the file system (server-side only)	Set *objvar* = CreateObject ("Scripting.FileSystemObject")
GetObject	Returns a reference to an ActiveX object	GetObject([*path*] [,*class*])
TextStream	Provides sequential access to a file	TextStream[.*property or method*]

Options Quick Reference

Keyword	Description	Syntax
Option Explicit	Forces explicit variable declaration	Option Explicit

Procedures Quick Reference

Keyword	Description	Syntax
Call	Calls a procedure	Call *FunctionName*
Function... End Function	Declares a function	[Private] [Public] Function *name*[(*arguments*)] *statements* End Function
Sub... End Sub	Declares a subroutine	[Private] [Public] Sub *name*[(*arguments*)] End Sub

Script Engine ID Functions Quick Reference

Keyword	Description	Syntax
ScriptEngine	Returns a string describing the scripting language in use	ScriptEngine
ScriptEngine BuildVersion	Returns the build number	ScriptEngineBuildNumber
ScriptEngine MajorVersion	Returns the major version number	ScriptEngineMajorVersion
ScriptEngine MinorVersion	Returns the minor version number	ScriptEngineMinorVersion

String Functions Quick Reference

Keyword	Description	Syntax
Asc, AscB, AscW	Returns the ANSI character code of the first letter in a string	Asc("x")
Chr, Chrb, ChrW	Returns the character for the specified character code	Chr(65)
Filter	Returns a filtered array containing a subset of a string array	Filter(*inputstrings, value*[,*include*[,*compare*]])

(continued)

String Functions Quick Reference (continued)

Keyword	Description	Syntax
FormatCurrency	Returns a string formatted as a currency value	FormatCurrency(*string* [,*decimalplaces* [,*inclleadingzero* [,*useparenthesis* [,*groupdigits*]]]])
FormatDateTime	Returns a string formatted as a date or a time value	FormatDateTime(*date*[,*format*])
FormatNumber	Returns a string formatted as a number	FormatCurrency (*string*[,*decimalplaces* [,*inclleadingzero* [,*useparenthesis* [,*groupdigits*]]]])
FormatPercent	Returns a string formatted as a percentage	FormatCurrency (*string*[,*decimalplaces* [,*inclleadingzero* [,*useparenthesis* [,*groupdigits*]]]])
Instr	Returns the position of the first occurrence in one string in another	Instr([*start*,] *string1*,*string2* [,*compare*])
InstrB	Same as Instr but uses byte data; returns the byte position	
InstrRev	Returns the position of the first occurrence of one string in another, beginning from the end	InstrRev(*string1*, *string2*[,*start*[,*compare*]])
Join	Returns a string constructed by joining substrings in an array	Join(*list*[,*delimiter*])
Len, LenB	Returns the number of characters in a string or the number of bytes required to store a variable	Len(*string or variable*)
LCase	Returns a string that has been converted to lowercase	LCase(*string*)
Left, LeftB	Returns the specified number of characters beginning from the left	Left(*string, number*)

(continued)

String Functions Quick Reference *(continued)*

Keyword	Description	Syntax
LTrim	Returns a string without leading spaces	LTrim(*string*)
Mid, MidB	Returns the specified number of characters	Mid(*string, start*[*,number*])
Replace	Returns a string in which a specified substring has been replaced a specified number of times	Replace(*string,s tringtoreplace, replacewith*[*,start*[*,count* [*,compare*]]])
Right, RightB	Returns the specified number of characters beginning from the right	Right(*string, number*)
RTrim	Returns a string without trailing spaces	RTrim(*string*)
Space	Returns a string consisting of the specified number of spaces	Space(*number*)
Split	Returns an array containing the specified number of substrings	Split(*string*[*,delimiter* [*,count*[*,compare*]]])
StrComp	Returns a value indicating the result of a string comparison	StrComp(*strint1, strin2*[*,compare*])
String	Returns a character string of a specified character of the length specified	String(*number,character*)
StrReverse	Returns a reversed string	StrReverse(*string*)
Trim	Returns a string without leading or trailing spaces	Trim(*string*)
UCase	Returns a string that has been converted to uppercase	UCase(*string*)

Variant Functions Quick Reference

Keyword	Description	Syntax
IsArray()	Boolean indicating whether a variable is an array	IsArray(x)
IsDate()	Boolean indicating whether a variable can be converted to a date	IsDate(x)

(continued)

Variant Functions Quick Reference *(continued)*

Keyword	Description	Syntax
IsEmpty()	Boolean indicating whether a variable has been initialized	IsEmpty(x)
IsNull()	Boolean indicating whether a variable is Null	IsNull(x)
IsNumeric()	Boolean indicating whether a variable can be evaluated as a number	IsNumeric(x)
IsObject()	Boolean indicating whether a variable references an OLE Automation object	IsObject(x)
TypeName()	String providing subtype information	TypeName(x)
VarType()	Value indicating the variant subtype	VarType(x)

VBScript Constants Quick Reference

Category	Constant	Value	Description
Color	vbBlack	0	Black
	vbRed	255	Red
	vbGreen	65280	Green
	vbYellow	65535	Yellow
	vbBlue	16711680	Blue
	vbMagenta	16711935	Magenta
	vbCyan	16776960	Cyan
	vbWhite	16777215	White
Comparison	vbBinaryCompare	0	Perform a binary comparison
	vbTextCompare	1	Perform a textual comparison
Date/Time	vbSunday	1	Sunday
	vbMonday	2	Monday

(continued)

VBScript Constants Quick Reference (continued)

Category	Constant	Value	Description
	vbTuesday	3	Tuesday
	vbWednesday	4	Wednesday
	vbThursday	5	Thursday
	vbFriday	6	Friday
	vbSaturday	7	Saturday
	vbFirstJan1	1	Use the week in which January 1 occurs (default)
	vbFirstFourDays	2	Use the first week that has at least four days in the new year
	vbFirstFullWeek	3	Use the first full week of the year
	vbUseSystem	0	Use the date format contained in the regional settings for your computer
	vbUseSystemDay OfWeek	0	Use the day of the week specified in your system settings for the first day of the week
Date Format	vbGeneralDate	0	Display a date and/or time
	vbLongDate	1	Display a date using the long date format
	vbShortDate	2	Display a date using the short date format
	vbLongTime	3	Display a time using the long time format
	vbShortTime	4	Display a time using the short time format

(continued)

VBScript Constants Quick Reference *(continued)*

Category	Constant	Value	Description
Drive Type	Unknown	0	Drive type cannot be determined
	Removable	1	Drive has removable media
	Fixed	2	Drive has fixed media
	Remote	3	Network drives
	CDROM	4	Drive is a CD-ROM
	RAMDisk	5	Drive is RAM memory acting as a drive
File Attribute	Normal	0	Normal file
	ReadOnly	1	Read-only file
	Hidden	2	Hidden file
	System	4	System file
	Volume	8	Disk drive volume label
	Directory	16	Folder or directory
	Archive	32	File has changed
	Alias	64	Link or shortcut
	Compressed	128	Compressed file
Error	vbObjectError	-2147745792	Object-generated error
File I/O	ForReading	1	Open a file for reading only
	ForWriting	2	Open a file for writing (overwrites the file if it already exists)
	ForAppending	8	Open a file and write from the end
MsgBox	vbOKOnly	0	Display OK button only
	vbOKCancel	1	Display OK and Cancel buttons

(continued)

VBScript Constants Quick Reference (continued)

Category	Constant	Value	Description
	vbAbortRetryIgnore	2	Display Abort, Retry, and Ignore buttons
	vbYesNoCancel	3	Display Yes, No, and Cancel buttons
	vbYesNo	4	Display Yes and No buttons
	vbRetryCancel	5	Display Retry and Cancel buttons
	vbCritical	16	Display Critical Message icon
	vbQuestion	32	Display Warning Query icon
	vbExclamation	48	Display Warning Message icon
	vbInformation	64	Display Information Message icon
	vbDefaultButton1	0	First button is the default
	vbDefaultButton2	256	Second button is the default
	vbDefaultButton3	512	Third button is the default
	vbDefaultButton4	768	Fourth button is the default
	vbApplicationModal	0	Application modal
	vbSystemModal	4096	System modal
MsgBox Return Values	vbOK	1	OK button
	vbCancel	2	Cancel button
	vbAbort	3	Abort button
	vbRetry	4	Retry button
	vbIgnore	5	Ignore button
	vbYes	6	Yes button
	vbNo	7	No button

(continued)

Category	Constant	Value	Description
String	vbCr	Chr(13)	Carriage return
	vbCrLf	Chr(13) & Chr(10)	Carriage return/linefeed combination
	vbLf	Chr(10)	Line feed
	vbNewLine	Chr(13) & Chr(10) or Chr(10)	Platform-specific new line character
	vbNullChar	Chr(0)	Character having the value 0
	vbNullString	-	String having value 0
	vbTab	Chr(9)	Horizontal tab
Tristate	TristateTrue	-1	True
	TristateFalse	0	False
	TristateUseDefault	-2	Use default setting
VarType	vbEmpty	0	Uninitialized (default)
	vbNull	1	Contains no valid data
	vbInteger	2	Integer subtype
	vbLong	3	Long subtype
	vbSingle	4	Single subtype
	vbDouble	5	Double subtype
	vbCurrency	6	Currency subtype
	vbDate	7	Date subtype
	vbString	8	String subtype
	vbObject	9	Object
	vbError	10	Error subtype
	vbBoolean	11	Boolean subtype

(continued)

VBScript Constants Quick Reference *(continued)*

Category	Constant	Value	Description
	vbVariant	12	Variant (used only for arrays of variants)
	vbDataObject	13	Data access object
	vbDecimal	14	Decimal subtype
	vbByte	17	Byte subtype
	vbArray	8192	Array

Intrinsic HTML Controls Quick Reference

Control	Properties	Events	Methods
Button	Form, Name, Value	OnClick	Click
Reset Button	Form, Name, Value	OnClick	Click
Submit Button	Form, Name, Value	OnClick	Click
Checkbox	Form, Checked, Name, Value	OnClick	Click
Combo Box	Form, Checked, List, ListCount, ListIndex, MultiSelect, Name, Value	OnClick, OnFocus, Focus, Add Item, Remove Item	Clear, Click
Radio Button	Form, Checked, Name, Value	OnClick	Click
Password Control	Form, Name, Value	OnBlur, OnChance, OnFocus, OnSelect	Blur, Focus, Select
Text Box Control	Form, Name, Value	OnBlur, OnChance, OnFocus, OnSelect	Blur, Focus, Select
Text Area Control	Form, Name, Value	OnBlur, OnChance, OnFocus, OnSelect	Blur, Focus, Select
Select or List	Form, Name, Length	OnBlur, OnChange	Blur, Focus

(continued)

Intrinsic HTML Controls Quick Reference *(continued)*

Control	Properties	Events	Methods
Box Control	Length, Options, SelectedIndex	OnFocus	Focus
Hidden Control	Name, Value	None	None

Scripting For Windows

Once you are comfortable with scripting, you'll find yourself wanting to use it everywhere. If you're running Windows 98, you'll be able to run scripts directly under Windows.

The two programs that allows this are WSCRIPT.EXE (the program that runs scripts under Windows) and CSCRIPT.EXE (an interpreter for console scripts). In general, these two interpreters are identical except for how they display output. For example, the **WScript.echo** command displays a message box under WSCRIPT.EXE and prints to the current console when using CSCRIPT.EXE.

Of course, there are some differences between scripting for Windows and browser scripting. The object models are necessarily different. To help you get started, "WScript Object Members Quick Reference" shows the members available in the **WScript** object. This object is always present, just like the **Window** object is in the browser.

You can use **CreateObject** to create any ActiveX object, including a special scripting object that allows you to access the shell (see "WshShell Members Quick Reference"). You can also create objects that let you work with network connections or any ActiveX object you need.

Although this book isn't about Windows scripting, you can find an example in Listing 5.28. This simple program dumps the environment. If you use CSCRIPT, the output appears in the console. If you use WSCRIPT, you'll see each environment string in a separate message box.

Listing 5.28   A Windows script.

```
Set WshShell = Wscript.CreateObject("Wscript.Shell")
Set env=WshShell.Environment("PROCESS") ' Only PROCESS allowed for Win95/98
for each s in env
  WScript.echo s
next
```

WScript Object Members Quick Reference

Member	Description
Application	The IDispatch for the WScript object
Arguments	A collection of the command-line arguments
FullName	The full pathname of the executable
Name	The name of the scripting object
Path	The directory that contains the script interpreter (WScript or CScript)
ScriptFullName	The full pathname of the current script
ScriptName	The file name of the current script
Version	The version of the script interpreter
CreateObject	Creates an ActiveX object
DisconnectObject	Releases an ActiveX object
Echo	Displays data
GetObject	Obtains an ActiveX object that corresponds to a file
Quit	Terminates execution of the script

WshShell Members Quick Reference

Member	Description
Environment	A collection of environment variables
SpecialFolders	A collection of special folder objects
CreateShortcut	Creates a shortcut
ExpandEnvironment Strings	Interprets strings with embedded environment variable references
Popup	Shows a message box
RegDelete	Deletes a Registry entry

(continued)

WshShell Members Quick Reference *(continued)*

Member	Description
RegRead	Reads the Registry
RegWrite	Writes to the Registry
Run	Runs a program

Chapter 6

Adding Client-Side JavaScript

JavaScript is a rich language, based on the popular Java, that is used to add programming logic to Web pages. Additionally, it is well supported by both Microsoft and Netscape.

Kim Barber

Notes…

Chapter 6

JavaScript is an *object-based* language developed by Netscape. Syntactically, it is similar to Java but is not a subset of it. JavaScript has a rich feature set that provides a very good environment for developing client and server applications and is well suited for quick development and easy maintenance of relatively small programs, such as those typically found in Web applications.

JavaScript is a scripting language that allows you to write programs that reside inside HTML documents. It is an interpreted language, so the host environment (the Web browser) must have a JavaScript scripting engine to execute the code. Web pages incorporating client-side scripting must be viewed by a browser with a built-in scripting engine or a plug-in. Both Microsoft's Internet Explorer and Netscape's Navigator support JavaScript.

With JavaScript, you can create Web pages that have application-like behavior. Many tasks that once required processing on the server can now be done on the client, thus limiting the number of requests made to the server. The client does most of the work, so the server has a reduced workload. For example, a single Web page can request user input, perform calculations or some other processing, and output the results. Using the CGI approach would require two HTML pages and a CGI script or executable on the server to perform the same task.

Performing calculations on the client is just one use of client-side scripting, which can also be used to process HTML forms and perform data validation. This ensures that form data is complete and correct prior to submitting the data to the server.

Script can respond to user actions (such as clicking an HTML button control) by executing blocks of code that you define. Script can interact with HTML elements, for example, by setting the values of text controls and setting radio button and checkboxes. JavaScript can also interface with ActiveX controls and Java applets and interact with the Web browser.

JavaScript, JScript, ECMAScript?

Netscape developed JavaScript, and, not surprisingly, Microsoft developed its own implementation of the language called JScript. As you might guess, the two implementations share many common features, but each has additional features that are intended to "enhance" the language. Although this is great for marketing, it can be a source of frustration for developers who must create Web pages that can be displayed in the most popular browsers.

To make the language compatible across multiple platforms, Netscape, Microsoft, and other vendors worked with the European Computer Manufacturers Association (ECMA) to develop a standard scripting language for the Internet. The specification uses JavaScript as its basis and is known as ECMA-262, or ECMAScript. The ECMA-262 specification is available at **www.ecma.ch/stand/ecma-262.htm**. Documentation for the Microsoft and Netscape versions is available on each company's Web site.

Although most of this chapter focuses on the features of the language supported by the ECMA-262 standard, mention is made of JScript features as well. The term *JScript* is used throughout this chapter to refer to the language. This chapter's JScript Quick Reference in the Practical Guide shows the ECMA-compliant (and other) features provided by JScript and JavaScript.

A Quick Example

Before going any further, let's take a look at a simple example of a JavaScript program. You have likely seen examples of the classic "Hello World" program in other languages. Here is what it looks like in JavaScript:

```
<HTML>
<HEAD>
<TITLE>Hello World</TITLE>
<SCRIPT LANGUAGE=JavaScript>
<!--
    alert ("Hello World");
// -->
```

```
</SCRIPT>
</HEAD>
<BODY>
</BODY>
</HTML>
```

This is an example of a fairly typical HTML file. JavaScript is embedded in the HTML with the **<SCRIPT>** tag, which is used to insert client-side script in HTML documents. This is a paired tag, meaning that it requires the **</SCRIPT>** ending tag. The script code is placed between this pair of tags. Like many HTML tags, the **<SCRIPT>** tag has attributes that allow the user to modify the tag's behavior. The **LANGUAGE** attribute must specify the scripting language in use, because browsers can support many different languages. SRC is another useful attribute. You can use SRC to specify the URL of a file that contains the script source code. This is convenient if you use the same script in several files. Also, an HTML document can contain multiple scripts in different languages.

The browser actually provides the **alert** function and displays the greeting in an alert box. (You'll read more about accessing browser objects in Chapter 7.) Notice the use of the HTML comment tags: **<!-- ... -->**. It's a very good idea to place script code within comment tags because some browsers don't support client-side scripting. These browsers ignore script placed within comment tags. Script displayed by nonscript-aware browsers will create undesirable effects in your pages and be confusing to your users. The HTML ending comment tag is slightly modified with **//**. These characters indicate JavaScript comments and are used to comment out the ending HTML comment tag. Interestingly, Internet Explorer does not require the **//** character, but Netscape Navigator does. To be safe, you should always include the character with the closing comment around a script block.

You can place JavaScript code anywhere in an HTML document, although it is often placed in the **HEAD** section. An exception to this general rule is that you might need to include inline script in the **BODY** section, commonly done to respond to events, such as a button click. The thing to remember is this: Code must be defined before it is referenced. (Later in this chapter, you'll learn about functions, which are blocks of code that you can refer to from other parts of your script.) The script code that defines a function must be placed in the HTML document before you try to call it.

The browser processes script code as the page loads. Code that isn't part of a procedure or inline event-driven code is executed immediately.

A Trio Of Scripting Tips

Here are three tips you'll find useful when using VBScript or JavaScript.

Using <NOSCRIPT>

It is good practice to protect your script code with HTML comments. This prevents older browsers from displaying your code as plain text. However, that doesn't allow you to take a different action for those browsers. That's when the **<NOSCRIPT>** tag comes in handy. It allows you to provide other information when the browser doesn't understand the **<SCRIPT>** tag. It also works when a script is in an unknown language or when the user disables scripts:

```
<SCRIPT type="vbscript">
  <!--
  Sub myfunction ()
…
  End Sub
  -->
</SCRIPT>
<NOSCRIPT>
<P>
Please go get a real browser at <a href=http://the.browsercompany.com>The
Browser Co.</a>
</NOSCRIPT>
```

This works because script-aware browsers know to ignore everything between **<NOSCRIPT>** and **</NOSCRIPT>** unless it purposely ignored the previous script. Older browsers don't understand **<NOSCRIPT>** so they ignore it and process everything between the two tags.

Setting Script Language

According to the HTML 4 documentation, you can use the **<META>** tag to set a default scripting language (instead of doing it each time you use the **<SCRIPT>** tag on a page). You do it by including a line like the following in the **<HEAD>**:

```
<META http-equiv="Content-Script-Type" content="text/vbscript">
```

At present, however, the current versions of Internet Explorer and Netscape don't support this particular command, and it has no effect. The HTML 4 specification also allows you to set the script type using the type modifier like this:

```
<SCRIPT type=text/vbscript>
```

This does work in IE 4 and Navigator.

Ending A Script

The HTML 4 specification specifically requires browsers to end a script at the first sign of any tag that starts with **</** followed by a letter. So while you usually use **</SCRIPT>** to end a tag, technically, anything that resembles an end tag should work. This is a problem when you write things like

```
document.write("<B>Bold</B>");
```

since the script language should end when it sees the **</B>** tag. Currently, Internet Explorer and Navigator don't follow the specification in this case. You must end with a **</SCRIPT>** tag. But other browsers might not. To be safe, you should write the preceding using a backslash escape character (for JavaScript, anyway):

```
document.write("<B>Bold<\/B>");
```

This has the same effect but doesn't confuse the scripting engine.

Advantages Of Client-Side Scripting

Client-side scripting offers some significant advantages over traditional methods of activating Web pages:

- *Processing on the client*—Processing can be performed on the client, thereby reducing the number of trips to the server as well as the work-load placed on the server. This improves the user's experience because the Web pages are more responsive.

- *Interactive*—You can create pages that involve the user by requesting information and displaying responses using functions, including program-mer-defined functions, provided by JScript. Web pages can also respond to user actions, such as clicking a button or changing a form element.

- *Access to ActiveX controls and Java applets*—Client-side script can control the appearance and behavior of ActiveX controls and Java applets. This allows you to add a very high level of richness and functionality to your Web pages.

- *Access to the browser*—Client-side script can interact with the Web browser itself and the documents contained within the browser (discussed in Chapter 7).

Disadvantages Of Client-Side Scripting

Client-side scripting is nice, but like many things it also has its disadvantages. The following are two of the more significant disadvantages of client-side scripting:

- *Browser dependency*—Client-side script is useful only if the user's browser supports it. Microsoft's Internet Explorer and Netscape's Navigator support JavaScript, but other browsers might require a plug-in to interpret the language or might not support it at all. A corollary to this is that code that works on one browser may not work on another because of differences in how the browser implements the scripting language.

- *Source viewable on client*—Just like HTML, client-side script code is viewable on the client. As a result, you're sharing your hard work and intellectual property with the world.

Language Details

The following sections of this chapter focus on many of the details of JScript. If you have experience using C, C++, or Java, you'll be familiar with much of this discussion. In this case, you might want to jump to this chapter's Practical Guide to review the language and to the JScript Quick Reference to get an idea of the many features available in the language.

A couple of useful tidbits of information are:

- JScript is case-sensitive. This is quite different from VBScript (covered in Chapter 5), which is case insensitive.

- The use of semicolons at the end of lines is optional but recommended.

Variables

JScript variables are the same as variables in other languages. Simply stated, they are placeholders in memory where data is stored. A variable name is assigned to the placeholder, and the data stored there is referenced by the name.

JScript variable names must comply with a few simple rules:

- The first letter must be a character, an underscore (_), or a dollar sign ($).

- The name can't be a reserved word.

- The name can't contain certain characters, such as a period.

JScript is case sensitive. This is important to remember because, to JScript, **Grossincome** and **GrossIncome** are different variables.

Declaring Variables

Variables are declared either *implicitly* or *explicitly*. You declare variables explicitly with the **var** statement:

```
var Hours;
```

Multiple variables are declared in the same statement by separating the variable names by a comma:

```
var Hours, Wage;
```

Hours and **Wage** are now declared but are **undefined**. Variables are undefined until a value has been assigned. In fact, JScript has a data type, **Undefined**, that it gives to declared but uninitialized variables. A variable is initialized when a value is assigned:

```
Hours = 40;
Wage = 23.50
```

Simply using a new variable declares it implicitly. The following statement implicitly declares the variable **GrossIncome**:

```
GrossIncome = Hours * Wage;
```

Usually, you can declare variables either implicitly or explicitly. However, it is considered good programming practice to declare variables explicitly. Getting into the habit of explicitly declaring variables reduces the chances of program errors due to typographical errors and generally improves the readability of the program. There is only one rule you need to remember: Variables that are local to a function must be declared explicitly with the **var** statement.

Variable Scope And Lifetime

Variable *scope* refers to where within a script a variable is available. JScript variables have two levels of scope: *global* and *local*. Global variables are declared outside of functions and are available throughout the script. Also, variables declared inside functions without using the **var** statement are global. Local variables are declared inside functions using the **var** statement and are visible only within the function in which they are declared.

Variable *lifetime* refers to the amount of time a variable exists. Global variables exist from the time they are declared until the script finishes running. Local variables exist from the time they are declared until the function finishes executing.

Data Types

JScript is a *loosely typed* language; that is, you don't specify the data type in a variable declaration as you do in Java and C++. You can store values of any type in a variable, and JScript will handle it appropriately. If a number is placed in the variable, it is treated as a number. If a string is stored, it is treated as a string. JScript is also clever enough to automatically convert data when an expression contains both numbers and strings. In this case, JScript temporarily converts the numeric values to strings in memory:

```
var a_string = "150", result;
result = a_string * 2;          // result = 300
```

The first statement defines a string variable containing the value "150". The second statement multiplies the string value by 2. To do this, JScript temporarily converts the string in memory to a number and then performs the operation. The numeric result is placed in **result**. String concatenation is another good example of JScript's ability to convert data types automatically:

```
var a_number = 456, a_string = "123", result;
result = a_string + a_number;    // result = "123456"
```

JScript uses the + operator for both addition and string concatenation. Because the preceding statement "adds" a number to a string, JScript assumes that you want to perform a concatenation operation, so it converts **a_number** temporarily to a string and stores the string result in **result**.

JScript is factory equipped with six data types:

- **string**—This is a sequence of characters enclosed in single or double quotation marks.

- **number**—JScript supports integer and floating point numbers. Numbers are represented as base 10 (decimal), base 8 (octal), or base 16 (hexadecimal). Octal numbers begin with 0 and contain the digits 0 through 7. Hexadecimal numbers begin with 0x and contain the digits 0 through

9 and the characters A through F. Octal and hexadecimal numbers can be negative but can't contain a decimal point. Exponential numbers are indicated with the letter "e" or "E" in decimal and octal numbers.

- **boolean**—Contains **true** or **false**, which equals 1 or 0, respectively.

- **object**—A collection of properties and methods.

- **null**—A data type that indicates no value.

- **undefined**—A value is given to a variable that is declared but hasn't had a value assigned to it.

JScript has four *primitive* types: **number**, **boolean**, **string**, and **function**. These are not called primitive types because they have a Neanderthal-like appearance and behavior. Instead, they are called primitives because they contain a single value that is easily manipulated by the interpreter. The interpreter manipulates **number** and **boolean** types *by value* and **string** and **function** type *by reference*. Accessing data by value and by reference is covered later in this chapter.

JScript has a number of built-in objects (covered in the next section). Object types are more sophisticated in that they contain an arbitrary number of properties and methods. Because object types vary in size, they are not as easily manipulated by the interpreter as are primitives. Therefore, they are manipulated by *reference*. You might be wondering why strings and functions are considered primitives because they do not have a fixed size. JScript views them as primitives because they are not objects.

Wrapper Objects

So, what's the difference between a primitive and an object? Objects can have properties and methods. However, JScript has a corresponding object type for each primitive type. Therefore, JScript has **number**, **boolean**, **string**, and **function** objects. These objects contain the same primitive data item, as well as properties and methods to operate on the data item, and are used as *wrapper objects* around the primitive types.

Listing 6.1 shows how wrapper objects give primitive types objectlike behavior.

Listing 6.1 A JScript wrapper object in action.

```
<SCRIPT LANGUAGE=JavaScript>
<!--
var a_string, new_string;
var len;

    a_string = "JScript is cool!";
```

```
new_string = a_string.toUpperCase();     // new_string = JSCRIPT IS COOL!
a_string.toUpperCase();                  // a_string still = JScript is cool!

len = a_string.length;                   // len = 16

// -->
</SCRIPT>
```

Listing 6.1 declares three variables and assigns **a_string** a string value. The **String** object's method **toUpperCase** returns a string converted to all uppercase characters. The statement

```
new_string = a_string.toUpperCase();
```

uses **a_string** in an object context, applies the **toUpperCase** method to the value stored in the variable, and stores the resulting uppercase string in **new_string**. The next statement retrieves the **String** object's **length** property and places it in **len**.

JScript automatically creates a temporary wrapper object when a primitive type is used as an object. In the preceding example, a string wrapper object is created that contains the value of the simple variable as well as the **String** object's properties and methods. The value of the original variable is not affected, but you have access to the functionality of the object.

The reverse of this is also true. JScript converts the value of objects to their corresponding primitive type when they are used as primitives, as in the following statements:

```
var a_string;
var a_string_obj = new String("JScript is ");
a_string = a_string_obj + "Cool!";
```

This example declares a string object and assigns it a value. The last statement performs string concatenation using the **String** object and the string primitive.

JScript's ability to treat primitives as objects is convenient and frequently more efficient than using an object type. The next section covers the built-in JScript objects, several of which have a corresponding primitive type.

JScript Objects

JScript is an object-based language, so it is not surprising that JScript supplies several built-in objects in addition to the primitive types. JScript has objects that conform to the ECMA-262 standard and objects that are specific to Microsoft's implementation. Netscape's JavaScript also has objects specific to its implementation. The JScript Quick Reference in this chapter's Practical Guide shows the differences between these implementations.

It is important to remember that the built-in objects are not the only objects available to your programs, as the browser exposes a set of objects that you can also use (see Chapter 7). This section covers only objects that are part of JScript.

This section describes JScript objects that conform to the ECMA-262 standard. JScript offers several additional objects to provide drive and file access (server-side scripting only) and other special-purpose functions.

It is also easy to create your own objects to provide needed functionality. Later in this chapter, you'll see how to roll your own objects and to extend the built-in objects.

JScript Arrays And The **Array** Object

An array is used to store a collection of related data items and can hold multiple values. The **Array** object provides support for arrays in JScript. Because JScript is loosely typed, arrays can hold any type of data.

You'll use the **var** keyword to declare an array. The following statement declares an array variable, **SalesRegion**, which will store sales data for four regions:

```
var SalesRegion = new Array(3);
```

The operator **new** creates a new object, in this case an **Array** object. The value in parentheses specifies the array size. This statement declares an array that can contain four items, or *array elements*. Arrays in JScript are *zero based*, which means that the first element in the array is element 0 (zero). Therefore, the number of array elements that the array can contain is the number in parentheses plus 1. The element number is referred to as the array *index*.

Specifying the element number in brackets ([ ]) references individual elements in an array. A string is stored in the first array element as follows:

```
SalesRegion[0] = "East";
```

You can also declare an array without specifying an initial size:

```
var SalesRegion = new Array();
```

SalesRegion has a size of zero, but you can still assign values to any array element, and JScript will automatically adjust the size (array size is stored in the **length** property). The statement

```
SalesRegion[0] = "East";
```

assigns a value to the first array element and adjusts the **length** property to 1. JScript arrays are *sparse,* meaning that array indices need not be contiguous. Assuming that the next assignment statement is

```
SalesRegion[3] = "South";
```

length is adjusted to 4. The **length** property does not equal the number of elements in the array but instead is equal to 1 plus the highest element defined in the array. What about elements 1 and 2? They are still available, but they are **undefined** at this time.

Arrays are initialized during declaration by specifying the values in parentheses instead of specifying the array size. The **length** property is then determined on the basis of the number of values provided. The following declaration initializes the **SalesRegion** array:

```
var SalesArray = new Array("East", "West", "North", "South");
```

Arrays And Objects

Arrays and objects are the same thing in JScript. You can prove this by using the **typeof** operator:

```
alert (typeof(SalesRegion));
```

The **typeof** operator returns the type of the expression in parentheses and returns **object** for arrays as well as objects.

Because an array is an object, it can have properties. This means that you can use non-numeric indexes as properties. Arrays are also indexed with property names. Continuing with the **SalesRegion** example, the statements

```
var SalesRegion = new Array();
SalesRegion.East = 200;
SalesRegion.West = 350;
SalesRegion.North = 180;
SalesRegion.South = 225;
```

declare the array, give it properties indicating the various regions, and assign values to each property. These statements reference the array properties by using dot notation. You can also access named elements of an array by placing the name string in brackets. This notation is similar to using associative arrays in languages such as AWK and Perl:

```
SalesRegion["East"] = 200;
```

However, you can't reference properties with a numerical index. The statement

```
SalesVol = SalesRegion[0];
```

does not assign a value to **SalesVol** because **SalesRegion[0]** is **undefined**.

There is a subtle but important difference between using dot notation and using property names in brackets. The property name is an identifier when dot notation is used and as such must be defined in advance. When used in brackets, the property name is a string. Strings can be manipulated at runtime, so property names can be defined dynamically while the program is executing. You have already seen that array elements can be added at any time and that the size of the array is automatically adjusted. This, coupled with the ability to generate property names at runtime, gives the user a very flexible and powerful capability. Objects used in this manner are called *associative arrays*. These arrays allow you to assign values to arbitrary strings dynamically. This is a very powerful feature. For example, you could define a phone book array that easily transforms names into phone numbers.

Multidimensional Arrays

JScript does not provide direct support for multidimensional arrays. However, you can simulate multidimensional arrays by defining arrays of arrays. Listing 6.2 defines an array of arrays to contain the following information on each of the four sales regions: region name, city, state, and sales volume.

Listing 6.2 Using an array of arrays to simulate multidimensional arrays.
```
<SCRIPT LANGUAGE=JavaScript>
<!--
var SalesRegion = new Array();
var i, j;

    for (i = 0; i <= 3; i++)
      SalesRegion[i] = new Array();

    SalesRegion[0][0] = "East";
    SalesRegion[0][1] = "New York";
    SalesRegion[0][2] = "NY";
    SalesRegion[0][3] = 200;
```

```
SalesRegion[1][0] = "West";
SalesRegion[1][1] = "Los Angeles";
SalesRegion[1][2] = "CA";
SalesRegion[1][3] = 350;

// and so on

// -->
</SCRIPT>
```

The **for** statement is a loop structure (covered later in this chapter), and you'll be familiar with it if you have experience with C, C++, or Java. The **for** loop is used here to iterate through the **SalesRegion** array and assign an **Array** object to each array element.

The statement

```
SalesRegion[0][0] = "East";
```

assigns the region name to the first element of the first **SalesRegion** array element. The next three statements assign the city, state, and sales volume values to the remaining three elements of the first **SalesRegion** array element. These steps are repeated for the rest of the **SalesRegion** array.

You can also implement this using an associative array of associative arrays. Listing 6.3 does this to store the sales region information.

Listing 6.3 Using an associative array of associative arrays.

```
<SCRIPT LANGUAGE=JavaScript>
<!--
var SalesRegion = new Array();
var SalesVol;

   SalesRegion.East = new Array();
   SalesRegion.East.City = "New York";
   SalesRegion.East.State = "NY";
   SalesRegion.East.Vol = 200;

   SalesRegion.West = new Array();
   SalesRegion.West.City = "Los Angeles";
   SalesRegion.West.State = "CA";
   SalesRegion.West.Vol = 350;

   // and so on
```

```
// -->
</SCRIPT>
```

Listing 6.3 defines elements of the **SalesRegion** array using property identifiers. The region property of each array is given the name of the region and assigned an array. Each region's array is then given properties for the various pieces of information that will be stored, and each property is assigned a value. The statement

```
SalesVol = SalesRegion.West.Vol;
```

retrieves the value of the **SalesRegion.West.Vol** property and places it in **SalesVol**.

Listing 6.4 is another example of the flexibility of associative arrays. This example uses an array of associative arrays.

Listing 6.4 Using an array of associative arrays.
```
<SCRIPT LANGUAGE=JavaScript>
<!--
var SalesRegion = new Array();
var SalesVol;
var i;

    for (i = 0; i <= 3; i++)
      SalesRegion[i] = new Array();

    SalesRegion[0]["Region"] = "East"
    SalesRegion[0]["City"] = "New York";
    SalesRegion[0]["State"] = "NY";
    SalesRegion[0]["Vol"] = 200;

    SalesRegion[1]["Region"] = "West";
    SalesRegion[1]["City"] = "Los Angeles";
    SalesRegion[1]["State"] = "CA";
    SalesRegion[1]["Vol"] = 350;

    // and so on

    SalesVol = SalesRegion[0].Vol;
    SalesVol = SalesRegion[1]["Vol"];

// -->
</SCRIPT>
```

Another way to simulate multidimensional arrays is to build composite string keys using a character as a separator. For example:

```
ary["10:3"]=0
```

This doesn't really place anything on the tenth row and third column; rather it simply associates a value with the string "10:3". However, if your program consistently uses this notation, it appears to create a two-dimensional array. Of course, you could easily add even more dimensions using the same technique.

Array Object Properties

Table 6.1 shows the **Array** object's properties.

The **constructor** property returns the function that created the object. This property is a member of every object that has a *prototype*, which is an object that defines the properties, methods, and constants for a class of objects. The **constructor** property is used as follows:

```
var Greeting = new String("Hello World!");
var Result = Greeting.constructor;
if (Result == String)
    document.write("It's a String!");
```

The **length** property returns a value equal to 1 plus the highest element in the array. It does not always mean the number of elements in the array because array elements are not always contiguous. The following statement retrieves the **length** property:

```
var SalesRegion("East", "West", "North", "South");
var UBound = SalesRegion.length;      // UBound equals 4
```

The **length** property is also used to set the highest element in the array. If the new value is less than the previous value, the array is truncated, and data in elements higher than the previous value is lost. If the new value is greater than the previous value, the array is expanded, and the new elements are **undefined**. The statement

```
SalesRegion.length = 6;
```

adds two elements to the **SalesRegion** array.

Table 6.1   The **Array** object's properties.

Property	Description	Syntax
constructor	Specifies the object's constructor function	arr.constructor;
length	Indicates the highest element in the array	arr.length;
prototype	Contains a reference to the object's prototype	arr.prototype;

The **prototype** property is used to define the properties, methods, and constants for a class of objects. All intrinsic JScript objects have a **prototype** property. New instances of the object inherit the features of the object. This property extends the functionality of an existing class of objects within the scope of the current script(for an example of this, see this chapter's Practical Guide). The **prototype** property adds a **count** method to the **Array** object. The **count** method returns the number of elements that actually are in an array.

Array Object's Methods

Table 6.2 shows the **Array** object's methods.

The **concat** method combines two arrays and returns a new array containing the two original ones. The method doesn't change the original arrays unless you name one of them on the left side of the assignment operator:

```
var SalesRegion = new Array("East", "West", "North", "South");
var NewRegion = new Array("Hawaii", "Alaska");
var AllRegions = SalesRegion.concat(NewRegion);
```

The **join** method converts array elements to a string and joins them. You'll pass a *separator* argument to specify the character used between the elements. If you

Table 6.2 The Array object's methods.

Method	Description	Syntax
concat	Combines two arrays	arr3 = arr1.concat(arr3);
join	Converts array elements to a string	arr2 = arr1.join(*separator*);
reverse	Reverses the array elements	arr.reverse();
slice	Returns a section of the array	arr2 = arr1.slice(*start*[,*stop*]);
sort	Sorts the array elements	arr.sort([*compare function*]);
toString	Returns a comma-separated string of the array elements	arr2 = arr1.toString();
valueOf	Returns a comma-separated string of the array elements	arr2 = arr1.valueOf();

omit the separator argument, the method uses a comma to separate the elements. The statements

```
var arr1 = new Array("1", "2", "3");
var arr2 = arr1.join("");
```

set **arr2** to the string "123".

The **reverse** method reverses the elements of the array. If the array is sparse, the method creates elements to fill in the missing elements:

```
var arr1 = new Array("a", "b", "c");
arr1.reverse();
```

The **slice** method returns a section of the array. This method takes an argument to specify a zero-based starting position and optionally takes a zero-based ending position. If you omit the starting position, **slice** copies to the end of the array. For example, if you have this declaration

```
var arr1 = new Array("a", "b", "c", "d", "e", "f");
```

followed (eventually) by this statement

```
arr2 = arr1.slice(1);
```

the result will be to copy from the second element of **arr1** to the end of the array. The statement

```
arr2 = arr1.slice(1, 4);
```

copies from the second element up to (but not including) the fourth element. If a negative value is specified for the starting position, that value is used as an offset from the end.

The **sort** method sorts the array elements. The **sort** method takes an optional argument of type **function** to specify the sort order. The method sorts the array in ascending order if the argument is omitted. The following statements define and sort an array in ascending order:

```
var arr1 = new Array("a", "f", "e", "b", "d", "c");
arr1.sort();
```

To sort the array in a different order, a comparison function is provided as an argument. The comparison function takes two arguments and returns a value as follows:

- **<0** First argument is less than the second argument.

- **0** Both arguments are equivalent.

- **>0** First argument is greater than second argument.

Listing 6.5 first sorts an array in ascending order and then sorts it in descending order using the function **compare** to compare the arguments.

Listing 6.5 Using the sort method.

```
<SCRIPT LANGUAGE=JavaScript>
<!--
var arr1 = new Array(12, 51, 32, 10, 16);

   function compare(a,b) {
     return b - a;
   }
   arr1.sort();              // sort ascending
   arr1.sort(compare);        // sort descending
// -->
</SCRIPT>
```

The **toString** method returns a comma-separated string type containing the array elements:

```
var arr1 = new Array("a", "f", "e", "b", "d", "c");
var arr2 = arr1.toString();
```

The **valueOf** method returns a comma-separated string object containing the array elements. The method converts the array elements to strings and concatenates them:

```
var arr1 = new Array(1,4,3,6,7);
var arr2 = arr1.valueOf();
```

The **valueOf** method acts like the **toString** method, except it returns an object.

The **Boolean** Object

The **Boolean** object creates a Boolean value and is also the wrapper object for the **Boolean** primitive type. It is useful for converting non-Boolean values to Boolean values. The statement

```
var bln = new Boolean(true);
```

creates a **Boolean** object with a value of **true**. If the value is not specified, it is **false**.

Boolean Object's Properties
Table 6.3 shows the **Boolean** object's properties.

Boolean Object's Methods
Table 6.4 shows the **Boolean** object's methods.

The **Date** Object

The **Date** object provides several functions for getting and setting date and time values. You define a **Date** object like this:

```
var theDate = new Date();
```

Here, the date object supplies the current date and time, and the script stores it in **theDate**. The declaration

```
var theDate = new Date("Nov 23, 1997 22:49:00");
```

specifies a date string to initialize **theDate**. You can also specify a number, which represents the number of milliseconds since January 1, 1970:

```
var theDate = new Date(880000000000);
```

The statement above initializes **theDate** to "Wed Nov 19 23:26:40 Eastern Standard Time 1997". You can also use this format:

```
var theDate = new Date(year, month, date[, hour[, minute[, second[,ms]]]])
```

Table 6.3   The Boolean object's properties.

Property	Description	Syntax
constructor	Specifies the object's constructor function	bln.constructor;
prototype	Contains a reference to the object's prototype	bln.prototype;

Table 6.4   The Boolean object's methods.

Method	Description	Syntax
toString	Returns a string representation	bln.toString();
valueOf	Returns a string representation	bln.valueOf();

Table 6.5 The Date object's constructor optional arguments.

Argument	Description
year	The year in the format 1997
month	The month expressed as an integer from 0 through 11
date	The date expressed as an integer from 1 through 31
hour	The hour expressed as an integer from 0 through 23
minute	The minutes expressed as an integer from 0 through 59
second	The seconds expressed as an integer from 0 through 59
ms	The milliseconds expressed as an integer from 0 through 999

Table 6.5 shows the descriptions for the arguments used in the preceding syntax.

The **Date** object is also used as a function. It returns the current date and time:

```
var theDate = Date();
```

What Is UTC?

Universal Coordinated Time (UTC) refers to the time as set by the World Time Standard and is, for practical purposes, equivalent to Greenwich Mean Time (GMT). Many of the **Date** object methods set or return time values in UTC.

Date Object Properties

The **Date** object has the **constructor** and **prototype** properties, which are used as described previously.

Date Object Methods

The **Date** object has several methods for getting and setting date and time values. Table 6.6 shows descriptions of the available methods.

The **Date** object has two static methods: **parse** and **UTC**. You don't call these against a particular object because they are static. You call them using the class name like this:

```
Date.parse(argument);
Date.UTC(arguments);
```

The **parse** method parses a date string and returns the number of milliseconds between midnight January 1, 1970, and that date.

Table 6.6 The Date object's methods.

Method	Description	Syntax
getDate	Returns the day of the month (1 through 31)	theDate.getDate();
getDay	Returns the day of the week (0 through 6)	theDate.getDay();
getFullYear	Returns the year	theDate.getFullYear();
getHours	Returns the hours (0 through 23)	theDate.getHours();
getMilliseconds	Returns the milliseconds past the second (0 through 999)	theDate.getMilliseconds();
getMinutes	Returns the minutes past the hour (0 through 59)	theDate.getMinutes();
getMonth	Returns the month (0 through 11)	theDate.getMonth();
getSeconds	Returns the seconds past the minute (0 through 59)	theDate.getSeconds();
getTime	Returns the time in milliseconds since midnight January 1, 1970	theDate.getTime();
getTimezoneOffset	Returns the difference in minutes between Universal Coordinated Time (UTC) and time on the host computer	theDate.getTimezone Offset();
getUTCDate	Returns the UTC day of the month (1 through 31)	theDate.getUTCDate();
getUTCDay	Returns the UTC day of the week (0 through 6)	theDate.getUTCDay();
getUTCFullYear	Returns the UTC year	theDate.getUTCFullYear();
getUTCHours	Returns UTC hours (0 through 23)	theDate.getUTCHours();
getUTCMilliseconds	Returns the number of milliseconds past the second according to UTC (0 through 999)	theDate.getUTC Milliseconds();
getUTCMinutes	Returns the number of minutes past the hour according to UTC (0 through 59)	theDate.getUTCMinutes();
getUTCMonth	Returns the UTC month (0 through 11)	theDate.getUTCMonth();
getUTCSeconds	Returns the number of seconds past the minute according to UTC (0 through 59)	theDate.getUTCSeconds();
getVarDate	Returns the VT_DATE*	theDate.getVarDate();

* **getVarDate** is used when working with objects that work with dates in the VT_DATE format. Netscape Navigator does not support this method.

(continued)

Table 6.6 The Date object's methods (continued).

Method	Description	Syntax
getYear	Returns the years past 1900	theDate.getYear();
setDate	Sets the numeric date	theDate.setDate(date);
setFullYear	Sets the year	theDate.setFullYear (year[,month[,date]]);
setHours	Sets the hours	theDate.setHours(hours [,mins[,secs[,millisecs]]]);
setMilliseconds	Sets the milliseconds	theDate.setMilliseconds (millisecs);
setMinutes	Sets the minutes	theDate.setMinutes (mins[,secs[,millisecs]]);
setMonth	Sets the month	theDate.setMonth (month[,date]);
setSeconds	Sets the seconds	theDate.setSeconds (secs[,millisecs]);
setTime	Sets the time and date	theDate.setTime(millisecs);
setUTCDate	Sets the numeric UTC date	theDate.setUTCDate(date);
setUTCFullYear	Sets the UTC year	theDate.setUTCFullYear (year[,month[,date]]);
setUTCHours	Sets the UTC hours	theDate.setUTCHours(hours [,mins[,secs[,millisecs]]]);
setUTCMilliseconds	Sets the UTC milliseconds	theDate.setUTC Milliseconds(millisecs);
setUTCMinutes	Sets the UTC minutes	theDate.setUTCMinutes (mins[,secs[,millisecs]]);
setUTCMonth	Sets the UTC month	theDate.setUTCMonth (month[,date]);
setUTCSeconds	Sets the UTC seconds	theDate.setUTCSeconds (secs[,millisecs]);
setYear	Sets the years past 1900	theDate.setYear(years);
toGMTString	Converts the date to a string using GMT format	theDate.toGMTString();

(continued)

Table 6.6 The Date object's methods (continued).

Method	Description	Syntax
toLocalString	Converts the date to a string using the current locale format	theDate.toLocalString();
toUTCString	Converts the date to a string according to UTC format	theDate.toUTCString();
toString	Returns a string representation of the date	theDate.toString();
valueOf	Returns the milliseconds since January 1, 1970	theDate.valueOf();

The **UTC** method returns the number of milliseconds between January 1, 1970, UTC and the specified date. The **UTC** method uses the syntax:

```
Date.UTC(year,month,day[,hours[,mins[,secs[,millisecs]]]]);
```

The **Function** Object

A function is a block of code that performs a specific task and can return a result. Functions are given names that they are called by throughout a program. Some functions take arguments containing values that the functions use to do their jobs. A function that calculates and returns a payment would accept arguments specifying the principal, interest rate, and number of payments.

JScript uses functions extensively and even has a primitive function type. The **Function** object is a wrapper object for the primitive type and is also used to create new functions. Creating user-defined functions is covered later in this chapter, but you no doubt have an inquiring mind and want to know. Therefore, the following statements create a function that calculates and returns the square of a number:

```
function sqr(x) {
   return x * x;
}
```

The keyword "function" is used to declare a function. This function is named **sqr** and takes one argument, **x**, which contains the value to operate on. The **return** statement returns the result to the caller.

Function Object Properties

The **Function** object has two properties in addition to the **constructor** and **prototype** properties. Table 6.7 shows descriptions of these.

Table 6.7 The **Function** object's properties.

Property	Description	Syntax
arguments	An array containing the arguments passed to the function	fctn.arguments[n];
caller	Contains a reference to the caller function	fctn.caller;

The **arguments** property is an array that contains the arguments passed to the function. Because it is an array, the **length** property is used to determine the number of arguments passed. Using the **sqr** function as an example, the statement

```
sqr.length;
```

returns the number of arguments passed to the function, which is 1. The following statement returns the argument value:

```
sqr.arguments[0];
```

The **length** and **arguments** properties are useful within functions to determine whether the correct number of arguments were passed and within writing functions that work with a variable number of arguments.

The **caller** property contains a reference to the function that called the current function. The value of **caller** is **null** when the function is called from the script's top level.

The **arguments** and **caller** properties are defined only while the function is executing.

Function Object Methods

Table 6.8 shows the **Function** object's methods, and you are already familiar with these: **toString** and **valueOf**.

Table 6.8 The **Function** object's methods.

Method	Description	Syntax
toString	Returns a string representation of the entire function	fctn.toString();
valueOf	Returns the entire function	fctn.valueOf();

The **Global** Object

The **Global** object contains all global methods. It is an intrinsic object, and you'll never create a variable of this type because JScript creates it for you. You can use the **Global** object's properties and methods without referencing the object itself.

Global Object Properties

Table 6.9 shows descriptions of the **Global** object's properties.

The **NaN** (Not a Number) value is returned when a mathematical operation returns an error or undefined result. For example, the **parseInt** method converts a string to its equivalent numerical value. **NaN** is returned if the string cannot be evaluated to a number. This is illustrated in the following statements:

```
var somenum;
somenum = parsInt("Hello");
```

The variable **somenum** equals **NaN** after the call to **parseInt**. You can't use **NaN** in comparisons directly. Instead, use the **isNaN** function to evaluate for the **NaN** value. If an expression is equal to **NaN**, **isNaN** returns **true**:

```
if (isNaN(somenum))
// statement(s) to execute
```

The **Infinity** and **-Infinity** values are returned when a positive or negative number is larger than the largest representable type.

Global Object Methods

Table 6.10 shows the **Global** object's methods.

The **escape** method applies HTML encoding rules to the specified character string. This method is useful when a script is dynamically constructing URL query strings:

```
theURL = "http://www.diningclub.com?" + escape("FavResturant=Luigi's Pizza
Parlor and Pub");
```

Table 6.9 The Global object's properties.

Property	Description
NaN	Indicates that a value cannot be evaluated as a numeric value
Infinity	Indicates that a value is larger than the largest representable value

Table 6.10 The **Global** object's methods.

Method	Description	Syntax
escape	Applies HTML encoding to the specified string	escape(*charstring*);
eval	Executes the specified code string	eval(*codestring*);
isFinite	Evaluates a number for **NaN** or **Infinity**	isFinite(*number*);
isNaN	Returns **true** if a value equals **NaN**	isNaN(*value*);
parseFloat	Converts a string value to a floating point value	parseFloat(*string*);
parseInt	Converts a string value to an integer value	parstInt(*string*[,*radix*]);
unescape	Returns a string without HTML encoding characters	unescape(*charstring*);

After this statement executes, **theURL** contains the following string:

```
"http://www.diningclub.com?FavResturant%3DLuigi%27s%20Pizza%20Parlor%20
and%20Pub"
```

The **unescape** method performs the opposite task of removing HTML encoding:

```
theURL = unescape(theURL);
```

The **eval** method evaluates a specified code string that can contain any number of JScript statements separated by semicolons. The statements

```
theURL = "http://www.diningclub.com?" + "FavResturant=Luigi's Pizza Parlor
and Pub";
codestring = "theURL = escape(theURL)";
eval(codestring);
```

assign a JScript statement to **codestring** and pass the string to the **eval** method, causing HTML encoding to be applied to the string stored in **theURL**.

isFinite returns **true** if the specified number is any value other than **Infinity**, **-Infinity**, or **NaN**.

The **parseInt** and **parseFloat** functions convert strings to integer and floating point numbers if the specified strings begin with characters that form numbers. If the strings cannot be converted to numeric values, both methods return **NaN**. Also, **parseInt** has an optional argument *radix,* which specifies the base of the number in *string*. Radix is a value between 2 and 36 and can also be specified as hexadecimal ("0xnnn") or octal ("0nnn"). The following statements contain expressions that can be converted:

```
parseInt("10");
parseInt("10.5");            // returns 10
parseInt("10 Hello");        // returns 10
parseFloat("10.5");
parseFloat("10.5 World");    // returns 10
```

The **Math** Object

The **Math** object provides math functions through several methods and properties. It is like the **Global** object in that it is not created with the **new** operator and its methods and properties are directly available.

Math Object Properties

Table 6.11 shows the **Math** object's properties.

Math Object Methods

Table 6.12 shows descriptions of the **Math** object's methods.

Table 6.11   The Math object's properties.

Property	Description	Syntax
E	Base of natural logarithms, approx. equal to 2.71828	Math.E
LN2	Natural logarithm of 2, approx. equal to .069314	Math.LN2
LN10	Natural logarithm of 10, approx. equal to 2.30258	Math.LN10
LOG2E	Base 2 logarithm of e, approx. equal to 1.44269	Math.LOG2E
LOG10E	Base 10 logarithm of e, approx. equal to .43429	Math.LOG10E
PI	Constant p, approx. equal to 3.14159	Math.PI
SQRT1_2	1 divided by the square root of 2, approx. equal to .70710	Math.SQRT1_2
SQRT2	Square root of 2, approx. equal to 1.41421	Math.SQRT2

Table 6.12 The **Math** object's methods.

Method	Description	Syntax
abs()	Absolute value	Math.abs(*number*);
acos()	Arc cosine	Math.acos(*number*);
asin()	Arc sine	Math.asin(*number*);
atan()	Arc tangent	Math.atan(*number*);
atan2()	Angle from the X axis to a point	Math.atan2(*x, y*);
ceil()	Rounds a number up	Math.ceil(*number*);
cos()	Cosine	Math.cos(*number*);
exp()	Computes e^x	Math.exp(*number*);
floor()	Rounds a number down	Math.floor(*number*);
log()	Natural logarithm	Math.log(*number*);
max()	Returns the larger of two values	Math.max(*n1, n2*);
min()	Returns the smaller of two values	Math.min(*n1, n2*);
pow()	Computes x^x	Math.pow(*base, exponent*);
random()	Returns a random number between 0 and 1	Math.random();
sin()	Sine	Math.sin(*number*);
sqrt()	Square root	Math.sqrt(*number*);
tan()	Tangent	Math.tan(*number*);

The **Number** Object

The **Number** object provides properties that are used as numeric constants and is the wrapper object for the **Number** primitive type.

Number Object Properties

In addition to the **constructor** and **prototype** properties, the **Number** object has the properties shown in Table 6.13.

Number Object Methods

Table 6.14 shows the **Number** object's methods.

Table 6.13 The Number object's properties.

Property	Description	Syntax
MAX_VALUE	Maximum JScript representable value	Number.MAX_VALUE;
MIN_VALUE	Minimum JScript representable value	Number.MIN_VALUE;
NaN	Indicates that an expression returned a non-numeric value	Number.NaN;
NEGATIVE_INFINITY	Indicates that a negative value is larger than the largest representable number	Number.NEGATIVE_ INFINITY;
POSITIVE_INFINITY	Indicates that a value is larger than the largest representable number	Number.POSITIVE_ INFINITY;

Table 6.14 The Number object's methods.

Method	Description	Syntax
toString	Returns a string representation of a number	toString(number);
valueOf	Returns the numeric value of a number	valueOf(number);

The **Object** Object

The **Object** object serves as the "mother of all objects" in JScript. That is, all objects derive from **object**. Therefore, its properties and methods are properties and methods available to all other JScript objects.

Object Object Properties

Table 6.15 shows descriptions of the **Object** object's properties.

You use the **prototype** property to define the properties, methods, and constants for a class of objects. All intrinsic JScript objects have a **prototype** property. New in-

Table 6.15 The Object object's properties.

Property	Description	Syntax
prototype	Contains a reference to the object's prototype	Object.prototype;
constructor	Specifies the object's constructor function	Object.constructor;

stances of the object inherit the features of the object. This property extends the functionality of an existing class of objects within the scope of the current script.

Listing 6.6 shows the use of the **prototype** and **constructor** properties. The code defines a constructor function for a very simple object, **MyObject**, which has just one property, **x**. The code adds the method **showme** to all instances of this object using the **prototype** property. Then it defines the variable **MyObject** and sets **x** to the string "JScript is cool!". Finally, the code calls the **showme** method to output the property value.

Listing 6.6   Using the prototype and constructor properties.

```
<SCRIPT LANGUAGE="JavaScript">
<!--
    // define a constructor function
    function MyObject(x) {this.x = x;}

    // give it a method
    MyObject.prototype.showme = new Function("document.write(this.x);");

    // create one
    var myobj = new MyObject("JScript is cool!");

    myobj.showme();

    document.write(MyObject.prototype);        // outputs [object Object]
    document.write(myobj.constructor);         // outputs function MyObject(x)
{ this.x = x; }


// -->
</SCRIPT>
```

Object Object Methods

Table 6.16 shows descriptions for the **Object** object's methods.

The **regular expression** Object

Regular expressions are patterns of characters used in pattern matching and substitution. The JScript regular expressions follow the Perl model. The **regular expression**

Table 6.16   The Object object's methods.

Method	Description	Syntax
toString	Returns a string representation of the object	Object.object();
valueOf	Returns the object primitive	Object.valueOf();

object stores patterns that are used when searching strings. These patterns are either passed to a string method or a string is passed to a **regular expression** method.

The **RegExp** object contains information about the last regular expression search and is updated automatically by the **regular expression** object and **String** object methods. You'll learn more about the **RegExp** object in the next section.

At the time of this writing, Internet Explorer 4 does not support all the properties and methods even though documented by Microsoft. Microsoft undoubtedly plans to implement all these features, so they might be fully functional by the time you read this.

The **RegExp** object supports two syntaxes:

```
var regexpr = /pattern/[switch];
var regexpr = new RegExp("pattern"[,"switch"]);
```

The *pattern* argument is required and specifies the regular expression pattern to use. The *switch* argument is optional and is one of the following:

- **i**—Ignore case

- **g**—Global search for all occurrences

- **gi**—Global search, ignore case

The first syntax is used when the search pattern is known when the script is written. The second syntax is used when the search pattern is unknown or subject to change.

regular expression Object Properties

Table 6.17 shows descriptions of the **regular expression** object's properties.

All the **regular expression** properties are read-only, except for **lastIndex**.

Table 6.17 The regular expression object's properties.

Property	Description	Syntax
global	Indicates whether the global switch was used	regexpr.global;
ignorecase	Indicates whether the ignore case switch was used	regexpr.ignorecase;
lastIndex	Specifies where to begin the next search	regexpr.lastIndex;
source	Indicates the regular expression pattern	regexpr.source;

Table 6.18   The regular expression object's methods.

Method	Description	Syntax
compile()	Compiles a pattern to an internal format	regexpr.compile(*pattern*);
exec()	Executes a search	regexpr.exec(*string*);
test()	Tests for a match	regexpr.test(*string*);

regular expression Object Methods

Table 6.18 shows descriptions of the **regular expression** object's methods.

The **compile** method converts the search pattern to a format that results in faster execution. You can invoke this method explicitly, but you don't need to. Search patterns are compiled when the script is loaded when the syntax

```
var regexpr = /pattern/[switch];
```

is used and are compiled just before searching when using the following syntax:

```
var regexpr = new RegExp("pattern"[,"switch"]);
```

The **exec** method executes a search on the specified string. If no match is found, it returns **null**; if one or more matches are found, it returns an array and updates the **RegExp** object.

The **test** method checks to see whether a pattern exists. If one does exist, the method returns **true**; if it doesn't exist, it returns **false**. The **test** method does not update the **RegExp** object.

Listing 6.7 shows the use of the first syntax to search for the pattern "JScript".

Listing 6.7   Using the regular expression object.

```
<SCRIPT LANGUAGE=JavaScript>
<!--
var regexpr = /JScript/gi;
var result;

    result = regexpr.exec("Programming in JScript is fun!");

    document.write(result + "<BR>");      // pattern found
    document.write(result.length + "<BR>");   // its an array and has a
length property
    document.write(result.lastIndex + "<BR>");
```

```
// -->
</SCRIPT>
```

Listing 6.8 shows the use of the second syntax.

Listing 6.8   Using an alternate syntax with the regular expression object.
```
<SCRIPT LANGUAGE=JavaScript>
<!--
var regexpr = new RegExp("JScript", "gi");
var result;

    result = regexpr.exec("Programming in JScript is fun!");

    document.write(result + "<BR>");        // pattern found
// its an array and has a length property
    document.write(result.length + "<BR>");
    document.write(result.lastIndex + "<BR>");

// -->
</SCRIPT>
```

The **RegExp** Object

JScript stores information on regular expression pattern searches in the **RegExp** object. This object has only properties and is updated by search methods of **regular expression** objects as well as **String** objects. The **RegExp** object is always available; you don't need to create it.

RegExp Object Properties

The **RegExp** object has several read-only properties that store information on regular expression pattern searches. Table 6.19 shows descriptions of the **RegExp** object's properties.

The **String** Object

The **String** object has several methods to format, manipulate, and search strings. Many of the **String** object's methods format strings in HTML. This object is also the wrapper object for the **string** primitive type. The **String** object's methods and properties are available with string primitives, string literals, and string objects:

```
var str = "JScript";
var len;
len = str.length;
len = "JScript".length;
```

Table 6.19 The RegExp object's properties.

Property Syntax	Description	Syntax Optional
$1...$9	Specifes the nine most recent matches	RegExp.$1;
index	Indicates where the first match begins	RegExp.index;
input	Contains the string on which a search was performed	RegExp.input; RegExp.$_;
lastIndex	Indicates where the last match begins	RegExp.lastIndex;
lastMatch	Contains the substring from the last match	RegExp.lastMatch; RegExp.$&;
lastParen	Specifies the last parenthesized substring match	RegExp.lastMatch; RegExp.$+;
leftContext	Specifies the string up to the most recent match	RegExp.leftContext; RegExp.$';
multiline	Indicates whether searching across multiple lines	RegExp.multiline; RegExp.$*;
rightContext	Specifies the string following the most recent match	RegExp.rightContext; RegExp.$';

String Object Properties

Table 6.20 shows descriptions of the **String** object's properties.

String Object Methods

Table 6.21 shows non-HTML related methods. Table 6.22 shows descriptions of the methods that format strings in HTML.

Table 6.20 The String object's properties.

Property	Description	Syntax
length	Returns the length of the string	str.length;
prototype	Contains a reference to the **String** object prototype	str.prototype;

Table 6.21 The String object's methods.

Method	Description	Syntax
charAt()	Returns the nth from a string	str.charAt(*n*);
charCodeAt()	Returns the Unicode value for the specified character	str.charCodeAt(*n*);
concat()	Returns the concatenation of two strings	str1.concat(*str2*);
fromCharCode()	Returns a string created from a series of Unicode values	String.fromCharCode (*code1, code2, ...*);
indexOf()	Finds the first occurrence of a substring in a string	str.indexOf(*substring*[, *startindex*]);
lastIndexOf()	Finds the last occurrence of a substring in a string	str.lastIndexOf(*substring*[, *startindex*]);
match()	Searches a string	str.match(*regexpr*);
replace()	Replaces text found with a regular expression	str.replace(*regexpr, newtext*);
search()	Searches for a regular expression match	str.search(*regexpr*);
slice()	Returns a segment of a string	str.slice(*start*[,*end*]);
split()	Removes a regular expression from a string	str.split(*regexpr*);
substr()	Returns a substring	str.substr(*start*[,*length*]);
substring()	Returns a substring	str.substring(*start, end*);
toLowerCase()	Returns the string in lowercase	str.toLowerCase();
toUpperCase()	Returns the string in uppercase	str.toUpperCase();
toString()	Returns a string object	str.toString();
valueOf()	Returns the string value	str.valueOf();

Table 6.22 The String object's HTML formatting methods.

Method	Description	Syntax	Equivalent HTML
anchor()	Adds an HTML anchor	str.anchor(*name*);	<A>*name*</A>
big()	Makes the string big	str.big();	<BIG>*string*</BIG>

(continued)

Table 6.22 The String object's HTML formatting methods (continued).

Method	Description	Syntax	Equivalent HTML
blink()	Makes the string blink	str.blink();	<BLINK>*string*</BLINK>
bold()	Makes the string bold	str.bold();	<B>*string*</B>
fixed()	Makes the string fixed width	str.fixed();	<TT>*string*</TT>
fontcolor()	Sets the string's font color	str.fontcolor(*color*);	<FONT COLOR=*color*>
fontsize()	Sets the font size	str.fontsize(*n*);	<FONT SIZE=*n*>
italics()	Makes the string italics	str.italics();	<I>*string*</I>
link()	Adds a hyperlink to the string	str.link(*URL*);	<A HREF=*URL*>*string*</A>
small()	Makes the text small	str.small();	<SMALL>*string*</SMALL>
strike()	Strikes through the string	str.strike();	<STRIKE>*string*</STRIKE>
sub()	Makes a string subscript	str.sub();	_{*string*}
sup()	Makes a string superscript	str.sup();	^{*string*}

JScript Operators

Operators are used to form expressions that perform calculations, comparisons, and logical operations. JScript has a complete range of operators that are extensively used in all but the simplest programs. You'll be familiar with JScript operators if you have programmed in C, C++, or Java. JScript has four classifications of operators: arithmetic, comparison, logical, and bitwise.

Arithmetic Operators

Arithmetic operators perform basic arithmetic operations on one or more variables. Also, some math operations in JScript are performed using the **Math** object, such as exponentiation. Table 6.23 shows JScript's arithmetic operators.

Comparison Operators

Comparison operators compare expressions and return **true** or **false**. JScript comparison operators fall into three general categories: relational, equality, and identity. Numbers, strings, and Booleans are compared by value. Objects, arrays, and functions are compared by reference on the basis of whether they refer to the same object. Table 6.24 shows JScript's comparison operators.

Table 6.23　JScript's arithmetic operators.

Operator	Operation	Description	Syntax
-	Unary negation	Returns the negative value of an expression	a = -b;
++	Increment	Increments the value by 1	a++; or ++a;*
–	Decrement	Decrements the value by 1	a--; or --a;*
*	Multiplication	Multiplies two numbers	a = b * c;
/	Division	Divides two numbers	a = b / c;
%	Modulo arithmetic	Divides two numbers and returns the remainder	a = b % c;
+	Addition	Adds two numbers**	a = b + c;
-	Subtraction	Finds the difference between two numbers	a = b - c;

* a++/a-- increments/decrements but returns the original value; ++a/--a increments/decrements the value and returns the new value.

** The + operator is also used in string concatenation operations.

Table 6.24　JScript's comparison operators.

Operator	Operation
<	Less than
>	Greater than
<=	Less than or equal to
>=	Greater than or equal to
==	Equality
!=	Inequality
===	Identity
!==	Nonidentity

When performing relational operations, JScript tries to convert both expressions into numbers. However, if both expressions are strings, a lexicographical string comparison is performed. In the case of equality operations, JScript tries to convert the expressions to strings, numbers, or Booleans if the expressions are different. Identity operators perform the same as equality operators except that no type conversion is done.

Logical Operators

Logical operators evaluate one or more logical expressions and return **true** or **false**. These operators are frequently used with comparison operators to evaluate multiple expressions. Table 6.25 shows JScript's logical operators.

Bitwise Operators

Bitwise operators perform low-level bit manipulation on integer values. These operators perform two general functions: logical operations on individual bits and shifting bits left or right. Table 6.26 shows the available bitwise operators.

Table 6.25 JScript's logical operators.

Operator	Operation	Syntax	Expression1	Expression2	Result
!	Logical negation	result = !expression1	True		False
			False		True
&&	Logical conjunction	result = expression1 && expression2	True	True	True
			True	False	False
			False	True	False
			False	False	False
||	Logical disjunction	result = expression1 || expression2	True	True	True
			True	False	True
			False	True	True
			False	False	False

Table 6.26 JScript's bitwise operators.

Operator	Description	Syntax
<<	Left shift	a = b << n
>>	Right shift	a = b >> n
>>>	Unsigned right shift	a >>> n
~	Not	a = ~b
&	And	a = b & c
^	Xor	a = b ^ c
		Or	a = b	c

The bitwise shift operators are useful for performing fast multiplication and division. Shifting bits left performs multiplication such that shifting left 1 bit multiplies by 2, shifting left 2 bits multiplies by 4, and so on. The number of places to shift left is an integer in the range of 1 through 31. As bits shift to the left, JScript fills the "vacated" positions on the right with zeroes.

Shifting bits right performs division in the same manner as shifting left performs multiplication. As bits shift right, the positions on the left are filled with the topmost bit of the original operand. This has the effect of preserving the number's sign. If you shift a negative number right, the result is still a negative number. The unsigned shift right operator fills the vacated positions on the left with zeroes.

Be careful not to confuse the negation operator (~) with the logical negation operator (!). What's the difference? The ~ operator flips all the bits in a number, making the ones into zeroes and vice versa. The ! operator simply returns **true** if a Boolean expression is **false** and **false** if the expression is **true**.

Assignment Operators

The assignment operator (=) assigns the value of the expression on the right side of the operator to the left side of the operator. The assignment operator expects a variable, an object property, or an array element to be on the left side:

```
a = b * 2;
```

JScript, like C, C++, and Java, lets you use compound assignment statements. This short-cut allows you to combine other operators with the assignment operator. The assignment operator is always the second operator when using this syntax. The statement

```
a += 2;
```

is equivalent to:

```
a = a + 2;
```

You can use compound assignments with arithmetic, logical, and bitwise operators.

A Few More JScript Operators

JScript has a few miscellaneous operators that defy classification.

The *conditional* Operator

The **conditional** operator is the only ternary (three-operand) operator in JScript. The **conditional** operator uses the syntax:

```
op1 ? op2 : op3;
```

The value of the first operand must be a Boolean value and is typically the result of some comparison. If the value of the first operand is **true**, the operator returns the value of the second operand. If the value of the first operand is **false**, the operator returns the value of the third operand. The following statement sets *result* to the value of *a* or *b*, whichever is larger:

```
result = a > b ? a : b;
```

The **conditional** operator performs the same function as the **if...else** statement (discussed later in this chapter) but is more concise.

The *typeof* Operator

The **typeof** operator returns a string indicating the type of an expression. The possible return values are:

- **boolean**
- **function**
- **number**

- **object**
- **string**
- **undefined**

The **typeof** has the following syntax:

```
typeof var;
typeof(var);
```

The *new* Operator

You have already seen examples of the **new** operator in this chapter. The **new** operator creates new objects using the syntax

```
new constructor[(argument list)];
```

where *constructor* is the object's constructor function. The **new** operator works by first creating a new object without any defined properties. It then calls the object constructor function and optionally passes arguments to the constructor. The constructor can then initialize the new object using the keyword **this**. The following statement defines a new string object:

```
var newstring = new String("I'm a string object!");
```

The *delete* Operator

The **delete** operator deletes variables, object and object properties, and arrays and array elements by undefining them. Unlike the C++ **delete**, it does not actually free up the memory associated with the variable or object being deleted. JScript has automatic garbage collection, so the **delete** operator doesn't need to free memory. Here's how you use **delete**:

```
delete expression;
```

The *void* Operator

The **void** operator evaluates an expression and returns **undefined**. This operator is useful when you want to evaluate an expression but not return the value:

```
void expression;
```

The *comma* Operator

The **comma** operator (,)evaluates multiple expressions sequentially. The statement

```
document.write("The Comma operator "), str="is little used.",document.write(str);
```

is equivalent to the statements:

```
document.write("The Comma operator ");
str="is little used.";
document.write(str);
```

The resulting return value is whatever the last expression returns. You won't use the comma operator much except in **for** loops, which are discussed shortly.

Operator Precedence

Operators are evaluated in a predetermined *order of precedence*. Often, this order of precedence is different than the order in which you write the operators. Arithmetic operators have a higher precedence than comparison operators, which have a higher precedence than assignment operators. There is also an order of precedence within some of the operator categories. Operators with equal precedence are evaluated left to right.

JScript evaluates operators in the following order, highest to lowest:

- **call, member** -- . [] ()
- **unary, object creation/deletion** --, ++, --, ~, !, typeof, new, void, delete
- **multiplication, division, modulo division** -- *, /, %
- **addition, subtraction, string concatenation** -- +, -, +
- **bitwise shifting** -- >>, <<, >>>
- **relational** -- <, <=, >, >=
- **equality, identity** -- ==, !=, ===, !==
- **bitwise and, exclusive or, or** -- &, ^, |
- **logical and, or** -- &&, ||
- **conditional** -- ?:
- **assignment** -- +, +=, -=, /=, %=, <<=, >>=, >>>=, &=, ^=, |=

You can override the standard order of precedence by enclosing operations in parentheses. Operations in parentheses take precedence over those not in parentheses, and normal precedence is maintained within parentheses. Nesting parentheses further controls the order of operation, and operations within the innermost parentheses are evaluated first.

The following statements illustrate how operator precedence and parentheses work:

```
A = B * C + D / E
A = B * (C + D) / E
```

These statements produce different results. In the first example, the product of B * C is added to the result of D / E. In the second example, the sum of C + D is multiplied by B and then divided by E. For a more numeric example, consider:

```
10+2*2
```

The correct result is 14 (not 24) because * has a higher precedence than +.

Controlling Program Flow

Most programs make decisions and do different things as a result. The program often makes these decisions on the basis of a variable's or object property's value. A program's ability to make decisions and execute code accordingly is provided by *conditional statements*. Conditional statements evaluate a condition and specify statements to execute as a result of the evaluation.

Programs commonly execute a block of code repeatedly, for example, to initialize an array. *Looping statements* provide a way for a program to repeat statements a specific number of times or while a condition is **true** or **false**.

Conditional Statements

Programs make decisions using conditional statements. The ability to make decisions and execute statements on the basis of decisions is useful in all but the most basic programs. JScript has the following conditional statements:

- **if...else**
- **switch**

The *if* And *if...else* Statements

The **if** statement evaluates a condition and executes a statement or group of statements if the condition is **true**:

```
if (condition == true) {
   statement(s) to execute
}
```

If the condition is **true**, the statements inside the curly braces ({ }) are executed. If you have only one statement you don't need to use the braces, but it is still a good practice to include them. Listing 6.9 shows the **if** statement in action.

Listing 6.9   The if statement.

```
<SCRIPT LANGUAGE=JavaScript>
<!--
var Sales, Commission;

   Commission = .05;
   Sales = 12500.00;

   if (Sales >= 10000.00)
     Commission = .10;

// -->
</SCRIPT>
```

You can also specify statements to execute on both a **true** condition and a **false** condition. The **else** clause specifies statements to execute if the condition is **false**:

```
if (condition == true) {
   statements to execute
}
else {
   statements to execute
}
```

Listing 6.10 uses the **else** clause to execute a statement when the condition is **false**.

Listing 6.10   Using the else clause in an if statement.

```
<SCRIPT LANGUAGE=JavaScript>
<!--
var Sales, Commission;

   Commission = .05;
   Sales = 12500.00;
```

```
   if (Sales >= 10000.00)
     Commission = .10;
   else
     alert ("You need to work harder.");

// -->
</SCRIPT>
```

It is very common to combine an **if** statement with a relational operator to further define the condition. Listing 6.11 uses relational operators with the **if** statement to determine whether a value is within a range.

Listing 6.11   Using relational operators in an if statement.

```
<SCRIPT LANGUAGE=JavaScript>
<!--
var Sales, Commission = 0.0;

   if (Sales < 1000.00)
     Commission = .05;
   else if (Sales >= 1000.00 && Sales < 5000.00)
     Commission = .10;
   else if (Sales >= 5000.00 && Sales < 10000.00)
     Commission = .15;
   else {
     Commission = .20;
     alert ("Wow! Great job!");
   }

// -->
</SCRIPT>
```

The *switch* Statement

The **switch** statement executes one of several blocks of statements on the basis of an expression's value. A statement block executes when the expression value matches a label, which is specified by the **case** clause. The **default** clause specifies statements to execute when there is no match.

The **switch** statement uses the syntax:

```
switch (expression) {
   case label:
     statements to execute
   case label:
     statements to execute
```

```
    default:
        statements to execute
}
```

You can find an example of the **switch** statement in Listing 6.15.

Loop Statements

Loops execute selected lines of code repeatedly. JScript has loop statements that repeat program statements a specific number of times or while a condition is **true**. Of course, by using the logical negation operator (!), you can easily reverse the sense of any loop statement to make it repeat while a condition is false. Here are the loop statements:

- **for**

- **for...in**

- **while**

- **do...while**

The **for** Statement

The **for** statement executes a block of statements a specific number of times. The **for** statement uses an integer counter variable to control the number of times the loop is repeated. The **for** statement modifies the counter variable each time through the loop.

The **for** statement uses the syntax:

```
for (init_counter; test_counter; increment/decrement_counter) {
    statements to execute
}
```

The loop initializes the counter variable before the loop begins and tests it at the beginning of each iteration. The loop repeats as long as the test returns **true**. You don't need the braces if only one statement is in the loop, but it is a good habit to include them anyway.

The following statement sets each element in an array to zero:

```
for (counter = 0; counter < 10; counter++)
    somearray[counter] = 0;
```

The **comma** operator is used to handle more than one counter variable in a **for** statement. This is one of the most common uses of the comma operator. The following statements show the use of the **comma** operator in a **for** statement:

```
for (i = 0, j = 10; i < 10; i++, j++)
   document.write (i + " " + j);
```

Although it is common to increment or decrement the loop counter as the last clause in the **for** loop, you may use any legal expression. For example:

```
for (x=0,y=0;x<100;x+=10,y+=10)
```

The *for...in* Statement

The **for...in** statement executes the loop one time for each element in an array or for each property in an object:

```
for (var in object) {
   statements to execute
}
```

Var is the name of a variable, an array element, or an object property. *Obj* is the name of an object or an array.

Arrays have a **length** property that returns the highest array index plus 1. JScript arrays can be sparse, so the **length** property might not return the actual number of array elements. Listing 6.12 uses **for...in** to count the actual number of elements in an array.

Listing 6.12   Using for...in to count array elements.

```
<SCRIPT LANGUAGE=JavaScript>
<!--
var Count = 0;
var SomeArray = new Array(10);

   // statements to initialize the array

   for (i in SomeArray)
     count++;

// -->
</SCRIPT>
```

An example in this chapter's Practical Guide uses the **for...in** statement to add a **count** property to the **Array** object.

Listing 6.13 shows how to use **for...in** to iterate through an object's properties.

Listing 6.13 Iterating through an object's properties.

```
<SCRIPT LANGUAGE=JavaScript>
<!--
var Place = new Object;
var Prop;

    Place["City"] = "Columbus";
    Place["State"] = "OH";
    Place["Zip"] = "43220";

    for (Prop in Place)
        document.write(Prop + ": " + Place[Prop] + "<BR>");

// -->
</SCRIPT>
```

The **while** Statement

The **while** statement executes a loop while a condition is **true**:

```
while (condition==true)
    statements to execute
```

The following statements use the **while** statement to output array element values:

```
var Count = 0;
var SomeArray = new Array(10);

// statements to initialize the array

while (count < 10) {
    document.write(SomeArray[count]);
    count++;
}
```

The **do...while** Statement

The **do...while** statement works much like the **while** statement, except that the body of the loop is executed at least once. This is because the statement doesn't evaluate the condition until the end of the loop:

```
do {
    statements to execute
} while (expression);
```

The following statements perform the same function as the previous example but with the **do...while** statement:

```
var Count = 0;
var SomeArray = new Array(10);

// statements to initialize the array

do {
   document.write(SomeArray[count]);
   count++;
} while (count < 10);
```

The *break* And *continue* Statements

The **break** statement causes a loop to exit early. Listing 6.14 searches an array for a value and breaks out when it finds a match.

Listing 6.14 Using the break statement.
```
<SCRIPT LANGUAGE=JavaScript>
<!--
var SomeArray = new Array(10);
var SearchItem;
var Found = false;

   // statements to initialize SomeArray
   // and SearchItem

   for (i = 0; i < 10; i++) {
     if (SearchItem == SomeArray[i]) {
        Found = true;
        break;
     }
}

// -->
</SCRIPT>
```

You'll recall that the **switch** statement also uses the **break** statement, as shown in Listing 6.15.

Listing 6.15 Using break in the switch statement.
```
<SCRIPT LANGUAGE=JavaScript>
<!--
var Commission = .0;
var Bonus = 0;
```

```
    switch (Commission) {
      case .05:
          Bonus = 0;
          break;
      case .10:
          Bonus = 500.00
          break;
      case .10:
          Bonus = 1000.00
          break;
      case .20:
          Bonus = 1500.00
          break;
      default:
          alert ("Invalid Bonus value");
}

// -->
</SCRIPT>
```

The **continue** statement stops the current iteration of the loop and starts a new one. The following example uses the **for** statement to sum the values of an array. If an array element is not a number, **continue** immediately starts a new iteration:

```
<SCRIPT LANGUAGE=JavaScript>
<!--
var a = new Array(10);
var asum;

    for (i = 0; i < 10; i++)
      a[i] = i;

    a[7] = "I'm not a number anymore.";
    asum = 0;
    for (i = 0; i < 10; i++) {
      if (isNaN(a[i]))
          continue;
      asum += a[i];
    }

// -->
</SCRIPT>
```

Functions

Most programs include sections of code that perform specific tasks and are used many times. Such sections of code in JScript are *functions*. Functions are blocks of code that perform a specific task for the rest of the program. Functions can accept arguments, accept values used by the function, and return a result.

JScript provides several built-in functions and also allows you to define your own functions. Functions are a major part of JScript programming and are even a type of data. Because a function is a data type, it can be assigned to a variable, an object property, or an array element and can be passed as an argument to another function. JScript also has a **Function** object, which is a wrapper object around the primitive **function** type.

Defining Functions

Defining a function is straightforward. A function definition consists of the **function** keyword, the name of the function, any arguments, and the statements that constitute the function body:

```
function name(argument1, argument2, …) {
    function statements
}
```

The following statements define a function that calculates the square of a number:

```
function sqr(x) {
    return x * x;
}
```

Argument **x** contains the value to square. The **return** statement returns the specified value (in this case, the result of the calculation) to the caller.

The statement

```
sqr(5);
```

calls the **sqr** function with 5 as the argument; **sqr** will return 25. However, in this example there is nothing to accept the returned value. Functions that return values are typically used in expressions on the right side of an assignment statement:

```
result = sqr(5);
area = Math.PI * sqr(radius);
```

By Value Vs. By Reference

JScript functions can manipulate arguments *by value* and *by reference*. When you pass a variable by value to a function, JScript actually passes a copy of the variable to the function. The function can change the value locally without changing the original value.

When you pass a variable by reference, JScript sends the function the variable's address in memory. The function can change the value stored at that address, and the change persists even after the function returns.

Some languages let you specify how to pass arguments, but JScript doesn't. Rather, JScript passes numbers and Booleans by value and passes objects and arrays by reference. Strings and functions are primitive types like numbers and Booleans, but their length can vary. Therefore, JScript passes them by reference, too.

The **Function** Constructor

In addition to defining functions with the **function** keyword, functions can be created using the **new** statement and specifying the **Function** object:

```
var sqr = new Function("x", "return x * x;");
```

This method uses the **Function** object constructor to create the function. The constructor takes any number of string arguments. The last string that is specified defines the function body.

Using the constructor function is convenient when you are defining a method for an object. The following statements declare an object variable **loan** and assign it a method that calculates a payment:

```
var loan = new Object;
var payment
loan.pmt = new Function("I", "P", "Amt", "return I / P * Amt;");
payment = loan.pmt(.07, 12, 200000);
```

Events And Event Handlers

An *event* is an action that (typically) the user generates. Some events originate from the operating system. However events are generated, they signal to your program that something interesting has happened. For example, when the user clicks on an HTML button, a *click* event occurs. Also, some objects (such as ActiveX controls) can fire events. An *event handler* is code that executes in response to an event.

You define event handlers like any other JScript function. Indeed, they are simply functions that the browser calls when an event occurs. You can also call a handler as you would any other function at any time. Listing 6.16 shows a function that calculates the area of a rectangle. When the user clicks an HTML button control, the browser calls the event handler.

Listing 6.16   A JScript event handler.

```
<HTML>
<HEAD>
<TITLE>Listing 6.16</TITLE>
<SCRIPT LANGUAGE=JavaScript>
<!--
   function calc_area(len, wid) {
     alert ("Area: " + len * wid);
   }
// -->
</SCRIPT>
</HEAD>

<BODY>

<FORM>
Length:<INPUT TYPE=TEXT NAME="length"><BR>
Width: <INPUT TYPE=TEXT NAME="width"><BR>
<INPUT TYPE=BUTTON NAME="calc" VALUE="Calculate"
OnClick="calc_area(length.value, width.value)">
</FORM>

</BODY>
</HTML>
```

You can embed JScript code directly into an HTML form definition and it will execute when a specified event occurs. For example:

```
<INPUT TYPE=BUTTON VALUE="Calculate"
OnClick="var area = length.value * width.value; alert('Area: ' + area);">
```

Creating Objects

JScript is an object-based language that provides several built-in objects. Additionally, JScript makes it easy to create your own objects.

The simplest method of creating an object is to declare it using the **Object** object. The statement

```
var myobj = new Object();
```

declares an object variable, but one of little use. We think of objects as collections of methods and properties. The object **myobj** is empty; that is, it has no properties or methods.

However, you can add properties to **myobj** by assigning it a value:

```
myobj.name = "John";
```

Now, **myobj** has a **name** property. You add methods in the same manner:

```
// define the method
function showname() {
   document.write(this.name);
}

// assign the method to the object
myobj.show = showname;
myobj.name = "John";
// now invoke the method
myobj.show();
```

Although easy to do, this method of creating an object has a slight problem. You must repeat the steps for every object that you want to use. So if you want 10 objects just like **myobj**, you'll need to do the same steps 10 times to initialize each new object. Wouldn't it be easier to define one object and declare objects that would automatically have all properties and methods? You bet, and it can be done using a constructor.

Using Constructors To Define Objects

A *constructor* is a function that defines an object's properties and methods and creates and initializes a new object. Constructor functions can take arguments like any other function but do not return a value (technically it can, but it rarely needs to). The following statements define a **Loan** object with three properties:

```
function Loan() {
   this.principal = 0;
   this.rate = 0;
   this.periods = 0;
}
```

The keyword **this** is used in the constructor function to refer to the object. It distinguishes constructor functions from ordinary functions.

In the statement

```
var newloan = new Loan();
```

the **newloan** properties are accessed just like properties of built-in objects:

```
newloan.principal = 12000.00;
newloan.rate = .18;
newloan.periods = 12;
```

Methods are added to the object by defining the necessary functions and then assigning them to object properties. The following example defines a function to calculate a loan payment. The object definition is shown again, but now it includes the method definition:

```
function payment() {
    return this.rate/this.periods * this.principal;
}

function Loan() {
    this.principal = 0;
    this.rate = 0;
    this.periods = 0;
    this.pmt = payment;
}
```

Now that the **Loan** object has a method, you can put it to work:

```
var newloan = new Loan();
var loanpmt;

newloan.principal = 12000.00;
newloan.rate = .18;
newloan.periods = 12;
loanpmt = newloan.pmt();
```

Remember, constructor functions can take arguments that initialize the object's properties. Here is a modification of the **Loan** object constructor that accepts arguments:

```
function Loan(princ, rate, pds) {
    this.principal = princ;
    this.rate = rate;
    this.periods = pds;
    this.pmt = this.rate/this.periods * this.principal;
}

var newloan = new Loan(12000.00, .18, 12);
```

Using The **prototype** Object

Another way of specifying methods and properties is to use the **prototype** object. The **prototype** object defines all the properties and methods for an object, and these become properties and methods of all objects of that type. Prototype properties are shared among all the objects of that type and can be read. However, setting an object property creates a copy of the property for that particular object. The sharing of prototype properties is memory efficient, because each object doesn't require a copy.

Here is an example of using **prototype**:

```
// constructor function
function Loan() {
    this.principal = 0;
    this.rate = 0;
    this.periods = 0;
}

// calculate payment function
function payment() {
    return this.rate/this.periods * this.principal;
}

// assign the payment function as a method
Loan.prototype.pmt = payment;

// declare a Loan object
var newloan = new Loan();
var loanpmt;

newloan.principal = 12000.00;
newloan.rate = .18;
newloan.periods = 12;

loanpmt = newloan.pmt();
```

The next statement adds a default property:

```
Loan.prototype.type = "Auto";
```

A default property can be overridden by assigning it a new value:

```
newloan.type = "RV";
```

Summary

Believe it or not, this chapter doesn't completely cover every feature available in JScript. However, it is easy to see that JScript is a rich, capable scripting language. The JScript Quick Reference in this chapter's Practical Guide lists many more language features. JScript, or ECMAScript, is an attractive choice for developing Web pages with client-side script because Microsoft, Netscape, and other vendors support it. Therefore, you can create pages that work in the most popular browsers without having to writing multiple versions of the same pages. In addition to the examples in the Practical Guide, the following chapters show you how JScript is used to do many interesting things.

Practical Guide To

Client-Side JScript

- Using JScript With HTML Forms
- Using JScript With ActiveX Controls
- Using The **prototype** Property
- JScript Quick Reference

This Prectical Guide shows you how to put JScript to work in HTML documents. You'll see how JScript can work with form elements and perform basic data validation. You'll see how JScript can respond to user events, such as clicking on an HTML button control. JScript can also interact with ActiveX controls to script a control's appearance and behavior. At the end of the Practical Guide, you'll find a language Quick Reference.

Using JScript With HTML Forms

Listing 6.17 shows an HTML document containing a form to collect new member registration information for the Community Dining Club application. This sample Web application is used in several chapters of this book to illustrate some of the many things that can be incorporated into active Web pages. This listing shows how JScript can access form elements and respond to an event and how to perform basic data validation.

Listing 6.17   Using JScript with an HTML form.

```
<HTML>
<HEAD>
<TITLE>New Member Registration</TITLE>
<SCRIPT FOR="cmdSubmit" EVENT="onclick" LANGUAGE=JavaScript>
<!--

    var TheForm;
    TheForm = document.RegistrationForm;

    if (TheForm.firstname.value.length == 0) {
        alert("Please enter your first name.");
    TheForm.firstname.focus();
    }

    else if (TheForm.lastname.value.length == 0) {
        TheForm.lastname.value = prompt("Please enter your last name.");
    if (TheForm.lastname.value.length != 0)
        TheForm.addr1.focus();
    }
    else if (TheForm.addr1.value.length == 0) {
        alert("Please enter your address.");
        TheForm.addr1.focus();
    }
     else if (TheForm.city.value.length == 0) {
        alert("Please enter the city.");
       TheForm.city.focus();
```

```
        }
    else if (TheForm.state.value.length != 2) {
        alert("Please enter the 2-letter state abbreviation.");
        TheForm.state.focus();
    }
    else if (TheForm.zip.value.length < 5) {
        alert("Please enter a valid zip code.");
        TheForm.zip.focus();
        TheForm.code.select();
    }
    else if (TheForm.code.value.length != 3 || isNaN(TheForm.code.value)) {
        alert("Please enter a valid area code.");
        TheForm.code.focus();
        TheForm.code.select();
    }
    else if (TheForm.phone.value.length != 7 || isNaN(TheForm.phone.value)) {
        alert("Please enter a valid phone number.");
        TheForm.phone.focus();
        TheForm.phone.select();
    }
// -->
</SCRIPT>
</HEAD>
<BODY>

<H1 Align=Center>Community Dining Club</H1>
<H2 Align=Center>New Member Registration</H2>
<HR SIZE=5 WIDTH=90%>


<TABLE>
<TD>
</TD>
<TD>
<PRE>
<FORM NAME="RegistrationForm">
<B>First Name:       </B><INPUT TYPE=TEXT NAME="firstname">
<B>Last Name:        </B><INPUT TYPE=TEXT NAME="lastname">
<B>Address1:         </B><INPUT TYPE=TEXT NAME="addr1">
<B>Address2:         </B><INPUT TYPE=TEXT NAME="addr2">
<B>City:             </B><INPUT TYPE=TEXT NAME="city">
<B>State:            </B><INPUT TYPE=TEXT NAME="state" MAXLENGTH=2 SIZE=2>
<B>Zip:              </B><INPUT TYPE=TEXT NAME="zip" MAXLENGTH=10 SIZE=10>
<B>Area Code/Phone: </B><INPUT TYPE=TEXT NAME="code" MAXLENGTH=3 SIZE=3>
<INPUT TYPE=TEXT NAME="phone" MAXLENGTH=7 SIZE=7>

<B>Preferred Cuisine: </B><SELECT NAME="cuisine" SIZE="1">
                        <OPTION VALUE="1">American
                        <OPTION VALUE="2">Chinese
```

```
                         <OPTION VALUE="3">French
                         <OPTION VALUE="4">German
                         <OPTION VALUE="5">Greek
                         <OPTION VALUE="6">Indian
                         <OPTION VALUE="7">Italian
                         <OPTION VALUE="8">Japanese
                         <OPTION VALUE="9">Other
                         </SELECT>

<INPUT TYPE=BUTTON NAME="cmdSubmit" VALUE="Submit"> <INPUT TYPE="RESET"
 VALUE="Clear">
</PRE>

</FORM>
</TD>
</TABLE>

</BODY>
</HTML>
```

The document's **BODY** section defines an HTML form to collect new member registration data. When the user clicks the **Submit** button, the browser calls an event handler to verify the form data. The **<SCRIPT>** tag in the document's **HEAD** section contains the event handler's definition. The **FOR** attribute specifies the control that the script handles and must equal the name assigned to a control with the **NAME** attribute. The **EVENT** attribute specifies the event that the script responds to.

The event handler first defines the variable **TheForm**, which is set to reference the form **RegistrationForm**. The form is a member of the currently loaded document and is referenced by way of the **document** object. (You'll read more about the **document** object and other browser objects in Chapter 7.) It isn't necessary to assign a reference to the **document** object to a variable, because form elements can be referenced using the syntax:

```
Document.RegistrationForm.firstname.Value . . .
```

However, assigning a variable to reference the form reduces typing and generally makes the script easier to read.

The rest of the event handler verifies the input. The first test is of the **Value** property of **firstname**. If the length is equal to 0, the script displays an alert box asking the user to enter a first name. The text box control's **Focus** method places the cursor in the correct text box.

If the user leaves **lastname** blank, a **prompt** box requests the last name. This is inconsistent with the rest of the code, but it does illustrate that HTML control properties are easily changed programmatically. The script checks the **Value** property again and sets the focus to the address box if data is entered.

If the information entered for **state** does not equal two characters, the script asks the user to enter a two-letter abbreviation and the text box control's **Select** method is called to highlight any text already entered. The rest of the script checks the remaining form elements, except for **cuisine**, which defaults to American.

Using JScript With ActiveX Controls

This example shows how JScript is used to interact with ActiveX controls. You set ActiveX control properties with the **<PARAM>** tag when the document is loaded. The properties are usually static, unless the control itself is changing them. JScript can access exposed control properties, methods, and events and can work with them programmatically. Therefore, the control's appearance and behavior can be modified dynamically. Of course, some ActiveX controls are not aware that a script might change their properties. These controls read their properties once, tuck the values away somewhere, and never read them again. This makes them not useful for scripting. Luckily, most modern controls don't have this problem.

Listing 6.18 adds a spinning billboard to the Community Dining Club New Member Registration page. The billboard uses two controls that Microsoft supplies with Internet Explorer: **Label** and **Timer**. The **Label** control displays text and has properties that specify how the text is displayed. The control also has events and one method, but these are not used in this example. The **Timer** control is not visible on the browser's screen, and its only purpose is to fire a **timer** event at a specified interval. This event controls the speed of the spinning text. JScript is used to "glue" the two controls together.

Listing 6.18   Using JScript with ActiveX controls.

```
<HTML>
<HEAD>
<TITLE>New Member Registration</TITLE>

<SCRIPT LANGUAGE=JavaScript>
<!--
var Angle;
var MsgNo, ColorNo;
```

```
var Message = new Array("Join Today!", "Fine Dining!", "Impress Friends!", "Save
Money!", "Be Cool!");

MsgNo = 0;
ColorNo = 1;
Angle = 0;
// -->
</SCRIPT>


<SCRIPT FOR="IeTimer" EVENT="timer" LANGUAGE=JavaScript>
<!--
    IeLabel.Caption = Message[MsgNo];
    IeLabel.Angle = Angle;
    Angle = Angle + 5;
    if (Angle > 360) {
        Angle = 0;
        MsgNo = MsgNo + 1;
        if (MsgNo > 4)
            MsgNo = 0;
        IeLabel.ForeColor = Math.random() * 16777215;
    }
// -->
</SCRIPT>

<SCRIPT FOR="cmdSubmit" EVENT="onclick" LANGUAGE=JavaScript>
<!--
    var TheForm;
    TheForm = document.RegistrationForm;

    if (TheForm.firstname.value.length == 0) {
        alert("Please enter your first name.");
        TheForm.firstname.focus();
    }
    else if (TheForm.lastname.value.length == 0) {
        TheForm.lastname.value = prompt("Please enter your last name.");
        if (TheForm.lastname.value.length != 0)
            TheForm.addr1.focus();
    }
    else if (TheForm.addr1.value.length == 0) {
        alert("Please enter your address.");
        TheForm.addr1.focus();
```

```
        }
    else if (TheForm.city.value.length == 0) {
        alert("Please enter the city.");
        TheForm.city.focus();
    }
    else if (TheForm.state.value.length != 2) {
        alert("Please enter the 2-letter state abbreviation.");
        TheForm.state.focus();
    }
    else if (TheForm.zip.value.length < 5) {
        alert("Please enter a valid zip code.");
        TheForm.zip.focus();
        TheForm.code.select();
    }
    else if (TheForm.code.value.length != 3 || isNaN(TheForm.code.value)) {
        alert("Please enter a valid area code.");
        TheForm.code.focus();
        TheForm.code.select();
    }
    else if (TheForm.phone.value.length != 7 || isNaN(TheForm.phone.value)) {
        alert("Please enter a valid phone number.");
        TheForm.phone.focus();
        TheForm.phone.select();
    }
// -->
</SCRIPT>
</HEAD>
<BODY>

<H1 Align=Center>Community Dining Club</H1>
<H2 Align=Center>New Member Registration</H2>
<HR SIZE=5 WIDTH=90%>

<OBJECT ID="IeTimer" WIDTH=39 HEIGHT=39
 CLASSID="CLSID:59CCB4A0-727D-11CF-AC36-00AA00A47DD2">
    <PARAM NAME="Interval" VALUE="50">
</OBJECT>

<TABLE>
<TD>

<OBJECT ID="IeLabel" WIDTH=150 HEIGHT=150
 CLASSID="CLSID:99B42120-6EC7-11CF-A6C7-00AA00A47DD2">
    <PARAM NAME="Caption" VALUE=" ">
    <PARAM NAME="Angle" VALUE="0">
    <PARAM NAME="Alignment" VALUE="4">
```

```
        <PARAM NAME="Mode" VALUE="1">
        <PARAM NAME="FillStyle" VALUE="0">
        <PARAM NAME="ForeColor" VALUE="#000000">
        <PARAM NAME="BackColor" VALUE="#COCOCO">
        <PARAM NAME="FontName" VALUE="Arial">
        <PARAM NAME="FontSize" VALUE="14">
        <PARAM NAME="FontItalic" VALUE="0">
        <PARAM NAME="FontBold" VALUE="1">
        <PARAM NAME="FontUnderline" VALUE="0">
        <PARAM NAME="FontStrikeout" VALUE="0">
        <PARAM NAME="TopPoints" VALUE="0">
        <PARAM NAME="BotPoints" VALUE="0">
</OBJECT>

</TD>
<TD>
<PRE>
<FORM NAME="RegistrationForm">
<B>First Name:      </B><INPUT TYPE=TEXT NAME="firstname">
<B>Last Name:       </B><INPUT TYPE=TEXT NAME="lastname">
<B>Address1:        </B><INPUT TYPE=TEXT NAME="addr1">
<B>Address2:        </B><INPUT TYPE=TEXT NAME="addr2">
<B>City:            </B><INPUT TYPE=TEXT NAME="city">
<B>State:           </B><INPUT TYPE=TEXT NAME="state" MAXLENGTH=2 SIZE=2>
<B>Zip:             </B><INPUT TYPE=TEXT NAME="zip" MAXLENGTH=10 SIZE=10>
<B>Area Code/Phone: </B><INPUT TYPE=TEXT NAME="code"
MAXLENGTH=3 SIZE=3> <INPUT TYPE=TEXT NAME="phone" MAXLENGTH=7 SIZE=7>

<B>Preferred Cuisine: </B><SELECT NAME="cuisine" SIZE="1">
                        <OPTION VALUE="1">American
                        <OPTION VALUE="2">Chinese
                        <OPTION VALUE="3">French
                        <OPTION VALUE="4">German
                        <OPTION VALUE="5">Greek
                        <OPTION VALUE="6">Indian
                        <OPTION VALUE="7">Italian
                        <OPTION VALUE="8">Japanese
                        <OPTION VALUE="9">Other
                        </SELECT>

<INPUT TYPE=BUTTON NAME="cmdSubmit"
VALUE="Submit"> <INPUT TYPE="RESET" VALUE="Clear">
</PRE>
```

```
</FORM>
</TD>
</TABLE>

</BODY>
</HTML>
```

The first **<SCRIPT>** tag contains code to define the variable used by the **Timer** control's **timer** event handler. This script is run when the page is loaded.

The next **<SCRIPT>** tag defines the event handler for the **timer** event for the control assigned the name **IeTimer**. This handler is called when the **Time** control fires a **timer** event, or every 50 milliseconds in this example. The event handler sets the **Label** control's **Caption** property from the **Message** array and sets the **Angle** property from a variable. The angle is incremented 5 degrees each time, and the script checks to see whether the angle is greater than 360 degrees. If it is, the angle is set to 0 and **MsgNo** is incremented so that the next message is displayed the next time the **timer** event fires. The handler also changes the text color randomly each time a new message is displayed.

Using The **prototype** Property

This example shows how easy it is to add a default property to built-in or programmer-defined objects. The **Array** object has a **length** property that returns the index of the highest array element plus 1. Because JScript arrays are sparse, this value might not necessarily specify the actual number of elements in the array. Sometimes it is useful to know how many elements an array has. With the **prototype** property, a default method can be added to report that information.

Listing 6.19 shows a function named **array_count**. This function uses a **for...in** loop statement to iterate through the array and count the number of array elements. The **array_count** function is added as a method to the **Array** object. All array objects created in this document will have this new capability.

Listing 6.19   Using the prototype method to add a default method.
```
<HTML>
<HEAD>
<TITLE>The Prototype Method</TITLE>
<SCRIPT LANGUAGE=JavaScript>
<!--
```

```
function array_count() {
    var count = 0;

    for (j in this)
    {
        ++count;
    }
    return count - 1;
}

Array.prototype.count = array_count;
var SalesRegion = new Array();

SalesRegion[0] = "East";
SalesRegion[5] = "West";
SalesRegion[10] = "North";

document.write(SalesRegion.count());
// -->
</SCRIPT>

</HEAD>
<BODY>

</BODY>
</HTML>
```

JScript Quick Reference

Category	Keyword/(Feature)	JScript	JavaScript	ECMAScript
Array Support	Array	✔	✔	✔
	concat	✔		✔
	dimensions	✔		
	getItem	✔		
	join	✔	✔	✔
	lbound	✔		
	length	✔	✔	✔

(continued)

JScript Quick Reference *(continued)*

Category	Keyword/(Feature)	JScript	JavaScript	ECMAScript
	reverse	✔	✔	✔
	slice	✔		
	sort	✔	✔	✔
	toArray	✔		
	ubound	✔		
	VBArray	✔		
Collections	Drives	✔		
	Files	✔		
	Folders	✔		
Comments	/*...*/	✔	✔	✔
	//	✔	✔	✔
Conditional Compilation	@cc_on	✔		
	Conditional_Compilation _Variables	✔		
	@if Statement	✔		
	@set Statement	✔		
Constants	Infinity	✔	✔	✔
	NaN	✔	✔	✔
	null	✔	✔	✔
	true, false	✔	✔	✔
	undefined	✔	✔	✔
Control Flow	break	✔	✔	✔
	continue	✔	✔	✔
	do...while	✔		

(continued)

JScript Quick Reference (continued)

Category	Keyword/(Feature)	JScript	JavaScript	ECMAScript
	for	✔	✔	✔
	for...in	✔	✔	✔
	if...else	✔	✔	✔
	Labeled	✔		
	return	✔	✔	✔
	switch	✔		
	while		✔	
	with	✔	✔	✔
Date/Time	Date	✔	✔	✔
	getDate	✔	✔	✔
	getDay	✔	✔	✔
	getFullYear	✔		✔
	getHours	✔	✔	✔
	getMilliseconds	✔		✔
	getMinutes	✔	✔	✔
	getMonth	✔	✔	✔
	getSeconds	✔	✔	✔
	getTime	✔	✔	✔
	getTimeZoneOffset	✔	✔	✔
	getUTCDate	✔		✔
	getUTCDay	✔		✔
	getUTCFullYear	✔		✔
	getUTCHours	✔		✔

JScript Quick Reference (continued)

Category	Keyword/(Feature)	JScript	JavaScript	ECMAScript
	getUTCMilliseconds	✔		✔
	getUTCMonth	✔		✔
	getUTCSeconds	✔		✔
	getVarDate	✔		
	getYear	✔	✔	✔
	parse	✔	✔	✔
	setDate	✔	✔	✔
	setFullYear	✔		✔
	setHours	✔	✔	✔
	setMilliseconds	✔		✔
	setMinutes	✔	✔	✔
	setMonth	✔	✔	✔
	setSeconds	✔	✔	✔
	setTime	✔	✔	✔
	setUTCDate	✔		✔
	setUTCFullYear	✔		✔
	setUTCHours	✔		✔
	setUTCMilliseconds	✔		✔
	setUTCMonth	✔		✔
	setUTCSeconds	✔		✔
	setYear	✔	✔	✔
	toGMTString	✔	✔	✔
	toLocaleString	✔	✔	✔

(continued)

JScript Quick Reference (continued)

Category	Keyword/(Feature)	JScript	JavaScript	ECMAScript
	toUTCString	✔		✔
	UTC	✔	✔	✔
Declaration	function	✔	✔	✔
	new	✔	✔	✔
	var	✔	✔	✔
Enumeration	Enumerator	✔		
	atEnd	✔		
	item	✔		
	moveFirst	✔		
	moveNext	✔		
File and File System Objects	Dictionary	✔		
	Drive	✔		
	File	✔		
	Folder	✔		
	FileSystemObject	✔		
	TextStream	✔		
Function Support	Function	✔	✔	✔
	arguments	✔	✔	✔
	caller	✔	✔	
	length	✔		✔
Global Methods	Global	✔		✔
	assign		✔	
	escape	✔	✔	✔

(continued)

JScript Quick Reference

Category	Keyword/(Feature)	JScript	JavaScript	ECMAScript
	eval	✔	✔	✔
	isFinite	✔	✔	✔
	isNaN	✔	✔	✔
	parseFloat	✔	✔	✔
	parseInt	✔	✔	✔
	toString	✔	✔	✔
	unescape	✔	✔	✔
	valueOf	✔	✔	✔
Math	Math	✔	✔	✔
	abs	✔	✔	✔
	acos	✔	✔	✔
	asin	✔	✔	✔
	atan	✔	✔	✔
	atan2	✔	✔	✔
	ceil	✔	✔	✔
	cos	✔	✔	✔
	E	✔	✔	✔
	exp	✔	✔	✔
	floor	✔	✔	✔
	LN10	✔	✔	✔
	LN2	✔	✔	✔
	log	✔	✔	✔
	LOG10E	✔	✔	✔

(continued)

JScript Quick Reference

Category	Keyword/(Feature)	JScript	JavaScript	ECMAScript
	LOG2E	✔	✔	✔
	max	✔	✔	✔
	min	✔	✔	✔
	PI	✔	✔	✔
	pow	✔	✔	✔
	random	✔	✔	✔
	round	✔	✔	✔
	sin	✔	✔	✔
	sqrt	✔	✔	✔
	SQRT1_2	✔	✔	✔
	SQRT2	✔	✔	✔
	tan	✔	✔	✔
Numbers	Number	✔	✔	✔
	MAX_VALUE	✔	✔	✔
	MIN_VALUE	✔	✔	✔
	NaN	✔	✔	✔
	NEGATIVE_INFINITY	✔	✔	✔
	POSITIVE_INFINITY	✔	✔	✔
Object Support	Object	✔	✔	✔
	assign		✔	
	constructor	✔	✔	✔
	new	✔		✔
	prototype	✔		✔

(continued)

JScript Quick Reference (continued)

Category	Keyword/(Feature)	JScript	JavaScript	ECMAScript
	this	✔	✔	✔
	toString	✔		✔
	valueOf	✔	✔	✔
Objects	Array	✔	✔	✔
	Boolean	✔	✔	✔
	Date	✔	✔	✔
	Enumerator	✔		
	Function	✔	✔	✔
	Global	✔		✔
	JavaArray		✔	
	JavaClass		✔	
	JavaMethod		✔	
	JavaObject		✔	
	JavaPackage		✔	
	Math	✔	✔	✔
	Number	✔	✔	✔
	Object	✔	✔	✔
	Packages		✔	
	RegExp	✔		
	Regular Expression	✔		
	String	✔	✔	✔
	VBArray	✔		

(continued)

JScript Quick Reference *(continued)*

Category	Keyword/(Feature)	JScript	JavaScript	ECMAScript
Operators	=	✔	✔	✔
	OP=	✔	✔	✔
	+, -	✔	✔	✔
	%	✔	✔	✔
	*, /	✔	✔	✔
	==, !=	✔	✔	✔
	<, <=	✔	✔	✔
	>, >=	✔	✔	✔
	===, !==	✔		
	&&, ||, !	✔	✔	✔
	&, |, ~, ^	✔	✔	✔
	<<, >>	✔	✔	✔
	>>>	✔	✔	✔
	?:	✔	✔	✔
	,	✔	✔	✔
	--, ++	✔	✔	✔
	delete	✔		✔
	typeof	✔	✔	✔
	void	✔	✔	✔
Script Engine Identification	ScriptEngine	✔		
	ScriptEngineBuildVersion	✔		
	ScriptEngineMajorVersion	✔		
	ScriptEngineMinorVersion	✔		

(continued)

JScript Quick Reference *(continued)*

Category	Keyword/(Feature)	JScript	JavaScript	ECMAScript
String Support	String	✔	✔	✔
	anchor	✔	✔	
	big	✔	✔	
	blink	✔	✔	
	bold	✔	✔	
	charAt	✔	✔	✔
	charCodeAt	✔		✔
	concat	✔		
	fixed	✔	✔	
	fontcolor	✔	✔	
	fontsize	✔	✔	
	fromCharCode	✔		✔
	indexOf	✔	✔	✔
	italics	✔	✔	
	lastIndexOf	✔	✔	
	length	✔	✔	✔
	link	✔	✔	
	match	✔		
	replace	✔		
	search	✔		
	slice	✔		
	small	✔	✔	
	split	✔	✔	✔

(continued)

JScript Quick Reference *(continued)*

Category	Keyword/(Feature)	JScript	JavaScript	ECMAScript
	strike	✔	✔	
	sub	✔	✔	
	substring		✔	
	sup	✔	✔	
	toLowerCase	✔	✔	✔
	toUpperCase	✔	✔	✔

The Dynamic HTML Object Model

Objects are everywhere. The Web browser gives you scripting access to browser functionality and contents through its object model.

Kim Barber

Notes...

Chapter 7

If anything stands out as a general theme in this book, it's objects. Practically every chapter discusses using objects in Web pages. Objects, such as ActiveX controls and Java applets, are embedded in HTML pages. Scripting languages make extensive use of objects in both client-side and server-side scripting. Both the Web browser and the Web server provide objects. You can even write your own objects for client and server applications.

It should, then, be no surprise that an HTML document is simply an object. Like any object, an HTML document has properties, methods, and events. The Web browser exposes documents (as well as itself) through a structured set of objects referred to as the Dynamic HTML Object Model. You use client-side scripting to access and manipulate objects belonging to this model.

Remember that you can't directly manipulate these objects from the server. However, you can use server-side script to write client-side code—the code the server generates then executes on the client and can manipulate the browser's objects.

The Dynamic HTML Object Model is part of the browser and provides a way to access and manipulate the browser and the documents it contains. The object model defines and exposes several objects through which browser elements and functionality are accessed. In addition, one object provides access to documents and their contents.

Before looking at the objects themselves, consider how a browser such as Internet Explorer operates. Figure 7.1 shows Internet Explorer's structure. The actual browser

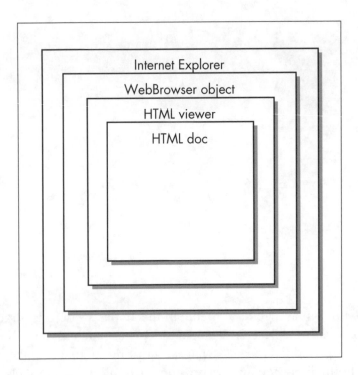

Figure 7.1

Internet Explorer's structure for displaying HTML documents.

application, **IEXPLORE.EXE**, is a relatively small executable that functions as a container for the **WebBrowser** object: **SHDOCVW.DLL**.

The **WebBrowser** object provides the browser's basic capabilities, such as navigation, refreshing pages, printing, and so on. This object doesn't display anything. To display an HTML page or other resource, it creates an ActiveX object from the appropriate document server. The document server actually displays the document. This allows the browser to display not only HTML pages but other documents as well, such as Word files (since Word is an ActiveX document server). Internet Explorer, then, can display any document that has an ActiveX document server.

Internet Explorer uses the Microsoft HTML viewer, **MSHTML.DLL**, to display HTML pages. The HTML viewer is an ActiveX server that displays HTML documents. It also provides client-side scripting. Figure 7.2 shows how the HTML viewer implements client-side scripting.

When a page contains the **<SCRIPT>** tag, the HTML viewer loads the scripting engine to execute the script. If the document specifies VBScript, the viewer loads

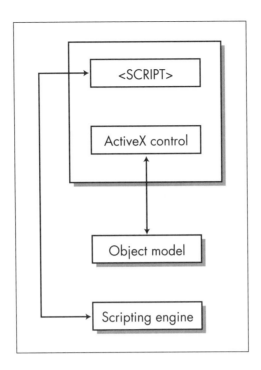

Figure 7.2

*Client-side scripting in **MSHTML.DLL**.*

VBSCRIPT.DLL. For JScript or JavaScript, the viewer loads **JSCRIPT.DLL**. The HTML viewer then passes the code in the **\<SCRIPT\>** tag to the scripting engine.

The HTML viewer also exposes objects that client-side script accesses. These objects include those embedded in the document with the **\<OBJECT\>** and **\<APPLET\>** tags as well as browser objects and objects of the loaded document. These objects constitute the Dynamic HTML Object Model, and the HTML viewer exposes the object model to scripting.

This chapter provides an overview of the objects and their properties, collections, methods, and events. You can find detailed information on the Microsoft Web site at **www.microsoft.com/msdn/sdk/inetsdk/help/dhtml/references/dhtmlrefs.htm**. Netscape Navigator uses a similar object model. Information on the Netscape implementation is available at **home.netscape.com/eng/mozilla/3.0/handbook/ javascript/index.html**. You'll read more about the features of the Dynamic HTML Object Model that allow you to add application-like behavior to your Web pages in Chapter 8.

The Object Hierarchy

The object model consists of a hierarchy of seven objects and one collection (see Figure 7.3). Some of the objects also contain other objects.

 This section provides a brief description of each of the objects. You'll find a quick reference to the objects and their properties, collections, methods, and events in this chapter's Practical Guide along with some sample Web pages.

The **window** Object

The **window** object is the top-level object and represents the browser's window. You access all other objects through the **window** object. In other words, the **window** object owns all the other browser objects. You are not limited to one **window** object. If

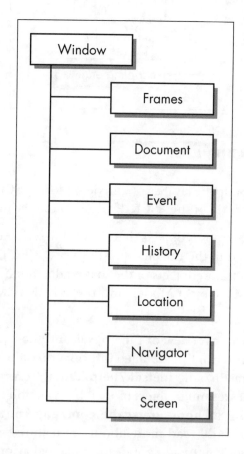

Figure 7.3

The object model hierarchy.

a document consists of frames, each frame will have a **window** object. The main window's object contains a **frames** collection. This collection contains the **window** objects that correspond to the frames.

While somewhat confusing, there is an object named **window** that represents the top-most window in the browser. This is an object of the **window** class. However, other **window** objects might have different names.

You access **window** object properties like this:

```
window.propertyname
```

If you are using the main window, you don't even have to specify the object:

```
propertyname
```

The **frames** Collection

The **frames** collection is the only collection in the **window** object. This collection contains a collection of all the **window** objects defined by a document or window. You access all **window** objects other than the top-most window through the **frames** collection.

If the document has a **<BODY>** tag, the **frames** collection contains one **window** object for each **IFRAME** element. If the document contains the **<FRAMESET>** tag, the **frames** collection contains one **window** object for each **<FRAME>** tag.

Specifying individual elements in the collection accesses frame windows. In VBScript, you use parentheses to access elements:

```
frames(0)                          // the current window
parent.window.frames(0)            // the parent window's first frame
top                                // references the top-most window
```

For JavaScript, use square brackets instead:

```
frames[0]
```

The **document** Object

The **document** object represents the page in the current browser window. The **document** object provides access to the elements contained in the page and specifies information about the document through the object's properties.

The **document** object also takes care of processing events. Chapters 5 and 6 describe how to handle events (such as a button click) in client-side scripting. The **document** object exposes events to script.

The **event** Object

The **event** object provides several items of information regarding the event being processed. The browser sets the **event** object's properties, most of which are read-only.

You also use the **event** object to cancel an event's default behavior and to prevent additional event handlers from being executed. The Dynamic HTML Object Model allows events to bubble up through the document hierarchy. The element that generates an event processes it first. Then the element's parent processes it. Then, the parent's parent element gets a chance. This continues until the **document** object receives the event. You can write your own event handlers to process events for several elements and then use the **event** object to cancel the default behavior of bubbling events up the hierarchy. You'll find a simple example of this in this chapter's Practical Guide.

The **history** Object

You use the **history** object to move forward and backward through the browser's history list. This object is exceedingly simple with only one property and three methods. You'll read more about the **history** object's members in this chapter's Practical guide.

The **location** Object

You can access and manipulate the URL of the current page with the **location** object. This object provides access to individual sections of the URL and to the entire URL. The complete URL is in the **href** property. The object also picks apart the URL into properties, such as **hostname** and **pathname**. Changing any property of the **location** object causes the browser to load a new URL.

The **navigator** Object

The **navigator** object provides information about the client browser, such as the application name and version number. It also has a **replace** method that causes the browser to load a new URL to replace the previous URL in the history list.

The **screen** Object

The **screen** object provides information about the client's screen and rendering capabilities. It is useful when you want to create a new window and set height and width, choose images to display, and so on.

Summary

Some of the objects of the Dynamic HTML Object Model, such as the **history** object, are seldom used, whereas others, notably the **window** and **document** objects, are often useful for accessing and manipulating the browser and the documents it contains.

In the following Practical Guide, you'll find many ways to use these objects from within client-side script. In the next chapter, you'll find even more powerful ways to manipulate these objects using dynamic HTML.

Practical Guide To

Dynamic HTML Object Model

- The **window** Object
- The **frames** Collection
- The **document** Object
- The **event** Object
- The **history** Object
- The **location** Object
- The **navigator** Object
- The **screen** Object
- Using The **window** Object
- Using The **document** Object
- Using The **event** Object
- Using The **location** Object
- Using The **screen** And **navigator** Objects

The **window** Object

The **window** object is the top-level object. It represents the browser's window and provides access to the browser and documents.

window Object Properties Quick Reference

Property	Description	Syntax
clientInformation	Returns the **navigator** object	*winobj*.clientInformation.appCodeName
closed	Indicates whether the window is closed	*winobj*.closed
defaultStatus	Specifies the default message in the status bar	*winobj*.defaultStatus = *status*
dialogArguments	Returns the variable of array of variables passed to the modal dialog window	*winobj*.dialogArguments
dialogHeight	Specifies the height of the dialog window	*winobj*.dialogHeight = *height*
dialogLeft	Specifies the left coordinate of the dialog window	*winobj*.dialogLeft = *coord*
dialogTop	Specifies the top coordinate of the dialog window	*winobj*.dialogTop = *coord*
dialogWidth	Specifies the width of the dialog window	*winobj*.dialogWidth = *width*
document	Represents the HTML document in a window	document.*member*
event	Represents the state of an event	*winobj*.event.*member*
history	Represents the browser history list	history.*member*
length	Returns the number of frames in a window	*winobj*.length
location	Contains information about the current URL	location.*member*
name	Specifies the name of a window or frame	*winobj*.name = *name*

(continued)

window Object Properties Quick Reference *(continued)*

Property	Description	Syntax
navigator	Contains information about the browser	navigator.*member*
offscreenBuffering	Specifies whether to use off-screen buffering	*winobj*.offscreenBuffering = *boolean*
opener	Specifies a reference to the window that created the current window	*winobj*.opener
parent	Returns the parent object	*winobj*.parent
returnValue	Specifies the return value from a modal dialog window	*winobj*.returnValue
screen	Represents information about the client's screen and rendering abilities	screen.*member*
self	References the current window	*winobj*.self
status	Specifies the status bar message	*winobj*.status
top	Specifies the top-most window	*winobj*.top

window Object's Collections Quick Reference

Collection	Description	Syntax
frames	Contains a collection of currently defined **window** objects	*obj*.frames(*index*)

window Object Methods Quick Reference

Method	Description	Syntax
alert	Displays an alert dialog box	*winobj*.alert(*optional message*)
blur	Causes an object to lose focus and fires the **onblur** event	*obj*.blur()
clearInterval	Cancels the interval set by setInterval	*winobj*.clearInterval(*intervalID*)

(continued)

window Object Methods Quick Reference *(continued)*

Method	Description	Syntax
clearTimeout	Cancels the timeout set by setTimeout	*winobj*.clearTimeout(*timeoutID*)
close	Closes the current window	*winobj*.close()
confirm	Displays a confirm dialog box	*winobj*.confirm(*optional message*)
execScript	Executes a script defined with the *expression* argument	*winobj*.execScript(*expression, language*)
focus	Causes a control to receive focus	*obj*.focus()
navigate	Navigates to the specified URL	*winobj*.navigate(*URL*)
open	Opens a new document	*winobj*.open([*URL*[,*name*[, *features*[,*replace*]]]])
prompt	Displays a prompt dialog box	*winobj*.prompt([*message*[, *inputDefault*]])
resizeBy	Changes the windows dimensions by the specified *x* and *y* relative offsets	*winobj*.resizeBy(*x, y*)
resizeTo	Sets the window's dimensions to the specified size	*winobj*.resizeTo(*x, y*)
scroll	Scrolls the window to the specified offset at the upper-left corner	*winobj*.scroll(*x, y*)
scrollBy	Scrolls the window relatively by the specified offsets	*winobj*.scrollBy(*x, y*)
scrollTo	Scrolls the window to the specified offsets at the upper-left corner	*winobj*.scrollTo(*x, y*)
setInterval	Repeatedly evaluates an expression at the specified interval in milliseconds	*winobj*.setInterval(*expression, msec*[,*language*])
setTimeout	Evaluates an expression after the specified interval has elapsed	*winobj*.setTimeout(*expression, msec*[,*language*])
showHelp	Displays a help file	*winobj*.showHelp(*URL*[,*contextID*])
showModalDialog	Creates and displays a modal dialog box *arguments*[,*features*]]])	*winobj*.showModalDialog(*URL*[,

window Object Events Quick Reference

Event	Description
onbeforeunload	Fires prior to a page being unloaded
onblur	Fires when the object loses input focus
onerror	Fires when a scripting error occurs
onfocus	Fires when the object receives input focus
onhelp	Fires when the user selects Help or presses F1
onload	Fires when the object is loaded
onresize	Fires when the object is resized
onscroll	Fires when the scroll box is repositioned
onunload	Fires just prior to a page being unloaded

The **frames** Collection

The **frames** collection contains a collection of all the **window** objects defined by a document or window.

frames Collection Properties Quick Reference

Property	Description	Syntax
length	Returns the number of elements in the collection	*winobj*.length

frames Collection Methods Quick Reference

Method	Description	Syntax
item	Returns a collection of elements	*elm = obj*.item(*index*[,*subindex*])

The **document** Object

The **document** object references the page in the current browser window.

document Object Properties Quick Reference

Property	Description	Syntax
activeElement	Identifies the element that has focus	*docobj*.activeElement
alinkColor	Specifies the color of the active link	*docobj*.alinkColor[=*color*]
bgColor	Specifies the background color	*docobj*;bgColor[=*color*]
charset	Specifies the document's character set	*docobj*.charset[=*charset*]
cookie	Specifies a string value of a cookie	*docobj*.cookie[=*cookie*]
defaultCharset	Specifies the document's default character set	*docobj*.defaultCharset[=*charset*]
domain	Specifies the document's security domain	*docobj*.domain[=*domain*]
expando	Specifies whether variables can be created within an object	*docobj*.expando[=*boolean*]
fgColor	Specifies the document's text color	*docobj*.fgColor[=*color*]
lastModified	Returns the document's last-modified date, if supplied	*docobj*.lastModified
linkColor	Specifies the color of the document links	*docobj*.linkColor[=*color*]
location	Specifies information on the current URL	*docobj*.location[=*location*]
parentWindow	Returns the document's **window** object	*docobj*.parentWindow
readyState	Specifies the current state of an object being downloaded	docobj.readyState
referrer	Returns the URL of the previous location	*docobj*.referrer
selection	Returns the action selection title	*docobj*.selection
url	Specifies the current document's URL	*docobj*.url[=*url*]
vlinkColor	Specifies the color of visited links	*docobj*.vlinkColor[=*color*]

document Object Collections Quick Reference

Collection	Description	Syntax
all	Returns a reference to a collection of the document's elements	*docobj*.all([*index*])
anchors	Returns a collection of the document's **\<A>** elements	*docobj*.anchors([*index*])
applets	Returns a collection of the document's **\<APPLET>** objects	*docobj*.applets([*index*])
children	Returns a collection of the document's children	*docobj*.children([*index*])
embeds	Returns a collection of the document's **\<EMBED>** elements	*docobj*.embeds([*index*])
forms	Returns a collection of the document's **\<FORM>** elements	*docobj*.forms([*index*])
frames	Returns a collection of the document's window objects	*docobj*.frames([*index*])
images	Returns a collection of the document's **\<IMG>** elements	*docobj*.images([*index*])
links	Returns a collection of the document's **\<A>** elements that have an **href** attribute and all **\<AREA>** elements	*docobj*.links([*index*])
plugins	Serves as an alias for the **embeds** collection	*docobj*.plugins([*index*])
scripts	Returns a collection of the document's **\<SCRIPT>** elements	*docobj*.scripts([*index*])
stylesheets	Returns a collection of the document's **stylesheet** objects	*docobj*.stylesheets([*index*])

document Object Methods Quick Reference

Method	Description	Syntax
clear	Clears the document's contents	*docobj*.clear()
close	Closes the output stream	*docobj*.close()

(continued)

document Object Methods Quick Reference *(continued)*

Method	Description	Syntax
createElement	Creates an element object for the specified tag	*docobj*.createElement(tag)
createStyleSheet	Creates a style sheet	docobj.createStyleSheet ([*url*[,*index*]])
elementFromPoint	Returns the element at the specified coordinates	*docobj*.elementFromPoint(x,y)
execCommand	Executes a command over the selection or text range	*docobj*.execCommand (Cmd[,*UserInterface*[,*Value*]])
open	Opens an output stream for **write** and **writeln** methods	*docobj*.open(*mimetype*[,*replace*])
queryCommand Enabled	Returns whether a command can be executed	*docobj*.queryCommandEnabled (*cmd*)
queryCommand Indeterm	Returns whether a command is in the indeterminate state	*docobj*.queryCommand Indeterm(*cmd*)
queryCommandState	Returns the command's current state	ocobj.queryCommandState(*cmd*)
queryCommand Supported	Returns whether the command is supported	*docobj*.queryCommand Supported(*cmd*)
queryCommandText	Returns the string associated with the command	*docobj*.queryCommantText(cmd)
queryCommandValue	Returns the current value of the command **ShowHelp**	ocobj.queryCommandValue(*cmd*)
write	Writes an HTML expression to the document	*docobj*.write(*exp*)
writeln	Writes an HTML expression followed by a carriage return	*docobj*.writeln(*exp*)

document Object Events Quick Reference

Event	Description
onafterupdate	Fires after data is transferred from the element to the data provider

(continued)

document Object Events Quick Reference *(continued)*

Event	Description
onbeforeupdate	Fires before data is transferred from the element to the data provider
onclick	Fires when the left mouse button is clicked
ondblclick	Fires when the left mouse button is double-clicked
ondragstart	Fires when the user starts to drag a selection
onerrorupdate	Fires when the **onbeforeupdate** event handler has canceled the data transfer
onhelp	Fires when the user presses F1 or the browser Help key
onkeydown	Fires when a key is pressed
onkeypress	Fires when a key is pressed
onkeyup	Fires when a key is released
onmousedown	Fires when a mouse button is pressed
onmousemove	Fires when the mouse is moved
onmouseout	Fires when the mouse pointer is moved out of an element
onmouseover	Fires when the mouse pointer is moved over an element
onmouseup	Fires when a mouse button is released
onreadystatechange	Fires when an object's ready state changes
onrowenter	Fires when the current row changes and new data is available
onrowexit	Fires when the data source control is changing the current row
onselectstart	Fires at the beginning of an element selection

The **event** Object

The **event** object contains information about the event being processed.

event Object Properties Quick Reference

Property	Description	Syntax
altkey	Returns the state of the ALT key	*event*.altkey
button	Returns which mouse button was pressed, if any	*event*.button
cancelBubble	Specifies whether the current event should bubble up	*event*.cancelBubble[=*bool*]
clientX, clientY	Returns the relative positions of the mouse click	*event*.clientx
ctrlKey	Returns the state of the CTRL (control key)	*event*.ctrlKey
fromElement	Returns the element being moved from	*event*.fromElement
keyCode	Specifies the Unicode key code associated with the key event	*event*.keycode[=*code*]
offsetX, offsetY	Returns container-relative positions	*event*.offsetX
reason	Returns the status of data transfer for a data source object	*event*.reason
returnValue	Specifies the return value from an event	*event*.returnValue[=*bool*]
screenX, screenY	Returns coordinates relative to screen size	*event*.screenX
shiftKey	Returns the state of the SHIFT key	*event*.shiftKey
srcElement	Returns the element that fired the event	*event*.srcElement
srcFilter	Returns the filter object that fired the **onfilterchange** event	*event*.srcFilter
toElement	Returns the element being moved to	*event*.toElement
type	Returns the event name or scripting language for the **event** object and the **script object**	*event*.type
x, y	Returns the position of the mouse click relative to an element	*event*.x

The **history** Object

The **history** object is used to navigate through the browser's history list.

history Object Properties Quick Reference

Property	Description	Syntax
length	Returns the number of elements in the history list	*history*.length

history Object Methods Quick Reference

Method	Description	Syntax
back	Loads the previous URL	*history*.back()
forward	Loads the next URL	*history*.forward()
go	Loads the specified URL	*history*.go(*integer* I *urlstring*)

The **location** Object

The **location** object specifies information about the URL of the current page.

location Object Properties Quick Reference

Property	Description	Syntax
hash	Specifies the section of the **href** attribute following the #	*loc*.hash[=*hash*]
host	Specifies the host:port section of the URL	*loc*.host[=*host*]
hostname	Specifies the host name section of the URL	*loc*.hostname[=*hostname*]
href	Specifies the entire URL	*loc*.href[=*url*]
pathname	Specifies the file or object path	*loc*.pathname[=*pathname*]
port	Specifies the port number in the URL	*loc*.port[=*port*]

(continued)

location Object Properties Quick Reference *(continued)*

Property	Description	Syntax
protocol	Specifies the URL access protocol	*loc*.protocol[=*protocol*]
search	Specifies the section of the URL following the ?	*loc*.search[=*querystring*]

location Object Methods Quick Reference

Method	Description	Syntax
assign	Sets the current location to the specified URL	loc.assign(url)
reload	Reloads the current page	loc.reload([bool])
replace	Replaces the current document with the specified document	loc.replace(url)

 ## The **navigator** Object

The **navigator** object provides information about the browser application.

navigator Object Properties Quick Reference

Property	Description	Syntax
appCodeName	Returns the code name of the browser	*nav*.appCodeName
appMinorVersion	Returns the application's minor version value	*nam*.appMinorVersion
appName	Returns the browser application's name	*nav*.appName
appVersion	Returns the browser application's version	*nav*.appVersion
browserLanguage	Returns the browser's language	*nav*.browserLanguage
connectionSpeed	Returns the session's connection speed	*nav*.connectionSpeed

(continued)

navigator Object Properties Quick Reference (continued)

Property	Description	Syntax
cookieEnabled	Returns whether client-side cookies are enabled	nav.cookieEnabled
cpuClass	Returns the client's CPU class	nav.cpuClass
onLine	Returns whether the system is in the global offline mode	nav.onLine
platform	Returns the client's platform	nav.platform
systemLanguage	Returns the system's default language	nav.systemLanguage
userAgent	Returns the client's HTTP user-agent header	nav.userAgent
userLanguage	Returns the current user language	nav.userLanguage
userProfile	Provides methods to request read access to a user's profile	nav.userProfile.method

navigator Object Collections Quick Reference

Collection	Description	Syntax
mimeTypes	Provided for compatibility, returns an empty collection for IE	nav.mimeTypes
plugins	Provided for compatibility, returns an empty collection for IE	nav.plugins

navigator Object Methods Quick Reference

Method	Description	Syntax
javaEnabled	Returns whether Java is enabled	nav.javaEnabled()
taintEnabled	Returns whether data tainting is enabled	nav.taintEnabled()

The **screen** Object

The **screen** object provides information about the client's screen and rendering capabilities.

screen Object Properties Quick Reference

Property	Description	Syntax
availHeight	Returns the working height of the system's screen	*scrn*.availHeight
availWidth	Returns the working width of the system's screen	*scrn*.availWidth
bufferDepth	Specifies an offscreen bitmap buffer	*scrn*.bufferDepth[=*bufferdepth*])
colorDepth	Returns the bits-per-pixel value used for colors	*scrn*.colorDepth
height	Returns the vertical screen resolution	*scrn*.height
updateInterval	Specifies the screen's update interval	*scrn*.updateInterval[=*msec*])
width	Returns the horizontal screen resolution	*scrn*.width

Using The **window** Object

Listings 7.1 through 7.4 are modifications of the Community Dining Club New Member Registration page that you saw in Chapters 5 and 6. This now consists of four pages: Listing 7.1 defines a frame set to contain the other three pages, Listing 7.2 displays the heading, Listing 7.3 displays the billboard, and Listing 7.4 collects and validates new member registration information.

Listing 7.2 contains a function "**window_onload**" that the browser calls when the **window** object fires the **onload** event. This function is like an ordinary JScript function, and the statement immediately following the function definition calls it. There is another way to respond to the **onload** event, as you'll see in a moment. The **window_onload** function sets background and text colors using the **document** object of the loaded document.

Listing 7.3 also responds to the **window** object's **onload** event but in a more direct way, using the **for** and **event** attributes of the **<SCRIPT>** tag. This event handler sets the background and text colors of the document as well as the initial text color of the ActiveX **Label** control. Rather than using the ActiveX **Timer** control to periodically update the label, the page uses the **window** object's **setInterval()** method. This method evaluates an expression at the specified interval. In this case, it calls the function **update_billboard()** every second. The **update_billboard()** function updates the label control's **Caption** and **ForeColor** properties.

Listing 7.4 also responds to the **onload** event to set background and text colors. The page also has script that sets the **defaultStatus** property to a string that displays the page's purpose. The script that validates the new member information changes the **defaultStatus** property.

Listing 7.1   The frame set page.

```
<!-- The frameset document -->
<HTML>
<HEAD>
<TITLE>Listing 7.1 Frameset</TITLE>
</HEAD>
<FRAMESET FRAMEBORDER=0 SCROLLING=NO ROWS="10%, 10%, *">
    <FRAME scrolling=no src="7-1_head.htm" name="header">
    <FRAME scrolling=no src="7-1_bill.htm" name="billboard">
    <FRAME src="7-1_reg.htm" name="register">
</FRAMESET>
</HTML>
```

Listing 7.2   The header page.

```
<HTML>
<HEAD>
<TITLE>Listing 7.2 Header</TITLE>
<SCRIPT LANGUAGE=JavaScript>
<!--
function window_onload() {
    document.body.bgColor="DARKBLUE";
    document.body.text="ALICEBLUE";
}

onload = window_onload;
// -->
</SCRIPT>
</HEAD>
<BODY>

<H2 ALIGN=CENTER>Community Dining Club</H2>

</BODY>
</HTML>
```

Listing 7.3 The billboard page.

```html
<HTML>
<HEAD>
<TITLE>Listing 7.3 Billboard</TITLE>
<SCRIPT for="window" event="onload" LANGUAGE=JavaScript>
<!--
     document.body.bgColor="ALICEBLUE";
     document.body.text="YELLOW";
     IeLabel.ForeColor=0x00FFFF;
// -->
</SCRIPT>

<SCRIPT LANGUAGE=JavaScript>
<!--
var MsgNo, ColorNo;
var Message = new Array("Join Today!", "Fine Dining!",
"Impress Friends!", "Save Money!", "Be Cool!");

MsgNo = 0;
ColorNo = 1;

setInterval("update_billboard()", 1000);

function update_billboard() {
     IeLabel.Caption = Message[MsgNo];
     MsgNo += 1;
     if (MsgNo > 4)
         MsgNo = 0;
     IeLabel.ForeColor = Math.random() * 16777215;
}

// -->
</SCRIPT>
</HEAD>
<BODY>
<P ALIGN=CENTER>
<OBJECT ID="IeLabel" WIDTH=150 HEIGHT=25
 CLASSID="CLSID:99B42120-6EC7-11CF-A6C7-00AA00A47DD2">
     <PARAM NAME="Caption" VALUE=" ">
     <PARAM NAME="Angle" VALUE="0">
     <PARAM NAME="Alignment" VALUE="4">
     <PARAM NAME="Mode" VALUE="1">
     <PARAM NAME="FillStyle" VALUE="0">
     <PARAM NAME="ForeColor" VALUE="#000000">
     <PARAM NAME="BackColor" VALUE="#C0C0C0">
     <PARAM NAME="FontName" VALUE="Arial">
     <PARAM NAME="FontSize" VALUE="14">
     <PARAM NAME="FontItalic" VALUE="0">
```

```
    <PARAM NAME="FontBold" VALUE="1">
    <PARAM NAME="FontUnderline" VALUE="0">
    <PARAM NAME="FontStrikeout" VALUE="0">
    <PARAM NAME="TopPoints" VALUE="0">
    <PARAM NAME="BotPoints" VALUE="0">
</OBJECT>
</P>
</BODY>
</HTML>
```

Listing 7.4 The new member registration page.

```
<HTML>
<HEAD>
<TITLE>Listing 7.4 Member Registration</TITLE>
<SCRIPT for="window" event="onload" LANGUAGE=JavaScript>
<!--
    document.body.bgColor="WHITE";
    document.body.text="BLUE";
// -->
</SCRIPT>

<SCRIPT LANGUAGE=JavaScript>
<!--
    defaultStatus="Community Dining Club New Member Registration";

//-->
</SCRIPT>

<SCRIPT FOR="cmdSubmit" EVENT="onclick" LANGUAGE=JavaScript>
<!--
    var TheForm;
    TheForm = document.RegistrationForm;

    defaultStatus = "Validating";

    if (TheForm.firstname.value.length == 0) {
        alert("Please enter your first name.");
        TheForm.firstname.focus();
    }
    else if (TheForm.lastname.value.length == 0) {
        TheForm.lastname.value = prompt("Please enter your last name.");
        if (TheForm.lastname.value.length != 0)
            TheForm.addr1.focus();
    }
    else if (TheForm.addr1.value.length == 0) {
        alert("Please enter your address.");
        TheForm.addr1.focus();
    }
```

```
        else if (TheForm.city.value.length == 0) {
            alert("Please enter the city.");
            TheForm.city.focus();
        }
        else if (TheForm.state.value.length != 2) {
            alert("Please enter the 2-letter state abbreviation.");
            TheForm.state.focus();
        }
        else if (TheForm.zip.value.length < 5) {
            alert("Please enter a valid ZIP code.");
            TheForm.zip.focus();
            TheForm.code.select();
        }
        else if (TheForm.code.value.length != 3 || isNaN(TheForm.code.value)) {
            alert("Please enter a valid area code.");
            TheForm.code.focus();
            TheForm.code.select();
        }
        else if (TheForm.phone.value.length != 7 || isNaN(TheForm.phone.value)) {
            alert("Please enter a valid phone number.");
            TheForm.phone.focus();
            TheForm.phone.select();
        }

// -->
</SCRIPT>
</HEAD>
<BODY>
<H2 Align=Center>New Member Registration</H2>
<HR SIZE=5 WIDTH=90%>

<P ALIGN=CENTER>
<TABLE>
<TD>
<PRE>
<FORM NAME="RegistrationForm">
<B>First Name:        </B><INPUT TYPE=TEXT NAME="firstname">
<B>Last Name:         </B><INPUT TYPE=TEXT NAME="lastname">
<B>Address1:          </B><INPUT TYPE=TEXT NAME="addr1">
<B>Address2:          </B><INPUT TYPE=TEXT NAME="addr2">
<B>City:              </B><INPUT TYPE=TEXT NAME="city">
<B>State:             </B><INPUT TYPE=TEXT NAME="state" MAXLENGTH=2 SIZE=2>
<B>Zip:               </B><INPUT TYPE=TEXT NAME="zip" MAXLENGTH=10 SIZE=10>
<B>Area Code/Phone: </B><INPUT TYPE=TEXT NAME="code" MAXLENGTH=3
SIZE=3> <INPUT TYPE=TEXT NAME="phone" MAXLENGTH=7 SIZE=7>

<B>Preferred Cuisine: </B><SELECT NAME="cuisine" SIZE="1">
                        <OPTION VALUE="1">American
                        <OPTION VALUE="2">Chinese
```

```
                              <OPTION VALUE="3">French
                              <OPTION VALUE="4">German
                              <OPTION VALUE="5">Greek
                              <OPTION VALUE="6">Indian
                              <OPTION VALUE="7">Italian
                              <OPTION VALUE="8">Japanese
                              <OPTION VALUE="9">Other
                              </SELECT>

<INPUT TYPE=BUTTON NAME="cmdSubmit"
VALUE="Submit"> <INPUT TYPE="RESET" VALUE="Clear">
</PRE>

</FORM>
</TD>
</TABLE>
</P>
</BODY>
</HTML>
```

Using The **document** Object

Listing 7.5 is similar to Listing 7.4, except that it uses the **document** object's **forms** collection to reference the **RegistrationForm** elements. The **forms** collection contains a collection of all the forms the document contains. This example uses only one form, so it is referenced in JScript at index 0 like this:

```
forms[0]
```

You can access the individual form elements using the **forms** collection's **item()** method, which also takes a zero-based index to reference form elements.

Listing 7.5 Using the **document** object.

```
<!-- The registration page -->
<HTML>
<HEAD>
<TITLE>Listing 7.5 Member Registration</TITLE>
<SCRIPT for="window" event="onload" LANGUAGE=JavaScript>
<!--
     document.body.bgColor="WHITE";
     document.body.text="BLUE";
// -->
</SCRIPT>

<SCRIPT LANGUAGE=JavaScript>
<!--
     defaultStatus="Community Dining Club New Member Registration";
```

```
//-->
</SCRIPT>

<SCRIPT FOR="cmdSubmit" EVENT="onclick" LANGUAGE=JavaScript>
<!--

    defaultStatus = "Validating";

    if (forms[0].item(0).value.length == 0) {
        alert("Please enter your first name.");
        forms[0].item(0).focus();
    }
    else if (forms[0].item(1).value.length == 0) {
        forms[0].item(1).value = prompt("Please enter your last name.");
        if (forms[0].item(1).value.length != 0)
            forms[0].item(1).focus();
    }
    else if (forms[0].item(2).value.length == 0) {
        alert("Please enter your address.");
        forms[0].item(2).focus();
    }
    else if (forms[0].item(4).value.length == 0) {
        alert("Please enter the city.");
        forms[0].item(4).focus();
    }
    else if (forms[0].item(5).value.length != 2) {
        alert("Please enter the 2-letter state abbreviation.");
        forms[0].item(5).focus();
    }
    else if (forms[0].item(6).value.length < 5) {
        alert("Please enter a valid ZIP code.");
        forms[0].item(6).focus();
        forms[0].item(6).select();
    }
    else  if (forms[0].item(7).value.length != 3 ||
        isNaN(forms[0].item(7).value)) {
        alert("Please enter a valid area code.");
        forms[0].item(7).focus();
        forms[0].item(7).select();
    }
    else if (forms[0].item(8).value.length != 7 ||
        isNaN(forms[0].item(8).value)) {
        alert("Please enter a valid phone number.");
        forms[0].item(8).focus();
        forms[0].item(8).select();
    }

// -->
</SCRIPT>
```

```
</HEAD>
<BODY>
<H2 Align=Center>New Member Registration</H2>
<HR SIZE=5 WIDTH=90%>

<P ALIGN=CENTER>
<TABLE>
<TD>
<PRE>
<FORM NAME="RegistrationForm">
<B>First Name:       </B><INPUT TYPE=TEXT NAME="firstname">
<B>Last Name:        </B><INPUT TYPE=TEXT NAME="lastname">
<B>Address1:         </B><INPUT TYPE=TEXT NAME="addr1">
<B>Address2:         </B><INPUT TYPE=TEXT NAME="addr2">
<B>City:             </B><INPUT TYPE=TEXT NAME="city">
<B>State:            </B><INPUT TYPE=TEXT NAME="state" MAXLENGTH=2 SIZE=2>
<B>Zip:              </B><INPUT TYPE=TEXT NAME="zip" MAXLENGTH=10 SIZE=10>
<B>Area Code/Phone:  </B><INPUT TYPE=TEXT NAME="code"
MAXLENGTH=3 SIZE=3> <INPUT TYPE=TEXT NAME="phone" MAXLENGTH=7 SIZE=7>

<B>Preferred Cuisine: </B><SELECT NAME="cuisine" SIZE="1">
                         <OPTION VALUE="1">American
                         <OPTION VALUE="2">Chinese
                         <OPTION VALUE="3">French
                         <OPTION VALUE="4">German
                         <OPTION VALUE="5">Greek
                         <OPTION VALUE="6">Indian
                         <OPTION VALUE="7">Italian
                         <OPTION VALUE="8">Japanese
                         <OPTION VALUE="9">Other
                         </SELECT>

<INPUT TYPE=BUTTON NAME="cmdSubmit" VALUE="Submit"> <INPUT TYPE="RESET"
VALUE="Clear">
</PRE>

</FORM>
</TD>
</TABLE>
</P>
</BODY>
</HTML>
```

Using The **event** Object

Listing 7.6 contains the new member registration page, which now contains a very simple example of using the **event** object. The **event** object contains a variety of data on the event being processed. Also, the Dynamic HTML Object Model uses an event model that allows events to bubble up through the object hierarchy. Events are first processed by the element firing the event and then by each of the parent elements up to the **document** object.

To illustrate event bubbling, this page has two new statements. First, look at the member registration page. The **alert()** method displays a message containing the name of the element that fired the event, in this case the **cmdSubmit** button. The event then bubbles up to the document's object level. The **document** contains an **onclick** handler that also displays the name of the element. If you click anywhere in the document except the Submit button, the document's **onclick** event handler fires. You can prevent the **cmdSubmit onclick** event from bubbling up to the document level by adding the statement

```
event.cancelBubble = true;
```

inside the **cmdButton onclick** event handler.

Listing 7.6   Using the **event** object.

```
<!-- The registration page -->
<HTML>
<HEAD>
<TITLE>Listing 7.6 Member Registration</TITLE>
<SCRIPT for="window" event="onload" LANGUAGE=JavaScript>
<!--
     document.body.bgColor="WHITE";
     document.body.text="BLUE";
// -->
</SCRIPT>

<SCRIPT LANGUAGE=JavaScript>
<!--
     defaultStatus="Community Dining Club New Member Registration";

//-->
</SCRIPT>

<SCRIPT FOR="document" EVENT="onclick" LANGUAGE=JavaScript>
<!--
     alert ("Now at document level: " + event.srcElement.name);
//-->
</SCRIPT>

<SCRIPT FOR="cmdSubmit" EVENT="onclick" LANGUAGE=JavaScript>
<!--
```

```
        defaultStatus = "Validating";
        alert ("Now at element level: " + event.srcElement.name);

    if (forms[0].item(0).value.length == 0) {
        alert("Please enter your first name.");
        forms[0].item(0).focus();
    }
    else if (forms[0].item(1).value.length == 0) {
        forms[0].item(1).value = prompt("Please enter your last name.");
        if (forms[0].item(1).value.length != 0)
            forms[0].item(1).focus();
    }
    else if (forms[0].item(2).value.length == 0) {
        alert("Please enter your address.");
        forms[0].item(2).focus();
    }
    else if (forms[0].item(4).value.length == 0) {
        alert("Please enter the city.");
        forms[0].item(4).focus();
    }
    else if (forms[0].item(5).value.length != 2) {
        alert("Please enter the 2-letter state abbreviation.");
        forms[0].item(5).focus();
    }
    else if (forms[0].item(6).value.length < 5) {
        alert("Please enter a valid ZIP code.");
        forms[0].item(6).focus();
        forms[0].item(6).select();
    }
    else if (forms[0].item(7).value.length != 3 ||
        isNaN(forms[0].item(7).value)) {
        alert("Please enter a valid area code.");
        forms[0].item(7).focus();
        forms[0].item(7).select();
    }
    else if (forms[0].item(8).value.length != 7 ||
        isNaN(forms[0].item(8).value)) {
        alert("Please enter a valid phone number.");
        forms[0].item(8).focus();
        forms[0].item(8).select();
    }

// -->
</SCRIPT>
</HEAD>
<BODY>
<H2 Align=Center>New Member Registration</H2>
<HR SIZE=5 WIDTH=90%>
```

```
<P ALIGN=CENTER>
<TABLE>
<TD>
<PRE>
<FORM NAME="RegistrationForm">
<B>First Name:       </B><INPUT TYPE=TEXT NAME="firstname">
<B>Last Name:        </B><INPUT TYPE=TEXT NAME="lastname">
<B>Address1:         </B><INPUT TYPE=TEXT NAME="addr1">
<B>Address2:         </B><INPUT TYPE=TEXT NAME="addr2">
<B>City:             </B><INPUT TYPE=TEXT NAME="city">
<B>State:            </B><INPUT TYPE=TEXT NAME="state" MAXLENGTH=2 SIZE=2>
<B>Zip:              </B><INPUT TYPE=TEXT NAME="zip" MAXLENGTH=10 SIZE=10>
<B>Area Code/Phone: </B><INPUT TYPE=TEXT NAME="code"
MAXLENGTH=3 SIZE=3> <INPUT TYPE=TEXT NAME="phone" MAXLENGTH=7 SIZE=7>

<B>Preferred Cuisine: </B><SELECT NAME="cuisine" SIZE="1">
                         <OPTION VALUE="1">American
                         <OPTION VALUE="2">Chinese
                         <OPTION VALUE="3">French
                         <OPTION VALUE="4">German
                         <OPTION VALUE="5">Greek
                         <OPTION VALUE="6">Indian
                         <OPTION VALUE="7">Italian
                         <OPTION VALUE="8">Japanese
                         <OPTION VALUE="9">Other
                         </SELECT>

<INPUT TYPE=BUTTON NAME="cmdSubmit"
VALUE="Submit"> <INPUT TYPE="RESET" VALUE="Clear">
</PRE>

</FORM>
</TD>
</TABLE>
</P>
</BODY>
</HTML>
```

 ## Using The **location** Object

When completed, the new member registration page needs a location to which to send the form data. Listing 7.7 modifies the registration page to use the **location** object to bundle the form data into a query string and send it to a page that will further process it, such as writing it to a database. All the work takes place inside the validation script. The script defines a few variables: **data_ok** is a Boolean that signals when the data is valid and ready for forwarding, and **submit_url** contains the name of the page that will receive the data, which is **7-7_mbr.asp**. This page is an *Active Server page*, thus the **.asp** extension. Active Server pages contain script that executes on the server (see Chapter 9). Finally, the **query_string** variable holds the form's name/value pairs that the form sends to the Active Server page.

If a data item is invalid, **data_ok** is set to **false**, and the user must reenter the data. When all the data is valid, the script constructs **query_string** from the form elements. The script uses a **for** loop that iterates through the **forms** collection for this form. The script appends each form item's **name** and **value** properties to **query_string**. An HTML query string's name/value pairs are separated with +, so the script must also insert this character in **query_string** after each name/value pair. When the loop completes, **query_string** has an extra + on the end. The script removes this unnecessary character with the JScript **string** object's **substr()** method. Finally, the script appends **query_string** to **submit_url** to construct the URL with the query string.

Changing any of the **location** object's properties causes the browser to load the new URL. Assigning **submit_url** to the **location** object accesses **7-4_mgr.asp** with the new member data.

Listing 7.7   Using the **location** object.

```
<!-- The registration page -->
<HTML>
<HEAD>
<TITLE>Listing 7.7 Member Registration</TITLE>
<SCRIPT for="window" event="onload" LANGUAGE=JavaScript>
<!--
     document.body.bgColor="WHITE";
     document.body.text="BLUE";
// -->
</SCRIPT>

<SCRIPT LANGUAGE=JavaScript>
<!--
     defaultStatus="Community Dining Club New Member Registration";

//-->
</SCRIPT>

<SCRIPT FOR="cmdSubmit" EVENT="onclick" LANGUAGE=JavaScript>
<!--
     var data_ok = true;
     var submit_url = "7-7_mbr.asp";
     var query_string = "?";

     defaultStatus = "Validating";
```

```
    if (forms[0].item(0).value.length == 0) {
        data_ok = false;
        alert("Please enter your first name.");
        forms[0].item(0).focus();
    }
    else if (forms[0].item(1).value.length == 0) {
        data_ok = false;
        forms[0].item(1).value = prompt("Please enter your last name.");
        if (forms[0].item(1).value.length != 0)
            forms[0].item(1).focus();
    }
    else if (forms[0].item(2).value.length == 0) {
        data_ok = false;
        alert("Please enter your address.");
        forms[0].item(2).focus();
    }
    else if (forms[0].item(3).value.length == 0) {
        forms[0].item(3).value = " ";
    }
    else if (forms[0].item(4).value.length == 0) {
        data_ok = false;
        alert("Please enter the city.");
        forms[0].item(4).focus();
    }
    else if (forms[0].item(5).value.length != 2) {
        data_ok = false;
        alert("Please enter the 2-letter state abbreviation.");
        forms[0].item(5).focus();
    }
    else if (forms[0].item(6).value.length < 5) {
        data_ok = false;
        alert("Please enter a valid ZIP code.");
        forms[0].item(6).focus();
        forms[0].item(6).select();
    }
    else if (forms[0].item(7).value.length != 3 || isNaN(forms[0].item(7).value))
{
        data_ok = false;
        alert("Please enter a valid area code.");
        forms[0].item(7).focus();
        forms[0].item(7).select();
    }
    else if (forms[0].item(8).value.length != 7 || isNaN(forms[0].item(8).value))
{
        data_ok = false;
        alert("Please enter a valid phone number.");
        forms[0].item(8).focus();
        forms[0].item(8).select();
    }
```

```
    if (data_ok) {
        for (i = 0; i < forms[0].length - 2; i++) {
            query_string += forms[0].item(i).name + "="
                + forms[0].item(i).value + "+";
        }
        query_string = query_string.substr(0, query_string.length-1);
        submit_url += query_string;
        location = submit_url;
    }

// -->
</SCRIPT>
</HEAD>
<BODY>
<H2 Align=Center>New Member Registration</H2>
<HR SIZE=5 WIDTH=90%>

<P ALIGN=CENTER>
<TABLE>
<TD>
<PRE>
<FORM NAME="RegistrationForm">
<B>First Name:       </B><INPUT TYPE=TEXT NAME="firstname">
<B>Last Name:        </B><INPUT TYPE=TEXT NAME="lastname">
<B>Address1:         </B><INPUT TYPE=TEXT NAME="addr1">
<B>Address2:         </B><INPUT TYPE=TEXT NAME="addr2">
<B>City:             </B><INPUT TYPE=TEXT NAME="city">
<B>State:            </B><INPUT TYPE=TEXT NAME="state" MAXLENGTH=2 SIZE=2>
<B>Zip:              </B><INPUT TYPE=TEXT NAME="zip" MAXLENGTH=10 SIZE=10>
<B>Area Code/Phone: </B><INPUT TYPE=TEXT NAME="code" MAXLENGTH=3 SIZE=3> <INPUT
TYPE=TEXT NAME="phone" MAXLENGTH=7 SIZE=7>

<B>Preferred Cuisine: </B><SELECT NAME="cuisine" SIZE="1">
                         <OPTION VALUE="1">American
                         <OPTION VALUE="2">Chinese
                         <OPTION VALUE="3">French
                         <OPTION VALUE="4">German
                         <OPTION VALUE="5">Greek
                         <OPTION VALUE="6">Indian
                         <OPTION VALUE="7">Italian
                         <OPTION VALUE="8">Japanese
                         <OPTION VALUE="9">Other
                         </SELECT>

<INPUT TYPE=BUTTON NAME="cmdSubmit" VALUE="Submit"> <INPUT TYPE="RESET"
VALUE="Clear">
</PRE>
```

```
</FORM>
</TD>
</TABLE>
</P>
</BODY>
</HTML>
```

 ## Using The **screen** And **navigator** Objects

Listing 7.8 uses the **screen** and **navigator** objects to retrieve information about the client browser. This example shows how to access this information, but it does not use that information for anything. This listing has an additional page that the registration page opens. The new page simply displays some of the client-application information.

Listing 7.8   Using the **screen** object.

```
<!-- The registration page -->
<HTML>
<HEAD>
<TITLE>Listing 7.8 Member Registration</TITLE>
<SCRIPT for="window" event="onload" LANGUAGE=JavaScript>
<!--
    document.body.bgColor="WHITE";
    document.body.text="BLUE";

// -->
</SCRIPT>

<SCRIPT LANGUAGE=JavaScript>
<!--
    var appName = navigator.appName;
    var appVersion = navigator.appVersion;
    var userAgent = navigator.userAgent;
    var screenHeight = screen.height;
    var screenWidth = screen.width;
    var screenAvailHeight = screen.availHeight;
    var screenAvailWidth = screen.availWidth;
    var screenColorDepth = screen.colorDepth;

    defaultStatus="Community Dining Club New Member Registration";

    open("7-5_stats.htm", null, "toolbar=0,location=0,status=0,menubar=0");
//-->
</SCRIPT>
```

```
<SCRIPT FOR="cmdSubmit" EVENT="onclick" LANGUAGE=JavaScript>
<!--
     var data_ok = true;
     var submit_url = "7-7_mbr.asp";
     var query_string = "?";

     defaultStatus = "Validating";

     if (forms[0].item(0).value.length == 0) {
         data_ok = false;
         alert("Please enter your first name.");
         forms[0].item(0).focus();
     }
     else if (forms[0].item(1).value.length == 0) {
         data_ok = false;
         forms[0].item(1).value = prompt("Please enter your last name.");
         if (forms[0].item(1).value.length != 0)
             forms[0].item(1).focus();
     }
     else if (forms[0].item(2).value.length == 0) {
         data_ok = false;
         alert("Please enter your address.");
         forms[0].item(2).focus();
     }
     else if (forms[0].item(3).value.length == 0) {
         forms[0].item(3).value = " ";
     }
     else if (forms[0].item(4).value.length == 0) {
         data_ok = false;
         alert("Please enter the city.");
         forms[0].item(4).focus();
     }
     else if (forms[0].item(5).value.length != 2) {
         data_ok = false;
         alert("Please enter the 2-letter state abbreviation.");
         forms[0].item(5).focus();
     }
     else if (forms[0].item(6).value.length < 5) {
         data_ok = false;
         alert("Please enter a valid ZIP code.");
         forms[0].item(6).focus();
         forms[0].item(6).select();
     }
     else if (forms[0].item(7).value.length != 3 || isNaN(forms[0].item(7).value))
  {
         data_ok = false;
         alert("Please enter a valid area code.");
         forms[0].item(7).focus();
         forms[0].item(7).select();
```

```
        }
    else if (forms[0].item(8).value.length != 7 || isNaN(forms[0].item(8).value))
{
        data_ok = false;
        alert("Please enter a valid phone number.");
        forms[0].item(8).focus();
        forms[0].item(8).select();
    }

    if (data_ok) {
        for (i = 0; i < forms[0].length - 2; i++) {
            query_string += forms[0].item(i).name + "="
                + forms[0].item(i).value + "+";
        }
        query_string = query_string.substr(0, query_string.length-1);
        submit_url += query_string;
        location = submit_url;
    }

// -->
</SCRIPT>
</HEAD>
<BODY>
<H2 Align=Center>New Member Registration</H2>
<HR SIZE=5 WIDTH=90%>

<P ALIGN=CENTER>
<TABLE>
<TD>
<PRE>
<FORM NAME="RegistrationForm">
<B>First Name:      </B><INPUT TYPE=TEXT NAME="firstname">
<B>Last Name:       </B><INPUT TYPE=TEXT NAME="lastname">
<B>Address1:        </B><INPUT TYPE=TEXT NAME="addr1">
<B>Address2:        </B><INPUT TYPE=TEXT NAME="addr2">
<B>City:            </B><INPUT TYPE=TEXT NAME="city">
<B>State:           </B><INPUT TYPE=TEXT NAME="state" MAXLENGTH=2 SIZE=2>
<B>Zip:             </B><INPUT TYPE=TEXT NAME="zip" MAXLENGTH=10 SIZE=10>
<B>Area Code/Phone: </B><INPUT TYPE=TEXT NAME="code" MAXLENGTH=3 SIZE=3> <INPUT
TYPE=TEXT NAME="phone" MAXLENGTH=7 SIZE=7>

<B>Preferred Cuisine: </B><SELECT NAME="cuisine" SIZE="1">
                        <OPTION VALUE="1">American
                        <OPTION VALUE="2">Chinese
                        <OPTION VALUE="3">French
                        <OPTION VALUE="4">German
                        <OPTION VALUE="5">Greek
                        <OPTION VALUE="6">Indian
                        <OPTION VALUE="7">Italian
                        <OPTION VALUE="8">Japanese
```

```
                    <OPTION VALUE="9">Other
                    </SELECT>

<INPUT TYPE=BUTTON NAME="cmdSubmit" VALUE="Submit"> <INPUT TYPE="RESET"
VALUE="Clear">
</PRE>

</FORM>
</TD>
</TABLE>
</P>
</BODY>
</HTML>
```

Listing 7.9   Accessing client statistics.

```
<!-- The client statistics page-->
<HTML>
<HEAD>
<TITLE>Listing 7.9 Client Stats</TITLE>
</HEAD>
<SCRIPT LANGUAGE=JavaScript>
<!--
    var appName = navigator.appName;
    var appVersion = navigator.appVersion;
    var userAgent = navigator.userAgent;
    var screenHeight = screen.height;
    var screenWidth = screen.width;
    var screenAvailHeight = screen.availHeight;
    var screenAvailWidth = screen.availWidth;
    var screenColorDepth = screen.colorDepth;

    document.write(appName + "<BR>");
    document.write(appVersion + "<BR>");
    document.write(userAgent + "<BR>");
    document.write(screenWidth + " x " + screenHeight + "<BR>");

//-->
</SCRIPT>
<SCRIPT FOR="close" EVENT="onclick" LANGUAGE=JavaScript>
<!--
    window.close();
//-->
</SCRIPT>
<BODY>

<INPUT TYPE=BUTTON NAME="close" VALUE="Close me">
</BODY>
</HTML>
```

Chapter 8

Dynamic HTML

The word "dynamic" is used a lot these days. The basic message is that Web pages don't have to be static anymore. Dynamic HTML makes every element on a page accessible to script. Add style sheets to this and you can also bring a lot of robustness (another popular term) to your Web pages.

Kim Barber

Notes…

Chapter 8

In Chapter 7, you learned how Internet Explorer uses the Dynamic HTML Object Model to expose documents to scripting. In this chapter, you'll see how these objects allow you to manipulate HTML elements. Simply stated, Dynamic HTML (DHTML) provides scripting access to all the elements in a page, including its properties, methods, and events. This means you can programmatically control the appearance and behavior of Web pages using client-side scripting.

In the not-so-old days of Web page development, you had to make all changes to a displayed Web page at the server. For example, if you wanted to change the text color, a new page had to be provided. Another example is that of displaying and manipulating data from a database. Let's assume you created a Web page that reads data from a database and displays it in an HTML table. If you wanted to give the user the capability of sorting the data in the table, it would require another request to the server and quite possibly an additional HTML document. With DHTML, you could implement both of these examples without additional server requests. This can reduce server loading and network traffic considerably.

Using DHTML, you can develop Web pages that have application-like behavior not typically found in HTML pages. You can change content and text styles, such as color, font face, and font size, on the fly. You can explicitly position HTML elements and later reposition them. Doing this repetitively can create simple animation. You can apply a variety of visual filters and transitions to create interesting effects. Additionally, you can bind data from a data source to HTML elements, allowing the user to access and manipulate data on the client without numerous requests to the server.

You can use most of DHTML's functionality without adding ActiveX controls or Java applets to your Web pages. One exception to this general rule is Data Binding, which uses an ActiveX control that is installed with Internet Explorer. This chapter introduces the following DHTML features:

- *Dynamic Style*
- *Dynamic Content*
- *Dynamic Positioning*
- *Filters And Transitions*
- *Data Binding*
- *Scriptlets*

Both Internet Explorer 4 and Netscape Navigator support DHTML, but, as you might expect, there are differences in the implementations. Both, however, support the World Wide Web Consortium's (W3C) proposed HTML 4 and Cascading Style Sheets (CSS) standards and plan to implement the eventual standards set by the consortium. Since this is an area of rapid change, you might check a few Web sites for current information on the proposed standard and the leading implementations:

- *Microsoft*—**www.microsoft.com/msdn/sdk/inetsdk/help/dhtml/dhtml.htm**
- *Netscape*—**developer.netscape.com/one/dynhtml/dynhtml.html**
- *W3C*—**www.w3c.org/TR/REC-html40**

Dynamic Style

Dynamic styles let you change the formatting and appearance of HTML elements without reloading the page. DHTML accomplishes this through a combination of the exposed object model, styles and CSS, and client-side scripting. In many cases, you can use dynamic styles without the need for script, but you can if you want to.

Styles usually use the **<STYLE>** tag or the inline **STYLE** attribute, which assigns a style to an HTML element. In either case, you can change the style settings dynamically in response to an event or via script logic.

Listing 8.1 uses the **<STYLE>** tag to define two styles. The **<STYLE>** tag uses CSS attributes to set various style properties and is usually placed in the **<HEAD>** section. Two styles are defined: **style1** sets the text color to blue, and **style2** sets the text color to red and the font size to 36 point. A level 2 header is defined and assigned the style **style1** with the **CLASS** attribute. When the mouse pointer is moved over the header, the **onmouseover** event fires, and the style is changed to **style2** in response. The style is reset to **style1** when the mouse pointer is moved away.

Listing 8.1 Dynamic styles with the <STYLE> tag.

```
<HTML>
<HEAD>
<TITLE>Listing 8.1 Dynamic Styles</TITLE>
<STYLE>
     .style1 {color:blue}
     .style2 {color:red;font-size:"36"}
</STYLE>
</HEAD>
<BODY>

<H2 CLASS=style1 onmouseover="this.className='style2'"
onmouseout="this.className='style1'">DHTML is flexible!</H2>

</BODY>
</HTML>
```

Listing 8.2 also changes the font color in response to events but calls JavaScript functions to get the job done. Also, notice that the functions use the DHTML event model (covered in Chapter 7).

Listing 8.2 Changing style with script.

```
<HTML>
<HEAD>
<TITLE>Listing 8.2 Script with style</TITLE>
<SCRIPT LANGUAGE="JavaScript">
<!--
function TurnRed() {
    window.event.srcElement.style.color = "red";
}

function TurnBlue() {
    window.event.srcElement.style.color = "blue";
}
// -->
</SCRIPT>
</HEAD>
<BODY>

<H2 STYLE=color:blue onmouseover="TurnRed()"
onmouseout="TurnBlue()">DHTML is flexible!</H2>
```

```
</BODY>
</HTML>
```

Notice that even browsers that don't understand DHTML will display the headings. They just won't change colors. This is an example of how you can jazz up your Web page without worrying about compatibility, if you are careful.

Positioning And Animation

You can explicitly place an HTML element at a specific location in a document using positioning. Positioning is an extension of CSS; therefore, you specify an element's position using the **STYLE** attribute. You can also specify the position with the **STYLE** object, allowing you to position elements with script and even create animation effects.

Elements are positioned either absolute or relative. When absolute positioning is used, the browser positions the element with respect to the top-left corner of the container, which is the document body by default. When you specify relative positioning, the browser places the element relative to its flow within the HTML document.

Elements are also positioned using x and y coordinates as well as a z-index. The z-index specifies how the element "stacks-up" with other elements. The element with the largest z-index is on top, and the element with the smallest z-index is on the bottom. You can use both positive and negative values for the z-index.

Consider the following:

```
<H3 STYLE="color:yellow">Using Positioning</H3>
<IMG STYLE="position:relative;top:0;left:0" SRC="turkey.gif">
```

The preceding HTML displays a header followed by an image. The image follows the header because the document specifies absolute positioning. The top and left coordinates are relative to the header. The following HTML displays the image over the header:

```
<IMG STYLE="position:absolute;top:0;left:0" SRC="turkey.gif">
```

You can control the overlapping and force the image under the header by specifying a z-index of -1:

```
<IMG STYLE="position:absolute;top:0;left:0;z-index:-1" SRC="turkey.gif">
```

You can produce some interesting effects by combining script, positioning, and dynamic style. An example in the Practical Guide in this chapter does this to display a billboard in various locations.

Dynamic Content

Dynamic content allows you to change the content of a Web page after it is loaded. Before DHTML, you had to request a new page from the server to reflect content changes. Now, you can manipulate a set of properties and methods to change the content of many HTML elements. Some of these features operate only on the text within an element; others operate on the text and the appearance of the element.

There are four properties you'll use to modify an element's contents. Assigning a string to these replaces the associated element's contents. You'll find these properties in Table 8.1.

Listing 8.3 defines a level 2 header with an ID of **aTag**. The **onload** event handler calls the function **ChangeHTML()** to change the contents of the header.

Listing 8.3 The innerText property.

```
<HTML>
<HEAD>
<TITLE>Dynamic Content</TITLE>
<SCRIPT LANGUAGE="JavaScript">
<!--
function ChangeHTML() {
     document.all.aTag.innerText = "Dynamic HTML is <I>dynamic!</I>";
}

// -->
</SCRIPT>
</HEAD>
<BODY onload="ChangeHTML()">

<H2 ID=aTag>DHTML is flexible!</H2>

</BODY>
</HTML>
```

Since the **innerText** property renders included HTML tags as text, the new header is:

```
Dynamic HTML is <I>dynamic!</I>
```

Table 8.1 Dynamic content properties.

Property	Description
innerText	Replaces the contents of the existing element and renders any included HTML tags as text
innerHTML	Replaces the contents of the existing element; renders included HTML tags as HTML
outerText	Replaces the entire element as text (may change the element type)
outerHTML	Replaces the entire element using HTML

You probably would prefer using the **innerHTML** property in this case. Then, the header looks like this:

```
Dynamic HTML is dynamic!
```

Using the same header, you could modify the **outerText** property instead:

```
document.all.aTag.outerText = "<H1>Dynamic HTML is <I>dynamic!</I></H1>";
```

This code changes the header to:

```
<H1>Dynamic HTML is <I>dynamic!</I></H1>
```

Setting **outerHTML** results in:

```
Dynamic HTML is dynamic!
```

Notice that using the outer properties, you can change the type of the element. The inner properties preserve the element's type. If you change the **outerHTML** property, you probably want to set the ID. Otherwise, the previous ID is no longer valid. You can also position text and HTML at the beginning or end of elements using the methods described in Table 8.2

Table 8.2 Dynamic content methods.

Method	Description
insertAdjacentText	Inserts text at the beginning or end of an element
insertAdjacentHTML	Inserts text and HTML at the beginning or end of an element

These methods take an argument that specifies where the new content is placed relative to the element:

- **BeforeBegin**—Inserts the text before the beginning tag
- **AfterBegin**—Inserts the text after the beginning tag
- **BeforeEnd**—Inserts the text before the ending tag
- **AfterEnd**—Inserts the text after the ending tag

Continuing with the heading defined in Listing 8.3, let's change the statement in the **ChangeHTML()** function to read:

```
document.all.aTag.insertAdjacentHTML("BeforeBegin", "<I>Wow!</I> ");
```

This statement produces the following:

```
Wow!
DHTML is flexible!
```

Changing the argument to **AfterBegin** produces:

Wow! DHTML is flexible!

The **TextRange** Object

The properties and methods just described are used with a specific element. You can also manipulate page contents using an entire range of text. The **TextRange** object lets you reference a part of the document. It doesn't actually hold any content, it just provides a reference to it. You can use the **TextRange** object to move through text and perform searches, select specific portions of text, and copy portions of text.

You create a **TextRange** object by calling the **createTextRange()** method of **BODY**, **BUTTON**, **TEXTAREA**, and text **INPUT** elements. Using **createTextRange()** with the **BODY** element returns a reference to the entire document.

The **TextRange** object has several properties and methods that provide information about the range, move through the text, compare selections, set text ranges, and more. Table 8.3 describes the **TextRange** object properties.

TextRange object methods are described in Table 8.4.

Listing 8.4 shows the use of the **TextRange** object to search a text range for a specified string. The function **SetRange()** creates a text range consisting of the contents

Table 8.3 **TextRange** object properties.

Property	Description
boundingHeight	Returns the height of the rectangle that bounds the range
boundingLeft	Returns the left coordinate of the rectangle that bounds the range
boundingTop	Returns the top coordinate of the rectangle that bounds the range
boundingWidth	Returns the width of the rectangle that bounds the range
htmlText	Returns the text ranges as an HTML fragment
offsetLeft	Returns the left position of the rectangle that bounds the range
offsetTop	Returns the top position of the rectangle that bounds the range
text	References the text contained in the range

Table 8.4 **TextRange** object methods.

Method	Description
collapse	Moves the insertion point to the beginning or end of the range
compareEndPoints	Compares the two end points
duplicate	Returns a duplicate of the range
execCommand	Executes a command over the specified range
expand	Expands the range so that partial units* are completely contained
findText	Searches for text
getBookmark	Returns a bookmark specifying a position
inRange	Returns whether one range is contained within another
isEqual	Returns whether the specified range is equal to the current range
move	Moves the start and end points a specified number of units
moveEnd	Moves the end position of the range
moveStart	Moves the start position of the range
moveToBookmark	Moves to a bookmark

* A unit is a character, word, sentence, or textedit.

(continued)

Table 8.4 TextRange object methods (continued).

Method	Description
moveToElementText	Moves the text range so that the start and end positions encompass the text in a specified element
moveToPoint	Moves the start and end position of the range to the specified point
parentElement	Returns the parent element of a specified range
pasteHTML	Pastes HTML and/or text into the current range
queryCommandEnabled	Returns whether the specified command can be executed
queryCommandIndeterm	Returns whether the specified command is in the indeterminate state
queryCommandState	Returns the current state of a specified command
queryCommandSupported	Returns whether a command is supported on the current range
queryCommandValue	Returns the current value of a specified command
scrollIntoView	Scrolls the range into view at either the top or bottom of the window
select	Makes the active selection equal to the current text range
setEndPoint	Sets the end point of one range based on the end point of another

of the **BODY** section. It then moves the element with the ID **theText** into the text range. The **doSearch()** function prompts the user to enter a search string and then calls the **Find()** function. If the search string is found, it is highlighted within the text range.

Listing 8.4   Using the **TextRange** object.

```
<HTML>
<HEAD>
<TITLE>Listing 8.4 The TextRange object</TITLE>
<SCRIPT LANGUAGE="JavaScript">
<!--
var theRange;
var fndText, searchStr;

function SetRange() {
    theRange = document.body.createTextRange();
```

```
        theRange.moveToElementText(theText);
    }

    function Find(s) {
        if (theRange.findText(s)) {
            fndText = "<FONT STYLE="+"COLOR:WHITE;BACKGROUND:BLACK" +">" +
                    theRange.text + "</FONT>";
            theRange.pasteHTML(fndText);
        }
    }
    }

    function doSearch() {
        searchStr = prompt("Enter search string:")
        Find(searchStr);
    }

    // -->
    </SCRIPT>
    </HEAD>
    <BODY onload="SetRange()">

    <H2>The TextRange Object</H2>
    <DIV ID=theText>You create a TextRange object by calling the createTextRange()
    method of BODY, BUTTON, TEXTAREA, and text INPUT elements. Using
    createTextRange() with the BODY element returns a reference to
    the entire document.</DIV>

    <INPUT TYPE=BUTTON VALUE="Search" onclick="doSearch()">
    </BODY>
    </HTML>
```

The *Selection* Object

Another way to create a text range is with the **Selection** object. A selection is a portion of text that has been selected by the user. The **Selection** object contains information about the current selection and provides methods to create a **TextRange** object and to clear and delete the selection.

The following statement creates a **TextRange** object using the **Selection** object:

```
theRange = document.selection.createRange();
```

The preceding statement could be included in an event handler that is called when the user releases the mouse button after making a selection.

You can also create selections in script by calling the **TextObject**'s **select()** method.

Filters And Transitions

Filters and transitions add special visual effects to elements. DHTML supports two types of filters: visual and transition. You use visual filters to change an element's appearance, such a flipping an image, adding a shadow, or adding a blur effect. You use transition filters when you want to change the display of an element gradually, such as transitioning from one image to another.

Filters and transitions are extensions to CSS and are implemented by setting style properties within a **<STYLE>** tag or with an element's **STYLE** attribute. You can add filter and transition effects without using script, but if you need to control these effects with script, you can do so with the **filters** collection. Each HTML control has a **filters** collection that provides script access to the filters. Also, filters have properties, methods, and events that control the appearance and behavior of the filter.

Filters can only be used with HTML elements that are controls. Control elements define a rectangular area in the display. You can add filters to the following controls:

- **BODY**
- **BUTTON**
- **DIV** (with a defined height, width, and absolute positioning)
- **IMG**
- **INPUT**
- **MARQUEE**
- **SPAN** (with a defined height, width, and absolute positioning)
- **TABLE**
- **TD**
- **TEXTAREA**
- **TFOOT**
- **TH**
- **THEAD**
- **TR**

Visual Filters

Visual filters modify a control's appearance. For example, you can use visual filters to add a shadow to text, flip an image horizontally or vertically, and apply other special effects. Table 8.5 describes the visual filters supported by Internet Explorer 4.

Filters are applied as a filter string, and you can apply multiple filters at the same time. The following HTML flips text vertically:

```
<SPAN ID="mySpan" HEIGHT=20 WIDTH=50
STYLE="position:absolute;top:0;left:0;font-size:24;color:blue;filter:flipv">
Using filters is easy</SPAN>
```

Some visual filters take arguments to specify how the filter will be applied. The **glow** filter takes up to two arguments to specify the color and strength. The following HTML adds a red glow effect to the text:

```
filter:glow(color=red)
```

Table 8.5   Internet Explorer 4 visual filters.

Filter	Description
alpha	Sets a transparency level
blur	Creates a movement effect
chroma	Makes a specified color transparent
dropshadow	Creates an offset silhouette
fliph	Creates a horizontal mirror image
flipv	Creates a vertical mirror image
glow	Creates a glow effect
grayscale	Removes color information from an image
invert	Reverses hue, saturation, and brightness values
light	Projects a light source onto the object
mask	Creates a transparent mask from the object
shadow	Creates a silhouette of an object
wave	Creates a sine wave distortion of an object
xray	Shows only the edges of the object

Listing 8.5 shows how you can add filters using script. When the user moves the mouse over the text, an event handler adds the glow effect.

Listing 8.5 Adding visual filters with script.

```
<HTML>
<HEAD>
<TITLE>Listing 8.5 Visual Filters</TITLE>
<SCRIPT LANGUAGE="JavaScript">
<!--
function addGlow() {
     mySpan.style.filter = "glow(red)";
}

// -->
</SCRIPT>
</HEAD>
<BODY>

<SPAN ID="mySpan" HEIGHT=20 WIDTH=50
onmouseover="addGlow()"
STYLE="position:absolute;top:0;left:0;
font-size:24;color:blue">
Using filters is easy</SPAN>

</BODY>
</HTML>
```

Transition Filters

You can use transition filters when you want to change a control's appearance over a period of time or gradually hide and reveal a control. This is commonly done in slide show presentations in the transition from one slide to another.

There are two types of transition filters: blend and reveal. Blend causes the control to gradually fade in and out. Reveal causes the control to gradually appear and disappear in one of 24 predefined patterns.

The **blendTrans** filter is very easy to use and takes one argument, **duration**, to specify the length of time the transition should take to complete. At the time of this writing, **blendTrans** doesn't work exactly as documented. You can, however, coerce it into working by using script. The following HTML uses the blend transition to fade in text over a five-second period:

```
<SCRIPT LANGUAGE=JavaScript>
<!--
```

```
function doTrans() {
    mySpan.filters.blendTrans.Apply();
    mySpan.innerText="Filters are easy!";
    mySpan.filters.blendTrans.play();
}
//-->
</SCRIPT>

<SPAN ID="mySpan" HEIGHT=20 WIDTH=50
STYLE="position:absolute;top:0;left:0;font-size:24;color:blue;
filter:blendTrans(duration=3)" onclick="doTrans()">
Click here to see blendTrans work!</SPAN>
```

The **revealTrans** filter causes the control to transition in and out using one of 24 patterns. This filter accepts two arguments to specify the duration in seconds of the transition and the transition pattern. Table 8.6 describes the available transition patterns.

Transition filters have a few methods that affect the transitions. The **apply()** method applies a transition to the specified object, **play()** causes the transition to happen, and **stop()** stops the transition play.

Table 8.6 Reveal filter transition patterns.

Transition Pattern	Value
Box in	0
Box out	1
Circle in	2
Circle out	3
Wipe up	4
Wipe down	5
Wipe right	6
Wipe left	7
Vertical blinds	8
Horizontal blinds	9
Checkerboard across	10

(continued)

Table 8.6 Reveal filter transition patterns *(continued)*.

Transition Pattern	Value
Checkerboard down	11
Random dissolve	12
Split vertical in	13
Split vertical out	14
Split horizontal in	15
Split horizontal out	16
Strips left down	17
Strips left up	18
Strips right down	19
Strips right up	20
Random bars horizontal	21
Random bars vertical	22
Random	23

Listing 8.6 uses the **revealTrans** transition filter to cycle through a series of images. An image is inserted into the document, and the **revealTrans** filter, with the random dissolve effect, is assigned. The **duration** property is set so that the transition occurs over a two-second period. When the document **onload** event fires, a call is made to the function **initTrans()**, which uses the **setInterval()** method to call the **doTrans()** function every three seconds. The **doTrans()** function cycles through the series of images. The **apply()** method applies the specified transition filter to the image element. The next image is assigned to the image element, and then the **play()** method is called to play the transition. The **play()** method can take an argument to specify the duration, which would override the initial setting.

Listing 8.6 Using transition filters.

```
<HTML>
<HEAD>
<TITLE>Listing 8.6 Transition Filters</TITLE>
<SCRIPT LANGUAGE="JavaScript">
<!--
```

```
var picNum = 0;
var pics = new
Array("turkey.gif","tbone.gif","beef.gif","desert.gif","fish.gif","tacos.gif","hotdog.gif");

function doTrans() {
    pic.filters.revealTrans.apply();
    picNum++;
    if (picNum > 6)
        picNum = 0;
    pic.src = pics[picNum];
    pic.filters.revealTrans.play();
}

function initTrans() {
    setInterval("doTrans()", 3000);
}
// -->
</SCRIPT>
</HEAD>
<BODY onload="initTrans()">

<IMG NAME="pic" SRC="turkey.gif"
STYLE="filter:revealTrans(duration=2, transition=12)"
WIDTH=100 HEIGHT=100>

</BODY>
</HTML>
```

Data Binding

Data binding allows you to develop Web pages that display and manipulate data on the client. Without data binding, if the user needs to manipulate the data (for example, search or sort), it would require a trip to the server. Also, if your page displays data one record at a time, then each time the user moved forward or backward in the data, it would result in a request to the server. With data binding, you can cache a record set on the client and allow the user to navigate, search, and sort the data without repeated requests to the server. Additionally, some elements can update the data if the data source supports updates.

Data binding binds database fields to HTML elements. The data binding architecture consists of four components: Data Source Objects (DSOs), data consumers, the binding agent, and the table repetition agent. Data Source Objects provide the data to the page. Internet Explorer 4 provides two DSOs: the Tabular Data Control and the Remote Data Service. The Tabular Data Control is useful for delimited text files, such as comma-delimited files, and does not support updates. The Remote Data

Service uses OLE-DB and ODBC data sources and supports updates. This chapter covers the simplest Data Source Object: the Tabular Data Control. (Chapter 10 covers using the Remote Data Service to access and update a database.)

Data consumers are HTML elements that display the data. The binding agent and table repetition agents take care of synchronizing the data provider with the data consumer. The binding agent binds single-value elements to data, and the table repetition agent binds the entire record set to multiple-value elements, such as HTML tables.

The Tabular Data Control

The Tabular Data Control is used to bind single-value elements, such as **<INPUT TYPE=TEXT>** or **<SPAN>,** to data. It can also bind multiple-value elements, such as **<TABLE>**, to data. Data source objects are embedded in a page with the **<OBJECT>** tag:

```
<OBJECT ID="restData" WIDTH=0 HEIGHT=0
CLASSID="CLSID:333C7BC4-460F-11D0-BC04-0080C7055A83">
     <PARAM NAME="DataURL" VALUE="restaurants.txt">
     <PARAM NAME="FieldDelim" VALUE=",">
     <PARAM NAME="UseHeader" VALUE=True>
</OBJECT>
```

The **DataURL** parameter specifies the URL of the data source. In this case, it is **restaurants.txt**, a comma-delimited file that contains restaurant information. **FieldDelim** specifies the character that separates the records. **UseHeader** specifies whether the data source contains field names in the first row.

Now, the data is ready to be bound to elements. The restaurant database consists of the following fields:

- **Name**
- **Cuisine**
- **Hours**
- **Address**
- **Phone**

Single-value elements are bound at design-time as follows:

```
<INPUT TYPE=TEXT ID=restName DATASRC="#restData" DATAFLD="Name">
```

This statement binds the **Name** field of the **restData** data source to the input text.

control. The attribute **DATASRC** is assigned the ID of the data source object. The hash mark, #, is required. The attribute **DATAFLD** is assigned the name of the field being bound to the element. Single-value elements can also be bound at runtime:

```
<SCRIPT LANGUAGE="JavaScript">
. . .
restName.dataSrc = "#restData";
resName.dataFld = "Name";
. . .
</SCRIPT>

<BODY>
<INPUT TYPE=TEXT NAME=restName>
</BODY>
```

Navigating With The Tabular Data Control

The data source has a **recordset** object that contains all the records in the data set. The **recordset** object has the following methods that let you move around in the data:

- **MoveFirst**

- **MoveNext**

- **MovePrevious**

- **MoveLast**

The **recordset** object also has properties that indicate whether the record pointer is at the beginning or the end of the record set; **BOF** is **true** if it's at the beginning, **EOF** is **true** if it's at the end.

Listing 8.7 binds single-value elements to records in a database. It also has buttons that let the user move forward and backward through the data.

Listing 8.7   Using single-value elements with the Tabular Data Control.
```
<HTML>
<HEAD>
<TITLE>Listing 8.7 Single-Value Data Binding</TITLE>
<SCRIPT LANGUAGE="JavaScript">
<!--

function BindData() {
    restName.dataSrc = "#restData";
    restName.dataFld = "Name";
    restCuisine.dataSrc = "#restData";
    restCuisine.dataFld = "Cuisine";
```

```
        restHours.dataSrc = "#restData";
        restHours.dataFld = "Hours";
        restAddress.dataSrc = "#restData";
        restAddress.dataFld = "Address";
        restPhone.dataSrc = "#restData";
        restPhone.dataFld = "Phone";
}

function next() {
        if (restData.recordset.EOF)
                restData.recordset.MoveFirst();
        else
                restData.recordset.MoveNext();
}

function gotoEnd() {
        restData.recordset.MoveLast();
}

function prev() {
        if (restData.recordset.BOF)
                restData.recordset.MoveLast();
        else
                restData.recordset.MovePrevious();
}

function gotoBegin() {
        restData.recordset.MoveFirst();
}
// -->
</SCRIPT>
</HEAD>
<BODY onload="BindData()">

<OBJECT ID="restData" WIDTH=0 HEIGHT=0
CLASSID="CLSID:333C7BC4-460F-11D0-BC04-0080C7055A83">
        <PARAM NAME="DataURL" VALUE="restaurants.txt">
        <PARAM NAME="FieldDelim" VALUE=",">
        <PARAM NAME="UseHeader" VALUE=True>
</OBJECT>

<INPUT TYPE=TEXT ID=restName><INPUT TYPE=TEXT ID=restCuisine>
<INPUT TYPE=TEXT ID=restHours><INPUT TYPE=TEXT ID=restAddress>
<INPUT TYPE=TEXT ID=restPhone><BR>
<INPUT TYPE=BUTTON onclick="next()" VALUE=">">
<INPUT TYPE=BUTTON onclick="gotoEnd()" VALUE=">>">
<INPUT TYPE=BUTTON onclick="prev()" VALUE="<">
<INPUT TYPE=BUTTON onclick="gotoBegin()" VALUE="<<">

</BODY>
```

```
</HTML>
```

When the document is finished loading, the function **BindData()** is called to bind the first record to the text controls. The page provides four buttons to allow the user to move to the next and previous records as well as to the first and last records. If the record pointer is at the first record and the previous button is pressed, the page displays the last record. Conversely, if the pointer is at the last record and the next button is pressed, the page shows the first record.

An example of using the Tabular Data Control with multiple-value elements is in the Practical Guide in this chapter.

Scriptlets

A *scriptlet* is an HTML page that contains script that has features normally associated with controls. Scriptlets can expose properties, methods, and events and are used much like ActiveX controls. In addition, they have full access to the DHTML Object Model. Internet Explorer 4 supports scriptlets, as does Visual Basic and the Active Desktop. The current version of Netscape Navigator, however, does not support scriptlets.

Scriptlets are easier to write and maintain than controls written in languages such as C, C++, and Java. One of the disadvantages of client-side script is the fact that your script code is visible in the browser. This is not the case with scriptlets. So if you want to provide rudimentary security to protect your intellectual property or prefer that your users not see your code for some other reason, you might want to use a scriptlet instead.

Using Scriptlets

Scriptlets are embedded into HTML documents using the **<OBJECT>** tag. Unlike ActiveX controls, scriptlets do not use the **CLSID** attribute. Instead, they are simply assigned an identifier with the **ID** attribute. A special MIME type is also specified using the **TYPE** attribute to inform Internet Explorer that the object is a scriptlet. The **DATA** attribute is used to specify the URL for the page containing the scriptlet's definition.

The following **<OBJECT>** tag inserts a scriptlet contained in the document **8-10.htm** (which is on the CD that accompanies this book). The scriptlet used in the example in this section outputs text and uses the identifier **Label1**:

```
<OBJECT ID="Label1"
```

```
       TYPE="text/x-scriptlet"
       DATA="8-10.htm">
       HEIGHT=50 WIDTH=150
</OBJECT>
```

Notice that the object's dimensions are specified using the **HEIGHT** and **WIDTH** attributes. The browser limits a scriptlet's display area to this size. Here's another way to insert a scriptlet:

```
<OBJECT ID="Label1" TYPE="text/x-scriptlet" HEIGHT=50 WIDTH=150>
     <PARAM NAME="url" VALUE="8-10.htm">
</OBJECT>
```

Writing A Scriptlet

Writing a scriptlet is straightforward. You declare the scriptlet by using one of two methods. The first method uses **public_description** object, which is a JavaScript object providing access to the object's properties and methods defined by its constructor function. The other method uses default interface descriptions. With this method, you must declare the properties and methods that are being exposed with the prefix **public_**. For example, to declare a public property called **Caption**, you would use the following syntax:

```
Dim public_Caption
```

The **public_description** object lets you explicitly declare properties and methods that are exposed and provides one area in the scriptlet where the public interface is declared. Anything declared outside the public description is not accessible outside the scriptlet. This method is used in this scriptlet example.

The following script contains the declaration for the **Label** scriptlet:

```
<HTML>
<HEAD>
<TITLE> The Label Scriptlet</TITLE>
</HEAD>
<BODY>
<SCRIPT LANGUAGE="JavaScript">

// Declaration
var public_description = new Label();
</SCRIPT>

</BODY>
</HTML>
```

Adding Properties And Methods

The **Label** scriptlet is a simple example that outputs text and provides properties to set the foreground and background colors as well as the text itself. After you declare the scriptlet, you must define the interface for any properties that are exposed to scripting.

You set and retrieve property values with expressions and functions. The code uses the **this** keyword to reference the property. The following uses a simple expression to set the background color:

```
function Label() {
     this.bgColor = window.document.bgColor;
}
```

Most of the time, you'll use functions to set and get property values. Functions to set property values have the prefix **put_**, and functions that return property values have the prefix **get_**. Remember, you don't use the prefixes when referencing the properties in the container (Internet Explorer, in this case). The following statements define the **Label** scriptlet's properties:

```
function Label() {
     this.put_bgColor = setbgColor;
     this.get_bgColor = getbgColor;
     this.put_fgColor = setfgColor;
     this.get_fgColor = getbgColor;
     this.put_Caption = setCaption;
     this.get_Caption = getCaption;
}
```

Each property in this example has two functions because programs can read and write the property values. However, you can make a property read-only by including only a function with the **get_** prefix. The properties are assigned functions that implement the setting and returning of values. The following code contains the function definitions:

```
function setbgColor(bgcol) {
     window.document.bgColor = bgcol;
     mbgCol = window.document.bgColor;
}

function getbgColor() {
     return mbgCol;
}
```

```
function setfgColor(fgcol) {
    window.document.fgColor = fgcol;
    mfgCol = window.document.fgColor;
}

function getfgColor() {
    return mfgCol;
}

function setCaption(cap) {
    theLbl.innerText = cap;
    mlblCap = theLbl.innerText;
}

function getCaption() {
    return mlblCap;
}
```

The variables **mfgCol**, **mbgCol**, and **mlblCap** are private variables that store the property values. They are declared in script outside of the public description. You can find the complete scriptlet listing at the end of this section if you would like to see where these variables first appear.

The scriptlet now has properties to set and return the background and foreground colors and the text that the scriptlet will display. Now, it's time to add a method. Here's how to expose a method called **about()** to the rest of the world:

```
this.about = about;
```

The **about()** method uses an **alert** box to provide version information. The **about()** function implements the method:

```
function about() {
    alert ("My Scriptlet v1.0");
}
```

Adding Events

Scriptlets can notify the container about two kinds of events: standard DHTML events and custom events. Standard DHTML events include:

- **onclick**
- **ondblclick**
- **onkeydown**
- **onkeypress**

- **onkeyup**

- **onmousedown**

- **onmousemove**

- **onmouseup**

The scriptlet notifies the container of a standard event using the **event** object. DHTML has an event model that "bubbles" events up the object hierarchy. Event bubbling is covered in Chapter 7. The following script bubbles an event when the user clicks on the label's caption:

```
<SCRIPT LANGUAGE="JavaScript" FOR="theLbl" EVENT="onclick">
    window.external.bubbleEvent();
</SCRIPT>
```

The **raiseEvent** method is used to notify the container of a nonstandard event. The following is a modification of the **setbgColor()** function that raises an event when the background color is changed:

```
function setbgColor(bgcol) {
    window.document.bgColor = bgcol;
    mbgCol = window.document.bgColor;
    window.external.raiseEvent("event_onsetbgColor",window.document);
}
```

The event is named by using the prefix **event_**. The container can respond to the **onsetbgColor** event much like responding to standard events.

Adding A Context Menu

Context menus appear when the user clicks the right mouse button over the scriptlet and are used to add functionality. They can be easily added using the **window** object's **setContextMenu()** method. To create a context menu, first define the menu as a series of array elements. Each menu item consists of two array elements: one for the menu selection and one for the function that is called when the item is selected.

The following statements add a context menu to the **Label** scriptlet. The menu has only one selection that displays the **about** box:

```
var menuItem = new Array(1);
menuItem[0] = "&About";
menuItem[1] = "about";
window.external.setContextMenu(menuItem);
```

The ampersand (&) is used to specify a hot key for the menu item. When the menu item is selected, the **about()** function is called to display the **about** box. This is the same function that the **about()** method uses.

The Label Scriptlet

In the previous section, you have seen the **Label** scriptlet in small pieces. Now, consider it as one entity. Listing 8.8 contains the complete code for the **Label** scriptlet. Notice the use of the **<SPAN>** tag to display the text. You'll also find a page that uses the scriptlet in Listing 8.9.

Listing 8.8   The Label scriptlet.

```
<HTML>
<HEAD>
<TITLE>Listing 8.8 The Label scriptlet</TITLE>
</HEAD>
<BODY onload="init()">

<SCRIPT LANGUAGE="JavaScript">
function init() {
    theLbl.innerText = mlblCap;
    window.document.fgColor = "yellow";
    window.document.bgColor = "blue";

    // The context menu
    var menuItem = new Array(1);
    menuItem[0] = "&About";
    menuItem[1] = "about";
    window.external.setContextMenu(menuItem);
}
</SCRIPT>

<SCRIPT LANGUAGE="JavaScript" FOR="theLbl" EVENT="onclick">
// Process a standard event
    window.external.bubbleEvent();
</SCRIPT>

<SCRIPT LANGUAGE="JavaScript">

// Declaration
var public_description = new Label();

var mbgCol = window.document.bgColor;
var mfgCol = window.document.fgColor;
var mlblCap = "I'm a scriptlet!";
```

```
// Definition
function Label() {
    this.put_bgColor = setbgColor;
    this.get_bgColor = getbgColor;
    this.put_fgColor = setfgColor;
    this.get_fgColor = getfgColor;
    this.put_Caption = setCaption;
    this.get_Caption = getCaption;
    this.about = about;
}

// Implementation
function setbgColor(bgcol) {
    window.document.bgColor = bgcol;
    mbgCol = window.document.bgColor;
    window.external.raiseEvent("event_onsetbgColor",window.document);
}

function getbgColor() {
    return mbgCol;
}

function setfgColor(fgcol) {
    window.document.fgColor = fgcol;
    mfgCol = window.document.fgColor;
}

function getfgColor() {
    return mfgCol;
}

function setCaption(cap) {
    theLbl.innerText = cap;
    mlblCap = theLbl.innerText;
}

function getCaption() {
    return mlblCap;
}

function about() {
    alert ("My Scriptlet v1.0");
}

</SCRIPT>

<SPAN ID="theLbl"></SPAN>

</BODY>
</HTML>
```

Listing 8.9 The Label scriptlet container.

```
<HTML>
<HEAD>
<TITLE>Listing 8.9 The Label scriptlet container</TITLE>
<SCRIPT LANGUAGE="JavaScript">
<!--

function SetbgColor() {
     Label1.bgColor = "red";
}
// -->
</SCRIPT>
<SCRIPT LANGUAGE="JavaScript" FOR="Label1" EVENT="onclick">
     SetbgColor();
</SCRIPT>

<SCRIPT LANGUAGE="JavaScript"
     FOR="Label1" EVENT="onscriptletevent(name)">
     alert ("Event: " + name + " occurred");
</SCRIPT>

</HEAD>
<BODY>

<OBJECT ID="Label1"
       HEIGHT=50 WIDTH=150
       TYPE="text/x-scriptlet"
       DATA="8-11.htm">
</OBJECT>

</BODY>
</HTML>
```

Summary

This chapter shows you what you can do with DHTML. By combining the many features and functions of DHTML with script, you can create interesting and highly functional Web pages. Additionally, you can put much of the work on the client and, thereby, reduce the load on the server and provide a better experience for the user.

Although this book is about ASP, which by definition is on the server, you'll often find it necessary to combine client-side techniques and server-side techniques. Even if you don't have to, pushing some processing off to the client allows your server to be more responsive and handle larger loads. DHTML gives you more opportunities than ever to move processing to the client computer.

Practical Guide To

Dynamic HTML

- Using Dynamic Styles
- Using The Transition Filter Control
- Data Binding With The Tabular Data Control

Using Dynamic Styles

Listing 8.10 uses dynamic styles to change the appearance of selected elements. Four styles are defined in the **<HEAD>** section. The page applies these styles to various elements in the **<BODY>** by assigning them via the **CLASS** attribute. It also defines a **<SPAN>** that contains underlined text. When the user moves the mouse over the text, the **onmouseover** event handler changes the style. The new style changes the font color and size and changes the mouse pointer to a hand, giving the appearance of a hyperlink. When the user moves the mouse away, the **onmouseout** event fires and the code restores the style to its previous setting. Also notice that as the text gets larger, the document layout changes with it. When the user clicks on the text, the event handler calls **OpenModal()**, which opens a modal dialog window to display another document. You'll read more about the function of the new document in a later example on the Tabular Data Control.

Further down in the document, you'll see another **<SPAN>** with an ID of **FREE**. When the document loads, the **onload** event handler calls **init()**. This function calls **setInterval()** so that the browser will call **blink()** every 200 milliseconds. The **blink()** function causes the text in the span to blink red and blue.

Finally, the page defines a hyperlink and assigns it the style **hot**. When the mouse pointer moves over the hyperlink, the link changes color and size.

Listing 8.10   Using dynamic styles.

```
<HTML>
<HEAD>
<TITLE>Listing 8.10 Community Dining Club</TITLE>
<STYLE>
     .s1 {color:blue;text-align:center}
     .s2 {color:red;font-size:"36";text-align:center}
     .normal {color:blue;font-size:"16"}
     .hot {cursor:hand;color:red;font-size:"18"}
</STYLE>

<SCRIPT LANGUAGE="JavaScript">
<!--
function blink() {
     if (free.style.color == "red")
          free.style.color = "blue";
     else
          free.style.color = "red";
}

function init(n) {
     setInterval("blink()", n);
}
```

```
function OpenModal() {
    window.showModalDialog("8-12.htm");
}


//-->
</SCRIPT>
</HEAD>
<BODY onload="init(200)">
<H1 class=s1 >Welcome To The</H1>
<H1 class=s1 >Community Dining Club!</H1>
<HR SIZE=5>
<P class=normal>The Community Dining Club is for those who enjoy
dining out and the convenience of the online world!</P>

<P class=normal>As a visitor, you can
<SPAN class=normal onmouseover="this.className='hot'"
onmouseout="this.className='normal'" onclick="OpenModal()">
<U>see the many fine participating restaurants.</U></SPAN>

As a member, you will enjoy the following benefits:</P>
<UL class=normal>
<LI>Online Reservations
<LI>10% Discount On All Meals
<LI>Special Discounts
<LI>Submit and Read Member Restaurant Reviews
<LI>Coolness
<LI>and More!
</UL>

<P class=normal>Best of all, membership is <SPAN ID=free class=hot>
FREE!</SPAN>

So why not <A class=normal onmouseover="this.className='hot'"
onmouseout="this.className='normal'"HREF="8-11.htm">
join today?</A></P>

</BODY>
</HTML>
```

Using The Transition Filter Control

Listing 8.11 contains the familiar Community Dining Club New Member Registration page. The page is a bit different than before because it uses a visual filter and a transition filter with dynamic positioning to display the billboard. The billboard consists of an array that contains the messages to display. When the document's **onload** event fires, the handler calls **startBillboard()**. The billboard is in the **<SPAN>** with the ID of **msg1**. The function applies the blur filter and the random dissolve transition and sets the billboard's starting position.

The **startBillboard()** function applies the transition using the **apply()** method. Then, it sets the first message in the sequence using the **innerText** property. Next, the call to the **play()** method causes the transition. Finally, the function uses **setInterval()** so that the browser will call **cycle()** every 2,500 milliseconds (2.5 seconds).

The **cycle()** function displays the appropriate message on the billboard. Assigning a value to the **top** property sets each message position. When the cycle completes, the code resets the property to the initial position.

Listing 8.11 Using the transition filter control.

```
<HTML>
<HEAD>
<TITLE>Listing 8.11 Member Registration</TITLE>
<STYLE>
        .s1 {color:blue;font-size:"18pt"}
        .s2 {color:blue;font-size:"12pt"}
        .s3 {color:red;font-size:"18pt"}
</STYLE>
<SCRIPT LANGUAGE=JavaScript>
<!--
var MsgNo, MsgTop;

var Message = new Array("Join Today!", "Fine Dining!",
                        "Impress Friends!", "Save Money!", "Be Cool!");

MsgNo = 0;
MsgTop = 125;

function startBillboard() {
    msg1.filters.revealTrans.apply();
    msg1.innerText = Message[MsgNo];
    msg1.filters.revealTrans.play();

    setInterval("cycle()", 2500);
}

function cycle() {
    MsgNo++;
    MsgTop += 35;
```

```
    if (MsgNo > 4) {
        MsgNo = 0;
        MsgTop = 125;
    }
    msg1.innerText = "";
    msg1.style.top = MsgTop + "px";
    msg1.filters.revealTrans.apply();
    msg1.innerText = Message[MsgNo];
    msg1.filters.revealTrans.play();
}

//-->
</SCRIPT>

<SCRIPT FOR="cmdSubmit" EVENT="onclick" LANGUAGE=JavaScript>
<!--
    // data validation here
// -->
</SCRIPT>
</HEAD>
<BODY onload="startBillboard()">

<SPAN ID=msg1 class=s3 style="position:absolute;top:125;left:0;
    filter:blur(add=1,direction=45,strength=3)
    revealTrans(transition=12 duration=8)"></SPAN>

<H2 class=s1 Align=Center>New Member Registration</H2>
<HR SIZE=5 WIDTH=90%>

<P ALIGN=CENTER>
<TABLE>
<TD>
<PRE>
<FORM NAME="RegistrationForm">
<B>First Name:        </B><INPUT TYPE=TEXT NAME="firstname">
<B>Last Name:         </B><INPUT TYPE=TEXT NAME="lastname">
<B>Address1:          </B><INPUT TYPE=TEXT NAME="addr1">
<B>Address2:          </B><INPUT TYPE=TEXT NAME="addr2">
<B>City:              </B><INPUT TYPE=TEXT NAME="city">
<B>State:             </B><INPUT TYPE=TEXT NAME="state" MAXLENGTH=2 SIZE=2>
<B>Zip:               </B><INPUT TYPE=TEXT NAME="zip" MAXLENGTH=10 SIZE=10>
<B>Area Code/Phone: </B><INPUT TYPE=TEXT NAME="code" MAXLENGTH=3 SIZE=3> <INPUT
TYPE=TEXT NAME="phone" MAXLENGTH=7 SIZE=7>
```

```
<B>Preferred Cuisine: </B><SELECT NAME="cuisine" SIZE="1">
                         <OPTION VALUE="1">American
                         <OPTION VALUE="2">Chinese
                         <OPTION VALUE="3">French
                         <OPTION VALUE="4">German
                         <OPTION VALUE="5">Greek
                         <OPTION VALUE="6">Indian
                         <OPTION VALUE="7">Italian
                         <OPTION VALUE="8">Japanese
                         <OPTION VALUE="9">Seafood
                         <OPTION VALUE="0">Other
</SELECT>

<INPUT TYPE=BUTTON NAME="cmdSubmit" VALUE="Submit"> <INPUT TYPE="RESET"
VALUE="Clear">
</PRE>

</FORM>
</TD>
</TABLE>
</P>
</BODY>
</HTML>
```

Data Binding With The Tabular Data Control

Listing 8.12 does a lot of work with surprisingly little script or HTML. It uses the Tabular Data Control to bind a comma-delimited data source to an HTML table. You will notice that the table definition has only one **<TR>** tag (table row) defined. The Tabular Data Control and the table repetition agent take care of binding each record to this one definition. The code sets the **DATAPAGESIZE** attribute to five to limit the number of rows displayed at a time. There are two navigation buttons at the top of the table for moving forward and backward a page at a time. Additionally, the **Name** and **Cuisine** columns have buttons that, when clicked, cause the page to sort the data.

Listing 8.12 Data binding with the Tabular Data Control.
```
<HTML>
<HEAD>
<TITLE>Listing 8.12 The Tabular Data Control</TITLE>
<SCRIPT LANGUAGE="JavaScript">
<!--

function sort(fld) {
    restData.sort = fld;
```

```
        restData.reset();
}

function fwd() {
    restSet.nextPage();
}

function back() {
    restSet.previousPage();
}
// -->
</SCRIPT>
</HEAD>
<BODY>

<OBJECT ID="restData" WIDTH=0 HEIGHT=0
CLASSID="CLSID:333C7BC4-460F-11D0-BC04-0080C7055A83">
    <PARAM NAME="DataURL" VALUE="restaurants.txt">
    <PARAM NAME="FieldDelim" VALUE=",">
    <PARAM NAME="UseHeader" VALUE=True>
</OBJECT>

<INPUT TYPE=BUTTON VALUE="<" onclick="back()">
<INPUT TYPE=BUTTON VALUE=">" onclick="fwd()">

<TABLE ID=restSet BORDER=1 DATASRC="#restData" DATAPAGESIZE="5">
<THEAD>
<TH><INPUT TYPE=BUTTON VALUE="Name" onclick="sort('Name')"></TH>
<TH><INPUT TYPE=BUTTON VALUE="Cuisine" onclick="sort('Cuisine')"></TH>
<TH>Hours</TH>
<TH>Address</TH>
<TH>Phone</TH>
</THEAD>
<TBODY>
<TR>
<TD><SPAN DATAFLD="Name"></SPAN></TD>
<TD><SPAN DATAFLD="Cuisine"></SPAN></TD>
<TD><SPAN DATAFLD="Hours"></SPAN></TD>
<TD><SPAN DATAFLD="Address"></SPAN></TD>
<TD><SPAN DATAFLD="Phone"></SPAN></TD>
</TR>
</TBODY>
</TABLE>

</BODY>
</HTML>
```

Chapter 9

Server-Side Scripting

Server-side scripting is a good choice when you can't depend on your user having a browser that supports client-side scripting or when you need access to sophisticated server components.

Kim Barber

Notes…

Chapter

9

Previous chapters focus on client-side scripting. Although client-side scripting has several advantages, it has disadvantages, as well, most notably that it is browser-dependent. Server-side scripting performs the processing on the server and pushes pure HTML to the client. As a result, your concerns about the client browser's capabilities will be reduced significantly. Other advantages of server-side scripting are discussed shortly.

What Is An Active Server Page?

An *Active Server page* is a page that contains server-side script and, possibly, HTML. Active Server pages can also push client-side script out to the client, so you may have a mix of client and server script commands intermixed with HTML. Active Server pages have the file name extension *.ASP*. When a client requests a file with an .ASP extension, Internet Information Server (IIS) passes the file to the scripting engine for processing. The server processes any sever-side script and passes any script output, as well as any HTML, to the client.

You can use Active Server pages to do a variety of things. For example, you can determine the brand and version of the browser and generate output dynamically based on the browser's capabilities. You can also create customized and personalized pages based on the user's preferences and interests.

Like client-side script, you can write server-side script in a number of languages, provided that the server has the appropriate scripting engine. The default language

343

for IIS is VBScript; a JavaScript engine is also available. It is worth mentioning that other scripting languages are available for other Web servers. For example, PHP works with many servers (see **www.php.net**), and there is even a PHP version that works with IIS. However, for the purposes of this book (which is, after all, the *ASP Black Book*), you'll look exclusively at ASP scripting.

Advantages And Disadvantages

Server-side script has several advantages, one being that it can be browser-independent. Because only HTML is sent to the browser, you don't have to worry about whether the client supports scripting, unless you're also sending client-side script in the output stream. Server-side script is generally easier and faster to write and maintain than CGI executables. You can make modifications to your code (which is conveniently in the file with your HTML), and the changes will take effect immediately with no need to recompile. Your source code is not visible to the user, allowing you to protect your intellectual property and the results of your hard work.

Server-side script can also use *components,* which are objects that execute on the server. Components perform tasks that would otherwise be difficult or impossible to do. The IIS provides several components, and you can write your own for additional functionality (see Chapter 13). You'll learn more about the components that IIS provides in Chapter 10. You can also use server-side script to access data sources, maintain persistent variables, and more.

There are very few disadvantages to server-side script. One disadvantage is that it places additional work on the server, and poorly written code can significantly affect server performance. Server-side script doesn't have much support for user interfaces. You can't use things such as **MsgBox()**, **Prompt**, and **Alert**. Instead, most scripts use HTML forms to gather information. Also, you must have access to a server to develop and test your code.

Script Delimiters

Server-side script is often embedded between <% and %> delimiters. The scripting engine processes script embedded in these delimiters on the server. You can't nest script delimiters inside each other, but you can use as many separate pairs of the tags as you need. Single statements as well as groups of statements can be placed within them.

The following is an example of a single VBScript statement in delimiters:

```
<% fontsize = 5 %>
```

As you can see, this is just a typical statement except that the delimiters tell the server to execute the code.

Here's an example of more than one statement inside a single set of delimiters:

```
<%
    Dim Commission, Sales
    Commission = .05
    Sales = 10000
    If Sales > 5000 Then Commission = .10
%>
```

The equal sign (=) is used to output the value of an expression. The following statement places the value of the variable **Commission** into the HTML output stream:

```
<%= Commission %>
```

Because you can use as many script delimiters as you need, it's easy to mix server-side script and HTML. Listing 9.1 does this to output text in font sizes from 1 through 7.

Listing 9.1 Mixing server-side script and HTML.
```
<% For fontsize = 1 to 7 %>
    <FONT SIZE=<% =fontsize %>>
    Server-side script!<BR>
    </FONT>
<% Next %>

<HTML>
<HEAD>
<TITLE>Listing 9.1 Server-Side Scripting</TITLE>
</HEAD>
<BODY>

</BODY>
</HTML>
```

Figure 9.1 shows the result of viewing this page in Internet Explorer.

Specifying The Default Language

VBScript is the default language for server-side script. The default language for a page is easily set to a different language, like this:

```
<%@ LANGUAGE="JavaScript" %>
```

You are not allowed to place any other elements within this delimiter pair. Also, you must insert a space between the **@** character and **LANGUAGE**.

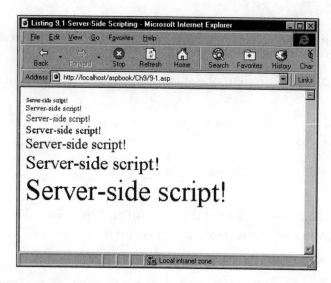

Figure 9.1

Output generated by server-side script.

You can set the default language on a more permanent basis by making a modification to the registry. The default scripting language is specified by the registry key **DefaultScriptLanguage**. This key is a subkey of **HKEY_LOCAL_MACHINE**, the full path is:

```
HKEY_LOCAL_MACHINE\System\CurrentControlSet\Services\W3SVC\ASP\Parameters
```

To make this change, start the registry editor, locate the registry key as described eariler, double-click **DefaultScriptLanguage**, enter the new default language, click OK, and close the registry editor.

The **<SCRIPT>** Tag

You can embed server-side script in the **<SCRIPT>** tag. When you use the **<SCRIPT>** tag, you must include the **RUNAT** attribute, which you set to **Server**. Listing 9.2 uses the **<SCRIPT>** tag to do the same as Listing 9.1.

Listing 9.2   Using the <SCRIPT> tag with server-side script.

```
<SCRIPT LANGUAGE=VBScript RUNAT=Server>

For fontsize = 1 to 7
    response.write("<FONT SIZE=" & fontsize & ">")
    response.write("Server-side script!<BR></FONT>")
Next
```

```
</SCRIPT>
<HTML>
<HEAD>
<TITLE>Listing 9.2 Using the <SCRIPT> Tag</TITLE>
</HEAD>
<BODY>

</BODY>
</HTML>
```

The **<SCRIPT>** tag isn't the only difference in this example. Notice that the script and HTML aren't mixed as they were in the previous example. Instead, the code places HTML in the output stream using the **Response** object, which is an intrinsic Active Server component that allows you to send output to the client. In this example, it's functionally equivalent to the = character that Listing 9.1 uses. You'll learn more about the **Response** object in Chapter 10.

Code in delimiters and the **<SCRIPT>** tag execute immediately, unless the code is within a procedure body (for example, a **SUB** or a **FUNCTION**).

Debugging Active Server Pages

Web pages containing server-side script can be inconvenient—at best—to debug. No debugger is available. Without a debugging tool, you have to resort to sending the values of variables and properties to the browser. Often this doesn't provide all the information you need, and it's difficult to trace code execution.

Debugging server-side scripts is now much easier with the Microsoft Script Debugger. Chapter 5 shows how to use the debugger with client-side script. With IIS 4, you can now debug server-side script.

But before you can debug server-side script, you must create an Active Server application. An application is a virtual directory marked as an application, and all the files and directories in the virtual directory are part of the application. You use the IIS Internet Service Manager program to create applications. You must also use the Internet Service Manager to enable server-side debugging. You'll see exactly how to do this in this chapter's Practical Guide.

Summary

Writing server-side script is fairly quick and easy. It lets you develop powerful Web pages without having to worry much, if at all, about browser compatibility. Scripting lets you have most (if not all) of the functions of CGI without the hassles that go along with CGI. This chapter introduces you to the syntax and mechanics of server-side scripting. Chapter 10 shows you the ActiveX server components you can use with server-side scripting. These components are key to the real power of server-side scripting.

Practical Guide To

Server-Side Scripting

- Creating An Active Server Application With IIS
- Creating An Active Server Application Using Personal Web Server
- Writing An Active Server Page
- Debugging Server-Side Script Using The Microsoft Script Debugger

Creating An Active Server Application With IIS

This example shows you how to create an Active Server application using IIS 4 Internet Service Manager. In addition to creating the application, you'll also enable server-side script debugging. This example assumes that a directory named myapp already exists and is a child directory of the IIS root directory **\inetpub\wwwroot**.

From the Start menu, select Programs|Microsoft Internet Information Server|Internet Service Manager. This might be different on your computer, depending on the installation. This runs the Microsoft Management Console (see Figure 9.2).

Right-click on myapp, then select Properties. This displays the myapp Properties dialog (see Figure 9.3). As you can see, you can set several properties for any given application. To create the application, select Create in the Application Settings section. Then, enter myapp in the Name text box. Also, make sure to select Script in the Permissions settings.

To enable server-side script debugging, select Configuration. This displays the Application Configuration dialog (see Figure 9.4).

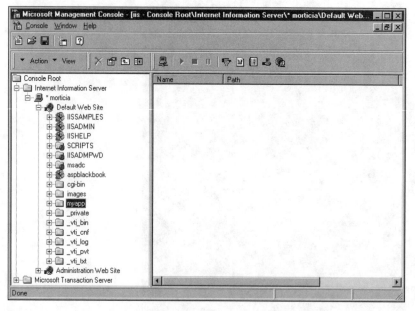

Figure 9.2

The Microsoft Management Console.

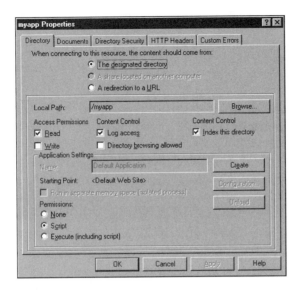

Figure 9.3

IIS's Properties dialog box for myapp.

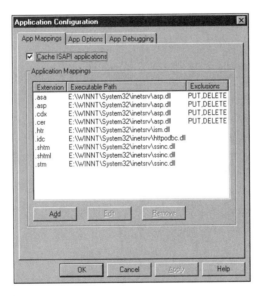

Figure 9.4

The Application Configuration dialog.

Figure 9.5 shows the dialog to set debugging options. Select Enable ASP server-side script debugging. This allows IIS to enter the Microsoft Script Debugger when processing server-side scripts. You'll want to turn this off when you place your application into production.

Click Apply, and click OK to close this dialog. Then, click Apply, and click OK to close the myapp Properties dialog.

The application is now created with debugging enabled.

Creating An Active Server Application Using Personal Web Server

You can use the Microsoft Personal Web Server (PWS) to write Active Server pages. Most of the functionality of Active Server pages is available in PWS; however, server-side script debugging isn't. Creating an Active Server application in PWS is very straightforward. This example assumes that a directory named myapp already exists and is a child directory of **Webshare\wwwroot**.

Using Windows Explorer, right-click on the directory myapp, and then select Sharing. This displays the myapp Properties dialog, as shown in Figure 9.6.

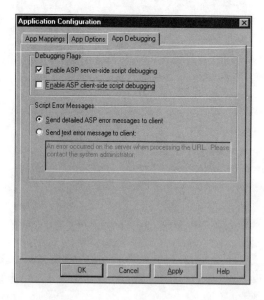

Figure 9.5

Enabling server-side script debugging.

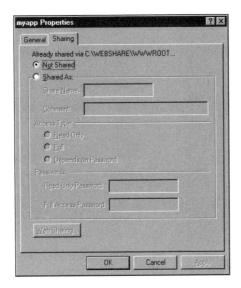

Figure 9.6

PWS's Properties dialog box for myapp.

Select Shared As (this also causes myapp to become the default share name), click on the Web Sharing button, and then select Execute Scripts to enable server-side scripting. To finish, click OK, and then click Apply and OK in the main properties dialog.

Writing An Active Server Page

This example shows a fairly common application of Web pages. Listing 9.3 displays an HTML form to collect sales information and calculates a commission on the basis of sales. To do this, the form posts the sales figure to a page on the server to perform the necessary calculation. Listing 9.3 shows an interesting use of Active Server pages. Rather than posting the sales data to a different page, the form posts the data to itself. To do this, however, you need some information from Chapter 10.

The **Request** object provides access to data in the HTTP Request Header, and the **Response** object provides access to data in the HTTP Response Header. Listing 9.3 uses the **Request** object to determine whether there is data. If data is not present, this must be a request to show the form. If data is present, the script should process it. The **Request** object retrieves the sales amount value. The script makes a function call to calculate the commission. The **Response** object then outputs the result. You'll learn more about all these objects in Chapter 10.

Listing 9.3   A typical use of server-side script.

```
<%@ LANGUAGE="VBSCRIPT" %>
<!-- Not purely necessary, but a good idea to include -->

<%
    Function CalcCommission(Sales)
        Commission = 0
            If Sales <= 1000 Then
                Commission = .05
            ElseIf Sales > 1000 And Sales <= 5000 Then
                Commission = .10
            ElseIf Sales > 5000 And Sales <= 10000 Then
                Commission = .15
            Else
                Commission = .20
            End If
            CalcCommission = Commission * Sales
    End Function
%>

<HTML>
<HEAD>
<TITLE>Listing 9.3 Server-Side Script</TITLE>
</HEAD>
<BODY>
<H2>Acme Commission Calculator</H2>

<% If Request("CONTENT_LENGTH") = 0 Then %> <!-- If no data, then show form -->
    <FORM NAME=calc METHOD=POST ACTION="9-3.asp"> <!-- post to self -->
    Enter sales amount:<INPUT TYPE=TEXT NAME="sales"><BR>
    <INPUT TYPE=SUBMIT VALUE="Calculate">
    <INPUT TYPE=Reset VALUE="Clear">
    </FORM>
<% Else %>  <!-- data detected, so do calculations -->
<%
    Comm = CalcCommission(Request.Form("sales"))
    Response.Write("Your commission is: $" & Comm)
%>
<% End If %>

</BODY>
</HTML>
```

Debugging Server-Side Script Using The Microsoft Script Debugger

Before you can use the Microsoft Script Debugger, you must enable server-side script debugging in the IIS software. Refer to "Creating An Active Server Application" earlier in this Practical Guide to see how to enable debugging. Additionally, debugging on a remote machine isn't supported; therefore, you must debug on the server locally.

This example will use Listing 9.3 to illustrate using the debugger. You can also find information about using the Microsoft Script Debugger in Chapter 5. In this example, you'll see how to invoke the debugger, view variable and form element values, set breakpoints, and step through a script.

Starting The Debugger

To start debugging, request the page from the server, in this case Listing 9.3. Then, start the debugger from the Start menu. Figure 9.7 shows the debugger with the Running Documents and Command Window windows open. If these are not already open, you can bring them up with the View menu.

In the Running Documents window, you can see Listing 9.3 under /**myapp**. Double-clicking 9-3.asp displays the script source (see Figure 9.8). The script debugger is read-only, so you'll have to use another editor to make changes.

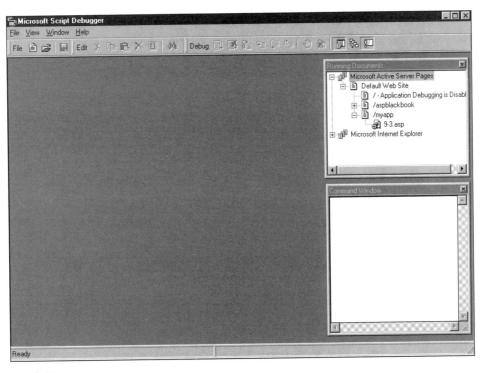

Figure 9.7

The Microsoft Script Debugger.

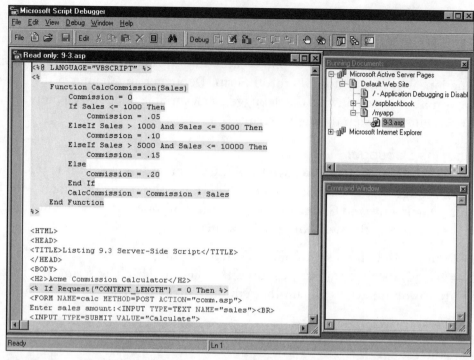

Figure 9.8

Server-side script source listing.

Setting Breakpoints

You can set a breakpoint by placing the cursor on the line where you want it and pressing F9. You can also select the Toggle Breakpoint icon (open hand) on the toolbar. Conversely, you can clear an existing breakpoint by placing the cursor on the line and pressing F9 (or the Toggle Breakpoint icon). You can also select the Clear All Breakpoints icon (open hand with a red X) on the toolbar to remove all breakpoints at once.

Figure 9.9 shows the debugger with a breakpoint set at the line that defines the form. You can tell there is a breakpoint at this line because there is a solid red circle in the left margin and the line is highlighted red.

To begin debugging, return to the browser and reload the page. When the page reloads, the script executes up to (but not including) the line with the breakpoint. When the debugger encounters the breakpoint, script execution halts, and focus returns to the debugger. Figure 9.10 shows the script source in the debugger. Now there is an arrow pointing to the line where the breakpoint stopped the script. This arrow indicates the next line to execution.

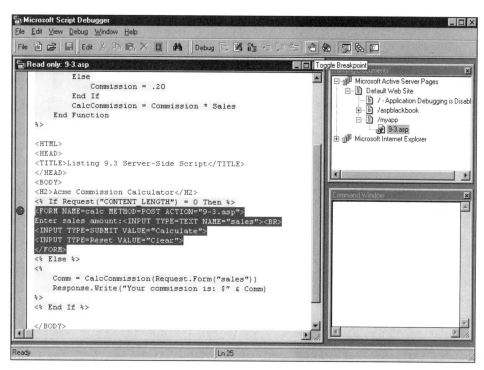

Figure 9.9

Setting breakpoints.

You can step through the program line by line using **Step Into** (F8), **Step Over** (Shift+F8), and **Step Out** (Ctrl+Shift+F8), which also have corresponding buttons on the toolbar.

- **Step Into** *(F8)*—This executes the next line of script. It allows you to follow the script line by line. If the next line is a procedure call, execution is followed into the procedure.

- **Step Over** *(Shift +F8)*—This steps over procedure calls. The called procedures are executed, but the debugger doesn't step through them.

- **Step Out** *(Ctrl+Shift +F8)*—This is used when **Step Into** stepped into a procedure and you want to step out of it and proceed to the next line following the procedure call.

If you press F8, the current line executes, and program flow continues on the line following the **End If** statement. Pressing F8 again causes you to return to the browser display. Now, you can enter a sales value and press the Calculate button. Focus then

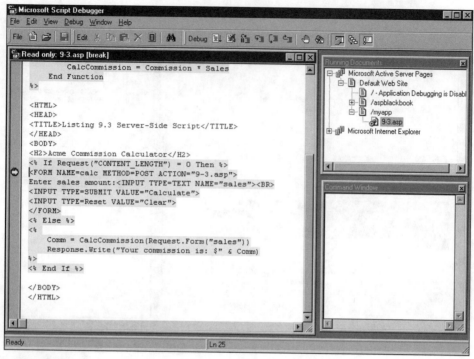

```
           CalcCommission = Commission * Sales
       End Function
%>

<HTML>
<HEAD>
<TITLE>Listing 9.3 Server-Side Script</TITLE>
</HEAD>
<BODY>
<H2>Acme Commission Calculator</H2>
<% If Request("CONTENT_LENGTH") = 0 Then %>
<FORM NAME=calc METHOD=POST ACTION="9-3.asp">
Enter sales amount:<INPUT TYPE=TEXT NAME="sales"><BR>
<INPUT TYPE=SUBMIT VALUE="Calculate">
<INPUT TYPE=Reset VALUE="Clear">
</FORM>
<% Else %>
<%
     Comm = CalcCommission(Request.Form("sales"))
     Response.Write("Your commission is: $" & Comm)
%>
<% End If %>

</BODY>
</HTML>
```

Figure 9.10

The arrow points to the next line to be executed.

switches back to the debugger, and the arrow appears on the line following the end of the **CalcCommission()** function.

You can use the Command Window to examine the value of a variable or property. To do this, click on the Command Window and enter "?" followed by the item you want to examine. Figure 9.11 shows the value of the **sales** element displayed in the Command Window.

If you continue to press F8, you'll step through the program and see the **CalcCommission()** function execute. Eventually, program flow will return you to the browser, where you'll see the result displayed.

You can also change the value of a variable during the debugging session. For example, if you want to change the value of the variable **Sales** to 5000 in the **CalcCommission()** function, you can do so by entering the statement

```
Sales = 5000
```

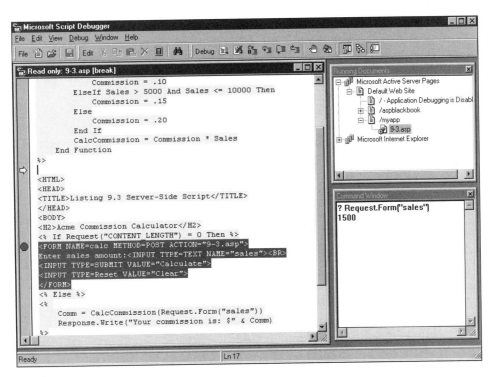

Figure 9.11

The Command Window.

in the Command Window. The script uses the new value until it finishes executing or something else changes the value.

The Microsoft Script Debugger isn't as rich with features as the Visual Basic or Visual C++ debugger, but it's certainly much better than the alternative (embedding output statements in your program, for example).

ActiveX Server Objects And Components

ActiveX server objects and installable components provide a great deal of functionality and enhancements that you can easily use in your Web applications. The server objects make it easy to perform the necessary tasks, and the installable components make it easy to add some interesting and powerful features, such as database access.

Kim Barber

Notes...

Chapter

10

One of the primary advantages to server-side scripting is the access it provides to ActiveX server objects and components. Internet Information Server (IIS) and Personal Web Server (PWS) provide built-in objects and installable components that you can use for a wide variety of tasks. Using the built-in objects, you can maintain state, perform per-application and per-user initialization, access information passed to and from the server in the Hypertext Transfer Protocol (HTTP) **Request** and **Response** headers, access information about the server, and more. Using the installable components, you can access files on the server, determine the client browser's capabilities, access databases, implement dynamic content and advertising, and much more. Additionally, you can install third-party components and write your own.

ActiveX server objects and components don't have a user interface. They perform all user input/output (I/O) via the HTML stream. Therefore, I/O is based on the capabilities of HTML, the target browsers, whether you're also using client-side script, and whether you're also using, for example, ActiveX controls and Java applets.

This chapter introduces you to ActiveX objects and components. As with everything associated with Web development, you're encouraged to visit Web sites that provide information on this topic, such as **www.microsoft.com/sitebuilder**. Also, IIS 4 and PWS will optionally install complete documentation.

What Is A Web Application?

First, you need to understand what a Web application is. In case you haven't read the previous chapter, a Web application consists of a virtual directory and all the files and directories belonging to that directory. A Web application starts when the first user requests any page in the application and ends when the server is shut down or when the application is unloaded with the IIS Service Manager. You also need to understand user sessions. The server automatically creates a session when users request their first page in the application and exists until it times out or is explicitly abandoned. The purpose of a session is to provide state for a single user. You manage applications and sessions using script and the events and objects the server provides.

The Global.asa File

Global.asa is an optional file that, as its name implies, is used globally by the application. You can have only one Global.asa file, and it lives in the application root directory. This file specifies scripts and objects that have application or session scope. It contains no content; rather, it's used mainly to manage the application and user sessions. It typically contains script to declare objects, declare and maintain global variables, maintain state, and process application and session events. Application events apply to information shared by all users, whereas session events apply to individual users.

Application Events

Application events have application-wide scope and all users share them. You might use an application event to maintain a hit counter, for example. Application events have access to the **Application** and **Server** objects (described later in this chapter). The two application events are:

- **Application_OnStart**

- **Application_OnEnd**

Application_OnStart occurs before the first user session is created and defines what happens when the application starts. **Application_OnEnd** occurs when the application quits.

The following script defines a hit counter in the **Application_OnStart** event code:

```
Sub Application_OnStart
    Application("hits") = 0
End Sub
```

Of course, this hit counter resets to zero each time the server or the application restarts. To increment the counter, a page could include this ASP code:

```
<% Application("hits")=Application("hits")+1 %>Session Events
```

Session events have session-wide scope and manage individual user sessions. For example, you can use session events to set user preferences or perform initialization and cleanup of data that applies to the session (a shopping cart, perhaps). Session events have access to all the ActiveX server objects. The two session events are:

- **Session_OnStart**

- **Session_OnEnd**

Session_OnStart occurs when the server creates a new session and processes any script prior to loading the first page. **Session_OnEnd** occurs when the session times out after a predetermined period or a script explicitly abandons it.

The following event procedure increments the site's hit counter when a new user session is created. Additionally, it defines a session variable that contains a visitor number:

```
Sub Session_OnStart
    Application("hits") = Application("hits") + 1
    Session("visitor") = Application("hits")
End Sub
```

Listing 10.1 contains all the script for the sample Global.asa file. At this point, the code doesn't attempt to handle the **Application_OnEnd** and **Session_OnEnd**.

Listing 10.1 The Global.asa file.

```
<SCRIPT LANGUAGE=VBScript RUNAT=Server>

Sub Application_OnStart
    Application("hits") = 0
End Sub

Sub Session_OnStart
    Application("hits") = Application("hits") + 1
    Session("visitor") = Application("hits")
End Sub

</SCRIPT>
```

Object Declarations

You are not required to declare intrinsic server objects, such as the **Application** and **Session** objects, before you reference them in script. You must, however, declare other objects, such as installable components, before referencing them. You can declare objects that have application or session scope in the Global.asa file or in any script in the application.

You'll use the **<OBJECT>** tag to declare objects in Global.asa:

```
<OBJECT RUNAT=Server SCOPE=Scope ID=Identifier {PROGID=ProgID | CLASSID=ClassID}
```

SCOPE is either **Application** or **Session**, (or you can omit the **SCOPE** clause for a page-level object). **ID** is a unique identifier used to reference an instance of an object, and **PROGID** is a class identifier for the object and is usually in the format:

```
[Vendor.]Component[.Version]
```

The following **<OBJECT>** tag declares an instance of the **AdRotator** component:

```
<OBJECT RUNAT=Server SCOPE=Application ID=MyAd PROGID="MSWC.AdRotator"></OBJECT>
```

Alternately, you can use the object's **CLASSID** to identify the object:

```
<OBJECT RUNAT=Server SCOPE=Application ID=MyAds
CLASSID="CLSID:1621F7C0-60AC-11CF-9427-444553540000"></OBJECT>
```

You also have the option of declaring objects in the documents where they are used. The **Server** object (discussed in the next section) provides the **CreateObject** method, which can create an object instance. If you use this method, the object's scope is limited to the current file (unless you store it in an application or session variable). Also, there's a slight performance penalty because the object is instantiated immediately. When the **<OBJECT>** tag is used in Global.asa, the object isn't instantiated until a script references it.

ActiveX Server Objects

Internet Information Server provides a number of built-in objects that provide a significant amount of functionality. Using these objects, you can access information coming from and going to the user, manage sessions, and access properties and methods on the server.

The built-in server objects are:

- **Application**
- **Session**
- **Request**
- **Response**
- **Server**
- **ObjectContext**

You need not instantiate these objects before using them. Generally, the built-in objects are almost always available, except as noted in the previous section. Only the **Application** and **Session** objects are available in the **Application_OnStart** and **Application_OnEnd** event handlers.

The **Application** Object

You use the **Application** object to share information among all users. You have already seen some use of this object because the **Application_OnStart** and **Application_OnEnd** events belong to it. Also, the hit counter in Listing 10.1 is stored in the **Application** object.

Methods

Because all users of your application share the **Application** object, you can use two methods to prevent multiple users from modifying information at the same time. These methods appear in Table 10.1.

The hit counter example is a good candidate for these methods because you don't want several users trying to increment the counter at the same time. You can modify the code in the **Session_OnStart** event to do this:

```
Sub Session_OnStart
    Application.Lock
    Application("hits") = Application("hits") + 1
    Application.Unlock
    Session("visitor") = Application("hits")
End Sub
```

This problem occurs because the script may run concurrently for multiple users. For example, suppose the hit count is currently 122. User A's script reads the value and

Table 10.1 **Application** object methods.

Method	Description
Lock	Prevents other users from modifying object properties
Unlock	Allows other users to modify object properties

adds one to it. Then the operating system preempts the thread for user A and begins user B's thread. User B's thread performs the same steps, reading 122 and adding one to it. User B's thread then stores the new value (123) before the A thread resumes. When it does, it also stores 123 in the application variable. This means you miss one count. This can also occur when the server utilizes multiple processors. Using **Lock** and **Unlock** prevents this from happening.

Collections

Two collections in the **Application** object contain items such as variables and objects. Information stored in these collections has application scope and is available throughout the application. Table 10.2 lists the **Application** object collections.

The **Contents** collection contains all items added through script, except objects defined with the **<OBJECT>** tag. *Key* specifies the name of the item. Using the hit counter, the following statement retrieves the counter's value:

```
t_hits = Application.Contents("hits")
```

You do not have to specify the **Contents** collection explicitly. The following statement produces the same result:

```
t-hits = Application("hits")Events
```

The **Application** object has only two events that you are already familiar with— **Application_OnStart** and **Application_OnEnd**.

Table 10.2 **Application** object collections.

Collection	Description	Syntax
Contents	Contains items that have been added to the object	Application.Contents(key)
StaticObjects	Contains objects created with the **<OBJECT>** tag that have application scope	Application.StaticObjects(key)

The **Session** Object

The **Session** object is very similar to the **Application** object, the primary difference being that you use the **Session** object to manage information on individual user sessions. A **Session** object is created when a user who doesn't already have a session accesses a page in the application. The object persists until it times out or is explicitly abandoned.

The **Session** object is a good place to store information about the user, including his or her color preferences, whether the client browser can display graphics or use ActiveX controls, and so on.

Methods

The **Session** object has only one method. The **Abandon** method destroys the session and all data maintained by the **Session** object for the session. By default, a user session lasts for 20 minutes (see the **Timeout** property in Table 10.3). If 20 minutes passes without the user requesting or refreshing a page, the session goes away. You can force this earlier by calling **Abandon**:

```
Session.Abandon
```

Properties

The **Session** object has the properties listed in Table 10.3.

CodePage is a character set that varies, depending on the language in use. For example, 1252 is the code page for English. An **LCID** uniquely identifies the language in use.

SessionID returns a unique identifier for each user. Don't store this ID for later use because it is valid only for the duration of the session.

Table 10.3 Session object properties.

Property	Description
CodePage	Specifies the character set code page
LCID	Specifies the locale identifier
SessionID	Returns a unique session identifier for the user
Timeout	Specifies the timeout period in minutes for the session

By default, sessions last for 20 minutes. If the user hasn't requested or refreshed a page after 20 minutes, the session goes away. You can change the 20-minute default by assigning a different value to the **Timeout** property:

```
Session.Timeout = 10
```

This statement causes the timeout to occur in 10 minutes. You can also change the timeout using the IIS Service Manager or by changing the Registry.

Collections

The **Session** object has two collections—**Contents** and **StaticObjects**. These function the same for user sessions as they do for the **Application** object. The **Contents** collection contains all the items defined for the session except those defined with the **<OBJECT>** tag. The **StaticObjects** collection contains objects defined with the **<OBJECT>** tag that have session scope.

Events

The **Session** object has the **Session_OnStart** and **Session_OnEnd** events. These events are described in the section "The Global.asa File."

The **ObjectContext** Object

You can use the **ObjectContext** object with Microsoft Transaction Server to commit or abort a transaction.

Methods

Table 10.4 describes the **ObjectContext** object's two methods.

SetComplete doesn't specifically complete the transaction. The transaction will complete when all the involved script components call **SetComplete**. Generally, you don't have to call **SetComplete** because it is assumed if none of the related script components call **SetAbort**.

Table 10.4 ObjectContext methods.

Method	Description
SetComplete	Indicates the script isn't aware of any reason for the transaction not to complete
SetAbort	Aborts the transaction

Events

The **ObjectContext** object's events are listed in Table 10.5.

The **Request** Object

You use the **Request** object to retrieve values passed from the user. This object is very useful because you can get the values sent from HTML forms or pull data directly out of the query string. Also, you can use this object to access several server environment variables. You will use the **Request** object frequently in your Web applications.

Methods

The one method in the **Request** object is the **BinaryRead** method, which is used to read the data sent from the user as part of an HTTP **POST** request and to store it in an array. Because form data is sent as a **POST** request, you can get form data with this method. However, if you do this, subsequent attempts to read the data from the **Form** collection will cause an error.

Properties

The **Request** object has one property—**TotalBytes**. This property specifies the total number of bytes being sent by the client. The following script uses **TotalBytes** and the **BinaryRead** method to read the data and to store it in an array:

```
<%
mybytes = Request.TotalBytes
myarray = Request.BinaryRead(mybytes)
%>
```

Collections

You can use several collections in the **Request** object to access server environment information, cookie data, client certificate information, and data sent in forms and query strings. Table 10.6 lists the **Request** object collections.

If a Secure Sockets Layer (SSL) protocol is in use, the **ClientCertificate** collection will contain the values stored in the certification fields. The Web server must be

Table 10.5 ObjectContext events.

Event	Description
OnTransactionCommit	Fires after the transaction commits
OnTransactionAbort	Fires when the transaction is aborted

Table 10.6 Request object collections.

Collection	Contents
ClientCertificate	The values stored in the client certificate fields
Cookies	Cookie values
Form	Form element values
QueryString	Variable values sent in the HTTP query string
ServerVariables	Environment variable values

configured to request client certificates before you can use this collection. This collection is used as follows:

```
Request.ClientCertificate(key[subfield])
```

Key specifies the name of the certification field and can be:

- **Certificate**—A string containing the entire certificate content

- **Flags**—Flags that provide additional client certificate information:

  - **ceCertPresent**—Indicates that a certificate is present

  - **ceUnrecognizedIssuer**—The last certification in the chain is unknown

- **Issuer**—A string containing a list of subfield values that contain information about the certificate's issuer

- **SerialNumber**—A string containing the certification serial number

- **Subject**—A string containing subfield values that contain subject information of the certificate

- **ValidFrom**—Specifies the date when the certificate became valid

- **ValidUntil**—Specifies the date when the certificate expires

 You must include the client certificate include file in your Active Server Pages if you use these flags. For VBScript, the include file is cevbs.inc. For JavaScript, the include file is cejavas.inc. The include files should be in the \Inetpub\ASPSamp\Samples directory.

Optionally, you can use subfield parameters with the **Issuer** and **Subject** keys. You specify the subfield by suffixing the key parameter with the following suffixes:

- **C**—Country of origin
- **CN**—User's common name (for use with the **Subject** key only)
- **GN**—A given name
- **I**—Set of initials
- **L**—Locality
- **O**—Company or organization name
- **OU**—Name of the organizational unit
- **S**—State or province
- **T**—Title of the person or organization

Using the **Cookies** collection, you can retrieve the values of cookies sent in the HTTP request. The following statement retrieves the value of a cookie named **CustomerID**:

```
t_custid = Request.Cookies("CustomerID")
```

The **Cookies** collection has an optional attribute—**key**—which you use to retrieve values from cookie dictionaries. Assuming that **CustomerID** is a dictionary with three keys—**FirstName**, **LastName**, and **AccountNumber**—you would use the following syntax to retrieve the customer's account number:

```
t_acctnum = Request.Cookies("CustomerID")("AccountNumber")
```

If you access a cookie dictionary without specifying the key, all the keys are returned as a single query string. The statement

```
t_custid = Request.Cookies("CustomerID")
```

returns

```
FirstName=thefirstname&LastName=thelastname&AccountNumber=theaccountnumber
```

The **Cookies** collection has one optional attribute—**HasKeys**—that returns **TRUE** if the cookie is a dictionary and **FALSE** if it isn't. This attribute is referenced as follows:

```
t_amiacookie = Request.Cookies("CustomerID").HasKeys
```

You can use the **Form** collection to retrieve the values of form elements passed by an HTTP **POST** request. This collection contains all the values a user entered into a form and submitted. The following syntax is used:

```
Request.Form(element)[(index)] | .Count]
```

Element specifies the name of the form element being accessed. The **Count** attribute returns the number of data items in the element. **Index** is an optional parameter that you use to access one of multiple form element values and is in the range of 1 to **Count**. For example, if you have a form element named **fish** that contains 5 values, you would access the third value as follows:

```
t_fish = Request.Form("fish")(3)
```

If you reference a form element that has multiple values and you don't specify an index, all the values will be returned in a comma-delimited string.

The following example consists of two listings. Listing 10.2 contains an HTML document with a form that collects pay data from the user. When the user clicks the Submit button, the form posts its data to the script in Listing 10.3, which retrieves the form data and calculates and displays the gross pay.

Listing 10.2   An input form.

```
<HTML>
<HEAD>
<TITLE>Listing 10.2</TITLE>
</HEAD>
<BODY>

<FORM METHOD=POST ACTION="10-3.asp">
<PRE>
Hours Worked: <INPUT TYPE=TEXT NAME="hours">
Hourly Wage:  <INPUT TYPE=TEXT NAME="wage">
<INPUT TYPE=SUBMIT VALUE="Calculate">
</PRE>
</FORM>

</BODY>
</HTML>
```

Listing 10.3   Retrieving values with the **Form** collection.

```
<HTML>
<HEAD>
<TITLE>Listing 10.3</TITLE>
</HEAD>
<BODY>
```

```
<%
   t_hours = Request.Form("hours")
   t_wage = Request.Form("wage")
   t_pay = t_hours * t_wage

  Response.Write("Gross pay: " + t_pay)
%>

</BODY>
</HTML>
```

The **Response** object is used to send output to the HTML stream and is discussed later. The **Request** object will give you a break if you don't like to type. Specifying the **Form** collection is optional. The statement

```
Request("hours")
```

also works.

The **QueryString** collection lets you retrieve the values of variables in an HTTP query string. The **QueryString** collection contains all the information passed as a parameter after the **?** in a URL or from a form if the action is **GET**. **QueryString** uses the syntax:

```
Request.QueryString("variable")[(index) | .Count]
```

Variable specifies the name of the variable name in the HTTP query string. **Index** is an optional parameter that you use to access one of multiple values for a variable. **Count** returns the number of variables in the collection.

The following HTML defines a hyperlink to a page called calcpay.asp and appends the hour and wage information as a query string to the URL:

```
<A HREF="calcpay.asp?hours=40&wage=10">Calculate Pay</A>
```

The following script in calcpay.asp uses the **QueryString** collection to retrieve the values and calculate the gross pay:

```
<%
    t_hours = Request.QueryString("hours")
    t_wage = Request.QueryString("wage")
    t_pay = t_hours * t_wage
%>
```

The **QueryString** collection is very useful if you need to retrieve values directly from a query. Using the pay calculator as an example, the following script retrieves the variable name and value from the query string:

```
<%
For Each item in Request.QueryString
    Response.Write(item + " " + Request.QueryString(item) + "<BR>")
Next
%>
```

You can use this method to retrieve name-value pairs without knowing anything about the query string.

The **ServerVariables** collection is useful for retrieving the values of several predefined environment variables. You'll find the variables in Table 10.7.

Table 10.7 The ServerVariables collection.

Variable	Description
ALL_HTTP	All HTTP headers sent by the client
ALL_RAW	All HTTP headers in raw form
APPL_MD_PATH	The metabase path for the application
APPL_PHYSICAL_PATH	The physical path for the application
AUTH_PASSWORD	The value in the client's authentication dialog box
AUTH_TYPE	The authentication method used to validate users
AUTH_USER	The raw authenticated user name
CERT_COOKIE	A unique ID for the client certificate
CERT_FLAGS	Bit 0 is set if the client certificate is present; bit 1 is set if the certifying authority isn't valid
CERT_USER	The issuer of the client certificate
CERT_KEYSIZE	The size of the SSL key in bits
CERT_SECRETKEYSIZE	The number of bits in the private key
CERT_SERIALNUMBER	The serial number of the client certificate
CERT_SERVER_ISSUER	The issuer of the server certificate

(continued)

Table 10.7 The ServerVariables collection (continued).

Variable	Description
CERT_SERVER_SUBJECT	The subject field of the server certificate
CERT_SUBJECT	The subject of the server certificate
CONTENT_LENGTH	The content length provided by the client
CONTENT_TYPE	The data type sent by the client
GATEWAY_INTERFACE	The version of the CGI specification in use by the server
HTTP_HeaderName	The value stored in the header specified by **HeaderName**
HTTPS	**ON** if the request came from a secure SSL channel; **OFF** if it came from a nonsecure channel
HTTPS_KEYSIZE	The size in bits of the SSL key
HTTP_SECRETKEYSIZE	The size in bits of the server certificate private key
HTTPS_SERVER_ISSUER	The issuer of the server certificate
HTTPS_SERVER_SUBJECT	The subject of the server certificate
INSTANCE_ID	The ID of the current instance is IIS
INSTANCE_META_PATH	The metabase path for the current instance of IIS
LOCAL_ADDR	The address on which the request came in
LOGON_USER	The NT account the user is logged into
PATH_INFO	Path information provided by the client
PATH_TRANSLATED	A version of **PATH_INFO** with any necessary virtual-to-physical mapping
QUERY_STRING	The query string
REMOTE_ADDR	The IP address of the machine making the request
REMOTE_HOST	The name of the host making the request
REMOTE_USER	The user name sent by the user
REQUEST_METHOD	The method used (for example, **POST** and **GET**)
SCRIPT_NAME	The virtual path to the executing script

(continued)

Table 10.7 The ServerVariables collection (continued).

Variable	Description
SERVER_NAME	The server's host name, DNS alias, or IP address
SERVER_PORT	The port number where the request was sent
SERVER_PORT_SECURE	Contains 1 if on a secure port; 0 if not on a secure port
SERVER_PROTOCOL	The name and version of the request information protocol
SERVER_SOFTWARE	The name and version of the server software
URL	The base URL

As you can see, the **ServerVariables** collection provides access to a lot of useful information. **CONTENT_LENGTH** is especially useful when processing forms. Using this variable, you can use the same document to collect information from the user and process the information. You can omit the collection name when using the **Request** object. If you do, IIS searches the collections in the following order: **QueryString**, **Form**, **Cookies**, **ClientCertificate**, and **ServerVariables**. The Practical Guide in Chapter 9 shows you how to do this in the example "Writing An Active Server Page."

The **Response** Object

The **Response** object provides access to the information sent in the HTTP **Response** header. You can use the **Response** object to create cookies, control caching, write content to the HTTP output stream, and several other functions.

Methods

Table 10.8 contains the **Response** object methods. In practice, you'll only use a few of these (notably **Write**).

AddHeader doesn't replace any existing header information with the same name; rather, it adds a new HTTP header. Normally, you don't need to use this method because other **Response** object methods usually provide all the functionality you need. **BinaryWrite** sends the specified data without any character conversion to the HTTP output stream. This method is useful for writing binary data, such as images.

The **Clear** method erases any buffered HTML output in the response body. You must be sure to set **Response.Buffer** to **TRUE** before using this method, or an error will occur. **End** causes the server to stop processing the ASP file and flush the buffer. Set **Response.Buffer** to **FALSE** to prevent the output to be returned. **Flush** will return an

Table 10.8 Response object methods.

Method	Description
AddHeader	Adds an HTML header
AppendToLog	Appends a string up to 80 characters to the Web server log file
BinaryWrite	Writes the specified information to the HTTP output stream
Clear	Erases any buffered HTML output
End	Stops processing of the HTML file and returns the result
Flush	Sends buffered output immediately
Redirect	Causes the browser to try connecting to another URL
Write	Writes a string to the HTTP output stream

error if **Response.Buffer** is not **TRUE**. The **Redirect** method causes the browser to try to connect to the specified URL and automatically generates a response body containing the redirect URL. Additionally, it sends the following explicit header:

```
HTTP/1.0 302 Object Moved Location URL
```

The **Write** method writes a string to the HTTP output stream and is generally equivalent to the = character used to send output in server-side script delimiters (**<%...%>**).

Properties

You'll find the list of **Response** object's properties in Table 10.9.

You use the **Buffer** property to specify whether to buffer output. If **Buffer** is set to **TRUE**, the server will not send a response until all the scripts in the current page are finished executing or until **Flush** or **End** are called. **FALSE** is the default setting. You use **CacheControl** to override the **Private** default value. Proxy servers can cache ASP output if you set this property to **Public**. **ContentType** is set to a string in the HTTP format **type/subtype**.

The **Expires** property controls when a page is reloaded. If the user refreshes a page before the specified time elapses, the page is read from the browser's cache. If it is refreshed after the time elapses, the page is reloaded. In some cases, you might want the user to get a new page every time he or she requests it. For example, the page might display the current outdoor temperature. To cause this to happen, set **Expires** to zero.

Table 10.9 **Response** object properties.

Property	Description
Buffer	Specifies whether to buffer output
CacheControl	Overrides the **Private** default value
Charset	Appends the character set name to the HTTP content-type header
ContentType	Specifies the HTTP content type for the response
Expires	Specifies the length of time before a cached page expires
ExpiresAbsolute	Specifies the date and time when a cached page expires
IsClientConnected	Indicates whether the client has disconnected from the server since the last **Response.Write**
Pics	Adds a value to the response header pics-label field
Status	Specifies the value of the HTTP status line returned by the server

You can use the **Status** property to specify the value of the HTTP status returned by the server. The status string consists of a three-digit number followed by a brief description.

Collections

The **Response** object has only one collection—**Cookies**. You use the **Cookies** collection to set cookie values. If the cookie doesn't exist, you create it with the following syntax:

```
Response.Cookies(name)[(key) | .attribute] = "value"
```

If you want to create a cookie dictionary, you specify the key name and assign it a value. For example, the following creates a cookie with two keys:

```
Response.Cookies("CustomerID")("LastName") = "Smith"
Response.Cookies("CustomerID")("FirstName") = "John"
```

The **Server** Object

The **Server** object provides access to properties and methods on the server. The methods provided are mainly utility functions.

Methods

Table 10.10 describes the methods available with the **Server** object.

You use **CreateObject** to create an instance of a server component, such as **AdRotator**. Recall from the discussion on Global.asa that you can also create an instance of a server component with the **<OBJECT>** tag. The server immediately instantiates objects created with **CreateObject**. If you use the **<OBJECT>** tag the server doesn't actually create the object until a script uses it.

The statement

```
<% Set myad = Server.CreateObject("MSWC.AdRotator")%>
```

sets **myad** to reference an instance of the **AdRotator** component.

Objects created with **CreateObject** have page scope by default. If you need an object to have application or session scope, create it with the **<OBJECT>** tag, and specify the scope or store the object in an application or session variable. The following statement creates an instance of the **AdRotator** component with the session scope:

```
<OBJECT RUNAT=Server SCOPE=Session
  ID=myad PROGID="MSWC.AdRotator">
</OJBECT>
```

HTMLEncode is used to apply HTML encoding to a string. This is frequently useful if you want to display unparsed HTML tags in the browser display. For example

```
<% s=Server.HTMLEncode("This is the <OBJECT> tag.") %>
```

sets variable **s** to:

```
This is the &It;OBJECT&gt; tag.
```

Table 10.10 Server object methods.

Method	Description
CreateObject	Creates an instance of a server component
HTMLEncode	Applies HTML encoding to the specified string
MapPath	Returns the physical path for the specified relative path
URLEncode	Applies URL encoding to the specified string

MapPath is useful if you need to write to disk and don't know, or don't want to know, what the physical path is. To illustrate this method, let's revise the sample Global.asa file to save the hit counter to disk. Listing 10.4 contains the revised script.

Listing 10.4 Using the **MapPath** method.

```
<SCRIPT LANGUAGE=VBScript RUNAT=Server>
Sub Application_OnStart
    Application("hits") = 0
    fname = Server.MapPath("/ch10") + "\hits.txt"
    Set fs = Server.CreateObject("Scripting.FileSystemObject")
    set out = fs.OpenTextFile(fname, 1, FALSE, FALSE)
    Application("hits") = out.ReadLine
    out.close
End Sub

Sub Session_OnStart
    Application.Lock
    Application("hits") = Application("hits") + 1
    Application.Unlock
    Session("visitor") = Application("hits")
    fname = Server.MapPath("/ch10") + "\hits.txt"
    Set fs = Server.CreateObject("Scripting.FileSystemObject")
    set out = fs.CreateTextFile(fname, TRUE, FALSE)
    out.WriteLine(Session("visitor"))
    out.close
End Sub

</SCRIPT>
```

In the **Application_OnStart** event handler, the **MapPath** method is used to assign the physical path with a file name to the variable **fname**. **MapPath** converts the logical application path, which on my computer is http://localhost/Ch10, to the physical path, which is C:\WebShare\wwwroot\Ch10. The **FileSystemObjet** component creates the file where the program will store the hit value. You'll read more about the **FileSystemObject** later in this chapter.

The **Session_OnStart** event handler updates hits.txt every time the server creates a new session.

URLEncode applies URL encoding to the specified string. This method is frequently useful if you are building HTTP query strings dynamically. Whenever the browser sends a string in a query string, it encodes spaces and other characters with special characters. This encoding is necessary for successfully transmitting the string.

Conclusion

The ActiveX server objects provide the functionality that is needed to manage the application and user sessions. The ability to tap into the HTTP **Request** and **Response** headers gives you substantial capability to retrieve and manage user input and to return output.

Although some of the server objects have obscure purposes, you'll find that many of the methods in **Response** and **Request** are crucial for handling forms. Once you are accustomed to using them, variables in the **Session** and **Application** objects are very handy as well.

ActiveX Components

ActiveX components are installable components that run on the server as part of the Web application. They are based on the Microsoft Component Object Model (COM), which is a standard that defines how programs can create and use binary objects (as opposed to, for example, C++ or Java objects, which are objects only at the source code level). Server components generally provide functionality that is routinely needed, such as database and file access. For the purposes of this book, you'll use ActiveX components only with Web pages, but you can also use them in many other types of applications, such as a Visual Basic or C++ program

You can include server components in your application using two methods. The first method uses the **Server** object **CreateObject** method:

```
<% Set myadd = Server.CreateObject("MSWC.AdRotator") %>
```

The second method uses the **<OBJECT>** tag:

```
<OBJECT RUNAT=Server SCOPE=Application ID=myad PROGID="MSWC.AdRotator"></OBJECT>
```

The first method causes the object to be instantiated immediately, and the scope of the object is limited to the document in which it is declared. When the second method is used, the object isn't instantiated until it is referenced in script, at which time it has either application or session scope. Therefore, you can reference the object anywhere it's in scope.

The remainder of this chapter introduces you to the components provided with IIS and PWS. Examples of using many of these components are in this chapter's Practical Guide. Microsoft provides the following base components:

- **AdRotator**

- **Browser Capabilities**

- **Content Linking**

- **Database Access**

- **File Access**

The **AdRotator** Component

Advertising is the traditional way to generate revenue from the Web. Many sites display ads and provide links to advertisers' Web sites. The **AdRotator** component makes it very easy to do this. This component automates the display of different advertisements each time the user opens or reloads a page and will optionally jump to the specified Web site when the user clicks on the ad. Using the **AdRotator** component requires three files: the ASP file that displays the ad, the Rotator Schedule file that manages the ads, and a redirection file that takes care of jumping to the advertiser's Web site (and possibly logging the hit).

The Rotator Schedule File

The **AdRotator** component uses a Rotator Schedule file to maintain information that it uses to manage and display the various ads. The Rotator Schedule file contains the details of each ad, including the size of the ad's display area, the percentage of time the ad is displayed, the image to display, and the advertiser's URL.

The Rotator Schedule file has two sections. The first section is optional and contains information that pertains to all ads in the schedule. The second section specifies information for each ad. An asterisk (*) separates the two sections. If you omit the first section, place an asterisk in the first line of the file.

The first section can take any of the optional parameters in Table 10.11.

The second section of the Rotator Schedule file contains up to four parameters for each ad. Table 10.12 lists the available parameters.

If the advertiser doesn't have a Web site, enter a hyphen (-) for the **adHomePageURL**. **Impressions** specifies the relative percentage of time an ad is displayed. The total for all ads in the file should be 100. Keep in mind that the component selects ads at random, using the **impressions** number as a guide.

Table 10.11   Optional Rotator Schedule file parameters.

Parameter	Description
Redirect	Path to the file that implements redirection
Border	Thickness of the border around the ad, default is 1
Height	Height of the display area in pixels, default is 60
Width	Width of the display area in pixels, default is 440

Table 10.12   Available advertisement parameters.

Parameter	Description
adURL	Location of the ad image file
adHomePageURL	Location of the advertiser's home page
text	Alternate text for nongraphical browsers
impressions	The percentage of time an ad is displayed

The Redirection File

You must supply a Redirection file to send the user to the advertiser's Web site. This file generally includes the following line of script that parses the query string sent by the **AdRotator** object:

```
<% Response.Redirect(Request.QueryString("URL")) %>
```

The *GetAdvertisement* Method

The **AdRotator** component has one method—**GetAdvertisement**—that retrieves the next ad from the Rotator Schedule file.

A complete example of using the **AdRotator** component is included in this chapter's Practical Guide.

The **Browser Capabilities** Component

The **Browser Capabilities** component provides information about the client browser's capabilities. When the client browser connects to the Web server, it sends an HTTP **Request** header, which sends a variety of information about the browser. One piece of information it sends—the **User-Agent** header—is a string that contains the browser name and version. You can use this information to send output that is customized according to the client's capabilities. For example, you don't want to send client-side VBScript to a browser that doesn't support it.

The **Browser Capabilities** component compares the **User-Agent** header to header entries in a special file, Browscap.ini, which is on the server in the directory \WINNT\system32\inetsrv in NT Server and \ProgramFiles\WEBSVR\SYSTEM\ASP \Cmpnts on PWS in Windows 95. This file contains information on the capabilities supported by various browsers, identified by the **User-Agent** header. It is important to realize that the server doesn't really know what the browser can or can't do—it only knows what the Browscap.ini file says about a given user agent string. The following is a sample browser definition:

```
; browscap.ini
[Netscape 3.0]
browser=Netscape
version=3.0
majorver=#3
minorver=#0
frames=TRUE
tables=TRUE
cookies=TRUE
backgroundsounds=FALSE
vbscript=FALSE
javascript=TRUE
ActiveXControls=FALSE

[Mozilla/3.0b5 (Win95; I)]
parent=Netscape 3.0
platform=Win95
```

The first line, a comment, is indicated by a semicolon. The **User-Agent** identifier is enclosed in brackets and is followed by the definitions for that browser. You can make changes to this file to add or remove capabilities and complete definitions.

Browser is an optional parameter that specifies the HTTP **User-Agent** header of a browser to use as a parent browser. **Parent** allows the second browser definition to inherit from the first. Inherited properties remain set unless they are overwritten in the browser definition.

Table 10.13 lists some of the possible entries in Browscap.ini.

An example of using the **Browser Capabilities** component is included in this chapter's Practical Guide.

Table 10.13 Possible Browscap.ini entries.

Property	Description
ActiveXControls	Indicates whether ActiveX controls are supported
backgroundsounds	Indicates whether background sounds are supported
beta	Indicates whether the browser is beta software
browser	Indicates the name of the browser
cdf	Indicates whether the browser supports the Channel Definition Format
cookies	Indicates whether cookies are supported
frames	Indicates whether frames are supported
Javaapplets	Indicates whether Java applets are supported
javascript	Indicates whether JavaScript is supported
platform	Indicates the platform the browser runs on
tables	Indicates whether tables are supported
vbscript	Indicates whether VBScript is supported
version	Indicates the version number of the browser

The **Content Linking** Component

Most Web pages contain links to other pages on the same site, and managing these links can sometimes be a bit of work. If your Web application consists of several pages with Next and Previous links, you often need to make changes to multiple pages as pages are added to or removed from the application.

The **Content Linking** component simplifies keeping track of these links by managing them as though the Web pages are pages in a book. Using this component, you can include jumps to the next or previous Web pages in a list of URLs you create that automatically change when your content changes. Better still, you can write script to handle the previous and next linking and include this one file in each page. Another possibility is to use the content linking component to automatically generate an index for your site.

The Content Linking List File

The **Content Linking** component references a Content Linking List file that contains a list of the linked Web pages. This file contains a line of information for each URL in the list. Only two pieces of information are necessary: the URL and a description. This information is separated by one **Tab**, and the line ends with a hard return (Enter):

```
Web page URL TAB description [TAB comment]CR
```

You can also include an optional comment. Be careful. The component insists that you separate the fields using a real tab character and not some number of blank spaces. Depending on the text editor you use, you may have to do something special to insert an actual tab.

The **Web page URL** is the relative, or virtual, URL of the Web page. You can't use absolute URLs, such as those that begin with **http:**, **//**, or ****.

Methods

The **Content Linking** component provides methods to move through and retrieve information from the Content Linking List file. These methods are listed in Table 10.14.

An example of using the **Content Linking** component is included in this chapter's Practical Guide.

Table 10.14 Content Linking component methods.

Method	Description
GetListCount	Returns the number of items in the list file
GetNextURL	Returns the URL of the next page in the list
GetPreviousDescription	Returns the description of the previous page in the list
GetListIndex	Returns the index of the current page in the list
GetNthDescription	Returns the description of the nth page in the list
GetPreviousURL	Returns the URL of the previous page in the list
GetNextDescription	Returns the description of the next page in the list
GetNthURL	Returns the URL of the nth page in the list

The **Database Access** Component

The **Database Access** component uses Active Data Objects (ADOs) to provide access to information stored in Open Database Connectivity (ODBC) data sources. You can easily add database access to your Web applications using ADO, which consists of an object model with the following objects:

- **Command**—Defines a specific command that can be executed against a data source

- **Connection**—Represents an open connection to a data source

- **Error**—Contains details pertaining to data access errors

- **Field**—Represents a column of data within a **Recordset**

- **Parameter**—Represents a parameter or argument associated with a parameterized **Command**

- **Property**—Represents a characteristic of an ADO object that is defined by the provider

- **Recordset**—Represents the set of records returned from a query

This chapter provides an introduction to ADO and uses only the **Connection** and **Recordset** objects to read and write to a database.

The **Connection** Object

A **Connection** object represents a unique connection to a data source. This object has several properties and methods that the underlying database may or may not support. Table 10.15 contains the **Connection** object properties. The **Connection** object's methods appear in Table 10.16.

The **Recordset** Object

The **Recordset** object is the main interface to the data. It represents the set of records from a table or the results of a command that has been executed. **Recordset** objects are constructed using records (rows) and fields (columns). The **Recordset** object references a single record at a time in the current record set.

The following script generates a record set from the data source **custdb**:

```
<%
Set Conn = Server.CreateObject("ADODB.Connection")
Conn.Open "custdb"
```

Table 10.15 Connection object properties.

Property	Description
Attributes	References one or more attributes of an object
ConnectionString	Contains information used to establish a connection to a data source
CommandTimeout	Specifies how long to wait while executing a command before timing out
DefaultDatabase	Specifies the default database
IsolationLevel	Specifies the level of isolation
Mode	Specifies the available permissions for modifying data in a connection
Provider	Specifies the provider's name
Version	Indicates the ADO version number

Table 10.16 Connection object methods.

Method	Description
BeginTrans	Begins a new transaction
Close	Closes an open object and dependent objects
CommitTrans	Saves changes and ends the transaction
Execute	Executes the specified query, SQL statement, or stored procedure
Open	Opens a connection to a data source
RollbackTrans	Cancels any changes and ends the transaction

```
Set RS = Conn.Execute("SELECT * FROM custinfo")
%>
```

You can also create **Recordset** objects without using a previously defined **Connection** object. You do this by passing a connection string with the **Open** method. Here is an example:

```
<%
Set RS = Server.CreateObject("ADODB.Recordset")
RS.Open "SELECT * FROM custinfo","custdb",3,3
%>
```

The **Open** method uses the following syntax:

```
recordset.Open source, ActiveConnection,CursorType,LockType
```

The ADO still creates a **Connection** object in the previous example but doesn't assign it to a variable. If you're assigning multiple **Recordset** objects over the same connection, you should explicitly create a **Connection** object. Otherwise, ADO creates a new **Connection** object for each **Recordset** object.

The **Recordset** object has two collections: **Fields** and **Properties**. The **Fields** collection consists of **Field** objects, each corresponding to a column in the record set. You can refer to a **Field** object by its **Name** property or by its number. For example:

```
RS.Fields.Item(0)
RS.Fields.Item("CustomerID")
RS.Fields(0)
RS.Fields("CustomerID")
RS.("CustomerID")
```

The **Properties** collection consists of **Property** objects. Each **Property** object corresponds to a characteristic of the ADO object specific to the provider. The following example displays the property names of a **Connection** object:

```
<%
Set Conn = Server.CreateObject("ADODB.Connection")
Conn.Open "custdb"
%>
<% For I = 0 to Conn.Properties.Count - 1 %>
<% =Conn.Properties(I) %>
<BR>
<% Next %>
```

The **Recordset** object's properties are listed in Table 10.17.

Table 10.18 lists the **Recordset** object's methods.

You'll find an example of using ADO to write to and read a database in this chapter's Practical Guide.

The **File Access** Component

The **File Access** component uses the **FileSystemObject** to provide access to the file system on the server. You can use the **FileSystemObject** to create, read from, and write to, disk files. The **FileSystemObject** has numerous methods for general use with VBScript and JavaScript, but only two are of interest here:

Table 10.17 Recordset object properties.

Property	Description
AbsolutePage	Specifies to which page to move for a new record
AbsolutePosition	Specifies the ordinal position of a **Recordset** object's current record
ActiveConnection	Specifies to which connection object the specified **Command** or **Recordset** object belongs
BOF	Indicates that the current record position is before the first record
Bookmark	Returns a bookmark that identifies the current record or sets the current record to the record identified by a valid bookmark
Cachesize	Specifies the number of records that are cached locally in memory
CursorLocation	Specifies the location of the cursor engine
CursorType	Specifies the cursor type
EditMode	Specifies the editing status of the current record
EOF	Indicates the current record position after the last record
Filter	Specifies a filter
LockType	Specifies the type of locks placed on records during editing
MarshalOptions	Specifies which records are to marshal back to the server
MaxRecords	Specifies the maximum number of records to return to a record set
PageCount	Specifies the number of pages of data the object contains
PageSize	Specifies the number of records constituting one page
RecordCount	Specifies the current number of records in the object
Source	Indicates the source of data or the name of the object or application that generated an error
State	Indicates the object's current state
Status	Indicates the current record's status with respect to batch updates or bulk operations

Table 10.18   Recordset object methods.

Method	Description
AddNew	Creates a new record
CancelBatch	Cancels a pending batch update
CancelUpdate	Cancels changes made to the current record or to a new record prior to calling the Update method
Clone	Creates a duplicate Recordset object from an existing object
Close	Closes an open object and dependent objects
Delete	Deletes the current record
GetRows	Retrieves multiple records into an array
Move	Moves the position of the current record
MoveFirst	Moves to the first record
MoveLast	Moves to the last record
MoveNext	Moves to the next record
MovePrevious	Moves to the previous record
NextRecordset	Clears the current object and returns the next record set by advancing through a series of commands
Open	Opens a cursor
Requery	Updates the record set by re-executing the query
Resynch	Refreshes the data in the current object
Supports	Determines whether a specified object supports a specified type of functionality
Update	Saves changes made to the current record
UpdateBatch	Writes all pending batch updates

- **Open Text File**—Opens the specified file

- **CreateTextFile**—Creates the specified file

The **FileSystemObject** appears earlier in this chapter during the discussion of the Global.asa file. There, it creates the hit counter's text file. The following script creates and writes to the file:

```
Set fs = Server.CreateObject("Scripting.FileSystemObject")
Set out = fs.OpenTextFile(fname, 1, FALSE, FALSE)
Application("hits") = out.ReadLine
out.close
```

OpenTextFile uses the following syntax:

```
object.OpenTextFile( fname[, iomode][, create][, format])
```

The optional parameter **Iomode** can indicate **ForReading** (1) or **ForAppending** (2). **Create** specifies whether the object can create a new file if one doesn't already exist. **Format** specifies the **Tristate** value to indicate the format of the opened file and can be one of the following:

- **TristateTrue**—Opens the file as unicode

- **TristateFalse**—Opens the file as ASCII (default)

- **TristateUseDefault**—Opens the file using the system default

CreateTextFile uses the following syntax:

```
object.CreateTextFile( fname,[overwrite][,unicode])
```

Overwrite is an optional value that indicates whether the object can overwrite an existing file (the default is **False**). **Unicode** is also optional. It indicates if the file uses UNICODE (16-bit characters). The default is **False**, which causes the file to use ASCII (or ANSI, if you prefer).

Both these methods return a **TextStream** object, which provides the actual file access. The **TextStream** object has the methods listed in Table 10.19.

The **TextStreamobject** has the properties listed in Table 10.20.

An example of using the **FileSystemObject** and **TextStream** object is included in this chapter's Practical Guide.

Summary

ActiveX server objects and components do a lot to extend the capabilities already provided by server-side script. As you have seen, the built-in objects give you the

Table 10.19 TextStream object methods.

Method	Description
Close	Closes the file
Read	Reads a specified number of characters
ReadAll	Reads all the characters from a file
ReadLine	Reads the next line
Size	Returns the size of the file in bytes
Skip	Skips a specified number of characters
SkipLine	Skips the next line
Write	Writes a string to a file
WriteLine	Writes a string followed by a new-line character
WriteBlankLines	Writes empty lines

Table 10.20 TextStreamObject properties.

Property	Description
AtEndOfLine	Returns TRUE if the file pointer is at the end of the line
AtEndOfStream	Returns TRUE if the file pointer is at the end of the file
Column	Returns the column number of the current character position
Line	Returns the current line number

needed access to the HTTP stream as well as access to information in the server environment. They also provide a very convenient way of managing the application and individual user sessions. The installable components go even further by providing powerful database access and other features to enhance your Web applications. In the Practical Guide, you'll see examples of using all the built-in objects and many of the installable components of ActiveX.

Using ActiveX Server Objects And Components

- Using Global.asa
- Using The **AdRotator** Component
- Using The **Database Access** Component
- Using The **Browser Capabilities** Component
- Using The **Content Linking** Component

Using Global.asa

Listing 10.5 contains a Global.asa file with scripts that manage the application's hit counter, user information, and cookies. Additionally, it uses the **FileSystemObject** to access disk files on the server.

The **Application_OnStart** event handler creates a hit counter variable. The value of the hit counter variable is saved to disk in the **Session_OnStart** event handler. The **Application_OnStart** event handler checks for the presence of this file in case the server is being restarted. The **Application_OnStart** event handler also checks for a file that stores the most recent customer number. This value is used to assign customer numbers to cookies.

The code in the **Session_OnStart** event handler increments the hit counter and assigns this value to a visitor variable for the individual session. The script then writes the value of the visitor variable to the hit counter file. Then the script checks to see whether a cookie was sent as part of the HTTP request. If it was not, the code assumes that this is a new visitor. Therefore, the script increments the customer number variable and assigns the new number as a cookie. Also set are the customer status (0 for a new customer) and the cookie's **Expires** property. To keep permanent track of the number, the code updates the customer number file with the new value. Finally, a session variable receives the customer number for future use during the session.

Listing 10.6 uses the cookie's **Status** value, which contains the script for the default page. If the status is 0, the page redirects the customer to the new member registration page. If the status is not 0, the redirection points to the site's home page.

Listing 10.7 contains the script for the site's home page. Returning customers automatically see this page. This simple example retrieves the customer's name and favorite cuisine information from the cookie and displays a welcome message.

Listing 10.5   A Global.asa file.

```
<SCRIPT LANGUAGE=VBScript RUNAT=Server>

Sub Application_OnStart
    Application("hits") = 0
    Application("cust_num") = 0
    fname = Server.MapPath("/ch10") + "\hits.txt"
    Set fs = Server.CreateObject("Scripting.FileSystemObject")
    Set out = fs.OpenTextFile(fname, 1, FALSE, FALSE)
    Application("hits") = out.ReadLine
    out.close
    fname = Server.MapPath("/ch10") + "\cust_num.txt"
    Set fs = Server.CreateObject("Scripting.FileSystemObject")
```

```
        Set out = fs.OpenTextFile(fname, 1, FALSE, FALSE)
        Application("cust_num") = out.ReadLine
        out.close
End Sub

Sub Application_OnEnd
        ' do any necessary cleanup
End Sub

Sub Session_OnStart
        Application.Lock
        Application("hits") = Application("hits") + 1
        Session("visitor") = Application("hits")

        fname = Server.MapPath("/ch10") + "\hits.txt"
        Set fs = Server.CreateObject("Scripting.FileSystemObject")
        Set out = fs.CreateTextFile(fname, TRUE, FALSE)
        out.WriteLine(Session("visitor"))
        out.close

        If Request.Cookies("CustomerID")("Cust_Num") = Empty Then
             Application("cust_num") = Application("cust_num") + 1
             Response.Cookies("CustomerID")("Cust_Num") = Application("cust_num")
             Response.Cookies("CustomerID")("Status") = 0
             Response.Cookies("CustomerID").Expires = #December 31, 1999#
             fname = Server.MapPath("/ch10") + "\cust_num.txt"
             Set fs = Server.CreateObject("Scripting.FileSystemObject")
             Set out = fs.CreateTextFile(fname, TRUE, FALSE)
             out.WriteLine(Request.Cookies("CustomerID")("Cust_Num"))
             out.close
        End If
        Application.Unlock
        Session("cust_num") = Request.Cookies("CustomerID")("Cust_Num")
End Sub

Sub Session_OnEnd
        ' do any necessary cleanup
End Sub
</SCRIPT>
```

Listing 10.6 The default page.

```
<%@ LANGUAGE="VBSCRIPT" %>
<%
If Request.Cookies("CustomerID")("Status") = 0 Then
        Response.Redirect "10-8.asp"
Else
        Response.Redirect "10-7.asp"
End If
%>
```

```
<HTML>
<HEAD>
<TITLE>The Default Page</TITLE>
</HEAD>
<BODY>
</BODY>
</HTML>
```

Listing 10.7   The site's home page.
```
<%@ LANGUAGE="VBSCRIPT" %>
<%
    fname = Request.Cookies("CustomerID")("fname")
    lname = Request.Cookies("CustomerID")("lname")
    cuisine = Request.Cookies("CustomerID")("cuisine")
%>


<HTML>
<HEAD>
<TITLE>Community Dining Club Home Page</TITLE>
</HEAD>
<BODY>

<FONT COLOR=BLUE>
<H1 ALIGN=CENTER>Community Dining Club</H1>
</FONT>
<FONT SIZE=4 COLOR=BLUE>
Welcome back <% =fname & " " & lname %>!<P>
</FONT>
</BODY>
</HTML>
```

Using The **AdRotator** Component

The new member registration page (see Listing 10.8) uses the **AdRotator** component to display advertising that changes when the page loads (or reloads). This
example contains only three ads: Al's Mexican Palace, Paul's China Garden, and
Kim's Steak House. When the user clicks on the ads, he or she sees the appropriate
Web page.

The **AdRotator** component uses a Rotator Schedule file to maintain information
about the ads. Listing 10.9 contains the code for this file. The **GetAdvertisement**
method retrieves the information from the Rotator Schedule file. Notice the equal
sign (=) preceding the call to **GetAdvertisement**. This is necessary but easy to forget.

If you forget to include this character, the component will not display the ad. In-stead, it will generate all the HTML required and the server will throw it away.

Listing 10.10 contains the script that implements the redirection to the advertiser's Web site.

Listing 10.8 The new member registration page.

```
<%@ LANGUAGE="VBSCRIPT" %>
<% Response.Expires = 0 %>
<% Set myad = Server.CreateObject("MSWC.AdRotator") %>
<% =myad.GetAdvertisement("10-9.txt") %>


<HTML>
<HEAD>
<TITLE>New Member Registration</TITLE>
</HEAD>
<BODY>
<H2 Align=Center>New Member Registration</H2>
<HR SIZE=5 WIDTH=90%>


<P ALIGN=CENTER>
<TABLE>
<TD>
<PRE>
<FORM METHOD=POST ACTION="10-11.asp">
<B>First Name:  </B><INPUT TYPE=TEXT NAME="firstname">
<B>Last Name:  </B><INPUT TYPE=TEXT NAME="lastname">
<B>Address1: </B><INPUT TYPE=TEXT NAME="addr1">
<B>Address2:  </B><INPUT TYPE=TEXT NAME="addr2">
<B>City:  </B><INPUT TYPE=TEXT NAME="city">
<B>State:  </B><INPUT TYPE=TEXT NAME="state" MAXLENGTH=2 SIZE=2>
<B>Zip:  </B><INPUT TYPE=TEXT NAME="zip" MAXLENGTH=10 SIZE=10>
<B>Area Code/Phone: </B><INPUT TYPE=TEXT NAME="code" MAXLENGTH=3 SIZE=3>
<INPUT TYPE=TEXT NAME="phone" MAXLENGTH=7 SIZE=7>

<B>Preferred Cuisine: </B><SELECT NAME="cuisine" SIZE="1">
                        <OPTION VALUE="1">American
                        <OPTION VALUE="2">Chinese
                        <OPTION VALUE="3">French
                        <OPTION VALUE="4">German
                        <OPTION VALUE="5">Greek
                        <OPTION VALUE="6">Indian
                        <OPTION VALUE="7">Italian
                        <OPTION VALUE="8">Japanese
                        <OPTION VALUE="9">Seafood
                        <OPTION VALUE="0">Other
                        </SELECT>
```

```
<INPUT TYPE=SUBMIT VALUE="Register"> <INPUT TYPE="RESET" VALUE="Clear">
</PRE>
</FORM>
</TD>
</TABLE>
</P>
</BODY>
</HTML>
```

Listing 10.9 The Rotator Schedule file.
```
--------------- Rotator Schedule ---------------------
REDIRECT 10-10.asp
width 440
height 60
border 0
*
als.bmp
http://morticia/ch10/als.asp
Enjoy Al's authentic Mexican food!
34
pauls.bmp
http://morticia/ch10/pauls.asp
Hunan is Paul's specialty!
33
kims.bmp
http://morticia/ch10/kims.asp
Huge Texas style steak!
33
```

Listing 10.10 The Redirect file.
```
<%@ LANGUAGE="VBSCRIPT" %>
<!-- Note: Could redirect to a local page that counts the hit and redirects to the
sponsor's URL. -->
<% Response.Redirect(Request.QueryString("URL")) %>
```

Using The **Database Access** Component

The **Database Access** component uses ADOs to access ODBC data sources. The ADO makes is very easy to write to and update databases. The following example uses ADO to write new member information to a Microsoft Access database named custdb.mdb.

The new member registration page shown in Listing 10.8 contains a form that collects information from the user. You can view Listing 10.8 in the previous example on the **AdRotator** component. The **ACTION** attribute specifies Listing 10.11 as the page to post the form data to.

The script in Listing 10.11 first creates a **Connection** object and then assigns it to **Conn**. The **Open** method opens a connection to the data source. **Custdb** is the Data Source Name (DSN) that references the database.

The script creates a **Recordset** object and assigns it to **RS**. Then the program uses the recordset to open a connection to the table **custinfo**, which holds all the data entered into the HTML form as well as the customer number and status (from the user's cookie).

Each field in the **custinfo** table receives values from the form. The **Request** object accesses the values posted to this page. When the program places data in the fields of the **Recordset** variable, it effectively places them in the database (subject to an **Update** call, of course).

After the program writes to the database and closes the connection, it updates the user's cookie with the additional information from the form.

Listing 10.11   Using Active Data Objects.

```
<%@ LANGUAGE="VBSCRIPT" %>
<%
set Conn = Server.CreateObject("ADODB.Connection")
Conn.Open "custdb"
Set RS = Server.CreateObject("ADODB.Recordset")
Conn.BeginTrans
RS.Open "custinfo",Conn,3,3
RS.AddNew
RS("fname") = Request("firstname")
RS("lname") = Request("lastname")
RS("addr1") = Request("addr1")
RS("addr2") = Request("addr2")
RS("city") = Request("city")
RS("state") = Request("state")
RS("zip") = Request("zip")
RS("area") = Request("code")
RS("phone") = Request("phone")
RS("cuisine") = Request("cuisine")
RS("cnum") = Request.Cookies("CustomerID")("cust_num")
RS.Update
Conn.CommitTrans
RS.Close
Conn.Close

Response.Cookies("CustomerID")("fname") = Request("firstname")
Response.Cookies("CustomerID")("lname") = Request("lastname")
Response.Cookies("CustomerID")("cuisine") = Request("cuisine")
Response.Cookies("CustomerID")("Status") = 1
```

```
%>
<HTML>
<HEAD>
<TITLE>New Member</TITLE>
</HEAD>
<BODY>
Member Registered
</BODY>
</HTML>
```

Listings 10.12 and 10.13 show how to access a specific record in the database. Listing 10.12 consists of a simple HTML document where the user enters a customer number. The script posts that value to Listing 10.13, which does the lookup and displays the record.

Listing 10.13 assigns an SQL query string to the variable **queryString** and passes the string to the **Connection** object's **Execute** method. You can access the results of the query using the record set variable **RS**, which will contain the complete set of records resulting from the query. In this example, it should return only one record, assuming that a record is found, because the customer number should be a unique value. The script in the document body is written to display all the records contained in a record set object in an HTML table.

Listing 10.12 A simple HTML form.
```
<HTML>
<HEAD>
<TITLE>Find Customer</TITLE>
</HEAD>
<BODY>

<H2 ALIGN=CENTER>Find Customer</H2>
<PRE>
<FORM METHOD=POST ACTION="10-13.asp">
Customer Number: <INPUT TYPE=TEXT NAME="cust_num">
                            <INPUT TYPE=SUBMIT VALUE="Find">
</FORM>
</PRE>
</BODY>
</HTML>
```

Listing 10.13 Searching with Active Data Objects.
```
<%@ LANGUAGE="VBSCRIPT" %>
<%
Set Conn = Server.CreateObject("ADODB.Connection")
Conn.Open "custdb"
```

```
queryString = "SELECT * FROM custinfo WHERE cnum = " & _
     "'" & Request("cust_num") & "'"
Set RS = Conn.Execute(queryString)
%>

<HTML>
<HEAD>
<TITLE>Customer Lookup</TITLE>
</HEAD>
<BODY>
<H2 ALIGN=CENTER>Find Customer</H2>
<TABLE BORDER=1>
<TR>
<% For i = 0 to RS.Fields.Count - 1 %>
<TD><B><% =RS(i).Name %></B></TD>
<% Next %>
</TR>
<% Do While Not RS.EOF %>
<TR>
<% For i = 0 to RS.Fields.Count - 1 %>
<TD VALIGN=TOP><% =RS(i) %></TD>
<% Next %>
</TR>
<%   RS.MoveNext
     Loop
     RS.Close
%>
</TABLE>
</BODY>
</HTML>
```

Using The **Browser Capabilities** Component

The **Browser Capabilities** component provides information about the capabilities of the client browser. It uses the **User-Agent** header passed in the HTTP **Request** header to search for browser data in the Browscap.ini file. If a match is found, the component assigns entries in Browscap.ini to the object variable's properties. You can use this information to customize output on the basis of the browser in use.

Listing 10.14 contains script to display the browser's capabilities in an HTML table.

Listing 10.14   Using the **Browser Capabilities** component.

```
<%@ LANGUAGE="VBSCRIPT" %>
<% Set bc = Server.CreateObject("MSWC.BrowserType") %>
<HTML>
<HEAD>
```

```
<TITLE>Browser Capabilities</TITLE>
</HEAD>
<BODY>
<H3>The following is a list of properties of your browser:</H3>
<TABLE BORDER=1>
<TR><TD>Browser Type</TD><TD><%= bc.browser %></TD>
<TR><TD>What Version</TD><TD><%= bc.Version %></TD>
<TR><TD>Major Version</TD><TD><%= bc.majorver %></TD>
<TR><TD>Minor Version</TD><TD><%= bc.minorver %></TD>
<TR><TD>Beta</TD><TD><%= bc.beta %></TD>
<TR><TD>Platform</TD><TD><%= bc.platform %></TD>
<TR><TD>Frames</TD><TD><%= bc.Frames %></TD>
<TR><TD>Tables</TD><TD><%= bc.Tables %></TD>
<TR><TD>Cookies</TD><TD><%= bc.cookies %></TD>
<TR><TD>Background Sounds</TD><TD><%= bc.BackgroundSounds %></TD>
<TR><TD>ActiveX Controls</TD><TD><%= bc.ActiveXControls %></TD>
<TR><TD>VBScript</TD><TD><%= bc.VBScript %></TD>
<TR><TD>JavaScript</TD><TD><%= bc.Javascript %></TD>
<TR><TD>Java Applets</TD><TD><%= bc.Javaapplets %></TD>
</TABLE>
</BODY>
</HTML>
```

 ## Using The **Content Linking** Component

The **Content Linking** component makes it easy to manage links among pages in your Web application. It uses a text file, Content Linking List, to maintain a list of URLs in the order you want them navigated. The **Content Linking** component provides methods to move through the list file. You can also build an index using the content linking component (see example in Chapter 12).

Listing 10.15 is an ASP file that implements the **Content Linking** component. It uses the Content Linking List file to build an HTML unordered list of hyperlinks.

Listing 10.16 is the Content Linking List file. It contains the URLs and descriptions of the three pages used in this example.

Listing 10.15   Using the **Content Linking** component.

```
<%@ LANGUAGE="VBSCRIPT" %>
<% Set NextLink = Server.CreateObject("MSWC.NextLink") %>

<HTML>
<HEAD>
<TITLE>Content Linking Component</TITLE>
</HEAD>
<BODY>
```

```
<% count = NextLink.GetListCount("10-16.txt") %>
<% i = 1 %>
<UL>
<% Do While(i <= count) %>
<LI><A HREF="<% =NextLink.GetNthURL("10-16.txt",i) %>">
<% =NextLink.GetNthDescription("10-16.txt",i) %></A>
<% i = i + 1 %>
<% Loop %>
</UL>
</BODY>
</HTML>
```

Listing 10.16   The Content Linking List file.
```
als.asp   Al's Mexican Palace
kims.asp  Kim's Steak House
pauls.asp  Paul's China Garden
```

Listing 10.17 contains script that is useful to include in each page listed in the list file. The script implements Previous and Next links on all the pages. To make it look a little better, this example uses graphics to add Previous and Next pointers. You can put this code in one file and use the **include** directive to include it in the pages:

```
<!-- #include file = "10-17.inc" -->
```

Listing 10.17   A handy include file.
```
<% Set NextLink = Server.CreateObject("MSWC.NextLink") %>
<A HREF="<% =NextLink.GetPreviousURL("10-16.txt") %> ">
<IMG SRC="u_prev_3.gif"></A>
<A HREF="<% =NextLink.GetNextURL("10-16.txt") %> ">
<IMG SRC="u_next_3.gif"></A>
<HR>
<A HREF="link.asp">Return to table of contents</A>
```

Chapter 11

Microsoft Personalization System

You can easily make your users feel at home by effectively using the Microsoft Personalization System. This easy-to-use tool will help you add a personal touch to your Web applications.

Kim Barber

Notes…

Chapter 11

I once had a job that required a lot of travel. I frequently traveled to the same location on the same airline and on the same flight and stayed at the same hotel. If you have had similar experiences, you know that, after a while, you become familiar with the people you come in contact with. Often, I felt a sense of "family" when arriving at a familiar and friendly establishment, such as a hotel where I often stayed. Perhaps you don't often travel to the same destination, but maybe you regularly shop or dine at the same place near home. If so, you might also experience the same feeling of familiarity and community.

A Web site that fosters the same sense of community is an incredibly valuable resource. The goal of the Microsoft Personalization System (MPS) is to provide this sense of community. You can use MPS to provide a community experience for your users, as it consists of a set of server components that provide support for personalization, opinion sharing, and feedback.

You may know MPS by its older name—the Internet Personalization System. At first, Microsoft provided this as an installable component. Then, it incorporated the package into Microsoft Site Server and changed the name to MPS.

MPS has three components: **User Property Database**, **User Voting**, and **Send Mail**. You can use these components to provide customized and personalized content, collect the feedback and opinions of your users, and mail feedback to them easily.

The **User Property Database** Component

The **User Property Database** (**UPD**) component lets you remember information about your users. You collect the property information from the user and can use it to personalize the content you provide. You can also collect information from other sources, such as the **Browser Capabilities** component (introduced in Chapter 10), and store it as user property information.

The **GUID**

For the **UPD** component to work, it must be able to recognize when a user returns to the Web site. The first time the user visits a Web application that uses the **UPD**, the system generates a unique identifier for that user and stores it as a client-side cookie. This identifier is a **Globally Unique Identifier**, or **GUID** (as defined by the Open Software Foundation Distributed Computing Environment, or OSF/DCE, specification). The **UPD** uses the **GUID** to identify the user later. When the user returns to the Web site, the **UPD** retrieves the **GUID** from the cookie and uses it to locate the user's property information in the database.

Because this method relies on a cookie on the client's computer, you need to be aware of a couple of considerations. First, the user's browser might not support cookies, or the user may disable cookie support. Second, the user might use more than one browser or computer. If the user returns to your Web site with another browser or with a different machine, the **UPD** will treat him or her as a different user. Of course, if the user deletes cookies (on purpose or by accident), your site will no longer recognize the user.

If you have an alternate way to authenticate users, you may be able to set your own user IDs and force the **UPD** to recognize authenticated users regardless of what browser or machine they use. However, if you authenticate users, you may want to use only the database component (see Chapter 10) to make your own property database and not use the **UPD**.

Properties

The **UPD** stores properties as name/value pairs. It can store single or multiple values in each property. You determine the property name and maintain any number of properties for each user. Additionally, the **UPD** treats all properties as strings.

Assuming that **Props** references an instance of the **UPD** component (created with **Server.CreateObject**), the following statement assigns a value to the single-value **Cuisine** property:

```
<% Props.Item("Cuisine") = "Chinese" %>
```

Item is a **UPD** method that assigns a value to a single-value property. The property value is retrieved as follows:

```
<% t_cuisine = Props.Item("Cuisine") %>
```

Item is the default **UPD** property, so you can also omit **Item** and simply refer to the property:

```
<% Props("Cuisine") = "Chinese" %>
<% t_cuisine = Props("Cuisine") %>
```

This is a nice shortcut that can save you some typing.

The **Append** method assigns values to multiple-value properties (similar to a collection):

```
<% Props.Append("favfood") = "pizza" %>
<% Props.Append("favfood") = "cheeseburgers" %>
```

The following statement retrieves the second value of the **favfood** property:

```
<% t_favfood = Props.Item("favfood")(2) %>
```

Alternately, you could retrieve the same value using the following statement:

```
<% t_favfood = Props("favfood")(2) %>
```

The **UPD** component has other properties and methods, as you'll see shortly.

Using The **UPD** Component

The **UPD** component is similar to other ActiveX installable components. You create an instance of the component and assign it to an object variable. You use the object variable to access the **UPD**. The following statements assign a **UPD** component object to the **Props** variable:

```
<% Set Props = Server.CreateObject("MPS.PropertyDatabase") %>
```

One important caveat: The **UPD** depends on modifying the outgoing HTML document's headers. That means that the call to **CreateObject** must appear before you create any HTML. Usually, it is a good idea to create the **UPD** component in the very first line in your HTML file. It is permissible to precede the line with server-side script but not with HTML.

There are typically three stages to using user properties:

- Collect the information

- Write the properties to the property database

- Retrieve and use the properties

Listing 11.1 uses an HTML form to collect two items of data from a user: the first name and a favorite color. Listing 11.2 processes the form submission.

Listing 11.1   Collecting user properties.

```
<HTML>
<HEAD>
<TITLE>Listing 11.1</TITLE>
</HEAD>
<BODY>
<H3 ALIGN=CENTER>Please tell us a little about yourself</H3>
<PRE>
<FORM METHOD=POST ACTION="11-2.asp">
First name:     <INPUT TYPE=TEXT NAME="fname">
Favorite Color: <INPUT TYPE=TEXT NAME="favcolor">
<INPUT TYPE=SUBMIT VALUE="Submit">
</FORM>
</PRE>
</BODY>
</HTML>
```

Listing 11.2 creates an instance of the **UPD** component and saves the information passed from Listing 11.1.

Listing 11.2   Saving user properties.

```
<%
    Set Props = Server.CreateObject("MPS.PropertyDatabase")
    Props("fname") = Request("fname")
    Props("favcolor") = Request("favcolor")
%>
<HTML>
<HEAD>
<TITLE>Listing 11.2</TITLE>
</HEAD>
<BODY>
<FONT SIZE=4 COLOR=RED>Properties saved.</FONT>
</BODY>
</HTML>
```

Now that the application saves user properties, it needs to retrieve them. Listing 11.3 checks to see whether a first-name property is present. If it is, it reads the properties from the database and uses them.

Listing 11.3 Retrieving and using user properties.

```
<%
     Response.Expires = 0
     Set Props = Server.CreateObject("MPS.PropertyDatabase")
%>
<HTML>
<HEAD>
<TITLE>Listing 11.3</TITLE>
</HEAD>
<BODY>

<% If Props("fname") <> "" Then %>
<FONT SIZE=4 COLOR=<% =Props("favcolor") %>>
Welcome back <% =Props("fname") %>
</FONT>
<% Else %>
<FONT SIZE=4>Hello stranger</FONT>
<% End If %>
</BODY>
</HTML>
```

Another way to determine whether properties exist for the user is to check the **Request** object's **ContentLength** property. If **ContentLength** is zero, there can't be any properties because there is no cookie data. Of course, a nonzero value doesn't necessarily imply properties since other data may be present. Listing 11.4 checks the **ContentLength** property to determine if properties exist. If no properties are present, the application displays the form to collect them. If properties are present, the page displays a welcome message and offers the user the opportunity to change his or her properties. Also notice that, in this case, the form controls already contain the existing **UPD** values.

Listing 11.4 Collecting and using properties in one file.

```
<% Response.Expires = 0 %>
<% Set Props = Server.CreateObject("MPS.PropertyDatabase") %>

<HTML>
<HEAD>
<TITLE>Lising 11.4</TITLE>
</HEAD>
<BODY>
```

```
<% If Request("ContentLength") = 0 Then %>
<FONT SIZE=4 COLOR=<% =Props("favcolor") %>>
Welcome back <% =Props("fname") %>
</FONT>
<PRE>
Complete the following form to change your settings.
<FORM METHOD=POST ACTION="11-2.asp">
First name:     <INPUT TYPE=TEXT NAME="fname" VALUE=<% =Props("fname") %>>
Favorite Color: <INPUT TYPE=TEXT NAME="favcolor" VALUE=<% =Props("favcolor") %>>
<INPUT TYPE=SUBMIT VALUE="Submit">
</FORM>
</PRE>

<% Else %>
<FONT SIZE=4>Hello stranger</FONT>
<PRE>
<FORM METHOD=POST ACTION="11-2.asp">
First name:     <INPUT TYPE=TEXT NAME="fname">
Favorite Color: <INPUT TYPE=TEXT NAME="favcolor">
<INPUT TYPE=SUBMIT VALUE="Submit">
</FORM>
</PRE>
<% End If %>
</BODY>
</HTML>
```

UPD Component Properties And Methods

The **UPD** has properties and methods that you use to create, update, and access user properties. You'll find a list of the **UPD** properties in Table 11.1.

Sometimes, it's convenient to set default values for items in the **UPD** if there is no existing entry. You use the **Defaults** property to do this. The following example sets the default text color property to green. If the user has set a favorite color, the code uses it. If not, the code uses green. Here's how you do it:

Table 11.1 UPD component properties.

Property	Description
Defaults	Specifies default properties
ID	Specifies the user's ID
ReadOnly	Specifies whether the properties are read-only
PropertyString	Returns the user's current properties

```
<% Response.Expires = 0 %>
<% Set Props = Server.CreateObject("MPS.PropertyDatabase") %>
<% Props.Defaults=("favcolor=GREEN") %>
<HTML>
<HEAD>
<TITLE>Setting Defaults</TITLE>
</HEAD>
<BODY TEXT=<% =Props("favcolor") %>>
<H3>Welcome</H3>
</BODY>
</HTML>
```

Also notice that the **Response** object's **Expires** property is set to zero. The **Expires** property specifies the amount of time in minutes before the page expires. If a page is requested before the specified time elapses, it is retrieved from the cache. If it is requested after the specified time elapses, it is reloaded. If you set **Expires** to zero, the page is reloaded every time it is requested. This is useful when the Web page contents change frequently and you want to use the most current data. You'll probably do this often in your Active Server Pages. This also prevents older proxy servers from showing one user's custom page to other users who areusing the same proxy.

The **ID** property contains the user's **GUID**. You can also use this property to override the system-selected **GUID**. The statement

```
<% =Props.ID %>
```

outputs the **GUID**. For example:

```
66b12ef1d26311d1a00200a024231ce9
```

PropertyString returns a string containing the current properties. For example,

```
<% =Props.PropertyString %>
```

displays

```
FAVCOLOR=Blue&ID=66b12ef1d26311d1a00200a024231ce9&FNAME=George
```

You might find the **PropertyString** variable useful if you want to shadow the property database using an SQL database. You might want to do this so you can easily manipulate the data or use the same data for groups of users. You would also want to look at the **LoadFromString** method.

Table 11.2 lists the **UPD** members.

Table 11.2 UPD component members.

Method	Description
Item	Reads and writes user properties
LoadFromString	Writes user properties from a URL-encoded query string

You can use the **Item** property to read from and write to the **UPD**. You'll find a typical use of the **Item** object earlier in this chapter in the introduction to **UPD** properties. This property works with both single- and multiple-value properties. Also, its use is generally optional, because it is the default property.

The **Item** object has the three methods described in Table 11.3.

Assume for a moment that **favcolor** is a multiple-value property. The following statement will append another color:

```
<% Props("favcolor").Append("Purple") %>
```

Also, notice that **Item** isn't specified. The statement

```
<% Props("favcolor").Remove(2) %>
```

removes the second item from the multiple-value property.

The **Item** method has one property, **Count**, which returns the number of items stored in the user property.

You can use the **LoadFromString** method to load properties directly to the database from the query string. This is typically used to load the database from data posted from a form:

```
<% Props.LoadFromString(Request.Form) %>
```

Table 11.3 Item object methods.

Method	Description
Append	Adds items to multiple-value properties
Item	Accesses a single value of a multiple-value property
Remove	Removes items from multiple-value properties

The **User Property Database** component is flexible and easy to use. With very little effort, you can easily maintain user information and preferences and add a personalized touch to your Web applications.

The **Voting** Component

I'm originally from West Virginia (okay, send your jokes to **kbarber@web. compuserve.com**), which isn't far from my current home in Ohio. Because it's so close, my wife, kids, and I often go back to visit. Depending on the time of the year, weather patterns, and cosmic phenomena, it sometimes seems like everyone has an opinion about everything, and they want to share it. It really isn't that my family is just highly opinionated (well, maybe just a little), but most people have opinions about a lot of things. You know what they say about opinions: Everybody has one.

Users of your Web applications often have something to say about them, and, equally as often, you are probably very interested in their feedback. Their feedback is useful, because you want your users to benefit from visiting your Web site, and you want them to come back. Therefore, you can use their opinions as input to making improvements. You might also want to collect their feedback on, for example, a restaurant or a movie review so that it can be shared with others. Well, how do you collect your users' feedback? You could create a form to collect the information, write server-side script to collect the data and store it in a database, and write more script to read the database and output the results. Or, you can use the **Voting** component and let it do all the work.

You can use the **Voting** component to allow users to provide their opinion on things and to see the opinions of others. The **Voting** component does all the work of submitting, counting, and storing the votes. You have very little to do other than creating a form to collect the input.

Using The **Voting** Component

The **Voting** component requires an Open Database Connectivity (ODBC) compliant database to store votes. MPS provides a Microsoft Access database (Vote.mdb) that you can use as well as an SQL script that creates an SQL database. Of course, you can create your own as long as it has the same structure. Usually, however, it's just as easy to use the standard database.

MPS automatically installs and prepares the Access database for use. If you create your own, you'll need to use the ODBC Data Source Administrator to configure the appropriate driver and other information about the datasource. Also, your database must contain the tables with the specified fields shown in Table 11.4.

Votes And Ballots

Votes are organized into ballots that can contain multiple questions, and each question can have multiple values. You can allow users to vote as often as they like or limit each user to one vote. The **Voting** component has five methods to set ballots and to submit and process votes. Table 11.5 describes the **Voting** component's methods.

GetVote displays the voting results in an HTML table. The table contains columns for the question, the number of votes per question, and the percentage of votes for each question. **GetVote** uses the following syntax:

Table 11.4 Voting component database requirements.

Table	Column Name		Data Type	Description
VoteMaster	Name	Character (255)		Ballot name
	VID	Integer		Unique ballot identifier
VoteQuestions	VID	Integer		Unique ballot identifier
	Question	Character (255)		Question name
	Value	Character (64)		Vote submission for the question
	VoteCount	Integer		Number of votes submitted for the ballot, question, and value
	Percentage	Integer		Percentage of total votes for the value
VoteRecord	VID	Integer		Unique ballot identifier
	VoterID	Character (50)		Unique identifier for the user submitting the vote

Table 11.5 Voting component methods.

Method	Description
GetVote	Displays voting results
GetVoteCount	Returns the number of votes
Open	Opens a connection to the Vote database
SetBallotName	Specifies the ballot to vote on
Submit	Submits the vote

```
GetVote([question][,value])
```

question specifies the question name, and **value** specifies the name of the specific value you want to count. Both **question** and **value** are optional, and the output of **GetVote** depends on whether they are specified. **GetVote** returns the following:

- An HTML table of the current ballot and all questions if you omit both **question** and **value**

- An HTML table containing the results for a specific question if you specify the **question** argument

- The vote count for a specific question if you supply both **question** and **value**

- An error message in the event an error occurs

GetVoteCount returns the number of votes per ballot, question, or value. You call it like this:

```
GetVoteCount([question][,value])
```

If you specify only the **question** argument, **GetVoteCount** returns the number of votes for that specific question. If you supply both arguments, the voting component returns the number of votes for the **question** and **value**. If you are keeping track of the user's identity with the **Submit** method and do not specify any arguments, **GetVoteCount** will return the number of people who voted for the current ballot. If you aren't tracking the user's identity and don't specify the arguments, a 0 is returned.

Open specifies the ODBC datasource where the voting results are stored:

```
Open(source, userID, password)
```

source identifies the datasource and is the Data Source Name (DSN) assigned when the datasource was configured using the ODBC Data Source Administrator, **userID** specifies the user ID required to log in to the datasource, **password** contains the required password to log in to the datasource, and **Open** returns **TRUE** if successful and **FALSE** if unsuccessful.

You use **SetBallotName** to specify the ballot to vote on:

```
SetBallotName(name)
```

name is the name of the ballot and is associated with records in the database, and **SetBallotName** returns **TRUE** if successful and **FALSE** if unsuccessful.

Submit adds a vote to the database:

```
Submit(question, value [,voterID])
```

question specifies the question to vote on, **value** contains the value selected by the user, and **voterID** identifies the user. If used, the system prevents users from voting more than once. Notice that this is often subject to the same limitations of the **UPD**, as you'll usually use the **UPD**'s **ID** property for this argument.

An example is worth a thousand words and probably more interesting. The following example lets users vote on their favorite car or truck. Listing 11.5 contains an HTML form to collect the votes. The code in Listing 11.6 processes the form.

Listing 11.5 Collecting user votes.

```
<% Response.Expires = 0 %>

<HTML>
<HEAD>
<TITLE>Listing 11.5</TITLE>
</HEAD>
<BODY>
<H3 ALIGN=CENTER>Vote For Your Favorite Car Or Truck!</H3>
<PRE>
<FORM METHOD=POST ACTION="11-6.asp">
<INPUT TYPE=RADIO NAME="favcar" VALUE="Corvette">Corvette
<INPUT TYPE=RADIO NAME="favcar" VALUE="Dodge Ram">Dodge Ram
<INPUT TYPE=RADIO NAME="favcar" VALUE="Ford F150">Ford F150
<INPUT TYPE=RADIO NAME="favcar" VALUE="Mustang">Mustang
<INPUT TYPE=RADIO NAME="favcar" VALUE="Porche">Porche
<INPUT TYPE=RADIO NAME="favcar" VALUE="Trans AM">Trans AM
<INPUT TYPE=SUBMIT VALUE="Vote">
</FORM>
</PRE>
</BODY>
</HTML>
```

Listing 11.6 accepts the vote and writes it to the database. In this example, users can vote as often as they want to because the script doesn't pass the user ID to the **Submit** method. The **Open** method uses a user ID of **guest** with no password. **Vehicle** is the name of the ballot (passes to **SetBallotName**). The **Submit** method specifies the question name *Favorite Vehicle* and uses the **Request** object to get the value of the form data. **GetVoteCount** displays the total number of votes for this question, and then the script uses **GetVote** to display the current voting results in a table.

Don't forget to use the **<%=** notation with **GetVote**. If you use only **<%**, the component will generate a nicely formatted table, but you'll throw it away. Of course, you could store the HTML in a variable and further manipulate it, but that would doubtless get troublesome rather quickly.

Listing 11.6 Processing a vote.

```
<% Response.Expires = 0 %>
<% Set vote = Server.CreateObject("MPS.Vote")
    If vote.Open("Vote","guest","") = TRUE Then
        bal_result = vote.SetBallotName("vehicle")
        vote_result = vote.Submit("Favorite Vehicle", Request("favcar"))
    %>
    Thanks for voting!
    <P>
    Total number of votes is: <% =vote.GetVoteCount("Favorite Vehicle") %>
    <P>
    <% =vote.GetVote %>
    <% Else %>
    The Voting component is not set up correctly.
<% End If %>

<HTML>
<HEAD>
<TITLE>Listing 11-6</TITLE>
</HEAD>
<BODY>
</BODY>
</HTML>
```

I think you will agree that the **Voting** component does a good bit of work for you. This example uses two documents to collect and process votes. The example in the Practical Guide does this using only one page and also limits voters to one vote.

The **Send Mail** Component

The **Send Mail** component gives you the ability to receive email feedback from your users. You can also use it to email information back to them. The **Send Mail** component is very easy to use and, like the **Voting** component, does most of the work.

To use the **Send Mail** component, you must have an SMTP mail server available. The component has only one method, **SendMail**:

```
SendMail(from, to subject, body)
```

from specifies a string that appears in the **From** field of the message header. It must be a valid email name in the format **name@domain**. **to** specifies a list of recipients. You must separate each recipient in the list with a semicolon. **subject** specifies a string that appears in the **Subject** filed of the message header. **body** specifies the message body. If you want to break the body into paragraphs, you must explicitly embed carriage returns into the message body. You can do this in VBScript by concatenating the constant **vbCrLf** into the body.

SendMail returns **TRUE** if it successfully sends the message or **FALSE** if it is unsuccessful.

You'll find a detailed example that uses the **Send Mail** component in the Practical Guide.

Summary

MPS provides three very interesting functions: persistent user properties, voting, and email. Microsoft provides each of these features to allow you to create an online community to attract and retain users.

Is there anything magic about MPS? No. These are nothing more than ActiveX controls for the server. However, they are very useful ActiveX controls. Although in theory you could write your own, none of these components is trivial.

For most Web sites, the **UPD**'s limitations are easy to ignore. However, if you are planning on a subscription service or other special site, be sure to plan carefully around the **UPD**'s limitations. For example, if I pay to subscribe to your site, I won't be happy if that subscription applies only to one browser on one machine. The **UPD** ID wouldn't be useful for limiting votes of real importance, either. It's too easy to delete a cookie or to change machines and vote multiple times.

Still, for most sites, these problems are minor in relation to the increased function that components like the **UPD** provide. Customizing content on the basis of user preferences can go a long way to building that all-important surfer loyalty.

Practical Guide To

Using The Microsoft Personalization System

- Using The **User Property Database** Component And The **Send Mail** Component
- Using The **Voting** Component

Using The **User Property Database** Component And The **Send Mail** Component

This example uses the **User Property Database** (**UPD**) component to get the user's dining reservation preferences. The application then uses the preferences later when the user makes a reservation online. This example also uses the **Send Mail** component to send confirmation to the user.

Listing 11.7 contains an HTML form to collect the data. Listing 11.8 processes the form data.

Listing 11.7 Getting the user's preferences.

```
<% Response.Expires = 0 %>

<HTML>
<HEAD>
<TITLE>Listing 11.7</TITLE>
</HEAD>
<BODY>
<FONT COLOR=BLUE>
<H1 ALIGN=CENTER>Community Dining Club</H1>
<HR SIZE=5>
<H3 ALIGN=CENTER>Reservation Preferences</H3>
<PRE>
<FORM METHOD=POST ACTION="11-8.asp">
Smoking?   <INPUT TYPE=RADIO NAME="smoking" VALUE="no">No
           <INPUT TYPE=RADIO NAME="smoking" VALUE="yes">Yes

Best Time: <INPUT TYPE=RADIO NAME="time" VALUE="5-6">5:00 PM to 6:00 PM
           <INPUT TYPE=RADIO NAME="time" VALUE="6-7">6:00 PM to 7:00 PM
           <INPUT TYPE=RADIO NAME="time" VALUE="7-8">7:00 PM to 8:00 PM
           <INPUT TYPE=RADIO NAME="time" VALUE="8-9">8:00 PM to 9:00 PM
           <INPUT TYPE=RADIO NAME="time" VALUE="9>">After 9:00 PM

Email Address: <INPUT TYPE=TEXT NAME="email">

<INPUT TYPE=SUBMIT VALUE="Submit">
</FORM>
</PRE>
</FONT>
</BODY>
</HTML>
```

Listing 11.8 creates an instance of the **UPD** and assigns the user's preferences. It then creates an instance of the **SendMail** component and sends confirmation to the user.

Listing 11.8 Processing the user's preferences.

```
<% Response.Expires = 0 %>
<% Set Props = Server.CreateObject("MPS.PropertyDatabase")
     Props("smoking") = Request("smoking")
     Props("time") = Request("time")
     Props("email") = Request("email")

     t_smoking = "Smoking"
     If Props("smoking") = "no" Then
          t_smoking = "Non-smoking"
     End If%>

<% Set sm = Server.CreateObject("MPS.Sendmail")
     email = Props("email")
     from = "webmaster@diningclub.com"

     sm.SendMail(webmaster,email,"Reservation Preferences", _
     ("Thank you." & vbCrLf & vbCrLf & _
     "Your reservation preferences are:" & vbCrLf & _
     "Smoking Preference: " & t_smoking & _
     "Preferred Time: " & Props("time")))
%>

<HTML>
<HEAD>
<TITLE>Listing 11.8</TITLE>
</HEAD>
<BODY>
Thank you!
</BODY>
</HTML>
```

Using The **Voting** Component

This example uses the **Voting** component to let users vote on their favorite restaurant. The **UserPropertyDatabase** component provides a unique identifier for each user. This identifier limits users to one vote each. Also, all processing occurs on a single page. Listing 11.9 contains the script.

Listing 11.9 Collecting and displaying user votes.

```
<% Response.Expires=0 %>
<% Set vote = Server.CreateObject("MPS.Vote") %>
<% Set Props = Server.CreateObject("MPS.PropertyDatabase") %>

<HTML>
<HEAD>
```

```
<TITLE>Listing 11.9</TITLE>
</HEAD>
<BODY>
<FONT COLOR=BLUE>
<H2 ALIGN=CENTER>Vote on your favorite Restaurant!</H2>
<HR SIZE=5>
<% If (Request("Content_Length")) = 0 Then %>
<PRE>
<FORM METHOD=POST ACTION="11-9.asp">
<INPUT TYPE=RADIO NAME="favrest" VALUE="Al's Mexican Palace">Al's Mexican Palace
<INPUT TYPE=RADIO NAME="favrest" VALUE="Paul's China Garden">Paul's China Garden
<INPUT TYPE=RADIO NAME="favrest" VALUE="Kim's Steak House">Kim's Steak House

<INPUT TYPE=SUBMIT VALUE="Vote">
</FORM>
</PRE>

<% Else %>
    <% If vote.Open("Vote", "guest", "") = TRUE Then %>
        <% ballot_result = vote.SetBallotName("restaurant") %>
        <% vote_result = vote.Submit("Favorite", Request("favrest"), Props.ID) %>
        <% If vote_result = TRUE Then %>
            Thanks for voting!
            <P>
            <% =vote.GetVote %>
        <% Else %>
            Oops, only one vote please.
        <% End If %>
        <% Else %>
            The voting component failed...
    <% End If %>
<% End IF %>
</BODY>
</HTML>
```

A Case Study

Sure, everyone wants to write an ASP-based site from scratch. But what happens when you have to convert an existing site?

Al Williams

Notes...

Chapter 12

Building a Web site is like building a house. None of the parts is overly difficult, but taken together it's a major undertaking. In this chapter, I'll show you a Web site I've used in training classes for several years where you can read about sightings of "The King," a near-mythical figure who seems to pop up everywhere. This chapter doesn't have a Practical Guide—it *is* a practical guide, and you'll find lots of little pieces in it to borrow. Here, I'll focus less on the details of each piece and more on how the pieces go together.

In the beginning, the Web site is fairly typical—just some static pages and a few images. In several steps, you'll see how to convert the pages to use VBScript on the client and server sides. The site also uses the Microsoft Personalization System (MPS, a part of Site Server) and has many interesting features, including:

- Access to a live database (updates and queries)

- Registration and user preferences (for example, graphics)

- Ad rotation

- Random content selection

- Rudimentary security to lock out certain users

- Hit counting

- Email notification and logging of user registrations

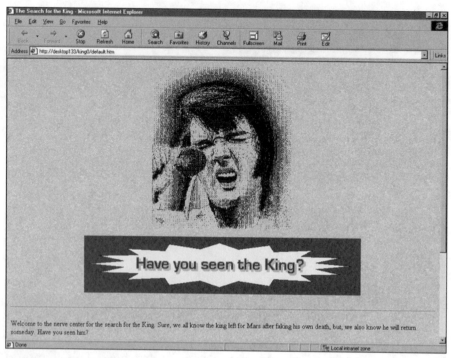

Figure 12.1

The original King home page.

Figure 12.1 shows the basic home page at the beginning of the project. Although certainly no paragon of site design, this is typical of the kind of site you might inherit. Also, it has a simple layout, so it will be easier to work with. The only advanced feature is an image map for navigation. However, many of the pages have inconsistent backgrounds and other design flaws.

The original site has 17 files (see Table 12.1). You'll also find the starting site in the KING0 directory for this chapter on the CD. The final Web site is in the KING1 (no MPS) and KING2 (MPS) directories.

Table 12.1   The original King site.

File	Description
AL_SM.GIF	GIF file of yours truly
DEFAULT.HTM	Main page

(continued)

Table 12.1 The original King site (continued).

File	Description
FACE.GIF	Picture of the King's Martian monument
FIND.HTM	Reports of sightings (static)
HISTORY.HTM	The history of the King
KAUFMAN.JPG	A picture of a man who did a pretty good King
KING1.GIF	The King's picture
KINGBAN.GIF	The King's site banner
KINGBAR.JPG	Navigation bar
LARROW.GIF	The usual left arrow graphic
MEN.HTM	One of these men may be the King?
PBML03.GIF	Used for some backgrounds
QUOTE.HTM	Read the quote of the day
REPORT.HTM	Report your sightings (not really functional yet)
TU.WAV	"Thank you very much"
VOTE.HTM	Nonfunctional voting page
WHO.GIF	Question graphic

Converting To ASP

Converting the site to utilize ASP is relatively straightforward. At first, you might try simply renaming the HTM files to ASP files. However, this won't work because the links between pages must also change.

A common mistake at this point is to copy the HTM files so that there are two versions of each file: one with an HTM extension and another with the ASP extension. Everything would appear to work. However, the links then take you to the HTM files, which do not support script. This can be very frustrating as you change your ASP file but never see any changes in the browser.

If you are in control of your server, you'll probably want to change the default page to DEFAULT.ASP. However, if some people still have DEFAULT.HTM bookmarked, you might want to supply a simple jump page (see Listing 12.1), which is a bridge that vectors users to the ASP file. Notice that you can't use **response.redirect** here, because, to use it, you would have to be in an ASP file. The entire point to the bridge is that it is an HTM file.

Listing 12.1 Bridging the old and the new.

```
<HTML>
<HEAD>
<META HTTP-EQUIV="REFRESH" CONTENT="1" URL="default.asp">

</HEAD>
Whoops... you probably meant to go to <A HREF="default.asp">HERE.</A>
</HTML>
```

Simple Enhancements

Once you have the files converted to ASP format, it is fairly simple to make some quick enhancements. For example, the quote feature is easy to enhance.

In the basic pages, the King's quote is always the same. Why not make the quote change at random? You can find a server-side solution for this in Listing 12.2. Of course, you could get the same effect with client-side script as well (see Listing 12.3).

It is interesting to see how the **RND** function works. Two things make this function odd. First, it employs a seed value. Given the same seed, **RND** will always produce the same sequence of numbers. That's fine if you want repeatable random numbers, but you'll usually want numbers that are unpredictable, in which case be sure to call **RANDOMIZE** first. This call sets the seed to an unpredictable value based on the current time.

The other oddity about **RND** is that it generates a number between zero and one. So, if you want to generate integers between 1 and 100, you need to compute:

```
x=Int(Rnd*99)+1
```

Next, you might add rotating advertisements. The **MSWC.AdRotator** component will do this, but it is somewhat cumbersome to use. Why not roll your own? It isn't much different than picking a random quote.

Listing 12.2 Server-side quotes.

```
<HTML>
<HEAD>
<META HTTP-EQUIV="REFRESH" CONTENT="15">
```

```
<TITLE>King's Quote for the Day</TITLE>

</HEAD>
<BODY <!-- #include file="stdbody.inc"-->>

<H1>The King's Quote of the Day</H1>

<HR>
<P>
&quot;
<%
  dim qt(10)
  qt(0)="Thank you very much!"
  qt(1)="Blue suede shoes"
  qt(2)="Uhhh huh huh...huh huh huh... yeah!"
  qt(3)="Man...that sucker's huge!"
  qt(4)="TCB!"
  qt(5)="If you play my records backwards, you can hear SIVLE!"
  qt(6)="They said they were just vitamins"
  qt(7)="I like sequins... a lot!"
  qt(8)="Can't get enough of them jumpsuits!"
  qt(9)="If they make a movie about me, don't let Roseanne play Pricilla!"
  qt(10)="One word: Hips!"
  Randomize
  n=Int(11*rnd)
%>
<%= qt(n) %>
<% if request("Debug")="1" then
    response.Write(" Debug=")
    response.Write(n)
    end if
%>
&quot;
</HTML>
```

Listing 12.3 Client-side quotes.

```
<HTML>

<HEAD>
<META HTTP-EQUIV="REFRESH" CONTENT="15">
<TITLE>King's Quote for the Day</TITLE>


</HEAD>
<BODY <!-- #include file="stdbody.inc"-->>

<H1>The King's Quote of the Day</H1>
```

```
<HR>

<P>
&quot;
<SCRIPT LANGUAGE=VBScript>
<!--
   ' Client side quote script
   dim qt(10)
   qt(0)="Thank you very much!"
   qt(1)="Blue suede shoes"
   qt(2)="Uhhh huh huh...huh huh huh... yeah!"
   qt(3)="Man...that sucker's huge!"
   qt(4)="TCB!"
   qt(5)="If you play my records backwards, you can hear SIVLE!"
   qt(6)="They said they were just vitamins"
   qt(7)="I like sequins... a lot!"
   qt(8)="Can't get enough of them jumpsuits!"
   qt(9)="If they make a movie about me, don't let Roseanne play Pricilla!"
   qt(10)="One word: Hips!"
   Randomize
   n=Int(11*rnd)
   document.Write(qt(n))
<% if request("Debug")="1" then %>
   document.Write(" Debug=")
   document.Write(n)
<% end if %>
-->
</SCRIPT>
&quot;
<P>
</HTML>
```

Listing 12.4 shows an ad rotation using the built-in component. Listing 12.5 shows an alternate scheme based on files. This code assumes that the ad banners are GIF files named Ad1.GIF, Ad2.GIF, and so on. You also create a corresponding SPONSORx.ASP file (where *x* is a number). This file should use the **response.redirect** call to vector the user to the correct page. The sponsor file might take other actions, too. For example, you could record the click in a file or a database. The sample files don't do anything but pop up an alert box.

The custom rotation code is in the ROTATE.INC file. This makes it easy to include anywhere you want a rotating advertisement. You can find ROTATE.INC in Listing 12.5. You'll see some similarity between this code and the random-quote-generation code you looked at earlier.

Listing 12.4 Standard ad rotation (excerpt from DEFAULT.ASP).

```
<% set ad=Server.CreateObject("MSWC.AdRotator") %>
<hr>
Please visit our sponsors:
<CENTER>
<%= ad.GetAdvertisement("ads.txt") %>
<hr>
</CENTER>
```

Listing 12.5 Custom ad rotation.

```
<!-- Rotate Ads -->
<%
  maxads=2    ' Set to maximum # of ads
  Randomize
  n=Int(maxads*rnd)+1
%>
<A HREF=SPONSOR<%= n %>.ASP><IMG SRC=AD<%= n %>.GIF></A>
```

With this simple scheme, it's trivial to have your ASP file pick a number and call up the right files. By placing the code in an include file, you can use it from many places easily.

Another simple enhancement is to allow the user to disable most graphics. This is easy to do by setting a session variable with a flag indicating whether graphics are off (the absence of the flag should mean that graphics are on, as this will be the default case). Then you bracket every nonessential graphic with an **if** statement so that it doesn't display when the flag is set. Listing 12.6 shows GOFF.ASP, which turns graphics off. Listing 12.7 shows an optional graphic.

Listing 12.6 GOFF.ASP.

```
<% Session("Graphics")="N" %>
<SCRIPT Language=VBScript>
location.pathname="default.asp"
</SCRIPT>
```

Listing 12.7 Making a graphic optional.

```
<CENTER>
<% if Session("Graphics")<>"N" then %>
<IMG Have you seen the King?  SRC="kingban.gif">
<% end if %>
</CENTER>
```

Of course, you don't want to disable all graphics for this site. The original site design depends on the graphics navigation bar to jump from the home page to the other pages on the site. Unless you add text-based navigation, you should leave the bar visible. This should be no problem because it will always appear unless you bracket it with an **if** statement.

An interesting effect is to use an **else** clause with an optional graphic. You could display some text or provide a link to turn graphics back on. You could even make the graphics flag select a level of graphics. Perhaps a value of zero means no graphics, 1 selects low-resolution images, and 2 turns on everything.

As it stands, the graphics flag survives only for the user's session because it's in a session variable. However, you could store the flag in the user property database if you are using the Microsoft Personalization System.

Although most users likely won't notice that the original site had inconsistent backgrounds, you can easily fix this by filling in each **<BODY>** tag with a server-side include. The STDBODY.INC file (Listing 12.8) allows you to easily change the background for each page.

Listing 12.8   STDBODY.INC.

```
BACKGROUND="pmb103.gif"
```

Another way to do this is by placing the entire **<BODY>** tag in the STDBODY.INC file. This has the advantage of allowing you to put other HTML or script in the STDBODY.INC file but the disadvantage of not allowing you to customize the **BODY** for individual pages.

Debugging

Debugging ASP is notoriously difficult because it all takes place on the server. Every programmer must debug sometimes, and a few tricks can help make your life easier.

Notice in the QUOTE.ASP file (shown in Listings 12.2 and 12.3) the debugging statements that print out key values for inspection (the ordinary user never sees these values).

The key is a session variable named **Debug**. The main page checks to see whether there is a query string named **Debug**. If there is, the value of the session variable becomes the value of this query string, and then any page that wants to print debugging information checks the state of the session variable first. If the variable is not **True**, the page skips the debugging code.

Hit Counting

Sometimes it seems as if creating hit counters was the reason they invented Web scripting. It's easy to create a counter using ASP. You simply increment the count in an application variable (see Listing 12.9). Be sure to lock the **Application** object before accessing it.

Listing 12.9   Hit counting.

```
<BR>
<% application.Lock
   application("Count")=application("Count")+1
   n=application("Count")
   application.Unlock
   set ofile=Server.CreateObject("scripting.FileSystemObject") '
   set file=ofile.CreateTextFile("kingcount.txt",TRUE) '
   file.WriteLine CStr(n)
   file.Close
 %>
You are visitor number <%= application("Count") %>
<P>
```

The catch here is that the server resets all application variables each time you restart the server, and you'd like a way to make your hit count persistent. Of course, you could read the count from a file when the application starts (in the GLOBAL.ASA file, as shown in Listing 12.10), but you can't write out the count when the application shuts down. By the time ASP informs you that the application is shutting down, most variables are already gone. Also, what happens if the server doesn't shut down in an orderly fashion?

Listing 12.10   Reading the hit count (excerpt from Global.asa).

```
<SCRIPT Language=VBSCRIPT RUNAT=Server>
   Sub Session_OnStart()
   End Sub

   Sub Application_OnStart()
   set ifile=Server.CreateObject("Scripting.FileSystemObject")
   set file=ifile.OpenTextFile("kingcount.txt",1,TRUE)
   s=file.ReadLine
   if s<>"" then
     application("Count")=CInt(s)
   else
     application("Count")=0
   end if
   End Sub
```

```
Sub Application_OnEnd()
  ' Can't write out here because everything is shut down!
End Sub
```

```
</SCRIPT>
```

The solution, then, is to write out the hit count when you update it, as Listing 12.9 does. Although this is reliable, it isn't as efficient because each hit produces a file write.

If you have several pages a user can visit directly and you want to keep track of unique visitors, try incrementing the hit count in the **Session_OnStart** event handler.

Content Linking

Often, it's useful to imagine your Web pages having a particular order (like the pages in a book). Although it is often a good thing in terms of usability, it can be a real nightmare in terms of maintenance.

The **MSWC.NextLink** component can be a real help in this case. This component uses an ordinary text file that contains the URLs in their correct order. When you ask the component to give you the next (or previous) URL, it locates the current URL in the list and returns the appropriate string.

Each line in the file consists of a URL, a tab character, a description, a tab character, and an optional comment. Although the description is optional, the tab preceding it is not (at least until Microsoft fixes this obvious bug). Also, you have to be careful that the text editor you use doesn't replace tabs with spaces.

You'll use this component mainly to generate hyperlinks, using the URL as the link's target and the description as the display portion. You can put a set of Previous and Next links in an include file (like the one in Listing 12.11) and easily place them on each page. Notice that each page ends with an include of a standard copyright file. This copyright file also includes the include file that handles the Next and Previous links (BROWSE.INC in Listing 12.11).

Listing 12.11   Using MSWC.NextLink.
```
<% set seq=Server.CreateObject("MSWC.NextLink") %>
<PRE>
<A HREF=<%=seq.GetPreviousURL("/index.txt")%>>Previous Page </A>
<A HREF=<%=seq.GetNextURL("/index.txt")%>>Next Page </A>
<A HREF=index.asp>Goto Index</A>
</PRE>
```

The **MSWC.NextLink** component also allows you to step through the entire list. This makes it easy to generate an index (see Listing 12.12 and Figure 12.2). Armed with these tricks, you can easily maintain the index and the Next links. Simply make an entry in the text file to add the new page to the list, and the scripts take care of the rest.

Listing 12.12   Automatically generating the index.

```
<HTML>
<HEAD>
<TITLE>The King's Page Index</TITLE>
</HEAD>
<BODY>
<% set link=Server.CreateObject("MSWC.NextLink")
   for i=1 to link.GetListCount("/index.txt") %>
<A HREF=<%= link.GetNthURL("/index.txt",i) %>>
   <%= CStr(i) + ". " %> ]
   <%= link.GetNthDescription("/index.txt",i) %>
</A><P>
<% next %>
</BODY>
</HTML>
```

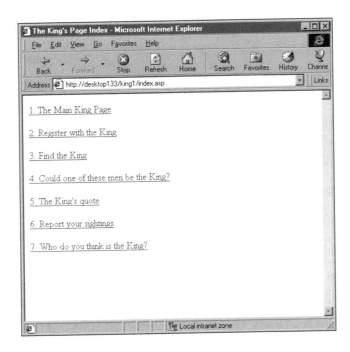

Figure 12.2

The index.

More Advanced Techniques

Using the User Property Database (UPD, part of the Microsoft Personalization System) allows you to make many other enhancements to the Web site. Notice in Listing 12.13 that the page greets the user by name, if it knows the user's name. If it doesn't, the user sees a link to a registration page. Because registration relies on cookies, the code doesn't present the registration option unless the browser capability object indicates that the browser supports cookies.

Listing 12.13 Excerpt from DEFAULT.ASP.

```
<% set prop = Server.CreateObject ("MPS.PropertyDatabase")
. . .
<P>
Welcome
<% if prop("Name")<>"" then %>
<%= prop("Name") %>
<% end if %>
to the nerve center for the search for the King. Sure,
we all know the king left for Mars after faking his own death,
but, we also know he will return someday. Have you seen him?
<P>
. . .
<% set binfo=Server.CreateObject("MSWC.BrowserType")
    if prop("Name")="" and binfo.Cookies<>"FALSE" then %>
    <A HREF=register.asp>Click here to register!</A>
    <% end if %>
<P>
```

When the user registers using the form in Listing 12.14, the script logs the entry in a file and sends email to the Webmaster. In this case, the registration is the user's name, but it could be anything.

Listing 12.14 Registration (REGISTER.ASP).

```
<% set prop = Server.CreateObject ("MPS.PropertyDatabase")
  response.Expires=0 %>
<HTML>
<HEAD>
<% if request("Content_Length")<>0 then %>
<!-- Client pull is OK, but leaves this page in the
     history. Better to use redirection. Try it!  -->
<META HTTP-EQUIV="REFRESH" CONTENT="5" URL="default.asp">
<% end if %>
<TITLE>Register with the King</TITLE>
<BODY <!-- #include file="stdbody.inc" -->>
<% if request("Content_Length")=0 then %>
<H1>Tell us your name!</H1><P>
<FORM NAME="Register" Action="register.asp" METHOD="POST">
```

```
Enter your name: <INPUT NAME="Name" Value= "<%= prop("Name") %>"    MAXLENGTH="60"
SIZE=60>
<INPUT TYPE=SUBMIT NAME="Enter" VALUE="Enter">
</FORM>
<% else
  prop("Name")=request("Name") %>
  Thanks for registering <%= prop("Name") %>

<!--Mail to Webmaster -->
<%  set mailer=Server.CreateObject("MPS.SendMail")
  mailer.SendMail "web1","bigdummyal@coriolis.com",
  "Registration",prop("Name")+" registered!" %>

<!-- Text log -->
<% set file=Server.CreateObject("Scripting.FileSystemObject")
   set tfile=file.OpenTextFile("register.log",8)
   tfile.WriteLine prop("Name")+" registered."
   tfile.Close
%>

<% end if %>
<!-- #include file="copyrigh.inc" -->
```

Another interesting effect of the UPD is allowing for the King pages to lock out un-
wanted users. If you ask for the King's history, the HISTORY.ASP file chastises you (see
Listing 12.15) and sets a flag in the UPD. If the main page detects this flag, it redirects
you to a page (see Listing 12.16) where you can redeem yourself and clear the flag.

Listing 12.15   Banishing the user.

```
<% set prop = Server.CreateObject ("MPS.PropertyDatabase")
  response.Expires=0 %>
<% prop("Banish")=1 %>
<HTML>

<HEAD>

<TITLE>History of the King</TITLE>


</HEAD>
<BODY <!-- #include file="stdbody.inc"-->>

<H1>About the King</H1>

<P>
You don't know every detail about the King? What shoe size did
he wear? What was odd about his ears? How many cars did he buy?
How many sequins were on his favorite jump suit?<BR>
```

```
<H2>WHAT!? You don't know these things? Then go away and never
return! You are banished from these pages forever!<BR>
<BR>
</H2>


</BODY>
</HTML>
```

Listing 12.16 Redeeming the user.

```
<% set prop = Server.CreateObject ("MPS.PropertyDatabase")
  response.Expires=0
  if request("Answer")=2 then
    prop("Banish")=""
    response.redirect("default.asp")
  end if
%>
<HTML>
<HEAD>
<TITLE>Your Chance to Redeem Yourself!</TITLE>
<BODY <!-- #include file="stdbody.inc"-->>
<H1>You blew it!</H1>
Yes, you blew it, bunky. You don't know beans about the King.
Well, here is your one chance to make good. If you can
answer the following question, we will forget all about
this unfortunate incident:
<P><P>
Pick the correct answer:<P>
The King was a burnin' burnin' hunka<P>
A. <A HREF=trivia.asp?Answer=1>Tire rubber</A><P>
B. <A HREF=trivia.asp?Answer=2>Love</A><P>
C. <A HREF=trivia.asp?Answer=3>Rubbish</A><P>
</BODY>
</HTML>
```

This isn't bulletproof, however, as a smart user can just delete your cookie to regain access. If you authenticate users, though, you could make a more secure system.

Database Access

Adding live access to a database is one of the most powerful features you can add to a Web site. The King pages allow you to enter and view sightings right from the Web site.

The first step to doing this is to create your database and install it as a system DSN (using the ODBC control panel). You can find the "sighting" database table on the CD and in Table 12.2.

Table 12.2 The "sighting" table.

Field	Description
Date	Date and time of sighting (not the entry date and time)
Before	True if user has seen the King before this sighting
Location	Where was the King?
Name	User's name
Comment	User's comments
subtime	System-generated submission time and date stamp

Assuming that you want only to display data, things are simple. The code in Listing 12.17 will convert any database table into an HTML table. It even labels the columns automatically. Often, this is all you need. The King pages modify this code just a little so that the last column doesn't display (see Listing 12.18).

Listing 12.17 Generic database table display.

```
<% Set Conn = Server.CreateObject("ADODB.Connection")
 ' Use your database info on the next 2 line
   Conn.Open "MyDB","guest",""
   SQL="Select * from SomeTable"
   set RS = Conn.Execute(SQL)
%>

<P>
<TABLE BORDER=1>
<TR>
<% For i = 0 to RS.Fields.Count - 1 %>
     <TD><B><%= RS(i).Name %></B></TD>
  <% Next %>
</TR>
<% Do While Not RS.EOF %>
  <TR>
  <% For i = 0 to RS.Fields.Count - 1 %>
       <TD VALIGN=TOP>
       <%= RS(i) %>
       </TD>
  <% Next %>
  </TR>
<%
  RS.MoveNext
  Loop
```

```
        RS.Close
        Conn.Close
    %>
    </TABLE>
```

Listing 12.18   The King database display.

```
<% set prop = Server.CreateObject ("MPS.PropertyDatabase")
   if prop("LastQuery")="" or request("RESET")=1 then
       prop("LastQuery")="01/01/80"
       noreset=1
   else
       noreset=0
   end if
   response.Expires=0
%>
<!--#include file="adovbs.inc" -->
<HTML>

<HEAD>

<TITLE>Find the King</TITLE>

</HEAD>
<BODY <!-- #include file="stdbody.inc"-->>

<H1>Recent King Sightings: </H1>

<% Set Conn = Server.CreateObject("ADODB.Connection") '***
   Conn.Open "KingSight","guest",""
   SQL="Select * from Sighting where subtime > CDate('"+prop("LastQuery")+"') or
isnull(subtime) order by date desc"
   set RS = Conn.Execute(SQL)
   prop("LastQuery")=now
%>

<P>
<TABLE BORDER=1>
<TR>
  <!-- last field is hidden -->
  <% For i = 0 to RS.Fields.Count - 2 %>
      <TD><B><%= RS(i).Name %></B></TD>
  <% Next %>
</TR>
<% Do While Not RS.EOF %>
  <TR>
  <% For i = 0 to RS.Fields.Count - 2 %>
      <TD VALIGN=TOP>
```

```
    <% if RS(i).Name<>"Before" then %>
        <%= RS(i) %>
    <% else %>
        <% if RS(i)=0 then %>
            N
        <% else %>
            Y
        <% end if %>
    <% end if %>
        </TD>
  <% Next %>
  </TR>
<%
  RS.MoveNext
  Loop
  RS.Close
  Conn.Close
%>
</TABLE>


<P>
<% if noreset=0 then %>
This page only shows sightings reported after <%= prop("LastQuery") %>
<A HREF="find.asp?RESET=1">Click here to see all sightings</A>
<P>
<% end if %>
Be sure to add your sightings by clicking <A HREF="report.asp">here</A>.

<P>
<A HREF="default.asp"><IMG SRC="larrow.gif" ALT="home"> Back to home page</A>
</BODY>
<!-- #include file="copyrigh.inc" -->
</HTML>
```

Why not display the last column? In this case, the last column stores the date and the time a user entered a sighting (not the date and time of the sighting). The code in Listing 12.18 remembers the time of the user's last query (using the UPD) and doesn't show data entered before that date and time. Presumably, the user already saw this data. However, setting the query string to **RESET=1** overrides this behavior and forces a complete display.

The display code in Listing 12.18 differs somewhat from that in Listing 12.17 in another way by converting the Boolean value in the **Before** field more meaningfully.

Entering data is straightforward (see Listing 12.19). The code automatically fills in the entry time stamp.

Notice that the display code uses an SQL query but that the data entry form uses a record set. Which is better? That depends. It's often more efficient to use an SQL statement to work with the database, but it can be very difficult to formulate a mix of HTML, SQL, and VBScript. Keeping the quotes straight is a major headache. In the end, you can use either method, or you can use both, as this example does.

Listing 12.19   Data entry.

```
<!--#include file="adovbs.inc" -->
<HTML>

<HEAD>

<TITLE>Report Your Sightings!</TITLE>

</HEAD>
<BODY <!-- #include file="stdbody.inc"-->>

<% if Request("Content_Length")=0 then %>
<H1>Report your King Sightings Here!<BR>
</H1>

<FORM NAME="KingForm" ACTION="report.asp" METHOD="POST">

<PRE WIDTH=132>
<FONT SIZE=2>Date:      </FONT><INPUT NAME="KDate" VALUE="" MAXLENGTH="8"
SIZE=8><FONT SIZE=2 FACE="Courier New">        I've seen the King before:
</FONT><INPUT TYPE="CHECKBOX" NAME="Before">

<FONT SIZE=2 FACE="Courier New">Location: </FONT><INPUT NAME="Loc" VALUE=""
MAXLENGTH="128" SIZE=64><FONT SIZE=2 FACE="Courier New">

<FONT SIZE=2 FACE="Courier New">Your name: </FONT><INPUT NAME="Name" VALUE=""
MAXLENGTH="128" SIZE=64><FONT SIZE=2 FACE="Courier New">


Comments:

</FONT>
<TEXTAREA NAME="Comment" ROWS=3 COLS=80>
</TEXTAREA>
</PRE>
<CENTER><INPUT TYPE=SUBMIT NAME="Enter" VALUE="Enter" >
</CENTER>
```

```
</FORM>
<%else %>
<% ' Using record set which is easy, but an Insert would
   ' have better performance (see FIND.ASP)
   Set Conn = Server.CreateObject("ADODB.Connection") '***
   Conn.Open "KingSight","guest",""
   set RS=Server.CreateObject("ADODB.RecordSet") '***
   Conn.BeginTrans ' start a unit of work
   rs.Open "Sighting", Conn, adOpenStatic, adLockOptimistic ' static open ***
   rs.AddNew ' new record
   rs("Date")=CDate(Request("KDate"))
   if Request("Before")="on" then
     rs("Before")=-1
   else
     rs("Before")=0
   end if
   rs("Location")=Request("Loc")
   rs("Name")=Request("Name")
   rs("Comment")=Request("Comment")
   rs("subtime")=now
   rs.Update
   Conn.CommitTrans
   rs.Close
   Conn.Close
%>


<H1> Thanks for your report </H1>
<% if Session("Debug")="1" then %>
Debug:<%= Request.Form %> <P>
<%end if %>
Your name is <%= Request("Name") %> and you saw the King
<% if Request("Before")="" then %>
for the first time
<% else %>
again
<% end if %>
on <%= Request("KDate") %> at <%= Request("Loc") %>
<P>Thank you very much!
<A HREF=find.asp>Click here to view recent sightings!</A>
<% end if %>
<P>
<A HREF="default.asp" ><IMG SRC="larrow.gif" ALT="home"> Back to home page</A>
</BODY>
<!-- #include file="copyrigh.inc" -->
</HTML>
```

Voting

Another part of the Microsoft Personalization System is the voting component. This component makes it simple to ask users questions and to have them reply. The component keeps a record of the vote in a database. You can ask the component to retrieve the results in a variety of ways. You can even ask the component to make a nicely formatted HTML table.

The voting component is very handy. If you want to do something fancier (for example, create a graph), you can ask the component for the raw data. Usually, you don't care exactly how or where the component stores its data.

A downside of the voting component is that you can't easily preload the choices without voting for them. So, if the question is "How much income tax would you be willing to pay?" and you don't preload any choices, the results will show only numbers that someone has already voted for. On the other hand, suppose you set a single vote at each 10 percent mark from 0 through 100—then someone might look at your results and think that someone really voted for 100 percent and 0 percent.

Another problem with the voting component is the lack of security. If you supply the user property ID with the vote, the component makes sure that the user did not previously vote. However, this makes the database grow quickly, because it has to store each ID. Also, savvy users can delete cookies, start other browsers, or change computers if they want to vote more than once.

VOTE.ASP (see Listing 12.20) shows how easy it is to integrate a form for voting and the voting component into one file. The script checks the content length. If the length is zero, the script shows the voting form. Otherwise, the script creates a vote object, opens the default voting database, sets the ballot name, and submits the question and the vote (there is only one question in this ballot). Next, the script shows the user the results obtained so far. Of course, you don't have to display the results to the public if you don't want to.

Listing 12.20 Voting.

```
<HTML>

<HEAD>

<TITLE>Vote for the King</TITLE>

</HEAD>
<BODY <!-- #include file="stdbody.inc"-->>
```

```
<% if request("Content_Length")=0 then %>
<!-- get vote -->
<H1>Vote for the King</H1>
<% set vt = Server.CreateObject("mps.vote") %>
<form action="vote.asp" method="post">
    Which of these men is the King: <BR>
    <input type=radio name=king value="Williams">Al Williams<BR>
    <input type=radio name=king value="Kaufman">Andy Kaufman<BR>
    <input type=radio name=king value="Simmons">Richard Simmons<BR>
    <input type=submit value="Vote">
    </form>
<% else %>
<!-- record and show votes -->
<% set vt=Server.CreateObject("mps.vote")
    if vt.Open("vote", "guest", "") = TRUE then
    ballotresult = vt.SetBallotName("King")
    voteresult = vt.Submit("King", Request("King")) %>
    Here are the results so far:
    <%= vt.GetVote("King") %>
    <% else %>
    Error! The Voting system is down. Please contact the web master!
    <% end if %>
<% end if %>
<P>
<A HREF="default.asp"><IMG SRC="larrow.gif" ALT="home"> Back to home page</A>
</BODY>
<!-- #include file="copyrigh.inc" -->
</HTML>
```

What If I Don't Have Site Server?

The enhanced site assumes that you have Site Server installed. However, Site Server won't work with the current version of Personal Web Server. If you still want to work with most of the examples, you can look in the KING1 subdirectory. This is a lite version of the final site that has most (but not all) of the features in the KING2 version.

If you want the advantages of the user property database without having Site Server, you can create a simple system that allows users to log in and have values associated with them using a custom database. Although this isn't exactly like the UPD, in some ways it's better since you don't have to rely on cookies.

Summary

This chapter gives you an inside look at converting an existing Web site into an ASP-based site. You've probably noticed that there is more than one way to do things. For quotes, you can use server-side or client-side script. For ad rotation, you can use an ActiveX component on the server or just write some script.

The best approach is to start with an idea of what you want to do and then let the solution suggest the way to do it. Of course, you can have too much of a good thing, so be sure to use active features only where they make sense.

Your Own Server-Side Components

Server-side components can add incredible power to your Web pages. But what happens if you can't find one that does what you want? Write your own, using Visual Basic.

Al Williams

Notes...

Chapter

13

Have you ever wondered how Microsoft server-side components work? Are they magical parts of IIS? No. Server-side components are simply ActiveX objects that Microsoft ships with IIS. Do you want your own components? Then, you need only write a custom ActiveX object.

Only? Writing ActiveX objects is a tough business, right? It's true that ActiveX programming has a bad reputation, but this reputation is not entirely deserved for several reasons. It's true that general-purpose ActiveX programming for large tasks (such as embedding documents) can be difficult. But the objects you need to build to make server-side components are much less complex. Besides, with new tools like Visual Basic (VB) 5, you can create components quite easily.

You can use any tool you like for developing ActiveX. Still, VB5 is probably the most approachable if you're not interested in becoming a full-time ActiveX programmer. When you write client controls (see the next chapter), you might not want to use languages like VB because they require large files that you must download to the client. But on the server side, these files are no problem at all. You just install them on the server, and you're done.

The Anatomy Of A Server-Side Component

A server-side component is simply an ActiveX object that implements the **IDispatch** interface. What does that mean? It means that it's a piece of code that supports a special interface for outside programs. This interface allows another program to set properties and call methods inside the ActiveX object. It also allows the external program to query the object about which properties and methods it supports.

How difficult is it to write an **IDispatch** interface in an ActiveX object? That depends. If you're willing to use VB5, it's not hard at all. If you use C++ or other languages, it gets more complex.

Each component resides in a DLL file. It is not unusual to make a single DLL that contains more than one component. When a page calls **Server.CreateObject** and passes the name of your component, IIS uses ActiveX to create an instance of your ActiveX object. Because there might be more than one page executing at one time, your object might have more than one instance active at any time.

The IIS calls a special event in your component immediately after it creates an instance of it (unless you don't provide a handler for it). It also calls another event when it's ready to delete an instance of your component. Other than these two calls, everything else happens because the ASP script calls a method or accesses a property.

Most high-level tools, including VB5, have special tools that make it easy to add properties and methods to an ActiveX **IDispatch** object. These tools can make it fairly easy to construct simple ASP components. However, because your component might have multiple instances active at once, you'll need to think about synchronizing between the multiple copies.

A number of ASP components are on the Web, so before you decide to write one, you might want to search to see whether someone else has already written it for you. A good place to start is **www.activeserverpages.com**.

Sometimes, however, there's no substitute for rolling your own component. Maybe you need to capture custom business rules or access a special device or database. You can do all this with components. In fact, anything you can do under Windows you can do with a server-side component.

Getting Started

Once you decide to write a server-side component, your first step should be planning and designing. Time you spend planning your component now will save you an enormous amount of trouble later.

As with other components, you can have any number of properties and methods. You can't readily support events, however, so don't design them in. You'll notice that only the ASP built-in objects, such as **Application** and **Session**, support events. The components (like the browser capability or ad rotation objects) also don't support events.

Properties can take several forms. To the ASP script, they always look like simple variables. But your program might see them differently. In their simplest form, properties look like variables to your program as well. Sometimes, though, they look like functions. Why? So you can modify your component's behavior.

Suppose you have a component that reads the temperature from an external sensor. You'd like to show the temperature on your Web page. Suppose the sensor reads in Celsius. Because most Web surfers live in the United States, however, you probably will want a Fahrenheit display.

Of course, you could just convert the reading to Fahrenheit before storing it in the property. But what about the Canadian branch office? It might prefer Celsius. You would be converting it once, and they would convert it right back.

Why not make two properties: **TempC** and **TempF**. When the script reads **TempC**, it invokes a function in your component that simply reads the temperature from the sensor. The **TempF** function, on the other hand, calls **TempC** and applies a conversion to the result before passing it back to the script. From the script's point of view, both are only variables.

Because these properties are variables, the script can write to them, which might not be a good idea if the property isn't something the script should change. When using functions internally, you can prohibit writing (or reading for that matter) by returning an error from the appropriate function.

Sometimes, you might want to write to the property. Suppose the component interfaces with a thermostat instead of a thermometer. It would then be reasonable to read and write the temperature value. Again, using a function you could convert incoming Fahrenheit values to Celsius.

Methods are subroutine, or function, calls that you create with VB5. However, you should consider whether a property would be more effective. Suppose you have a component that breaks a line of text into multiple lines on the basis of a width. You have at least two choices here. The obvious one is to write a method that accepts the text and width as parameters. The method returns the new string.

Another choice is to use three properties. For example, the script sets the **Width** and the **InString** properties, and then it can read the **OutString** property to learn the result. Which method is best? It depends on your needs and your personal preferences. Either way works well.

When you plan your component, remember that you'll have access to all the built-in IIS objects (such as **Application**, **Session**, **Request**, and **Response**). However, you won't have easy access to the other components (such as the ad rotation component). You also can't handle events from the built-in objects. That's up to the script. Of course, if you tell the script author to call your object during an event, you can process events, but it's up to the script author to decide that.

Getting Started With VB5

When you use VB to create a server-side component, you'll actually create an ActiveX DLL. Technically, it's possible for IIS to use ActiveX EXEs as well, but this can result in performance problems. Unless you know what you're doing and have a very good reason to do so, stick with the DLLs.

When you start VB, you'll see a dialog like the one shown in Figure 13.1. Simply select ActiveX DLL, and click Open. Of course, if you're in the middle of a project, you can click on the Recent tab and reopen it instead of creating a new one.

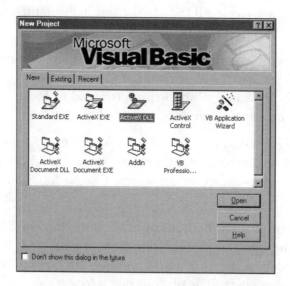

Figure 13.1

Starting VB.

Visual Basic assigns a name to your project and a name to the class module that contains your component. If you want more than one component in a DLL, you can add more class modules. If your project name is **ASPDLL** and the class module name is **TestComponent**, scripts will use the string **ASPDLL.TestComponent** to name your object for **Server.CreateObject**. Therefore, the first thing you should do is change the default names (unless you really want to use **Project1.Class1**—a bad idea).

To change the project name, select the project in the Project Explorer window (see Figure 13.2) and then change the name in the Properties window (see Figure 13.3). If you don't see these windows, use the View menu to bring them up.

Figure 13.2

The Project Explorer window.

Figure 13.3

The Properties window.

Changing the class name is just as easy. Just select the class in the Project Explorer window and change its name in the Properties window. You should not change the other available property—**Instancing**. Leave this value set at 5, which means that your object can service multiple instances at once.

Fleshing It Out

If you're an experienced VB programmer, you might want to jump right in and start writing methods and properties in the Code window (see Figure 13.4). Public **SUB**s and **FUNCTION**s become methods, and any public global variables become properties.

However, there's an easier way to proceed. Pull down the Add-Ins menu. Chances are, you won't see an entry there for the Class Builder Utility. If you do, that's great. If you don't, click on Add-In Manager (under the same menu), select the checkbox next to the Class Builder Utility (see Figure 13.5) and click OK.

Either way, you should now see the Class Builder Utility when you pull down the VB Add-Ins menu. Selecting the utility shows you the dialog in Figure 13.6. You might get a warning that the utility found a class already there, but don't worry. By selecting the proper class in the left-hand portion of the dialog, you can see all the properties and methods for that class (and events, but then, you can't use events). Right now there are no properties and methods, so the dialog is blank.

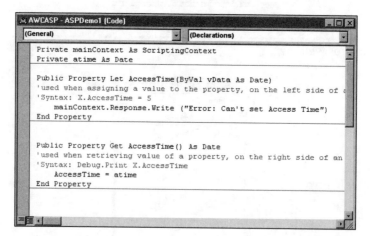

Figure 13.4

The Code window.

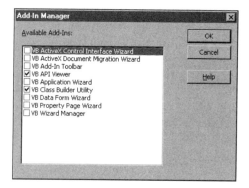

Figure 13.5

Adding Class Builder.

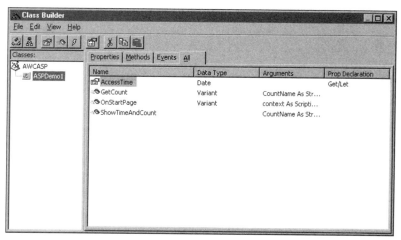

Figure 13.6

Using Class Builder.

Creating Methods

Creating a method is very simple. You can click on the small, green, box in the toolbar and select File|New|Method, or you can right-click the class name and select New|Method. In either case, you'll see the screen shown in Figure 13.7. Here, you can specify the name of the method, its return value, and any arguments it takes. For the purpose of ASP components, the Declare as Friend? checkbox is meaningless, and you'll rarely use the Default Method? checkbox.

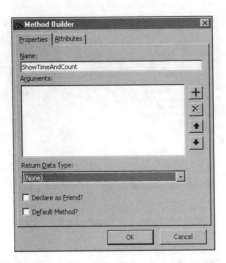

Figure 13.7

Adding a method.

You can click the Attributes tab if you want to describe the method and specify a help file ID for it. This does not mean a lot for pure ASP scripting, but some development tools might make use of this information.

Creating Properties

Properties are just about as easy to add as methods. You can either click the icon that has a hand pointing to some paper or pick File|New|Property. You can also right-click the class name and select New|Property. Any of these actions will make the dialog shown in Figure 13.8 appear.

Again, you need to specify a name and a type. You can also choose whether you want a simple variable or whether you want to use public properties to manipulate the variable. You won't use the Friend Variable selection, so don't worry about that.

When you pick Public Member as the property type, Class Builder will put two functions in your program. One looks like this:

```
Public Property Let AccessTime(ByVal vData As Date)
'used when assigning a value to the property, on the left side of an
assignment.
'Syntax: X.AccessTime = 5
. . .
End Property
```

This subroutine assigns the value from the script (passed in as **vData**) to the property.

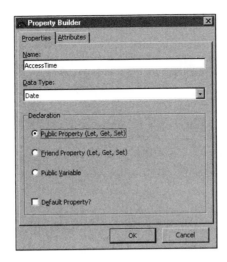

Figure 13.8

Adding a property.

The other subroutine is this:

```
Public Property Get AccessTime() As Date
'used when retrieving the value of a property, on the right side of an
assignment.
'Syntax: Debug.Print X.AccessTime
   . . .
End Property
```

As you can guess, this piece of code fetches the value of the property and returns it. Class Builder puts example code in these skeletons to get you started. It's up to you to add any data validation, conversion, or other operations to the basic skeleton.

Finishing Up

After you finish your methods and properties, you can add more classes. Each class will be a separate ASP object (but will reside in the same DLL file). When you're satisfied, exit the utility, which will ask you whether you want to update your project. Click Yes, or it will discard everything you just did.

Now your component has the skeleton for the methods and properties functions. You'll need to fill in any custom processing (for example, converting Fahrenheit to Celsius).

Once you have finished that, you'll want to save everything (just to be on the safe side) and build your project. You build your project by selecting File|Make *project name* (the actual menu item will have the name of your project on it). This saves your project as a DLL file that you can now integrate with an ASP script.

Remember, unless you're developing on your server, you'll need to put this DLL file on the server, register it (using REGSVR32), and be sure that all the VB support files are present.

How do you know which VB files you need? One way is to run the VB Application Setup Wizard (look for it on the Start menu in the VB group). It will create an entire setup program for you. You can run the setup program on the server, and everything (including the registration) will happen automatically.

You can also ask the program to show you what files you need and then manually copy them over. You'll need to open a command window first, change the directory to where you placed the DLL, and run REGSVR32 with your DLL on the command line. If your DLL is AWCASP.DLL, you would enter "REGSVR32 AWCASP.DLL". Remember, if you're developing on the machine that is also running the Web server, you don't need to do any of this. Just build the DLL, and you're ready to go.

Trying It Out

After you have all the files in place, how can you test your new object? By writing a script, of course. If you're lucky, everything will work the first time. If you're not lucky, you'll need to fix your program.

If you try to rebuild the DLL, you'll find that IIS is holding it open, so you can't rebuild it. Even if you're developing on a different machine, you'll find that you can't copy the new file over the old one because the old one is open.

The solution is to stop IIS and restart it. This once meant stopping the W3SVC service. However, the newest versions of IIS will still hold your component open when W3SVC shuts down. To completely shut down, you need to stop IISADMIN (which will also stop any other IIS services, not just the Web server). Then you can restart W3SVC (which automatically starts IISADMIN) and any of the other services you want.

You can shut these down from the Control Panel or a command prompt. From a command prompt, enter "NET STOP IISADMIN" followed by "NET START W3SVC". This should cause the server to close your component until a page requests it again. I usually rebuild the DLL between the STOP and the START just to be sure. Obviously, you don't want to develop ASP components on a production server.

Using C++ Or Java

What if you don't like VB? That's OK—ActiveX works with many languages, including C++ and Visual J++ (Microsoft's flavor of Java). If you can build an **IDispatch** interface, you're in business.

Details

As with most things, the devil is in the details. Sure the Class Builder will put skeletons in for your property functions and methods. It will even add internal private variables for your properties. But how do you flesh out your code?

A complete treatment of VB is beyond the scope of this book. However, if you have followed the discussion of VBScript in the earlier chapters, you probably won't have much trouble anyway.

So the only question left is, How do I work with IIS? Luckily, that's not difficult at all. The key is that IIS will call an event in your component every time a page creates or destroys the object. You need not supply code for either of these events, but usually you'll supply **OnStartPage** (the creation event). Why? Because IIS passes this event a magic object (a **ScriptingContext**) that allows you to access the IIS internal objects.

 ## Using **ScriptingContext**

*The only way to get a **ScriptingContext** object is from the **OnStartPage** event. However, if a script creates an object with Application scope, this event doesn't fire (neither does **OnEndPage**). Therefore, objects that expect to reside at the application level can't really use the internal IIS objects.*

The Events

To know that IIS created your object, you should write a function named **OnStartPage**. Here's how it should look:

```
Public Function OnStartPage(context As ScriptingContext)
. . .
End Function
```

Of course, VB doesn't know what a **ScriptingContext** object looks like, so you must tell it. Select Project|References on the VB menu. Then, locate the entry that says Microsoft Active Server Pages 1.0 Object Library (your version number might be different). Select the checkbox next to this item and click OK. Now VB knows about all the objects in IIS (press F2 to open the object browser if you want to examine them). You must do this one time for each new project you create.

Some components don't care about the scripting context. Suppose your component just wants to write a time stamp to a file. No problem. You could write it from inside **OnStartPage**. Although you'll still need the **context** argument, you can ignore it.

On the other hand, suppose you want the script to call your **WriteTimeStamp** method to do this work. In this case, you don't need an **OnStartPage** routine at all. However, if you want to work with any of the built-in IIS objects, you must provide an **OnStartPage** routine. You'll probably want to save the **context** argument to some private global variable so you can use it later.

Using The Objects

Suppose you want a component that will write out a palindrome. Your **OnStartPage** routine would look like this:

```
Public Function OnStartPage(context As ScriptingContext)
context.response.write("A man, a plan, a canal, Panama!")
End Function
```

Of course, this is no big deal. You could do the same job in script. But what if the string came from a database or perhaps a network socket connected to an MOTD (Message Of The Day) server? In this case, there might be some real value in using a component that has access to the **Response** object.

All the objects you expect are available: **Application**, **Session**, **Response**, **Request**, and **Server**. You can either use them right in place or make copies of them. For example:

```
Context.response.write("Howdy!")
```

Or you could write:

```
Dim ResponseObj as Response
Set ResponseObj = context.Response
ResponseObj.write("Howdy!")
```

An Example

Now that you've seen what is required, let's tackle a complete project. To keep things simple yet interesting, let's look at an object that counts page hits and page access times.

Remember: Planning (design) first! Then you can move on to coding and finally testing. Let's discuss these in order.

Planning

It's relatively easy to count hits and track access times in regular script, but some problems can occur. One problem is that the counts reset when the server restarts unless you write them somewhere. Tracking time is easy, but you must allocate storage for the time if you want to use it in more than one place.

To make life easier, you can build a component that counts hits and then stores them in the registry. It will manage different counters by using a unique name for each counter. You should be able to increment the count and retrieve it, or you can simply get the current count. As a by-product, it will also store the time at which you accessed the page. It shouldn't let you change that time, of course. Also, it would be nice if the object could display a preset message with the access time and count nicely formatted.

To accommodate this, I decided to allow for a read-only property (**AccessTime**), a method named **GetCount**, and another method named **ShowTimeAndCount**. The **GetCount** method accepts a string and returns the updated count for that string. If you pass an optional second argument as **False**, **GetCount** doesn't increment the count before it returns it. Therefore, assuming that our object is in an object reference variable **obj**, you would write:

```
' Assume Count is now 10
x=obj.GetCount("AWC")  ' x=11; count now =11
x=obj.GetCount("AWC",TRUE")   ' x=12; count now=12
x=obj.GetCount("AWC",FALSE)    ' x=12; count now=12
obj.ShowTimeAndCount "AWC"    ' writes formatted string to HTML
```

Getting Started

With the design firmly in hand (and in mind), it's time to start a new VB ActiveX DLL project. The first thing to do is rename the project and class module. The project name is **AWCASP** and the class name **ASPDemo1**, meaning that a script that wanted to create this object would write:

```
<% Set obj=Server.CreateObject("AWCASP.ASPDemo1") %>
```

Next, you must add the ASP Object Library to the project references with the Project|References menu. Then, VB will know about all the IIS objects, including **ScriptingContext**.

This component definitely needs to use the **ScriptingContext** object, so it will need an **OnStartPage** event handler. This handler only has to store away the context and the current time and date for later. Here's the code to do that:

```
Public Function OnStartPage(context As ScriptingContext)
Set mainContext = context
atime = Now
End Function
```

You also must declare global variables for **mainContext** and **atime**. You can see exactly where to declare these in Listing 13.1, which contains the complete listing.

Listing 13.1 The component.

```
VERSION 1.0 CLASS
BEGIN  MultiUse = -1  'TrueEND
Attribute VB_Name = "ASPDemo1"
Attribute VB_GlobalNameSpace = True
Attribute VB_Creatable = True
Attribute VB_PredeclaredId = False
Attribute VB_Exposed = True
Attribute VB_Ext_KEY = "SavedWithClassBuilder" ,"Yes"
Attribute VB_Ext_KEY = "Top_Level" ,"Yes"
' Everything from this point up is automatically put in by VB -
don't type it in!
' From here down is the stuff you type in
Private mainContext As ScriptingContext
Private atime As Date

Public Property Let AccessTime(ByVal vData As Date)
'used when assigning a value to the property, on the left side of an
assignment.
'Syntax: X.AccessTime = 5
    mainContext.Response.Write ("Error: Can't set Access Time")
End Property


Public Property Get AccessTime() As Date
'used when retrieving value of a property, on the right side of an
assignment.
'Syntax: Debug.Print X.AccessTime
    AccessTime = atime
End Property


Public Function GetCount(CountName As String, Optional flag)
ct = GetSetting("AWCASP", "Counter", CountName, 0)
If IsMissing(flag) Then flag = True
```

```
If flag = True Then
  ct = ct + 1
  SaveSetting "AWCASP", "Counter", CountName, ct
End If
GetCount = ct
End Function


Public Sub ShowTimeAndCount(CountName As String)
ct = GetCount(CountName)
mainContext.Response.Write "<BR><B><I>At " & atime & " you were the " & ct & "
visitor!</I></B><BR>"
End Sub


Public Function OnStartPage(context As ScriptingContext)
Set mainContext = context
atime = Now
End Function
```

Adding Properties

Using the Class Builder Utility (on the Add-Ins menu), you can add the single property **AccessTime**. If you don't see the Class Builder on the menu, use the Add-In Manger to include it.

At first it might be tempting to simply use a regular variable for the **AccessTime** property, but that won't do. Why not? Because the property is read-only. Instead, use Public Members for the properties. Then you can raise an error in the subroutine that attempts to set the value.

Although Class Builder creates a variable to correspond to the **AccessTime** property, you don't need that variable because **atime** already stores the time. After you close Class Builder, you can delete its variable and change the reference in the **AccessTime Get** function to **atime**.

Because this property is read-only, you can get rid of everything in the **Let** function. You can raise a VB error (using the built-in **Err** object) or just write an error out to the HTML using the **Response** object. Usually, writing the HTML error is a better idea.

Adding Methods

Class Builder adds the methods, but it really doesn't know what to do with them. It's up to you to flesh them out with meaningful code.

The **GetCount** function uses several tricks that might not be obvious at first glance. Notice in the argument list that the **flag** argument has the keyword **Optional**. This means that the caller doesn't need to supply it. However, if it's not present and you try to use it, an error will occur.

The trick is to use the **IsMissing** function (see Listing 13.1). If **IsMissing** returns **TRUE**, you can set a default value before proceeding.

The other interesting part of the **GetCount** method is how it manipulates the registry. Instead of using the Windows API, it uses the ultrasimple **GetSetting** and **SaveSetting** calls. Of course, you can call the Windows API from VB, but that's beyond the scope of this book. Besides, why not use these simple calls? They work very well.

There's one potential problem with the way the object stores counts. If the server is very busy accessing the same page for more than one client, it's possible that two copies of the object will try to access the count at one time. This can cause small inaccuracies in the count.

For example, suppose I pull up the page with the counter in it at the same time you do. The IIS creates one object for me and another for you. Suppose my object reads the current count from the registry as 9. The Windows scheduler puts my object to sleep and starts yours. Your object also reads a 9 from the registry, adds 1 to it, and puts it back. Then your object sleeps. When my object resumes processing, it will add 1 to the 9 it read before and write the resulting 10 to the registry. Now we both think we are the tenth visitor.

This is not a serious problem, however, because it's very unlikely to happen unless your site is heavily loaded and often gets multiple simultaneous hits. Even if it does happen, it means only that your count is off by 1. If you have a busy site, though, this might be a concern. Also, if you're giving away $1 million to your one-millionth visitor, you sure wouldn't want it to double up on the 1 million count!

In cases where it matters, you need to use a *mutex*, which is a Windows object that lets one object claim ownership of a resource. That's an advanced technique, but you can do it, even in VB. For most people, however, the component is fine the way it is.

The **ShowTimeAndCount** method is very simple because the first thing it does is call **GetCount**. This is a good example of how you can reuse parts of your component. Just because the script calls **GetCount** doesn't mean you too can't call it. After **GetCount** returns the correct count, a single line of code formats it and writes it using the **Response** object.

Trying It Out

Using the component is really quite simple. Listing 13.2 shows a simple ASP script that tests the basic functions of the component. Because it's so simple, I didn't even bother making it a proper HTML file. Once you view the script, refresh the screen and you'll see the count increase and the time change.

Listing 13.2   Test script.

```
<% Set obj=Server.CreateObject("AWCASP.ASPDemo1") %>  <!-- Sets time string -->
<P>Access time:
<%= obj.AccessTime %>
<P>This page accessed: <%= obj.GetCount("TestCounter") %> times. <P>
Again, that was: <%= obj.GetCount("TestCounter",FALSE) %> times. <P>


-Or-

<% obj.ShowTimeAndCount("AltCounter") %>
```

Summary

Although it isn't trivial, you can create your own ASP components. With Visual Basic, it isn't very difficult, and custom components can be the answer to getting just the effect you want in your Web page.

There are three major obstacles to creating your own ASP components. First, you need to learn a programming language that supports ActiveX. Second, you need to take multitasking issues into account. Third, and perhaps most frustrating, it's very difficult to debug your code once you have written it.

It's worth noting that some languages, like C++, have debuggers that can attach to IIS and let you step through component code. However, this isn't trivial, and the extra learning curve that comes with C++ makes this approach of interest mainly to experienced C++ programmers.

Practical Guide To

Server-Side Components

- Designing A Component
- Starting A Project
- Starting Class Builder
- Handling Multithreading
- Accessing IIS Objects And Affecting HTML
- Registration Of Components
- Debugging Tips

Designing A Component

The first step to building a component is to plan (design) it. Before you start, you should have a clear idea of all the properties and methods you'll use.

In addition, you should know whether properties will be read/write, read-only, or write-only. You should also know whether you expect them to be simple variable types or whether they will require public functions.

You should plan which arguments the methods will take and the values, if any, they return. It's also important to have a good idea of what the methods are supposed to do. Often, it's helpful to note which properties a method uses and which properties a method affects.

Finally, you should decide whether you need to write **OnStartPage** and **OnEndPage** event handlers. If you need to know when IIS instantiates your object or you need to use the built-in IIS objects, you need an **OnStartPage** handler. If you need to clean up anything you have created earlier, you'll want to write an **OnEndPage** handler.

Starting A Project

To start coding, you need to start a new VB project. Be sure the project is set to be an ActiveX DLL. Here are the steps you'll need to follow:

1. Start a new project.

2. Rename the project to something meaningful.

3. Rename the class module to something meaningful.

4. Add the ASP Object Library to the project references.

Starting Class Builder

The easiest way to add properties and methods to your component is with VB's Class Builder, which you can find on the Add-Ins menu. If it isn't there, click on the Add-In Manager menu item (also under Add-Ins) and select Class Builder.

Not all functions of Class Builder are relevant to ASP components. You'll add only properties and methods. You can also add new class modules if you want more than one component in a single file.

Handling Multithreading

It's important to realize that your object might run in a thread that is scheduled with other threads that are working for other clients. This means that if your component depends on sharing a file, a registry entry, or any other object, it should be prepared to deal with others trying to use it at the same time. This very complex subject requires an understanding of Windows synchronization objects (such as mutexes, semaphores, and events).

For many simple components, however, this isn't a real problem. Just be aware of it, and try to think through what would happen if two components were active at the same time.

Accessing IIS Objects And Affecting HTML

If you need to access IIS objects like **Session**, **Application**, **Request**, **Response**, or **Server**, you'll need to handle the **OnStartPage** event. This event receives a single argument—a **ScriptingContext** object.

You can use the **ScriptingContext** object right away or cache it away for later use. It has five members: **Session**, **Application**, **Request**, **Response**, and **Server**. You can use these members to access any property or method of the corresponding server object. Notice, however, that you can't handle events.

For example, here's how you would write something to the HTML stream if you had a **ScriptingContext** named **context**:

```
context.Response.Write("Howdy!")
```

Registration Of Components

Don't forget that you must install the component you write on the Web server. If you're developing on the server, that's fine. If you're not, you need to install the DLL file and any support files the DLL requires and register the DLL. You can do this manually if you know which files you need. Simply copy them to the server and run REGSVR32 (on the server) specifying the DLL's file name. This makes entries in the system registry so that IIS (and other ActiveX programs) can find it.

What if you don't know which files you need? For a VB program, you can run the Application Setup Wizard (from the Start menu in the VB group). This program can tell you which files a VB project requires and can create a setup program that will do all the installation work (even the registration) for you.

Debugging Tips

Debugging server components is notoriously difficult. If you're using C++ or other advanced languages, you might be able to run IIS as a debugged program (which has a lot of overhead, as you might expect).

If you're using VB or you don't want to run IIS as a debugged process, you'll need to resort to writing debugging information out to the HTML stream or a file. Although this is not ideal, you can usually get a handle on things by doing this.

Another way to approach a VB project is to add an ordinary VB EXE project to your DLL project. Then you can write simple routines that create your IIS object and call the routines in it. However, if you're using the **ScriptingContext** object, you'll have trouble simulating it and will be stuck, again, with peppering your code with debugging output.

More Information

This chapter only scratches the surface of ActiveX programming. If you want to know more, you might be interested in some other Coriolis books I have written. For C++ programmers, check out *Developing ActiveX Web Controls*. Visual Basic programmers should read *Visual Developer: Developing ActiveX Controls With VB5*.

ActiveX is a broad topic and has many uses. Writing server-side components is one of them. You can also use ActiveX to create client-side controls, as you'll see in Chapter 14. There are many other uses for ActiveX as well.

Time spent learning ActiveX will eventually pay off. Most new features in Windows use ActiveX (including Microsoft Transaction Server, Microsoft Message Queue, and advanced MAPI).

You can also find more information about ActiveX on the Web. My site (**www.al-williams.com**) is one place to start. You might also check out **www.microsoft.com/activex** and **www.program.com**.

Chapter 14

Your Own Client-Side Objects

What happens when you can't find the right ActiveX control or Java applet? Write your own, of course!

Al Williams

Notes...

14

I've been an amateur radio operator for over 20 years and an electronics hobbyist for longer than that. One odd phenomenon that affects people like me is the do-it-yourself syndrome. I've seen folks like me build their own computers (or televisions or radios) and spend double what it would take to simply buy the thing in the store.

Is this crazy? Maybe. But those of us afflicted with this malady will tell you that there's a certain satisfaction in doing something yourself. Besides, once you build something, you know it inside and out. You can also make it just the right size and with just the right mix of features.

There are plenty of ActiveX objects and Java applets on the Web that you can borrow for your Web site. On the other hand, there is the satisfaction of making your own. When you make your own objects, you can forge them to best meet your needs.

Surely making your own objects is difficult, right? Well, *difficult* is a relative term, and making objects with Visual Basic 5 really isn't that hard at all. Visual J++ and Visual C++ will work as well, but they are a bit harder. Even so, I believe that writing an ActiveX control with Visual C++ is easier than writing a complete Windows application.

Downsides

Is there a downside to all this? Unfortunately, yes. Writing your own objects requires you to buy a development tool and learn it. Visual Basic is probably the most approachable, but if you're not a programmer, you'll need to spend some time getting familiar with it.

Another concern that is true only for ActiveX controls is download efficiency. Sure, VB5 and Visual C++ (using Microsoft Foundation Classes, or MFC) can make it easy to create ActiveX controls. However, that simplicity depends on large DLLs that the tools use, and most of the code is in those libraries. If the user already has the library for some reason (for example, from downloading someone else's control), that's great. If they don't, they'll need to wait for a lengthy download before they can see your award-winning control.

Does it have to be this way? For VB, the answer is probably yes. For Visual C++, however, you can write minimalist controls that are much more efficient by using straight C++ or a tool called the Advanced Template Library (ATL). However, neither of these approaches is simple. You need an advanced understanding of ActiveX and C++ to create controls without the MFC library.

On the other hand, because many people do use these tools to build ActiveX controls, there is a good possibility that the libraries already exist on the user's computer. Also, as connection speeds continue to increase, the penalty for these downloads becomes less important.

Using VB5

All this changes with the release of VB5, which allows you to create controls as easily as you currently create form-based applications. It also lets you create ActiveX controls, which, in theory, you can use in VB, Web pages, C++, Delphi, PowerBuilder, and any other environment that understands ActiveX controls.

If you are already a VB programmer, you'll have little or no trouble creating controls. If you haven't tried VB, it isn't difficult to get started. Also, Microsoft has introduced a new user interface that is more comfortable for programmers who are accustomed to their Microsoft Developer's Studio program.

ActiveX Fundamentals

If you've ever used any kind of component software, you won't be surprised to hear that the fundamental pieces of an ActiveX control are properties, methods, and events. VB-created ActiveX controls are no different.

Properties are similar to variables. They are values that the program using the component (the container) can set or read. In VB, you can place these values in variables or connect them to components that you use to create your component. You'll see how this works shortly.

Methods are simply functions and subroutines that the container can call. Again, you can define your own, or you can expose methods from components that you use internally.

Events notify the container when something interesting happens. Guess what? You can define custom events or pass events from other components.

Fail To Plan—Plan To Fail

To get the most from an ActiveX control, you should carefully plan which properties, methods, and events it will handle. You can tweak things later, but it helps if you have a good idea from the start about what you want to use. The sample control I'll show you in this chapter is a simple scanning bar of lights (see Figure 14.1)—you know, the sort of thing you see under the view screen on the Enterprise (the original one). It exposes four properties:

- **Delay**—The number of milliseconds to delay between each lamp turning on.

- **Direction**—**TRUE** to scan from left to right, or **FALSE** to scan from right to left.

- **ForeColor**—The color of lights when they are on.

- **Hold**—Stops the lights from scanning when **TRUE**.

The control also supports a single event, **TICK**, which fires each time the lights change state (that is, once for each period set by **Delay**). The control has no methods.

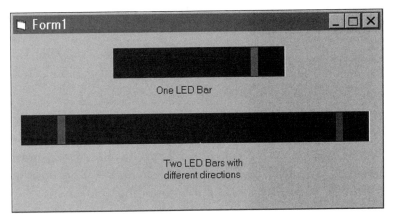

Figure 14.1

The scanning LED bar.

Laying Out The Control

Once you have a plan, you can fire up VB5. From the startup dialog box, select ActiveX Control from the New tab. The program will create an empty project.

If you start VB5 (and you have the default screen layout), you'll notice that a property browser window appears. Beneath that is a description window that describes the selected property. When you create a component, you'll want to control what appears in this window when programmers use your component. Even farther down is a layout window that shows where your form will appear when it runs. If you right-click on this window, you can create grid lines to show you the common screen resolutions and select options for where your forms will show up when your program runs.

In the center of the screen, you'll see windows that hold forms and Basic code. By default, the code window shows you all the code at once and draws lines between sections. If you prefer the old style, you can click the small button at the bottom-left corner of the code window. In fact, you can change just about any aspect of the interface and easily move, resize, or hide any of the windows or toolbars. You can customize everything. Right-clicking anywhere brings up interesting menus.

Defining The Interface

To create the **LEDBar** control (the scanning lights), I used the normal Basic shape component. Each of the 20 lights is a rectangle shape. I created the first one, copied it to the clipboard, and then pasted it to form a control array. Then I pasted it 18 more times to complete the array. By using a control array, I can refer to each light as an element in an array (or collection, if you prefer). The array's name is **LED0**, and the elements range from 0 through 19.

The control also needs a timer. Each time the timer expires, the control should turn off the current light and then turn on the light to the right or left of the current light (depending on the setting of the **Direction** flag).

At this point, you could start writing code to take care of the logic. However, you'll need some of the properties (for example, **Direction**), and they don't exist yet. To define properties, methods, and events, you'll use the Interface Wizard (from the Add-Ins menu). This wizard (see Figures 14.2 through 14.5) allows you to select members (that is, properties, methods, and events) that many controls support (see Figure 14.2). You can also create custom members (see Figure 14.3). On the next screen (see Figure 14.4), you attach the members to corresponding members in the components that the control contains. I attached the **Delay** property directly to the

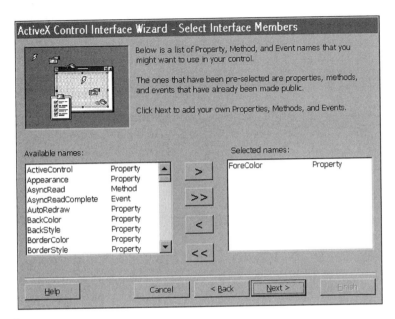

Figure 14.2

The Interface Wizard's first screen.

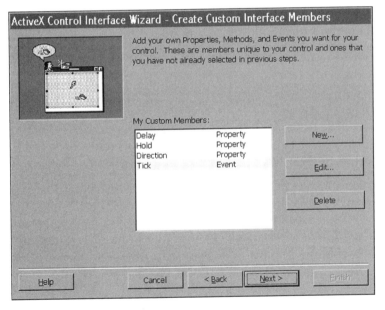

Figure 14.3

Creating custom members.

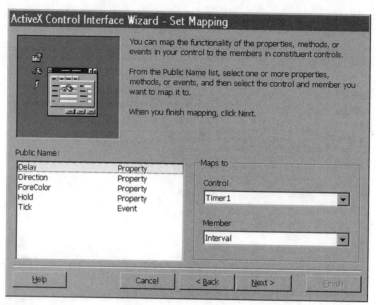

Figure 14.4

Mapping members.

Timer component and the **ForeColor** property to the **UserControl** component (**UserControl** corresponds to a form in a regular VB program).

At this point, it would be tempting to attach the **Tick** event to the timer's **Timer** event. You can do this as long as you haven't already put a **Timer** handler in the code. If you have an existing handler, the wizard will write an extra event handler that causes a compile error.

On the final wizard screen (see Figure 14.5), you can define any unattached members. The description text will appear in the design environment (below the property browser). You can also specify types, properties, and so on. The wizard creates variables for your unattached properties. For example, the **Direction** property causes the wizard to create a variable named **m_Direction**. Methods get skeletal function definitions that you must complete. The wizard also handles events. Of course, any members that you connect to other components don't show up on this screen.

After you complete this wizard, all your external members are complete. Of course, you'll need to write code that handles any custom methods and fires any custom events at the appropriate time. You'll also need to write all the other code that makes your control work.

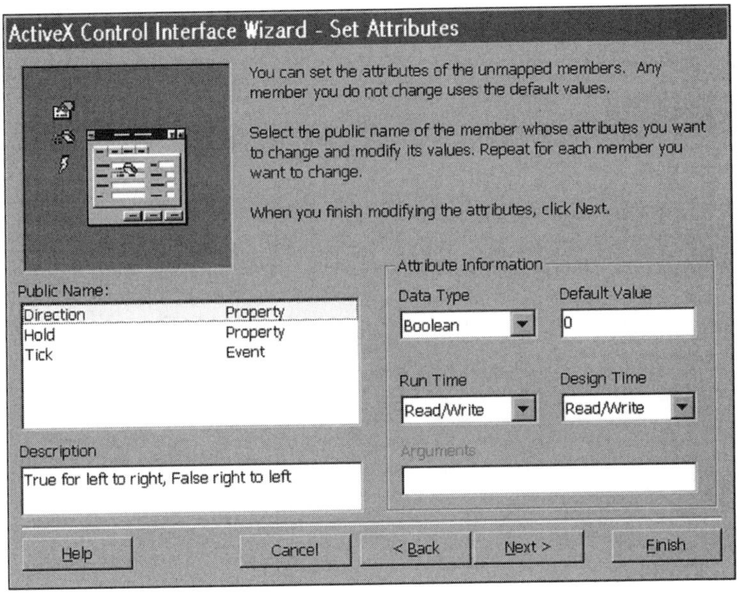

Figure 14.5

Setting member attributes.

Writing The Code

The code to handle the light bar is fairly simple. A **Timer** event handler cycles the lights on the basis of the **m_Direction** flag (see Listing 14.1). Also, the **UserControl_Initialize** event takes care of some setup issues. If you attached the **Tick** event to the **Timer** control, you already have a **Timer** handler. It will contain the line:

```
RaiseEvent Tick
```

You can simply add your code in the same handler. If you didn't hook up the **Tick** event, you can now create a **Timer** handler and add the **RaiseEvent** line to raise your custom event.

Listing 14.1   The LEDBar control.

```
VERSION 5.00
Begin VB.UserControl LedBar
   BackColor       =    &H00FFFFFF&
   ClientHeight    =    432
   ClientLeft      =    0
   ClientTop       =    0
   ClientWidth     =    4788
   FillColor       =    &H00FFFFFF&
   PropertyPages   =    "ledbar.ctx":0000
```

```
ScaleHeight       =    432
ScaleWidth        =    4788
ToolboxBitmap     =    "ledbar.ctx":001A
Begin VB.Timer Timer1
   Interval       =    125
   Left           =    4212
   Top            =    0
End
Begin VB.Shape LED0
   FillStyle      =    0   'Solid
   Height         =    492
   Index          =    19
   Left           =    4560
   Top            =    0
   Width          =    252
End
Begin VB.Shape LED0
   FillStyle      =    0   'Solid
   Height         =    492
   Index          =    18
   Left           =    4320
   Top            =    0
   Width          =    252
End
Begin VB.Shape LED0
   FillStyle      =    0   'Solid
   Height         =    492
   Index          =    17
   Left           =    4080
   Top            =    0
   Width          =    252
End
Begin VB.Shape LED0
   FillStyle      =    0   'Solid
   Height         =    492
   Index          =    16
   Left           =    3840
   Top            =    0
   Width          =    252
End
Begin VB.Shape LED0
   FillStyle      =    0   'Solid
   Height         =    492
   Index          =    15
   Left           =    3600
   Top            =    0
   Width          =    252
End
```

```
Begin VB.Shape LED0
   FillStyle      =   0  'Solid
   Height         =   492
   Index          =   14
   Left           =   3360
   Top            =   0
   Width          =   252
End
Begin VB.Shape LED0
   FillStyle      =   0  'Solid
   Height         =   492
   Index          =   13
   Left           =   3120
   Top            =   0
   Width          =   252
End
Begin VB.Shape LED0
   BackColor      =   &H00000000&
   FillStyle      =   0  'Solid
   Height         =   492
   Index          =   12
   Left           =   2880
   Top            =   0
   Width          =   252
End
Begin VB.Shape LED0
   BackColor      =   &H00000000&
   FillStyle      =   0  'Solid
   Height         =   492
   Index          =   11
   Left           =   2640
   Top            =   0
   Width          =   252
End
Begin VB.Shape LED0
   BackColor      =   &H00000000&
   FillStyle      =   0  'Solid
   Height         =   492
   Index          =   10
   Left           =   2400
   Top            =   0
   Width          =   252
End
Begin VB.Shape LED0
   FillStyle      =   0  'Solid
   Height         =   492
   Index          =   9
   Left           =   2160
```

```
            Top             =    0
            Width           =    252
         End
         Begin VB.Shape LED0
            FillStyle       =    0   'Solid
            Height          =    492
            Index           =    8
            Left            =    1920
            Top             =    0
            Width           =    252
         End
         Begin VB.Shape LED0
            FillStyle       =    0   'Solid
            Height          =    492
            Index           =    7
            Left            =    1680
            Top             =    0
            Width           =    252
         End
         Begin VB.Shape LED0
            FillStyle       =    0   'Solid
            Height          =    492
            Index           =    6
            Left            =    1440
            Top             =    0
            Width           =    252
         End
         Begin VB.Shape LED0
            FillStyle       =    0   'Solid
            Height          =    492
            Index           =    5
            Left            =    1200
            Top             =    0
            Width           =    252
         End
         Begin VB.Shape LED0
            FillStyle       =    0   'Solid
            Height          =    492
            Index           =    4
            Left            =    960
            Top             =    0
            Width           =    252
         End
         Begin VB.Shape LED0
            FillStyle       =    0   'Solid
            Height          =    492
            Index           =    3
            Left            =    720
```

```
         Top             =     0
         Width           =     252
      End
      Begin VB.Shape LED0
         FillStyle       =     0    'Solid
         Height          =     492
         Index           =     2
         Left            =     480
         Top             =     0
         Width           =     252
      End
      Begin VB.Shape LED0
         BackColor       =     &H00000000&
         FillStyle       =     0    'Solid
         Height          =     492
         Index           =     1
         Left            =     240
         Top             =     0
         Width           =     252
      End
      Begin VB.Shape LED0
         BackColor       =     &H000000FF&
         FillColor       =     &H000000FF&
         FillStyle       =     0    'Solid
         Height          =     492
         Index           =     0
         Left            =     0
         Top             =     0
         Width           =     252
      End
   End
End
Attribute VB_Name = "LedBar"
Attribute VB_GlobalNameSpace = False
Attribute VB_Creatable = True
Attribute VB_PredeclaredId = False
Attribute VB_Exposed = True
Attribute VB_Ext_KEY = "PropPageWizardRun" ,"Yes"

Dim n As Integer
'Default Property Values:
Const m_def_Direction = True
Const m_def_Hold = False
'Const m_def_ForeColor = 255
'Property Variables:
Dim m_Direction As Boolean
Dim m_Hold As Boolean
'Dim m_ForeColor As OLE_COLOR
'Event Declarations:
```

```vb
Event Tick()
'Event Timer() 'MappingInfo=Timer1,Timer1,-1,Timer

Private Sub Timer1_Timer()
If m_Hold = True Then Exit Sub
LED0(n).FillColor = vbBlack
If m_Direction Then
  If n = 19 Then n = 0 Else n = n + 1
Else
  If n = 0 Then n = 19 Else n = n - 1
End If
LED0(n).FillColor = UserControl.ForeColor
RaiseEvent Tick
End Sub


Private Sub UserControl_Initialize()
n = 0
LED0(0).FillColor = UserControl.ForeColor
Hold = False

End Sub


Private Sub UserControl_Resize()
For i = 0 To 19
  LED0(i).Width = (ScaleWidth \ 20) * 20 / 20!
  LED0(i).Height = ScaleHeight
  LED0(i).Top = 0
  LED0(i).Left = i * (ScaleWidth \ 20) * 20 / 20!
Next i
End Sub
''WARNING! DO NOT REMOVE OR MODIFY THE FOLLOWING COMMENTED LINES!
''MappingInfo=UserControl,UserControl,-1,BackColor
'Public Property Get BackColor() As OLE_COLOR
'     BackColor = UserControl.BackColor
'End Property
'
'Public Property Let BackColor(ByVal New_BackColor As OLE_COLOR)
'     UserControl.BackColor() = New_BackColor
'     PropertyChanged "BackColor"
'End Property
'
'Public Property Get ForeColor() As OLE_COLOR
'     ForeColor = m_ForeColor
'End Property
'
'Public Property Let ForeColor(ByVal New_ForeColor As OLE_COLOR)
'     m_ForeColor = New_ForeColor
'     PropertyChanged "ForeColor"
'End Property
```

```
'WARNING! DO NOT REMOVE OR MODIFY THE FOLLOWING COMMENTED LINES!
'MappingInfo=Timer1,Timer1,-1,Interval
Public Property Get Delay() As Long
Attribute Delay.VB_Description = "Returns/sets the number of milliseconds between
calls to a Timer control's Timer event."
    Delay = Timer1.Interval
End Property

Public Property Let Delay(ByVal New_Delay As Long)
    Timer1.Interval() = New_Delay
    PropertyChanged "Delay"
End Property

'Initialize Properties for User Control
Private Sub UserControl_InitProperties()
'    m_ForeColor = m_def_ForeColor
    m_Hold = m_def_Hold
    m_Direction = m_def_Direction
End Sub

'Load property values from storage
Private Sub UserControl_ReadProperties(PropBag As PropertyBag)

'    UserControl.BackColor = PropBag.ReadProperty("BackColor", &HFFFFFF)
'    m_ForeColor = PropBag.ReadProperty("ForeColor", m_def_ForeColor)
    Timer1.Interval = PropBag.ReadProperty("Delay", 125)
    UserControl.ForeColor = PropBag.ReadProperty("ForeColor", &H80000012)
    m_Hold = PropBag.ReadProperty("Hold", m_def_Hold)
    m_Direction = PropBag.ReadProperty("Direction", m_def_Direction)
End Sub

'Write property values to storage
Private Sub UserControl_WriteProperties(PropBag As PropertyBag)

'    Call PropBag.WriteProperty("BackColor", UserControl.BackColor, &HFFFFFF)
'    Call PropBag.WriteProperty("ForeColor", m_ForeColor, m_def_ForeColor)
    Call PropBag.WriteProperty("Delay", Timer1.Interval, 125)
    Call PropBag.WriteProperty("ForeColor", UserControl.ForeColor, &H80000012)
    Call PropBag.WriteProperty("Hold", m_Hold, m_def_Hold)
    Call PropBag.WriteProperty("Direction", m_Direction, m_def_Direction)
End Sub

'WARNING! DO NOT REMOVE OR MODIFY THE FOLLOWING COMMENTED LINES!
'MappingInfo=UserControl,UserControl,-1,ForeColor
Public Property Get ForeColor() As OLE_COLOR
Attribute ForeColor.VB_Description = "Returns/sets the foreground color used
to display text and graphics in an object."
    ForeColor = UserControl.ForeColor
End Property
```

```
Public Property Let ForeColor(ByVal New_ForeColor As OLE_COLOR)
    UserControl.ForeColor() = New_ForeColor
    PropertyChanged "ForeColor"
End Property

Public Property Get Hold() As Boolean
Attribute Hold.VB_Description = "Set to TRUE to freeze LEDs"
    Hold = m_Hold
End Property

Public Property Let Hold(ByVal New_Hold As Boolean)
    m_Hold = New_Hold
    PropertyChanged "Hold"
End Property

Public Property Get Direction() As Boolean
Attribute Direction.VB_Description = "True for left to right, False right to left"
    Direction = m_Direction
End Property

Public Property Let Direction(ByVal New_Direction As Boolean)
    m_Direction = New_Direction
    PropertyChanged "Direction"
End Property
```

With those two handlers in place, the control will work as advertised. However, you must make the control the exact size of the 20 shape controls—not very programmer friendly. To improve the behavior, you can add a **UserControl_Resize** event handler to resize the shape controls dynamically.

To calculate the new size and position for each shape control, take the **ScaleWidth** of the **UserControl** object and round it so that it is divisible by 20 (the number of shape controls), then divide it by 20. Given the width of each control, it's easy to determine where the left edge of each control should be. You can set the height of the shape controls to the **UserControl**'s **ScaleHeight** property.

Finishing Touches

Now you are almost finished. You can set the **ToolboxIcon** property to a bitmap so that your control shows up with your choice of pictures in toolboxes. You can also edit the project properties and change the name of the control.

If you want a property sheet for the control, just run the Property Sheet Wizard. It will allow you to select a standard page to select colors (in this case, the foreground color). You can also define custom pages and place properties (such as **Direction** and **Hold**) on them. The wizard automatically creates appropriate pages (see Figures 14.6 and 14.7).

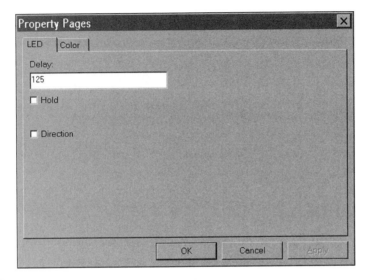

Figure 14.6

A custom property page.

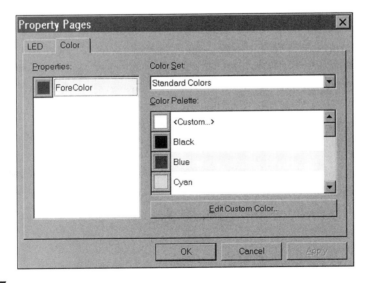

Figure 14.7

A stock property page.

Using The Control

When you are finished, you can test the control. Simply select Add Project from the File menu. When you are prompted, tell the environment that you want an EXE file project. You'll see your control appear in the toolbox. Simply grab it and place it on the form as you would any other component. Use the object browser to set the properties, then double-click the control to write event handlers. It's easy.

If you want to use the control in a regular VB project or a Web page, generate an OCX file (you'll find the choice on the File menu). Then you'll need to add the component to your toolbox using the Components command on the Project menu, and you're ready to go. Some other environments might require you to register your control, but that's no problem because VB5 generates self-registration code automatically. Simply run REGSRVR32.EXE and specify the OCX file that contains your control.

Packaging Your Control

What happens if you want to distribute your control to other users? To help you create distributions, VB5 provides a special tool that you run directly from the Start menu (or Program Manager if you are using NT 3.51). It allows you to create setup files for your project or files appropriate to download over the Internet. Simply tell it what project you want to distribute, and it does the rest.

VB Summary

All this sounds too good to be true, right? Well, there is one catch. Your control requires a special runtime DLL before it can run. If you're using your control with conventional programs, this isn't a big problem. However, if you want users to download your control over the Internet, it could be annoying. The good news is that after users download the DLL once, they don't need to download it again—they need only download your control.

Speaking of the Internet, you can even set up asynchronous properties using VB5. This advanced technique allows you to load a large property (perhaps a picture) over the network without waiting.

Writing A Java Applet

Although Microsoft bills its Visual J++ 1.1 product as a visual development language, you might wonder what Microsoft was thinking when it decided to do that. Don't get me wrong—there's nothing wrong with Visual J++. It's a very capable (and speedy)

Java environment. However, calling it *visual* is a bit of a stretch. On the plus side, it does have a familiar environment and integration with ActiveX.

In this section, I'll show you a calendar applet developed with Visual J++. Along the way, I'll tell you a bit about Java's development philosophy and why you might use Java (and why you might not as well). I'll also tell you why I don't think Visual J++ is very visual.

About Java

Just in case you've been living in a cave lately, I'll tell you briefly about Java, which is a language similar to C++. As an old-time C and C++ programmer, I think this is probably its chief disadvantage to me. When I use VB or Delphi, it's clear to me, almost immediately, that I'm not using C++. I enter a few too many equals signs once or twice until I shift mental gears, then I don't have any more problems. With Java, I never shift gears. It's very much like C++, so I never get used to the differences (and there *are* differences).

Of course, if you have no predisposition to C++, Java is just another language to learn. It has many nice features, including automatic garbage collection and built-in support for multithreading. However, the overriding question is, Why another language?

The answer to this question is one word: portability. Java is typically interpreted by a simple virtual machine, or Java Virtual Machine (JVM). If you can write the relatively simple JVM on your computer, you can run Java programs. Of course, other systems have tried this (remember UCSD Pascal?), but Sun (the developer of Java) has made two realizations:

- The Web needs a programming language that works on disparate platforms.

- Programs that run on the Web should have security constraints to prevent them from harming the system or performing malicious activity over the network.

Because any computer that uses a JVM can run a Java program, the first requirement is satisfied. Because Java runs through an interpreter, you can enforce any security restrictions you like. For example, most Web browsers don't allow Java programs to access local files. They also prohibit programs from opening network connections, unless it's back to the server that provided the program.

If you want to create programs that run on many different platforms, Java is your best chance at doing that. If you want the programs to run on the Web, it's your only chance (for now, anyway). ActiveX works very well on the PC but lacks Java's broad platform support. Even on platforms that support ActiveX, you usually need separate object files for each platform. Because Java is interpreted, a Java class file will run on any computer with a JVM.

Many people think that Java is a major innovation in language design, but it's really just an ordinary object-oriented language that is very similar to C++. The power that people associate with Java is really due to the class library. The same is true for C or C++. C isn't a very sophisticated language. Most of the interesting things you can do in C are really calls to the library. By itself, C (or C++) does very little.

Although Java includes several libraries, the most interesting is the Abstract Windows Toolkit (AWT). This library allows you to create windows, menus, and other user-interface items. If you are accustomed to Windows programming, you'll find the AWT somewhat anemic. For example, the concept of a resource does not exist in a Java program. Dialog boxes and menus require code to create and manage them. However, Microsoft has a clever wizard (discussed later) that helps you with this. Many Windows controls have no equivalent in Java.

On the plus side, Java has some things not readily available in Windows. For example, layout managers control the size and position of other windows, so you might have a layout manager that resizes all the controls in a user interface when the main window resizes.

Java programs come in two flavors: applications and applets. An application is a standalone program. It has its own main window and behaves like any other program on the target system. An applet doesn't have its own main window. Instead, it relies on another program to contain it. Usually, this program is a Web browser, but it can be any Java-aware program.

When you create a Java program, you'll usually start with the Microsoft Wizard, which will give you the option of creating an applet or a program that can be either an applet or an application. If you select the dual option, the program detects whether it's an application at runtime. If it's an application, it creates a main window and uses it to host the core applet. If the program runs as an applet, it doesn't create a main window. You'll find out more about the Microsoft Wizard shortly.

The Visual J++ Environment

The Visual J++ environment is simply the familiar Developer's Studio product that is also integral to Visual C++ and Visual InterDev. If you're familiar with these products, that's a big plus. However, many of the tools you expect from Visual C++ don't exist for Java programs. For example, Class Wizard isn't part of VJ++, so you'll need to handle most events manually.

If you find that you use Visual J++ and Visual C++, you might want to consider Microsoft's new Visual Studio 97 product. This is little more than Visual C++, Visual J++, Visual Basic, FoxPro, and Visual InterDev in one box. You also get a special version of the Microsoft Developer's Network (MSDN) CD. Even if you don't use all the products, the price is low enough to make it worthwhile, even if you use only two of the packages.

Wizards

Like other Microsoft products, Visual J++ comes with several wizards to help you work. Two wizards are of interest in Visual J++. The first one, the Java Applet Wizard, creates a new Java project. You can specify many details, including:

- The project name, directory, and main class name.

- Whether the project should create an applet or a dual applet/application.

- The initial size of the application window.

- Whether the applet will utilize multithreading.

- Sample animation code created by the wizard (if the applet is multithreading).

- Whether you would like to handle certain mouse events.

- Any parameters the applet will use to accept data from the outside world.

- A copyright string.

If you want it to, the wizard will also generate helpful comments and a sample HTML file that uses the applet. Once you are finished with this wizard, you can't run it again (except, of course, to create a new project). Be sure to make the right selections the first time because you won't get a second chance.

The other wizard that Microsoft supplies is the Resource Wizard. This wizard exists because Java doesn't use resource templates the way that Windows does. With ordinary Windows programming, you'll often design dialog boxes and menus visually during development and store them in resources. Then, at runtime, your program can retrieve the template and create the object with almost no effort on your part.

Java doesn't use resources, so you must create any dialog boxes and menus by using Java programming code. This is tedious at best. The Resource Wizard allows you to visually design resources using any standard tool (including the resource editor built into Developer's Studio). The wizard processes these resources into Java code that you can then use in your application or applet.

Although this is better than creating everything from scratch, a couple of problems exist. First, the resource doesn't become part of your project. If you make changes to the resource later, you must remember to rerun the Resource Wizard. Second, and worse, if you change your Java code, you can't preserve those changes if you rerun the wizard. Still, using the wizard is better than nothing—you just need to have a little discipline.

So how is Visual J++ visual? This depends on your definition of visual. Languages such as VB, Delphi, and Optima++ are very visual, Visual C++ somewhat less so. Sure, you use the Class Wizard to wire up events, and you can draw dialog boxes and menus, but there is very little visual integration except for the Resource Wizard.

Developing The Calendar

To test drive Visual J++, I decided to develop a simple calendar applet that you can place on a Web page (see Figure 14.8). This is a simple application and doesn't require any dialog boxes, multithreading, or much of anything special. All you need is a simple applet, some code to draw the calendar, and enough smarts to figure out which day of the week corresponds to a given date.

To start this project, I used the Java Applet Wizard. Because the calendar is simple, I turned off multithreading but didn't change anything else. For parameters, I added the ones shown in Table 14.1. The wizard does some of the work for you when you name parameters here, so it's better to specify too many parameters than

Table 14.1 Calendar parameters.

Parameter	Definition
MONTH	Month (0=January)
YEAR	Year
FGCOLOR	Foreground color (RGB format)
BGCOLOR	Background color (RGB format)

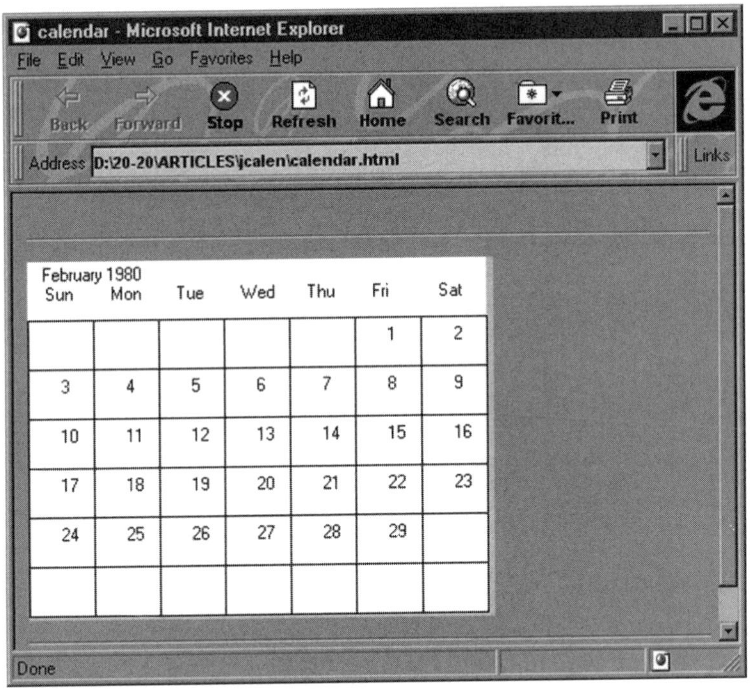

Figure 14.8

The calendar applet.

not enough. You can add parameters later, but it's easier to remove them later if you create too many.

The wizard makes a perfectly adequate applet for you. The only code I added was in the **paint** routine (see Listing 14.2). This code calculates the dimensions for the calendar and then draws it. It also computes the date/day relationship. Instead of writing a standard Zeller's congruence function to handle things, I relied on a standard Java class, **Date**. The **getDay** function for this class knows how to convert a date to a day of the week. My code uses this to correctly assign the date's position on the calendar.

Listing 14.2 The calendar.

```
//********************
// calendar.java:        Applet
//
//********************
import java.applet.*;
import java.awt.*;
import java.util.Date;
```

```java
//=================================
// Main Class for applet calendar
//
//=================================
public class calendar extends Applet
{
        // PARAMETER SUPPORT:
        // Parameters allow an HTML author to pass
        // information to the applet;
        // the HTML author specifies them using the
        // <PARAM> tag within the <APPLET>
        // tag.  The following variables are used to
        // store the values of the
        // parameters.
    //--------------------------------

    // Members for applet parameters
    // <type>         <MemberVar>    = <Default Value>
    //--------------------------------
        private int m_month = 0;
        private int m_year = 1980;
        private int m_bgcolor = 16777215;  // white
        private int m_fgcolor = 0;

    // Parameter names.  To change a name of a
    // parameter, you need only make
    // a single change.  Simply modify
    // the value of the parameter string below.
    //--------------------------------
        private final String PARAM_month = "month";
        private final String PARAM_year = "year";
        private final String PARAM_bgcolor = "bgcolor";
        private final String PARAM_fgcolor = "fgcolor";

        // calendar Class Constructor
        //--------------------------------
        public calendar()
        {
                // TODO: Add constructor code here
        }

        // APPLET INFO SUPPORT:
        // The getAppletInfo() method returns a string
        // describing the applet's
        // author, copyright date,
        // or miscellaneous information.
```

```java
//---------------------------------
    public String getAppletInfo()
    {
     return "Name: calendar\r\n" +
        "Author: Al Williams alw@al-williams.com\r\n" +
        "Created with Microsoft Visual J++ Version 1.1";
    }

    // PARAMETER SUPPORT
    // The getParameterInfo() method returns an
    // array of strings describing
    // the parameters understood by this applet.
    //
// calendar Parameter Information:
//   { "Name", "Type", "Description" },
//---------------------------------
    public String[][] getParameterInfo()
    {
            String[][] info =
            {
             { PARAM_month, "int", "Month" },
             { PARAM_year, "int", "Year" },
             { PARAM_bgcolor, "int",
                "Background color" },
             { PARAM_fgcolor, "int",
                "Parameter description" },
            };
            return info;
    }

    // The init() method is called by the
    // AWT when an applet is first loaded or
    // reloaded. Override this method to
    // perform whatever initialization your
    // applet needs, such as initializing
    // data structures, loading images or
    // fonts, creating frame windows,
    // setting the layout manager, or adding UI
    // components.
//---------------------------------
    public void init()
    {
      // PARAMETER SUPPORT
      // The following code retrieves the
      // value of each parameter
      // specified with the <PARAM> tag
      // and stores it in a member
      // variable.
```

```
                //-----------------------------
        String param;

        // month: Month
        //---------------------------
        param = getParameter(PARAM_month);
        if (param != null)
            m_month = Integer.parseInt(param);

        // year: Year
        //---------------------------
        param = getParameter(PARAM_year);
        if (param != null)
            m_year = Integer.parseInt(param);

        // bgcolor: Background color
        //---------------------------
        param = getParameter(PARAM_bgcolor);
        if (param != null)
            m_bgcolor = Integer.parseInt(param);

        // fgcolor: Parameter description
        //---------------------------
        param = getParameter(PARAM_fgcolor);
        if (param != null)
            m_fgcolor = Integer.parseInt(param);
    }

// Place additional applet cleanup code here.
// destroy() is called
// when your applet is terminating
// and being unloaded.
//-----------------------------
public void destroy()
{
        // TODO: Place applet cleanup code here
}

// calendar Paint Handler
//-------------------------------
public void paint(Graphics g)
{
        FontMetrics fm;
        int margin;
        int i,j;
        // height and width of each cell
        int cellheight,cellwidth;
        String months[]= // names of months
        {
```

```
    "January","February","March", "April",
    "May", "June", "July", "August",
    "September", "October", "November",
    "December"
    };
String days[]= // names of days
{
        "Sun","Mon","Tue",
        "Wed","Thu","Fri","Sat"
};
int len[]= { // 30 days hath September...
 31, 28, 31, 30, 31,
 30, 31, 31, 30, 31, 30, 31 };
int row=0;  // current drawing row
String title;  // title at top
Color fg,bg;  // colors
Rectangle r;
r=bounds();
fm=g.getFontMetrics();
margin=3*fm.getHeight(); // top portion
cellwidth=r.width/7;
cellheight=(r.height-margin)/6;
fg=new Color(m_fgcolor);
bg=new Color(m_bgcolor);
g.setColor(bg);
// draw header
g.fillRect(0,0,7*cellwidth,margin);
Integer yr;
yr=new Integer(m_year);
title=months[m_month]+" "+yr.toString();
g.setColor(fg);
g.drawString(title,10,fm.getHeight());
// draw cells
for (j=0;j<7;j++)
{
    g.drawString(days[j],
      j*cellwidth+cellwidth/2-10,
      fm.getHeight()*2); // day names
    for (i=0;i<6;i++)
    {
        g.setColor(bg); // draw inside
        g.fillRect(j*cellwidth,margin+
            i*cellheight,cellwidth,
            cellheight);
        g.setColor(fg); // draw outside
        g.drawRect(j*cellwidth,
            margin+i*cellheight,
            cellwidth,cellheight);
    }
```

```
        }
        j=len[m_month];
        // add one for leap years
        if (m_month==1 && m_year%4 == 0) j++;
        // draw dates
        for (i=0;i<j;i++)
        {
            Date date = new Date(m_year-1900,
                m_month,i+1);
            Integer day= new Integer(date.getDay());
            Integer I= new Integer(i+1);
            g.drawString(I.toString(),
                day.intValue()*cellwidth+cellwidth/2,
                margin+cellheight*row+cellheight/2);
            if (day.intValue()==6) row++;
        }
    }


    // The start() method is called
    // when the page containing the applet
    // first appears on the screen.
    // The Applet Wizard's initial implementation
    // of this method starts
    // execution of the applet's thread.
    //-------------------------------
    public void start()
    {
            // TODO: Place additional applet start code here
    }


    // The stop() method is called
    // when the page containing the applet is
    // no longer on the screen. The Applet Wizard's
    // initial implementation of
    // this method stops execution of the
    // applet's thread.
    //-------------------------------
    public void stop()
    {
    }




    // TODO: Place additional applet code here


}
```

Using The Calendar

You can use the **<APPLET>** tag to include the calendar applet in a Web page (see Listing 14.3). The code in the listing is essentially the sample file generated by the wizard. If you care only about compatibility with Internet Explorer, you could also use the **<OBJECT>** tag to include the applet.

Listing 14.3   Using the calendar.

```
<html>
<head>
<title>calendar</title>
</head>
<body>
<hr>
<!applet
    code=calendar.class
    name=calendar
    ID=cal
    width=320
    height=240>
    <param name=month value="1">
    <param name=year value="1980">
    <param name=events value="">
    <param name=bgcolor value=16777215>
    <param name=fgcolor value=0>
</applet>
<object classid=calendar.class height=240 width=320 Name=cal>
    <param name=month value="1">
    <param name=year value="1980">
    <param name=events value="">
    <param name=bgcolor value=16777215>
    <param name=fgcolor value=0>
</object>
<hr>
<SCRIPT>
<!--
 cal.year=1997
//-->
</SCRIPT>
</body>
</html>
```

You'll notice a series of **<PARAM>** tags in Listing 14.3. These tags set the initial values for the parameters in the applet. The wizard writes code so that variable **m_month**, for example, gets the value for the **MONTH** parameter. If the HTML doesn't supply a value, the wizard arranges for the default values you specified at design time.

Notice that the code that reads the parameters is in the **init** routine, meaning that once you read the parameters, their value is fixed. This is unlike ActiveX controls, in which you can change properties at any time using script.

Networking With Java

The biggest problem I see with Java is that it's too much like C++. Of course, some people see this as an advantage. I've been programming in C++ (and C) for a long time, so I have two problems. First, because Java is so much like C++, I think I know it better than I actually do. Second, I find it difficult to switch mental gears when I work with Java. If I'm writing, for example, in VB, it's very easy to change your mindset from C++ to Basic because the two languages are very, very different. However, Java *feels* like C++ enough to prevent me from making the shift. This is compounded by the fact that Visual J++ (the Java development system I use) uses the same environment that Visual C++ uses.

My Web page (**www.al-williams.com**) uses a small Java applet to scroll current news at the bottom of the screen (see Figure 14.9). Originally, I used an applet I found on the Web in some library of free applets, but this applet didn't include source code. There were some things I didn't like about it, but I couldn't change anything

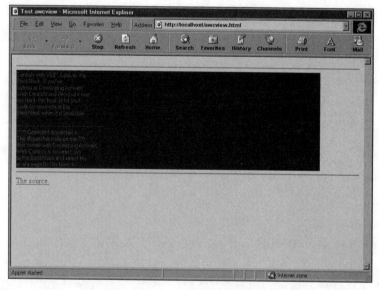

Figure 14.9

The AWCVIEW scroller.

because I only had the class file. Eventually, I decided to write my own version of the applet so I could eventually incorporate the features I wanted. I had written some applets that loaded images across the Web—that's easy. I found that loading text or other document types is a bit more involved. I also found that my common sense assumptions about double buffering were incorrect.

In this section I'll show you my text-scrolling applet. You'll find out how Java loads data from the Web and how you can customize the process. Along the way, you'll see how to draw off-screen (double buffering) and why doing so might not be a good idea.

Java's Library

Like most languages, Java isn't very powerful by itself. The real power comes from the libraries and tool kits that come with Java. These libraries contain classes that do useful things. In this case, the important objects are **URL**, a class that manages Internet connections, and **Thread**, a class that creates an executable thread.

The **URL** class (part of the **java.net** package) really does more than its name implies. It not only stores a URL but also manages a connection over the network and transfers data.

Of course, if you want a picture or a sound, the **Applet** class automatically loads your file through the **getImage** and **getAudioClip** functions. But what about other types? That's where the **URL** class comes into play. First, you need to construct the object. Usually, you'll pass the constructor two arguments: the base URL and the URL of the item in question. If the second URL is a full path (for example, **www.coriolis.com/xyz.txt**), the first argument is meaningless. However, if the second argument is not a full path, the constructor uses the first argument to build a full path to the correct name. Where do you get the base URL? The **Applet** class provides two handy calls—**getCodeBase** and **getDocumentBase**—to do the trick. The first call returns the URL that corresponds to the location that contains the applet's class file. The **getDocumentBase** function returns the URL that points to the document containing the applet.

Once you construct the URL, what do you have? Not much. However, the **URL** object has many functions that you can now use. For example, **openStream** allows you to obtain an **InputStream** object that corresponds to the URL. Armed with this, you can create a **BufferedInputStream** or a **DataInputStream**. You can then use these streams as though they were files.

However, an even easier way is to use the **getContent** method, which essentially is shorthand for **openConnection().getContent()**. To establish the connection (a **URLConnection** object), follows these steps:

1. If the application has previously set up an instance of **URLStreamHandler-Factory** as the stream handler factory, the library code calls the factory's **createURLStreamHandler** method, with the protocol string as an argument, to create the stream protocol handler.

2. If the previous step fails (no factory exists or the method returns **null**), the constructor tries to load the class named **sun.net.www.protocol.Handler**, where **protocol** is the name of the protocol. If this class doesn't exist, or if the class exists but it isn't a subclass of **URLStreamHandler**, the method throws a **MalformedURLException**.

If you look at your Java source code, you'll see many protocol classes (**http**, **news**, **ftp**, and so on). To actually acquire content, Java looks to another special class:

- If the application has set up a content handler factory instance using the **setContentHandlerFactory** method, the **createContentHandler** method of that instance is called with the content type as an argument. The result is a content handler for that content type.

- If no content handler factory has been set up yet, or if the factory's **createContentHandler method** returns **null**, the application loads the class named **<prefix>.<contentType>**. The prefix is one of the strings in the system property **java.content.handler.pkgs**—you separate the strings with a pipe character (I). You'll form **<contentType>** by taking the content type string and replacing each slash character with a period (.) and all other non-alphanumeric characters with the underscore character (_). If the specified class does not exist or is not a subclass of **ContentHandler**, an **UnknownServiceException** is thrown.

By default, the **java.content.handler.pkgs** property is set to **sun.net.www**. Again, the library contains many appropriate objects for various content types (for example, **text/plain**, **image/gif**, and **image/jpeg**). These collect and return objects of the appropriate type. For example, the **sun.net.www.text.plain** object returns a string.

You can use this knowledge to build your own content handlers. However, for the text scroller, the default plain text handler will work fine.

You might wonder why a simple text-scrolling application requires the **Thread** object. The answer is simple. The program requires a periodic nudge to cause the lines of text to scroll. However, you can't just sleep in the main program, as that would prevent the program from functioning correctly. Instead, the main program starts a thread that sleeps for the correct interval, then the thread forces the main program to repaint when it changes the displayed lines.

The Basic Program

Armed with this information, you can easily create the scroller (see Listing 14.4). The Visual J++ Applet Wizard created a lot of the code. The first interesting method, **init**, reads the parameters (the Applet Wizard wrote that code). It also creates a URL (on the basis of the **m_file** variable) and loads the entire file as a string. Next, the program breaks the string into individual lines and places them in the **lines** array.

Listing 14.4   The scroller applet.

```
//*************************************
// awcview.java:        Applet
//
//*************************************
import java.applet.*;
import java.awt.*;
import java.net.*;
import java.io.*;
import sun.net.www.*;
//===============================================
// Main Class for applet awcview
//
//===============================================
public class awcview extends Applet implements Runnable
{
    //-----------------------------------------------

    // Members for applet parameters
    // <type>        <MemberVar>    = <Default Value>
    //-----------------------------------------------
        private String m_file = "";   // file to scroll
        private int m_bgcolor = 65535;  // BG color
        private int m_fgcolor = 0;       // FG color
        private int m_speed = 5;        // speed of scroll in ms
        private int m_step=1;           // size of step
        private URL url;                // our URL
        private String content;         // string containing text
        private String[] lines;         // array containing text
        private int linect;             // # of lines
        private int current=0;          // current line at top
```

```
        private boolean first=true;  // first paint pass
        private boolean lock=false;  // don't scroll
        private int offset;              // where to paint 1st line
        private int fonth;  // font height
        private Thread timer;  // timer thread
// Only for double buffering
//          private Image img;
    // Parameter names.  To change a name of a parameter,
    // you need only make
    // a single change.  Simply modify the value of the
    // parameter string below.
    //-----------------------------------------------
        private final String PARAM_file = "file";
        private final String PARAM_bgcolor = "bgcolor";
        private final String PARAM_fgcolor = "fgcolor";
        private final String PARAM_speed = "speed";
                private final String PARAM_step="step";

        // awcview Class Constructor
        //-----------------------------------------------
        public awcview()
        {
        }


        // APPLET INFO SUPPORT:
        // The getAppletInfo() method
        // returns a string describing the applet's
        // author, copyright date, or miscellaneous information.
    //-----------------------------------------------
        public String getAppletInfo()
        {
                return "Name: awcview\r\n" +
                    "Author: Al Williams\r\n" +
                    "An applet to scroll textr\n" +
                    "";
        }


        // PARAMETER SUPPORT
        // The getParameterInfo() method returns an array of
        // strings describing the parameters understood
        // by this applet.
        //
    // awcview Parameter Information:
    //  { "Name", "Type", "Description" },
    //-----------------------------------------------
        public String[][] getParameterInfo()
        {
```

```
                String[][] info =
                {
                    { PARAM_file, "String", "File to read" },
                    { PARAM_bgcolor, "int", "background color" },
                    { PARAM_fgcolor, "int", "foreground color" },
                    { PARAM_speed, "int", "Speed" },
                    { PARAM_step, "int", "Step size"},
                };
                return info;
        }

// Count lines in content
        private int CountLines()
        {
                int n=0;
                int i;
                if (content==null)
                  content="Can't read source file.\n";
                for (i=0;i<content.length();i++)
                {
                        if (content.charAt(i)=='\r'||
                            content.charAt(i)=='\n')
                        {
                                n++;
                                i++;
                                while (i<content.length()&&
                                        (content.charAt(i)=='\r'||
                                        content.charAt(i)=='\n'))
                                            i++;

                        }
                }
        return n;
        }
        // The init() method is called by the AWT
        // when an applet is first loaded or
        // reloaded.
    //----------------------------------------------
        public void init()
        {
                // PARAMETER SUPPORT
                // The following code retrieves the value
                // of each parameter specified with the
                // <PARAM> tag and stores it in a member
                // variable.
                //----------------------------------------
                String param;
                int start,end, i;
                char termchar='\n';
```

```
// file: file to read
//-----------------------------------------
param = getParameter(PARAM_file);
if (param != null)
        m_file = param;

// bgcolor: background color
//-----------------------------------------
param = getParameter(PARAM_bgcolor);
if (param != null)
        m_bgcolor = Integer.parseInt(param);

// fgcolor: foreground color
//-----------------------------------------
param = getParameter(PARAM_fgcolor);
if (param != null)
        m_fgcolor = Integer.parseInt(param);

// speed: speed
//-----------------------------------------
param = getParameter(PARAM_speed);
if (param != null)
        m_speed = Integer.parseInt(param);

// step parameter
param = getParameter(PARAM_step);
if (param != null)
        m_step = Integer.parseInt(param);

// Read File!
try {
        url=new URL(getDocumentBase(),m_file);
        content=(String)(url.getContent());
    }
catch (MalformedURLException e)
  {
      content="Bad URL: "+url.toString()+"\n"+e.getMessage();
  }
catch (IOException e)
  {
      content="I/O exception: " + url.toString()+"\n"+e.getMessage();
  }
catch (Exception e)
  {
      content="Unknown error: "+url.toString()+"\n"+e.getMessage();
  }
// Break into lines;
lines=new String[linect=CountLines()];
```

```
                start=0;
                if (content.indexOf('\r',0)!=-1) termchar='\r';
                for (i=0;i<linect;i++)
                {
                        end=content.indexOf(termchar,start);
                        if (end==-1)
                                lines[i]=content.substring(start);
                        else
                                lines[i]=content.substring(start,end);
                        start=end;
                        while (start<content.length()&&
                                (content.charAt(start)=='\n'
                                || content.charAt(start)=='\r')) start++;

                }

        }

        // Place additional applet cleanup code here.
        // destroy() is called when
        // your applet is terminating and being unloaded.
        //------------------------------------------
        public void destroy()
        {
        }

// This routine does the actual painting.
// Since it is here, we can call it from anywhere.
        public void doPaint(Graphics g)
        {
                Color c;
                int i,ln;
                Rectangle r=bounds();
                c=new Color(m_bgcolor);
//                g.setColor(c);
//                g.fillRect(0,0,r.width,r.height);
                if (linect==0) return;  // nothing to do
                c=new Color(m_fgcolor);
                g.setColor(c);
                ln=current;
                for (i=offset;i<=r.height+fonth;i+=fonth)
                {
                        g.drawString(lines[ln++],0,i);
                        if (ln>=linect) ln=0;
                }
        }

        // awcview Paint Handler
        //------------------------------------------------
```

```java
        public void paint(Graphics g)
        {
                Rectangle r=bounds();
                Color c=new Color(m_bgcolor);
                if (first)  // initial setup
                {
                        FontMetrics fm;
                        fm=g.getFontMetrics();
                        fonth=fm.getHeight();
                        if (m_step<0) m_step=fonth/-m_step;
                        if (m_step==0) m_step=1;
                        current=0;
                        offset=r.height-fonth;
// This line used only for double buffering
                        //img=createImage(r.width,r.height);
                        setBackground(c);
                        first=false;
                }
 // this line for double buffering
                //g.drawImage(img,0,0,this);
// this line for normal drawing
                                        doPaint(g);
        }

        // The start() method is called when the page
        // containing the applet first appears on the screen.
        //-----------------------------------------------
        public void start()
        {
                if (timer==null) timer=new Thread(this);
                timer.start();
        }

        // The stop() method is called when the page
        // containing the applet is
        // no longer on the screen.
        // The Applet Wizard's initial implementation of
        // this method stops execution of the applet's thread.
        //-----------------------------------------------
        public void stop()
        {
                if (timer!=null) timer.stop();
        }

        public void run()
        {
                Graphics g0;
                while (timer!=null)
```

```
            {
                try
                {
                    timer.sleep(m_speed);  // wait
                } catch (InterruptedException e) {}
                if (first||lock) continue;  // not started yet
// advance scroll
                offset-=m_step;
                if (offset<=-fonth)
                {
                    offset=0;
                    if (++current>=linect) current=0;
                }
// comment the next 2 lines for normal drawing
        //      g0=img.getGraphics();
        //      doPaint(g0);
                repaint();
            }
        }


        //-----------------------------------------------
        public boolean mouseDown(Event evt, int x, int y)
        {
            lock=!lock;
            return true;
        }

        //-----------------------------------------------
        public boolean mouseUp(Event evt, int x, int y)
        {
            // Nothing for now
            return true;
        }



}
```

The line-breaking logic is a bit odd because I wanted to handle both Windows- and Unix-style files. The code examines the entire string for any \r (carriage return) characters. If there is even one, the file is likely to be a Windows text file, so the program splits lines on the \r character. If there are no \r characters, lines end with \n (line feed) characters. In any case, the code skips all \r and \n characters that it finds grouped together, meaning that the scroller doesn't recognize completely blank lines. If you need a blank line, simply make a line that contains a space or two.

The **paint** routine takes special action the first time you call it. The program needs to know some things about the **Graphics** object it will use, so the **paint** method calculates the font height and other interesting values. Every call to **paint** results in a call to **DoPaint**, which actually calculates the lines to display. This applet does not use double buffering (although it can; see the section "Paint Now Or Later?"). Instead, it draws the lines each time.

The **start** method kicks off the new thread. Notice that the same object that represents the main program also takes care of the thread. This is possible because the object implements the **runnable** interface. Passing **this** to the **Thread** object informs the thread to use the same object.

The code for the thread is in the object's **run** method. This code runs in an endless loop, sleeping most of the time. When it awakes, the thread examines the **first** and **lock** flags. If either is set, the thread goes back to sleep. The first flag indicates that processing hasn't started yet. The second flag tells the thread that the program is paused.

If the thread is active, it alters the **offset** and **current** variables to reflect what line to begin drawing at and where to draw the line on the screen. **DoPaint** uses these variables to draw in response to the **paint** method. Finally, the thread triggers a repaint for the applet and goes back to sleep.

The only other interesting function is the **mouseDown** handler, which toggles the **lock** flag. This allows users to stop scrolling by clicking on the applet. Clicking again resumes the scroll.

Another Way To Load A URL

As usual, you can write a program in more than one way. It's somewhat wasteful to read the entire file as a string and then chop it up into an array. If you prefer, you could use **openStream** on the URL and use the stream it returns to construct a **BufferedInputStream**. You could then construct a **DataInputStream** with the **BufferedInputStream** and use **readLine** to read lines from the **DataInputStream**. This is a bit more complicated, but it's more efficient. The only problem is that you can't know how many lines you'll need until you read the entire stream (not a problem if you use a **Vector** object instead of an array). Listing 14.5 shows an excerpt from the same applet that sets up the data input stream object and reads one line at a time.

Listing 14.5 Using a stream.

```java
//****************************************
// awcview.java:          Applet
//
//****************************************
import java.applet.*;
import java.awt.*;
import java.net.*;
import java.io.*;
import sun.net.www.*;
import java.util.Vector;
     .
     .
     .
     private Vector lines;
     .
     .
     .

     public void init()
     {
     .
     .
     .

              try {
                  InputStream is;
                  String s;
                  BufferedInputStream bis;
                  DataInputStream dis;
                  String line;
                  url=new URL(getDocumentBase(),m_file);
                  is=url.openStream();
                  bis=new BufferedInputStream(is);
                  dis=new DataInputStream(bis);
                  do
                  {
                     s=dis.readLine();
                     if (s!=null)
                     {
                        lines.addElement(s);
                        linect++;
                     }
                  } while (s!=null);   // EOF is s==null
              }
            catch (MalformedURLException e)
            {
              lines.setSize(linect=2);
              content="Bad URL: "+url.toString()+"\n";
```

```
              lines.setElementAt(content,0);
              lines.setElementAt(e.getMessage(),1);
          }
          catch (IOException e)
          {
            lines.setSize(linect=2);
            content="I/O exception: " + url.toString()+"\n";
            lines.setElementAt(content,0);
            lines.setElementAt(e.getMessage(),1);
          }
          catch (Exception e)
          {
            lines.setSize(linect=2);
            content="Unknown error: "+url.toString()+"\n";
            lines.setElementAt(content,0);
            lines.setElementAt(e.getMessage(),1);
          }
      }

   .
   .
   .

      public void doPaint(Graphics g)
      {
              Color c;
              int i,ln;
              Rectangle r=bounds();
              c=new Color(m_bgcolor);
              g.setColor(c);
              g.fillRect(0,0,r.width,r.height);
              if (linect==0) return;  // nothing to do
              c=new Color(m_fgcolor);
              g.setColor(c);
              ln=current;
              for (i=offset;i<=r.height+fonth;i+=fonth)
              {
                      g.drawString((String)lines.elementAt(ln++),0,i);
                      if (ln>=linect) ln=0;
              }
      }

   .
   .
   .
```

Paint Now Or Later?

When I first started this program, I was sure that drawing directly to the screen would result in an annoying flicker. Therefore, I used a technique called *double buffering*.

The process is simple. First, the **paint** routine (on its initial pass) creates an **Image** object from the applet that is the same size as the applet window. Then the paint routine simply copies the image to the screen (using **drawImage**). Then, when any portion of the program wants to draw, it can obtain a **Graphics** object from the image, draw to it, and trigger a repaint.

This technique works, but I was surprised at how much flickering occurred when I used it. I modified the code to draw directly on the window, and the flickering decreased significantly.

Why did this happen? I'm not sure. However, it seems to me that my test case had text that didn't stretch across the window. Drawing the image each time requires you to draw the entire applet window. Drawing only the text disturbs less of the screen. Your mileage can vary, so I left the double-buffering code in (but commented out). You could easily add a parameter to switch the drawing mode if you wanted to do so.

Another mistake I made in the beginning was to try to erase the background using **fillRect** during drawing. This leads to a great deal of flicker because the applet shows its background color for a split second before you can draw. The answer here is easy: Simply call **setBackground** to make the background color what you want. The applet will smoothly display the background color with no effort on your part.

Using The Scroller

Using the scroller could hardly be simpler. You can find a sample HTML file in Listing 14.6 and the parameters you need to set in Table 14.2. The **SPEED** parameter is in milliseconds. The **STEP** parameter, if it is positive, indicates the number of pixels to scroll on each step. If the parameter is negative, it indicates a fraction of the

Table 14.2 Scroller parameters.

Parameter	Type	Description
FILE	String	URL (relative or absolute) of file to display
BGCOLOR	int	Background color
FGCOLOR	int	Foreground color
SPEED	int	Delay between scroll steps in milliseconds
STEP	int	Size of scroll steps (see text)

character height. Therefore, when **STEP** is -1, the scrolling is in whole-character increments. When **STEP** is -2, the scrolling is in half-character units and so on. If the resulting number is 0, the code adjusts it so that **STEP**'s size is 1.

Listing 14.6   Using the scroller.

```
<html>
<head>
<title>Test awcview</title>
</head>
<body>
<hr>
<applet
    code=awcview.class
    name=awcview
    width=640
    height=200>
    <param name=file value="test.txt">
    <param name=bgcolor value=0>
    <param name=fgcolor value=255>
    <param name=speed value=500>
    <param name=step value=-2>
</applet>
<hr>
<a href="awcview.java">The source.</a>
</body>
</html>
```

Don't forget that the file you supply is a text file, not an HTML file. Java doesn't know how to interpret HTML. You could write an HTML parser in Java, but that would be quite a bit of work.

Another thing to watch out for is line width. The applet doesn't wrap your lines, so the lines must fit inside the applet window. This can be a problem if you design your Web page on a 1024x768 screen but your users have 640x480 screens. This is a good place to set your screen resolution down temporarily or to use a laptop to look at the page.

Future Plans

You could make many enhancements to this text scroller. For example, it would be nice to allow for font effects (bold and italic, for example). It might be nice to allow the user to scroll manually with the mouse if the **lock** flag is **TRUE**. None of these additions would be very difficult.

A more advanced improvement would use the **URLConnection** to detect when the source file on the server changes. Then the program could reload the file and start over again.

The Scroller In Review

If you are a C++ programmer, take heart. You can learn Java with a minimum of fuss. It just seems to take forever to break your old C++ habits. Although Java development tools are still not as nice as some C++ environments, the networking library is quite impressive. If you aren't a C++ programmer, Java is still approachable. Many of the features that make C++ hard to learn are absent from Java.

Don't get me wrong. I still enjoy using C++, but for Internet programming Java has several distinct advantages. The best way to learn is to dive right in, pick a small project, and write it.

Of course, there are always those who won't try a new language no matter what. Maybe we can port the Java library to C++ for them and make a few dollars in the process.

Is Java as easy as VB? Not unless you're already a Java or C++ programmer. Even then, VB is really easy to use and learn. However, only Java applets can currently claim to run on a wide variety of platforms.

Client Control Summary

Using VB makes it easy to create ActiveX controls. Visual J++ simplifies writing Java applets, but that's only part of the story. If you're a C++ programmer, you can certainly write ActiveX controls using C++. Microsoft Foundation Classes (MFC) help out a lot but tend to make large controls. The ActiveX Template Library (ATL), also from Microsoft, makes leaner controls but takes more effort to master.

On the Java side, many environments promise to simplify Java development. Sun and Symantec are both well known for Visual Java tools, and Borland's tools are well respected.

So, if you need client controls or applets, don't be afraid to write your own. With a little practice, you'll find it great fun and maybe even profitable.

Practical Guide To

Writing Client Controls

- Available Tools
- Planning A Control Or Applet
- Summary Of Steps For Using VB5
- Summary Of Steps For Using Visual J++

Available Tools

Although this chapter is mostly about VB and Visual J++, many other tools are available to help you build client-side components. Some of these are more visual and some more like traditional programming environments. However, programming in a language you know might be better than learning a new language, even if the new language is easier.

Nearly all C++ compilers can now generate ActiveX, including Visual C++ and Borland's C-Builder. Delphi, also from Borland, will create ActiveX controls as well. C++ allows you to create very efficient ActiveX controls but with great difficulty. Most compilers also have a simplified approach (like MFC, for example), but here the controls are less efficient than they would be had they been properly written without those tools.

Many Java tools are available, ranging from Sun's ultravisual Java Studio to the straight Java JDK (also from Sun). In between are respectable Java tools from Borland (JBuilder), Symantec (Visual Café), IBM (Visual Age for Java), and many others. Visual Studio in particular is very visual and requires almost no programming for many types of applets.

Of course, new tools for both technologies appear every day. You can search the Web or look in one of the many Java resources on the Web (try **www.stars.com**).

Planning A Control Or Applet

When you want to build your own ActiveX control or Java applet, the most important step is planning. For an ActiveX control, you should have a good idea concerning which properties, methods, and events you will support. For a Java applet, you need to identify parameters. In both cases, you need to have a clear idea of what each piece will do before you start; otherwise, you run the risk of painting yourself into a corner or forgetting to add some important piece.

Summary Of Steps For Using VB5

Using VB5 to create an ActiveX control takes a few simple steps:

1. Start VB5.

2. Select ActiveX Control from the New tab of the initial dialog box.

3. Add the VB controls you want to use in your ActiveX control (you can even use other ActiveX controls if you like). These are constituent controls.

4. Start the Interface Wizard (from the Add-Ins menu).

5. Select the properties, methods, and events you want to support.

6. Create custom members.

7. Attach your control's members to members of the constituent controls.

8. Define any unattached members.

9. Write code to handle unattached properties and methods.

10. Write code to fire unattached events when appropriate.

11. Write any code that implements logic for the control.

12. Set the **ToolboxIcon** property to set the design-time icon the control displays.

13. If you want a property sheet, run the property sheet wizard.

14. Build your OCX (from the File menu).

You can find the details for this procedure in the examples in this chapter.

Summary Of Steps For Using Visual J++

Using Visual J++ to create Java applets takes a few simple steps:

1. Open Developer's Studio.

2. Select File|New.

3. Select a project name, Java Applet Wizard, and click on OK.

4. On screen 1, select the applet support options, the applet's class name, and the level of comments you want in the code.

5. On screen 2, select whether you want a sample HTML file and the initial size of your applet window.

6. On screen 3, select multithreading code, animation support, and mouse event handlers. For your first attempts, disable multithreading (which disables animation automatically).

7. On screen 4, select any properties you want to expose to the outside world.

8. On screen 5, enter the information that the applet will return in response to **getAppInfo** calls.

9. Search for **TODO** comments (if enabled), and add code in the appropriate places. For many simple applets, you need only add code to **paint**.

10. Use the Build menu to build your applet.

You can find more details about building Java applets in this chapter.

More Information

You can find a great deal of information on both ActiveX and Java technologies. From Coriolis, I have two books on ActiveX: *Developing ActiveX Web Controls* (C++) and *Visual Developer: Developing ActiveX Controls With Visual Basic 5* (VB5). For Java, see *Visual J++ Programming FrontRunner*, *Exploring Java*, and *Java Programming Explorer*.

Chapter 15

Where To On The Web

Now that you have a solid back-ground in active Web pages and scripting, where do you go from here? This chapter ties up the lessons of this book, gazes into a crystal ball, and provides a list of links and resources.

Paul Newkirk

Notes…

Chapter

15

Early in my professional life, I heard of a study that split technical readers into two groups: those who read manuals from cover to cover like they read novels, and those who read only what they need to do a particular task. If you're in the former group, it's easier to summarize the places this book has taken you, from HTML to creating your own objects. If you're in the latter group, it could be harder to summarize unless we can assume you skipped the parts you already knew.

In either case, this book provides you with a wealth of practical how-to experience on Web development. It is modularized and serialized so that you can get what you want out of either a pick-and-choose or a novel-reading approach. Blended in with the how-to experience is a substantial amount of background information provided through the hard knocks endured by the three of us. Sometimes, it is as fundamentally important to know the *why* as it is to know the *how*. Why do backgrounds look nice and at the same time create problems? Why is VBScript a nice language to use, and, at the same time, when can its powers be rendered useless outside the Microsoft world (for example, if you have users who use the Netscape browser)?

In the following pages, I recap where we've been, make some conclusions, stick my head out and make some prognostications, and provide some links and resources.

Early Lessons

This book begins with an overview of the Web. It isn't an overview from a bearded, suspender-wearing old-time Internet user. It isn't the view of someone who builds networks for a living. Instead, we provided an overview by people in the business for people in the business world.

Some of the ideas from this book's early chapters follow:

- There are still a lot of technical people out there who, for one reason or another, haven't fully exploited the Web.

- The technology of the Web isn't that hard if you have the time to look around for an expert guide.

- Several interesting things are happening to the Web. On the one hand, it is leaving HTML as most people know it and moving to a more traditional programming paradigm. On the other hand, programming is being made easier so that nontraditional programmers can get in on the act. Also, everyone is going there, which will continue to change and enrich the flavor of the Web as people from different professions affect the direction of Web evolution.

In addition, we've tried to remain less partial and more practical, avoiding "religious wars" where possible. You want to focus on getting practical things done in the best way possible. You probably don't own stock in Netscape, Microsoft, or Sun, but you do need to use their tools and understand their ways to make Web sites work. And in lieu of finalized standards, when two or more standards running off in slightly different directions seems to be the rule, it's people like you and me who have to figure out the differences and make corresponding usability decisions.

If you read the early chapters, you know that HTML is essentially a 30-year-old formatting language. In addition, you'll note the Web and Internet were designed to be conservative about how the data gets back and forth across the network, but not so much about how it looks at the receiving end. One reason for this is that the Web encompasses a diverse population of people browsing the Net on 20-inch color monitors and 9-inch black and whites. If you are developing for a defined intranet, where you know what all the PCs look like and the software they run, you can afford to develop a one-size-fits-all solution. But most people have to be careful about how they develop their sites. For every fancy piece of technology or graphics that you consider when designing your site, you need to at least consider, and hopefully make allowances for, the effect on your varied audiences.

A lot of work on a page can be worthless if you forget these issues. I've seen pages that look beautiful at one resolution become unusable and amateurish at another.

I've seen sites that are superb when run on one browser but are impossible to navigate on another. Two similar rules come to mind. One is from the programming world (at least that's where I heard it): KISS, or Keep It Simple Stupid (no offense intended). The other, Occam's Razor, is from the world of science: The simplest solution is the most likely.

I have always been a believer in function over form. If it's usable on all possible clients, that's a passing mark. If it's spectacular on some sites and unusable on others, the end result is a failing mark regardless of how spectacular it would have been *if they could have only seen it.* Public speaking guru Bert Decker always says, "You've got to be believed to be heard." On the Web, you might well turn that around to be, "You've got to be seen to be believed." To start with, then, the best design solution is to keep it simple and functional. From there, you can add the bells and whistles. On top of that, although it might sound contradictory, the better *looking* sites are often more believable than the most authoritative sites. So, you have to keep that in mind.

It really is a tough game, knowledgeably weighing the different technologies (VBScript or JavaScript), tools (Internet Explorer or Netscape), and areas of emphasis (pretty or usable). One goal of this book is to help you make those decisions. More important, this book is a gateway to show you how to create your own active Web pages, providing fun, profit, and room for development (not necessarily in that order).

Instant Replay

You should now have a good grasp of HTML (if you didn't already). At its simplest, HTML is just a way to format text on a page. Furthermore, if used correctly, the formatting for simple HTML should be more of a hands-off formatting, letting the language and the browser do the work.

As we get a little more complicated, HTML lets you add functionality and charm to your pages with graphics, image maps, tables, frames, forms, and style sheets.

Graphics can replace standard buttons or rule lines to give one level of sophistication. You can use graphics as hot links, looking very much like buttons, to give another level. Image maps let you take advantage of a visual medium, providing countless ways to interact and navigate a page through clickable regions on a graphic.

Tables let you organize your pages and even do some advanced layout.

Frames are another advanced layout method fraught with disadvantages and advantages. One undeniable advantage of frames is that you can use it to keep one frame on the page and target the changes in another frame. The tabular alternative can require that you have many versions of the same page (more files to maintain), whereas the frame version is more complicated to keep track of and has some navigational issues (like frames within frames and the issue of the Back button).

One of the first limitations pointed out about frames regarded navigation with the Browser's Forward and Back buttons. With frames, for example, you can have three "pages" loaded in three separate frames. When you press Back on your browser, where do you go? Do you dump all three frames and go back to the page you were at before arriving at the framed page, or do you go back within the context of one of the frames? The answer has been improved upon since frames first came out, because you can now click your mouse in a specific frame and your browser's Forward and Back buttons will work within the context of that frame. Good frame designers build in a ton of navigational aids to obviate this problem, and a well-designed framed page can be a navigational joy, once you understand the site's design and means of navigation. But if you are new to frames, you need to consider the navigation issue carefully if you plan to design framed pages.

Forms are a predefined HTML way to collect user input. As you likely noticed, the controls of HTML forms (buttons, text boxes, and so on) are often used in scripts for collecting user input.

Style sheets are a way to set a style for your page, changing attributes on your page in one file instead of each time the attribute appears. Thus, you could set the background and all the headers and text to something other than the default HTML styles and, instead of doing it all with thousands of uses of the **<FONT>** tag, for example, do it once with a style sheet. Furthermore, style sheets are easier to update because the style (if done right) defines these attributes once and in one place.

After HTML and more advanced HTML, you learned the basics of how to insert scripts. Originally, there were the **<SCRIPT>** and **<APPLET>** tags, which you will still find heavily used on the Web. In fact, most Java examples still show the **<APPLET>** tag. However, with HTML 4, you should start to use and find more examples of the **<OBJECT>** tag.

Then, you found out about client-side VBScript and client-side JavaScript (or JScript). VBScript is a language that almost looks like Visual Basic in many areas. It is, of course, from Microsoft, and it is an easy-to-use language for adding functionality to the client and server side of your Web site. JavaScript, not really a subset of Java, is a product originally developed by Netscape. Currently, three versions of JavaScript are on the market: Microsoft's, Netscape's, and the European Community's (ECMA). The advantage of JavaScript over VBScript is that both major browsers currently support it but in somewhat different ways. The disadvantage of VBScript is that only Internet Explorer natively supports it.

You saw the benefits and defects of client-side scripting, which are nearly the same for VBScript and JavaScript. One benefit is the added functionality on the client side. If you fetch data to the browser, for example, you can sort it on the browser without having to go back to the server each time. A defect is that all your hard-developed script code is viewable by anyone with a Web browser.

Next, you saw the Dynamic HTML Object Model and how it fits in with the browser and allows you to manipulate the browser and the documents it contains. The next step is to actually use the object model by writing Dynamic HTML. The way HTML is evolving is causing the functionality everyone wants to become available in a fairly standardized way. One thing I always loved about the Unix world was that whenever I wanted to do something, either someone had created an application that let me do it or it was fairly easy to write a shell script to do it yourself. Unix always provided. I teach the same thing in beginning HTML classes: HTML provides. If you want to quote the text of Hamurabi, don't use italics, use **<BLOCKQUOTE>**. If you don't want to convert RGB values to Hex, now you can specify normal color names, like "red." Dynamic HTML (and HTML 4, for that matter) lets you have application-like functionality without necessarily needing ActiveX controls or Java applets, yet another way that HTML provides for you needs.

After Dynamic HTML, the other end of the spectrum is sever-side scripting. This might not be a great option if your server gets heavier use than it can handle. However, server-side scripting can work regardless of your user's browser. In fact, you can use VBScript for server-side scripting even if Netscape's browser, for example, doesn't support VBScript. All the processing occurs on the server. Another advantage is that your users might never see your actual script source. Most examples of sever-side scripting shove the output of the script (raw HTML) out to the browser, and what goes on behind the scenes is your secret.

ActiveX Server Objects, stock components, and MPS build on this idea, allowing you to use the wealth of components and objects already written and available. Because of these, many of the applications you write might already exist in a stock component. If not, you can always be the first and write your own component in the form of a Java applet or an ActiveX control.

Conclusions

It's hard to tell what conclusions to draw from this book or the state of the industry at the time of this writing, because everything is changing so fast and so much can change in a short time. I don't know when that will not be the case, but, to play it safe, I include things closer to facts here and leave things closer to speculation to the following "Prognostications" section.

Security

In terms of guaranteeing the safety of active content, the security model of the Internet and Web is insufficient for the demands that will be placed on it. "What are you talking about?" some people might ask. It has to become seamless, unobtrusive, and foolproof. You don't worry about security when you change channels on your TV, nor should you do so on the Web. The current models offer more or less security with corresponding better or worse performance. Although Microsoft is the unstoppable train, my bet is on Java and JavaScript until someone comes out with a better security model.

Browsers

Some time ago, I would have said that at some date in the future you could stop worrying about Netscape and its browser. Now, I'm not so sure. This is not a comment on the relative quality of the browsers. It's just that Microsoft is a huge company that makes a lot of money, and Netscape is a company for which I have yet to figure out how it generates cash to validate its stock price other than by stock sales. Microsoft can afford to give away a browser because it has other sources of income, but how can Netscape make money when everyone gets the browser free? Yet there are a lot of other players in that game, like the Justice Department, AOL, Sun, and IBM, so who knows?

One thing you do know is that Netscape currently dominates the market or at least has enough of a share that you have to take both browsers into consideration when designing your site (unless you work in a closed system, such as an intranet, where all software can be specified top-down). The safest bet for all is either Java and client-side JavaScript, or server-side scripting and controls. This is not necessarily the fastest or the easiest bet, but it is the safest.

Server Or Client?

Do you create scripts and applets for the server or for the client? A lot depends on what kind of environment you expect (intranet or Internet). By default, I think the answer is server, unless you write your client-side applications so that they have the ability to punt if the browser doesn't support what you're trying to do.

Speed
What's the fastest? After the initial download of a control, ActiveX wins in terms of performance. If you depend on that performance, its other shortcomings diminish. Of course, depending on how you write the control, the download time might be incredible, depending on a variety of factors.

HTML 4/Scriplets/Applets/JScript/ActiveX/VBScript
By now, all these terms should no longer seem like a confused mess of alphabet soup. Furthermore, you should know how to make decisions regarding using the technologies and be well informed about their strengths and weaknesses. However, you should also realize that no one answer is always best.

Combination Of Technologies
If there is one thing you should walk away from this book with it is this realization: You'll often need a combination of techniques to produce the results you want. It is tempting to go with the tools you know, but you need a big enough tool set to get the job done. You wouldn't build a house with only a screwdriver, so why create a Web site with only one tool?

Prognostications
This section is almost a freebie for an author, like being an economist or a weatherman. Maybe that's a cheap shot, however, because they supposedly keep their jobs only when they make more right guesses than wrong ones. Usually, though, you have to be rich or famous before you get a chance to prognosticate while people listen. Although you may have no more inside information than they do, you're just richer or more famous because of one thing or another and people listen. I am neither rich nor famous, so this is my golden opportunity to speak my mind.

But the *almost* in "almost a freebie" is a keyword. Those who do not read history are doomed to repeat it, someone once said, and you can gain a lot from the voice of experience. What, then, does the future hold?

I've seen the online world go from scrolling ASCII text to pretty front ends with graphics and sounds. I've seen the Internet go from ASCII news and mail readers to fantastic-looking Web applications. I heard the sound of the waves going by as the

Web lapped the online world, and I watched the online (information service) world groan and creak and wobble to attempt to catch up to a business that it had been doing for years. I've also seen the thrashing of the whole computer and business world as everyone tried (and is still trying) to figure out what to make of the Web.

When I worked at AT&T, I learned a lot about the future. For example, one veteran there had a nifty dust collector on his desk—a video phone. It was a great idea. It had three views you could use, displaying your face, the table in front of it (to show a document that both sides of the conversation could look at), and the other person's camera. I think it was from the 1960s, but it was ahead of its time. At that time, there wasn't enough bandwidth in the copper lines or enough computing power to make up for the difference.

Another funny point to consider in computing history is the laptop. Remember back, if you can, to the time that the "IBM world" discovered mice. The early "IBM" (as opposed to "Mac") laptops were masterpieces of third-rate engineering. That is, the mice were tacked on in any number of ways, mostly as variations on little clips that made the mouse stick out the side. It was horrible engineering. By comparison, when the Mac laptops came along with a built-in trackball, they were artistry. When you shut your laptop, you didn't have to unclip the clip-on mouse and find a place to store it. Yet, despite brilliance versus Elbonian engineering, which side has clearly won?

All this goes to show you some important points. Having the best product doesn't always matter. Being first doesn't always matter. Twenty years of great products and high standing in the industry doesn't guarantee you a place for life (the examples of this in the past few years are numerous).

What should be exciting (or frightening) for everyone reading this book is the potential for profit and change and the explosive development of exciting new technologies. At the '97 Professional Developers Conference, one of Microsoft's bigwigs showed a chart that compared the technological life cycles of radio, television, and microwave oven. According to my understanding of what was said, all these products have similar growth curves. These curves grew slowly at first (early adopters), steadily climbed for so many years, and then leveled off. For example, either you or your parents (or, heaven forbid, your grandparents) remember when the first family on the block got a television set (perhaps a Dumont with a tiny, round screen). Then, it seemed like everyone had a television, and now everyone has two or three. Of course, many of them are huge and almost always in brilliant color, if not stereo sound.

The curve that Microsoft's exec showed indicated that we in the Internet/Web world are past the early adopter's stage and at the bottom of a staggeringly upward rise during which time every household will soon come to own one or two equivalents of "televisions, microwaves, or radios." But in the case of the Internet and Web, what does that mean?

Certainly, we will leave behind the hardware and network limitations we faced yesterday and even today. Cable modems are promising exciting new speeds, some communities are going fiber-optic, and parts of the old copper-wire network are being replaced by (or are at least competing against) fiber. Then, there are satellites.

Sitting on our desktop—everyone's desktop—are not the junky old 8088s, 386s, or 486s but faster processors with more RAM, bigger hard drives, CD players, speakers, sound cards, and bigger and better-quality monitors. I looked at buying a new PC recently and had to ask myself whether I was buying a PC or a home entertainment system. I mean, you have to have the upgraded speakers, the television and radio tuner, and the bigger and better monitor, don't you? Whoa! Wait a minute. This PC now is a major purchase and has more doodads than the rest of my house. I'll have to upgrade my house to keep up!

But the prices will come down (as they always do), and everyone will have not only a PC but a multimedia PC. Furthermore, I think the revolution will go way beyond that. I'm talking about a browser in every room of every building, on every toaster and bank machine, in every booth in restaurants and bars, and as an interface to vending machines.

At one time, Bill Gates may have dreamed that Windows would be that interface— the interface to the modern world. But I think he has since realized something different, which is why I think he doesn't want to divorce Internet Explorer from the Windows operating system as the Justice Department wants him to. Much more is at stake than just cheating in the traditional way to browbeat your competitors. Browsers are not just another piece of commodity software to be sold on the shelf like compilers, word processors, and sound editors. They likely will be the front end to the entire computer. In many people's minds, it will probably be as important or indistinguishable from what folks like us understand as the operating system.

Imagine Internet Explorer (or Netscape Navigator, or some other browser) on every pop machine, toaster, and TV in the world. Imagine the power you have if you control that front end and the power you don't have if you can't. On the one hand, you have to define the direction; on the other, you have to follow it and hope to keep up. This sounds like the kind of power any company would enjoy, at least until the Department of Justice steps in to the fray.

And if that isn't enough of a struggle, there is the battle between Microsoft and Sun. In most cases, anyone who wants to argue with Microsoft gets left behind in the jet fumes. Regardless of who is right or wrong (or who built the better laptop), Microsoft has a focus on the future and is racing full speed ahead toward it. While others whine about standards and old battles, Microsoft has already leaped ahead 10 battles. That is a luxury of having a powerful and focused chief stockholder (and the majority of the installed base of operating systems). Regardless of what you might think of Microsoft's megalithic powers, its focus and energy should be admired and emulated by all, and its products are (finally, some would say) getting really good.

Aside from the pie-in-the-sky speculating, what does that mean for the Web hacker making scripts? It means that whether you are programmer, a graphic artist, or a technical writer, you will have ample opportunity to make your mark in any number of these new areas. The explosion from 10 Web surfers on every block to 2 Web-surfing tools in every building means an explosion in opportunity; and, while the technology gets more complex, the tools for delivering it are becoming easier to use. The best way to stay on top of it and be a part of it is to keep your hands in the business and, wherever possible, take advantage of other people's homework, like you did with this book.

It also means you will have to pick and choose among the competing technologies and tools as they continually develop. Keep your learning hat on and hold on tight.

Whatever the future, I'd like to wish you luck in this exciting new age. And, when you see the first toaster with a Web browser on it, with clickable regions for light, medium, dark, and bagel, let me know.

Lists Of Links And Resources

- **www.internic.net**—Internic is an organization that, among other things, provides really good Internet end-user information. Be sure to check out its 15-minute series of educational topics (covering TCP/IP, HTTP, and so on—**rs.internic.net/nic-support/15min**).

- **www.netscape.com**—Netscape is currently one of the big three (with Sun and Microsoft) who are setting the directions of the industry. If you are looking for information or want to stay current, it never hurts to check out Netscape's site. You can find references on technology, tips, and information about its browser and JavaScript. You especially want to head to the areas for developers (**developer.netscape.com/index_home.html**).

- **www.sun.com**—Currently the only credible competitor to Microsoft, Sun is the developer of Java and holding tightly onto it. This is another site that you should check out if you are looking for information or trying to stay on top of things. Look for developer areas.

- **www.microsoft.com**—Regardless of what some people say about Microsoft, it has become very good at what it does, and it does almost everything. It has a lot of information, and it is a great site to use to stay on top of things. Microsoft is the leader in tools and technology, and the wealth of information on its Web site is considerable (that is, assuming you're running some version of a Windows or NT shop). For the good stuff, you currently have to register, but it doesn't cost anything and you have to hand over only an email address and some other harmless information. When the system is up, it really provides a lot of information, like documentation, articles, and so on that you can quickly search.

- **www.cnet.com**—Along with other things, like news and so on, Cnet is the best place to find browsers (like Internet Explorer and Netscape Communicator)—even better than Microsoft or Netscape's sites.

- **www.w3.org**—If Microsoft, Sun, or Netscape have their slants, the standards body World Wide Web Consortium heralds back in my mind to the old Internet days, where you had semi-academic bodies responsible for standards. The W3C is vendor-neutral, and it works with the global community to "produce specifications and reference software that is made freely available throughout the world." In other words, if you want to find the latest HTML specifications, you go here.

Appendix A

Top 10 ASP Tips

This appeared in a slightly different form in Web Techniques *magazine and is reused with permission. You can find my Java column in that same magazine* (*www.webtechniques.com*).

Al Williams

Notes...

Appendix

A

Most of this book talks about Active Server Pages in a tutorial style. Now that you know about ASP programming, this appendix might give you some new ideas on how to use ASP in your pages. So, in true David Letterman style, I present my top 10 ASP tips and tricks.

10. Setting A Session Debug Flag

One area in which ASP files are badly deficient is debugging. I usually resort to writing debugging information in the script using **<%=** or **response.write**. The problem is that the minute you remove the debugging code, you find that you need it again.

A better idea is to set a session variable (perhaps named **Debug**) to control the debugging output. For example:

```
<% For x=0 To 10 %>
<% If Session("Debug")=True Then %>
    <BR>Debug: Current x= <%= x %>
<% End If %>
    . . .
```

Then, you can use any of a variety of methods to set the session variable. I like to use a special file, debug.asp (Listing A.1), to do the job. Once set, your debugging code is on for your session. Other users don't see it, and the flag resets when your session expires (or when you abandon the session).

9. Performing Array Tricks

Although the **Session** and **Application** objects look like ordinary collections, they are not. For example, you can't enumerate the **Session** variables using **ForEach**. Therefore, it's often handy to store an array in the object. That should be simple because the objects contain **Variant** data, right? Wrong.

Look at the code in Listing A.2. If you execute this code, you'll find that you can read the original data from the array but that you can alter it. The trick (see Listing A.3) is to copy the session variable array to a local variant, modify it, and then replace the array in the session variable. Although this is ugly, it works.

Of course, the real value to this trick is when the array is used in multiple ASP files or is set during one pass and used in another. In Listing A.3, there is no real reason to store the array in the **Session** object other than to illustrate the quirk.

8. Displaying Forms And Processing Data In One File

One thing I never liked about traditional CGI programming is that you need to store forms in one place (an HTML file) and process the data for that form in another place (typically a Perl script). There is plenty of opportunity to get the files out of sync with one another.

However, ASP offers a better solution. You can easily detect whether form data is present by examining **Request("Content_Length")**. Even if the form data is blank, the length will still be nonzero because the request will still contain the names of the form fields.

Using this bit of information, you can easily put your forms and the related processing in one place (see Listing A.4). If **Request("Content_Length")** is zero, display the form. Make the form submit its data to the same ASP file. Then, when the content length is not zero, process the data.

At times, separate form files could be an advantage. Perhaps you have multiple, related forms that submit to the same script, or you might have forms in different languages. On the other hand, you could easily select the correct form on the basis of a query string or session variable and still keep everything in one file.

7. Using VB5 To Create New Objects

All the objects that Internet Information Server (IIS) allows you to create with **Server.CreateObject** are simply external ActiveX objects. If those objects don't suit your needs, you can write your own. You can use any language that creates ActiveX objects, but VB5 is likely the easiest. For server-side controls, you don't need to create an actual ActiveX control—a simple ActiveX DLL will do just fine.

If you want to know more about this, check out Chapter 13, where you'll find a complete example.

6. Using ActiveX To Learn The Screen Size

Speaking of ActiveX controls, you can use client-side controls to pass data to your ASP script. For example, wouldn't it be nice to know the exact size of the user's screen in your ASP file? You can do it with an ActiveX control (see Listings A.5 and A.6). This trick uses an ActiveX control that you can download from my Web site (**www.al-williams.com**). Of course, it requires an ActiveX-capable browser to work because it uses a client-side control.

Here's how it works. The size.htm file (Listing A.5) loads an ActiveX control that learns the size of the screen. It also contains an invisible form. When the page loads, some client-side VBScript takes over, stores the screen size in the invisible fields of the form, and submits the form to size.asp (Listing A.6). Then the ASP file can read the screen size directly from the **Request** object (just as it can read any form data).

5. Avoiding Global.asa

Usually, you'll want to avoid placing code in the Global.asa file for two reasons. First, it's difficult to make the server reload the page. Second, because Global.asa doesn't generate HTML, it's often difficult to see errors that occur.

Sometimes you can't avoid Global.asa, but with some ingenuity you can often find a better answer. For example, suppose you want to set a hit counter to 500 every time your server starts (or better, read the value from a database). Your first thought might be to initialize in the **Application_OnStart** event in Global.asa, but you can write this code where you want to update the hit count:

```
<% if IsEmpty(Application("Hits")) then Application("Hits")=500 %>
<% Application("Hits")=Application("Hits")+1 %>
<%= Application("Hits") %>
```

By testing for an empty variable, you move the initialization from Global.asa to a normal file where you can see errors and make changes easily.

4. Creating Reusable Libraries With SSI

If you want to make routines that you can reuse, place them in a file and include them using server-side includes (SSIs). For example, you might write:

```
<!--#include file="library.inc" -->
```

3. Using Virtual Tags

If you're worried about compatibility with different browsers, you might consider using different tags based on information from the browser capability object (**MSWC.BrowserType**).

For example, consider tables, which some older browsers don't support. Listing A.7 shows a table using virtual tags. The script creates an **MSWC.BrowserType** object. If the object indicates that the browser supports tables, the script sets up variables named **Table**, **EndTable**, **TR**, **EndTR**, **TD**, and **EndTD**. These variables contain the appropriate HTML tags for tables. If the browser doesn't support tables, the script still sets these variables, but, in this case, it uses characters designed to somewhat mimic the look of a table (see Figure A.1). Of course, this is just one possible scheme. You could change the look to suit your needs.

When constructing the table, replace all occurrences of **<TABLE>** with **<%=TABLE%>** and each **</TABLE>** with **<%=EndTABLE%>**. Make similar changes for **<TD>** and **<TR>** tags. Now the table appears formatted properly for all browsers. If you want to test the layout and your browser supports tables, temporarily reverse the sense of the **If** statement.

2. Scripting Buttons On The Server

What do you do when you want to attach server-side script to a button? This isn't trivial because the button is on the client computer. If the buttons are simple push buttons, this is easy. Simply make each button a Submit button for a form and use the script to determine which button the user pushed (see Listing A.8).

That's fine, but what happens if you want something fancier, like radio buttons? A little client-side script can help out in this case (see Listing A.9). Simply handle the

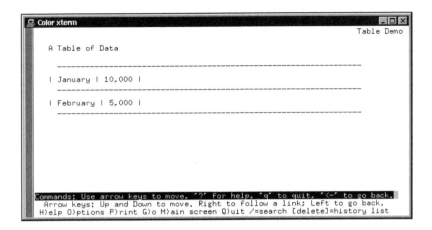

Figure A.1

A table in a browser that doesn't support tables.

button's **onClick** event with a small piece of code that submits the form to the server (the **Go** routine in this example). With a little ingenuity, you can adapt this technique to many different types of form controls.

1. Using An Image As A Histogram

The whole often is greater than the sum of the parts. This is certainly true when you mix the power of script with HTML. Suppose that you want to display some percentages graphically. You might think about using script to create a GIF file on the fly or perhaps using an ActiveX object, but why not use HTML's built-in ability to scale graphics?

Look at Figure A.2. The code to draw these graphs is surprisingly simple (see Listing A.10). The script calculates the percentage of each value and uses it to stretch the width of a 5-pixel-wide GIF file (hist.gif). Of course, if you wanted vertical bars, you could stretch the height instead.

Summary

I hope these tips have fired your imagination. Although the code in these examples uses VBScript, you can do the same things with JavaScript as well. So what are you waiting for? Go write some script!

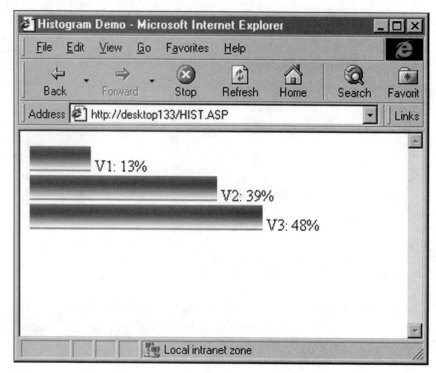

Figure A.2

An ASP-generated histogram.

Listing A.1 The debug.asp file.

```
<HTML>
<HEAD>
<TITLE>For internal use only</TITLE>
</HEAD>
<BODY>
<% If Session("Debug")=True Then
        Session("Debug")=False
      Else
          Session("Debug")=True
      End If  %>
Debugging is
<% If Session("Debug")=True Then %>
 On
<% Else %>
 Off
<% End If %>
</BODY>
</HTML>
```

Listing A.2 An example of a bad array.

```
<HTML>
<HEAD>
<TITLE>Bad Array Code</TITLE>
</HEAD>
<BODY>
<% ' Initialize
   Dim ary(10)
   For i = 0 to 10
      ary(i)=i
   Next
   Session("Array")=ary
' Dump it out to prove it is there
   For i=0 to 10 %>
     <%=Session("Array")(i) %><BR>
   <% Next

' Change it
   For i=0 to 10
      Session("Array")(i)=-i
   Next %>
Making Array Negative<BR>

<% ' Dump it again?
   For i=0 to 10 %>
     <%=Session("Array")(i) %><BR>
   <% Next %>

</BODY>
</HTML>
```

Listing A.3 The proper use of an array.

```
<HTML>
<HEAD>
<TITLE>Good Array Code</TITLE>
</HEAD>
<BODY>
<% ' Initialize
   Dim ary(10)
   For i = 0 to 10
      ary(i)=i
   Next
   Session("Array")=ary
' Dump it out to prove it is there
   For i=0 to 10 %>
     <%=Session("Array")(i) %><BR>
   <% Next
```

```
' Change it
   localary=Session("Array")
   For i=0 to 10
      localary(i)=-i
   Next
   Session("Array")=localary  ' replace old array %>
Making Array Negative<BR>

<% ' Dump it again?
   For i=0 to 10 %>
     <%=Session("Array")(i) %><BR>
   <% Next %>

</BODY>
</HTML>
```

Listing A.4   A self-submitting form.

```
<HTML>
<HEAD>
<TITLE>Form Demo</TITLE>
</HEAD>
<BODY>
<% If Request("Content_Length")=0 Then ' show form %>
<FORM ACTION="ASP3.ASP" METHOD=POST>
Your Name: <INPUT NAME="Name"><BR>
<INPUT TYPE=SUBMIT>
</FORM>

<% Else  ' Process Data %>

Thank you <%= Request("Name") %>.

<% End If %>
</BODY>
</HTML>
```

Listing A.5   Learning the screen size (part 1).

```
<HTML>
<HEAD>
<SCRIPT LANGUAGE="VBScript">
<!--
Sub window_onLoad()
  DataForm.ScrWidth.Value= ScreenMachine.ScreenWidth
  DataForm.ScrHeight.Value=ScreenMachine.ScreenHeight
  DataForm.Submit
end sub
-->
</SCRIPT>
```

```
<TITLE>Please wait!</TITLE>
</HEAD>
<BODY>
<H1>Sensing display... please wait</H1>
    <OBJECT ID="ScreenMachine" WIDTH=105 HEIGHT=83
     CLASSID="CLSID:8528EC66-ACC9-11D0-BC98-00400526DBEA"
     CODEBASE="AWC.CAB#version=1,0,0,0">
        <PARAM NAME="_ExtentX" VALUE="2778">
        <PARAM NAME="_ExtentY" VALUE="2170">
    </OBJECT>
    <FORM ACTION="SIZE.ASP" METHOD="POST" NAME="DataForm">
        <INPUT TYPE=HIDDEN NAME="SCRWIDTH">
        <INPUT TYPE=HIDDEN NAME="SCRHEIGHT">
    </FORM>

</BODY>
</HTML>
```

Listing A.6 Learning the screen size (part 2).

```
<HTML>
<HEAD>
<TITLE>Main Page</TITLE>
</HEAD>
<BODY>

Greetings!<P>
I see your screen is <%= request("SCRWIDTH") %> X <%= request("SCRHEIGHT") %><P>
</BODY>
</HTML>
```

Listing A.7 Virtual tags for tables.

```
<HTML>
<HEAD>
<TITLE>Table Demo</TITLE>
</HEAD>
<BODY>
<% Set bc=Server.CreateObject("MSWC.BrowserType")
   If bc.Tables=True Then
      Table="<TABLE BORDER=1>"
      EndTable="</TABLE>"
      TR="<TR>"
      EndTR="</TR>"
      TD="<TD>"
      EndTD="</TD>"
   Else
      Table="<BR>"
      EndTable="<BR><HR>"
      TR="<HR>| "
      EndTR=""
```

```
        EndTD=" | "
        TD=""
   End If %>


A Table of Data<BR>
<%=TABLE%>
<%=TR%><%=TD%>January<%=EndTD%> <%=TD%>10,000<%=EndTD%> <%=EndTR%>
<%=TR%><%=TD%>February<%=EndTD%> <%=TD%>5,000<%=EndTD%> <%=EndTR%>
<%=EndTABLE%>


</BODY>
</HTML>
```

Listing A.8   Server-processed buttons.

```
<HTML>
<HEAD>
<TITLE>Button Demo</TITLE>
</HEAD>
<BODY>
<% if Request("Content_Length")=0 then %>
   <FORM ACTION=ASP5.ASP METHOD=POST>
   <INPUT TYPE=SUBMIT NAME="Lion" VALUE="Lion">
   <INPUT TYPE=SUBMIT NAME="Tiger" VALUE="Tiger">
   <INPUT TYPE=SUBMIT NAME="Bear" VALUE="Bear">
   </FORM>
<% else %>
   <%   Lion=(request("Lion")="Lion")
        Tiger=(request("Tiger")="Tiger")
        Bear=(request("Bear")="Bear") %>

<% if Lion then %>
  Lions!
<% end if %>

<% if Tiger then %>
  Tiger!
<% end if %>

<% if Bear then %>
  Bear!
<% end if %>

Oh My!


<% end if %>
```

```
</BODY>
</HTML>
```

Listing A.9   Server-processed radio buttons.

```
<HTML>
<HEAD>
<TITLE>Button Demo</TITLE>
</HEAD>
<BODY>
<% if Request("Content_Length")=0 then %>

    <FORM NAME=aForm ACTION=ASP6.ASP METHOD=POST>
    Lion <INPUT TYPE=RADIO onClick=Go Language="VBScript" NAME="Animal"
    VALUE="Lion">
    Tiger <INPUT TYPE=RADIO onClick=Go Language="VBScript" NAME="Animal"
    VALUE="Tiger">
    Bear <INPUT TYPE=RADIO onClick=Go Language="VBScript" NAME="Animal"
    VALUE="Bear">
    </FORM>
<SCRIPT LANGUAGE=VBScript>
<!--
  Sub Go
  Document.aForm.Submit
  End Sub
-->
</SCRIPT>
<% else %>

<%= Request("Animal") %>

Oh My!


<% end if %>


</BODY>
</HTML>
```

Listing A.10   Histograms.

```
<HTML>
<HEAD>
<TITLE>Histogram Demo</TITLE>
</HEAD>
<BODY>
<% if Request("Content_Length")=0 then %>

    <FORM NAME=aForm ACTION=ASP7.ASP METHOD=POST>
Input three numbers:<BR>
    <INPUT NAME=V1><BR>
```

Appendix B

Managing Microsoft Internet Information Server

If you have an NT Server, Microsoft Internet Information Server is easy to install and administer and has plenty of functionality. This appendix provides an overview of running servers, an overview of IIS, and helpful hints for running your own IIS server. It also covers basic administrative issues.

Paul Newkirk

Notes…

Appendix B

Designing a Web site is only half the battle. You also have to put it on the air, so to speak. Sometimes, it seems as if it is as difficult to run a busy Web server as it is to develop a modern site. Before we get into the actual details of administering IIS, let's take a bird's-eye view first.

What Do You Need To Run A Server?

Let's say that you've never run a server. You've read this book, and maybe many others, and you now know how to make files for the Web. However, you've always just given your HTML and ASP files to someone else to stick on the server. What is the process for getting your files onto a server, and where do you put them?

Let's look at this from the perspective of a new server administrator (as opposed to someone who is paying an administrator to host a Web page). First, you must install the server. I have installed three servers: the EMWAC server, the Spry Safety Web server, and IIS. In all three cases, installation was mostly a case of finding the software and responding yes a few times to prompts. (Note: This section assumes that you have a connection to the Internet and an IP address. It also assumes that you have the correct operating system.)

Because installation (especially with IIS) in the past has been a nonissue, and because IIS comes with NT Server CDs, let's assume that you have installed NT correctly, have your connection to the Internet set up correctly, and have an IP address. You have either installed IIS when you installed NT Server (version 4 or later) or you went back and added IIS from the NT CD. Where do you go from here?

Well, let's backtrack once more before we go on. Realistically, you need to install IIS on NT Server 4 with Service Pack 3 installed and have Internet Explorer 4 installed if you are using IIS 4. (Note: Technically, you can install IIS 4, Personal Web Server, on NT 4.0 Workstation, but it limits the number of simultaneous connections to 10, and the administration interface is different.)

Server Root

What's a *server root*? Almost everyone knows what a root directory is. On DOS-type machines, the root directory is usually C:\. In the Unix world, it is just /. There is nothing above the root, but there are subdirectories below it, such as util, msoffice, and so on. Well, just like your machine has a root directory, so does your Web server. The installation process determines where that root is. The IIS default is \INETPUB\WWWROOT on the same drive that holds the \WINDOWS directory. The default for Spry's Safety Web includes the IP address of the server. This was handy for running multiple IPs on the same server but forced you to do a lot of typing.

So, what does the concept of server root mean? Let's say that you've installed IIS, you have your IP address, and you've registered the WWW.BREWSER.COM domain (named after my neighbor's yellow Lab). Your friends and business associates, who want to see your Web site, fire up their browsers and enter **www.brewser.com**. What happens? Their browser calls your server, and your server gives them a Web page. The browser can request a specific page or settle for the default. By default, most servers are set up to return a file called either default.htm or index.htm (or their ASP equivalent) unless the browser requests a specific page.

When you install IIS, it provides a default page for you that is basically an advertisement for IIS. One of the first things you will want to do with your new server is to replace the default.htm you're given with your own top page. Just change their default.htm to another file name (or delete it) and stick your own default.htm in the same directory. You can also specify a different file as your default page, but for now, just use default.htm.

At this point, what can the average Web surfer see at your site? Can they see your whole machine's hard drive, cruise your Excel files, or read your confidential Word documents? No. They can see only those files in INETPUB\WWWROOT or subdirectories below that. Thus, you should put any files that you want a Web browser to see in INETPUB\WWWROOT or a subdirectory. Web surfers cannot go above that directory, because it is like C:\ to them. They cannot see directories above the server root, only below it.

This affects you, the administrator, in two ways. First, it lets you know (for the most part) that you do not have to worry about people cruising the rest of your hard drive if you hook up to the Internet (more on this later). Second, it lets you know where you need to place all your files.

For example, let's say that BREWSER.COM is a site devoted to Labs and their owners. The main page is about your dog (Brewser), yellow Labs, and beer. However, for a small fee, you let other people put their pages on your site. Administratively, how will this work from a DOS and a Web perspective?

From a DOS perspective, the first files on your site might look like this:

```
C:\INETPUB\WWWROOT\DEFAULT.HTM  --your top page
C:\INETPUB\WWWROOT\BREWSER.GIF  --Brewser's picture
C:\INETPUB\WWWROOT\BREWSER.WAV  --a Wave file of Brewser barking
C:\INETPUB\WWWROOT\BANNER.JPG   --a colorful banner
```

Let's say that all these files make up your top page, which includes some text about the site, a picture of Brewser, a colorful banner, and a hot link that you can click to hear Brewser bark. What does the Internet see this site as?

Web surfers come in to the top page, using either

```
http://www.brewser.com
```

for which your server gives them the default page, with the pictures and the sounds, or they enter

```
http://www.brewser.com/default.htm
```

which gives them the same thing.

Now, as administrator, you have your first server up and your first files, and you're in business. Way to go! But you have a couple of things to consider at this point. Yes, you can continue to stick all your files and all your friend's files in C:\INETPUB\WWWROOT. It won't hurt the server's feelings. However, as an administrator, after adding 40 or more files, you might find it hard to keep everything straight.

What's the answer? Subdirectories? Yes, subdirectories, but it is not as simple as that. A little planning now might save you a lot of work later. For example, I once ran a site with five or so distinct subsites. For each subsite, I had a whole host of associated graphics, because I had built each site separately. After the separate sites became large and time wiped my fragile memory, I found myself having to search to figure out where a graphic file was if I wanted to borrow it, reuse it, or change it. Now, you *can* use a tool like LVIEW or Paint Shop Pro to show you little thumbnails of all the graphics in a subdirectory, but that's not the best answer. A better example is a good directory plan and very explicitly named files.

For example, at BREWSER.COM, I know I want to maintain a page about Brewser, and I want to let other people have pages. And, if you noticed the pun on his name, you'll realize I also want a page to burden the world with my opinions about beer. Accordingly, here are some directories I might want to create:

```
C:\INETPUB\WWWROOT\                    --the default root directory,
                                         created upon IIS installation
C:\INETPUB\WWWROOT\GRAPHICS\           --a directory for all pictures used in
                                         the WWWROOT directory
C:\INETPUB\WWWROOT\SOUND\              --for all sound files
C:\INETPUB\WWWROOT\BMOVIES\            --for all AVI and such
C:\INETPUB\WWWROOT\BREW\               --for the beer pages
C:\INETPUB\WWWROOT\BREW\GRAPHICS\      --for the beer page graphics
C:\INETPUB\WWWROOT\DOGHOUSE\           --the subdirectory below which you will
                                         place all the other people's sites you
                                         host
```

So, for example, you create a page called myhomebrew.htm to describe your latest batch of beer, called Northwood Park Honey Stout #3. Where does it go on your hard drive?

```
C:\INETPUB\WWWROOT\BREW\MYHOMEBREW.HTM
```

How does the Web world see it?

```
HTTP://WWW.BREWSER.COM/BREW/MYHOMEBREW.HTM
```

You have five friends, with dogs, who maintain a presence on your server. Dan has a big black Lab named Hudy (after Hudepohl beer). Dan gives you five files for his site: hudytop.htm, hudytop1.gif, hudytop.wav, hudytopjump.jpg, and topbanner.bmp. Where do you stick them?

```
C:\INETPUB\WWWROOT\DOGHOUSE\HUDY\
```

How does the world see Dan's pages?

```
WWW.BREWSER.COM/DOGHOUSE/HUDY/HUDYTOP.HTM
```

Now you have some basic idea of how to administer a Web site, as far as directories and placement of files are concerned. This background information will help you whether you are running your own server, trying to place files on another person's server, or trying to figure out Web sites.

Not too long ago, a friend of mine called me up in alarm. The Web wizard at his wife's company had left in a huff and yanked the company's extensive and important Web site. The company managed to grab the source code for the top page before the blackout but, knowing little about the Web, felt unhappily exposed to the elements with no idea what to do next. On a hunch, I started testing all the links that formerly were on the top page. It turns out, to my chagrin, that the wizard had merely yanked the top page's file from the server (which would be enough to make the whole site seem to disappear if you didn't know any better). By working fast and understanding the basics of site setup, we were able to methodically grab every file and graphic before they were more effectively removed. Then we put them on another server (with appropriately changed paths and links) that same night. So, understanding server basics can be very helpful to you.

Of course, tools like Microsoft FrontPage provide tools for managing a site with a graphical interface. For example, in the scheme described for BREWSER.COM, if you go moving files around, you must manually check and change all the links. If, on the other hand, you use the FrontPage interface, it will let you move files by dragging and dropping, and it will either change your links for you or, at worst, tell you which ones have become suspect since the move. It also practically forces everyone who wants to add files to your site to use FrontPage.

Administering IIS

For the longest time, most servers were Unix based. Although Unix servers still seem to dominate the Web, IIS really is turning into a nice product. It has a graphical interface for administration that makes administration tasks very simple. In addition, IIS runs on NT, which is fast becoming (or already is) a strong selling point to a lot of people, including me. Below are just a few of the benefits of IIS:

- Provides a graphical administrative interface (two versions available in 4—Web and traditional)

- Integrates with NT (lets you administer using NT features that you already know, such as NT security)

- Runs on NT (a very stable and widely supported platform)

- Uses built-in tools and wizards (these can make your administration job easier and faster)

- Appears to be a Microsoft juggernaut (the tools and features being added to IIS will likely continue coming at a pace the other server developers will find hard to match, which means that functionality may spring up easily available on IIS but require custom work on other servers)

Covering all the administrative elements of IIS is more properly the province of a book or a training class than an appendix. For example, you could spend a lot of time learning about the proxy server, media server, merchant server, virtual directories, and virtual servers, and learning how to monitor server information to troubleshoot or tune. When coverage of these topics is needed in the context of an example or explanation for a chapter of this book, they are covered in that chapter (for example, a discussion of IIS debugging in Chapter 9). The rest of this appendix concentrates on providing an overview of the main administrative screens of IIS and some additional information (for example, on security).

The goal is to give you an overview of administering IIS from a "let's get up and get started" perspective and to provide some guidance. If you choose to learn more about IIS, you'll find that its administrative features provide you with many powerful tools.

Classic Vs. HTML

With IIS 4, Microsoft provides two administrative interfaces you can use: a traditional sort of NT interface and a new Web administration interface (that still has a few rough edges). If you have used IIS before version 4, the first difference you'll notice is that, after installation, you navigate from the Start menu to find two options where there used to be one:

- Internet Service Manager (HTML)

- Internet Service Manager

The HTML option is a newer wrinkle from Microsoft, and it promises some interesting things (like remote administration from any Web browser) and heralds an emphasis or even a direction that Microsoft will be going. There are still a few issues to be resolved between Microsoft and the U.S. Justice Department, and now the Microsoft rivals have hired some heavy Washingtonian insiders to weigh in on their side. But if Microsoft has its way and doesn't have to back down too far, it seems like the traditional Windows interface will be going away to be replaced by a new Web interface. This is neat and exciting but also creates some problems.

The Web interface to the desktop, as you now see it, has some rough edges. Why is this? Because the juxtaposition of the context of the Web and the context of a PC has yet to be ironed out. The traditional and original Web interface was designed around files and data; design for applications came later. Yet the Windows interface is still centered around applications. For those of us old enough to remember, there was a time you could load only one program at a time on your PC, and sharing between programs was certainly cumbersome (you had to shut down one application to open another—none of this drag and drop and cut and paste with a mouse malarkey).

It is a different shift that Microsoft and the world will have to deal with. You are used to the Windows interface (you know where the help buttons are and how to open files), and you are used to the Web interface (you can navigate through pages and use framed pages). But what does a Web interface to your PC look like? Does it look like Windows or does it look like the Web?

Here's my guess about the outcome. Where it is convenient for the Web interface to stay looking like the traditional Web interface, and where it doesn't interfere with a direction Microsoft wants to go, it will stay that way. Wherever Microsoft decides it needs to do something different, it will, and the rest of us will gripe and complain and follow along. Or maybe we'll rejoice, if it's a good thing.

But you can see from the Web interface to IIS that Microsoft has yet to standardize it into a new and stable context (give it time; Microsoft's had years to make Windows work sensibly). Many issues need to be resolved in adapting a Web front end or interface to what has more traditionally been the domain of PC applications. One example of this is on the IIS administrative screen (HTML based) for managing MIME types (see Figure B.1). You can alphabetize the two lists on your screen either by extension or MIME type simply by clicking on a button.

But the buttons look like HTML hot link buttons, not alphabetizing buttons. And after you've clicked on one, you can come back to the page later, and the button you previously clicked on might be highlighted (changed to blue). This is correct in the traditional Web context because it's a link you've already visited. But in the PC context, you look at it and assume "Oh, that one is highlighted, so the list must be alphabetized by extension" (or whichever button you previously clicked), which may or may not be the case.

Figures B.2 and B.3 show the two faces of IIS from the top level, called the Internet Service Manager or Microsoft Management Console (MMC), depending on which view you are using.

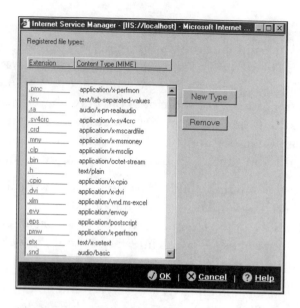

Figure B.1

The screen for managing MIME types shows some issues in the HTML interface.

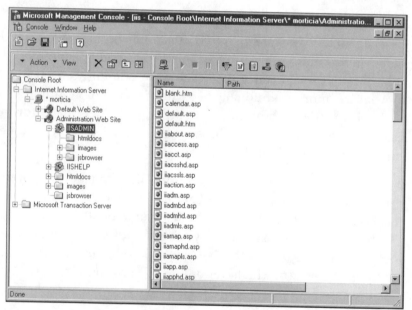

Figure B.2

Use this sheet to manage IIS in the traditional way through the Microsoft Management Console.

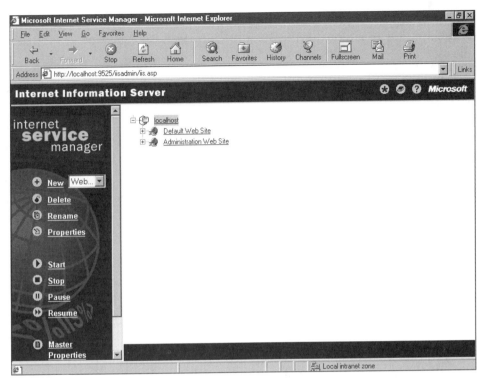

Figure B.3

Use this Web page to manage IIS through the IIS Internet Service Manager.

As I said earlier, going over every screen and prompt would fill another book. But take some time to poke around these different ways of looking at your Web server. Double-click on things to see what happens. Right-click on things to see what happens. Then tour through the pull-downs on the Management Console and the left frame of the Internet Service Manager. In each case, you have two ways to get at properties and settings. I found the Web interface strange and unintuitive to start with, but it eventually grew on me after I used it for a while.

Some Long-Term Implications For Running IIS

If you're not used to running a server, it may not seem obvious, but you'll probably need to leave your server on 24 hours a day, 7 days a week. After all, what good is a Web site that is available only during restricted hours? So, don't install it on a laptop or something you want to turn off, unless you plan to use it only for debugging. You don't need to leave the monitor on (or even connected) to run IIS, so that's one way of cutting down on the heat generated. In my experience, you can leave your server up and running for long periods without worrying about it (like weeks or months, depending on how reliable your local power company is and how prone your area is to storms).

You should probably also set IIS to restart when the machine reboots. If it isn't installed that way, you can go into Control Panel (from the Start menu) and double-click Services. There you will see a list of services on your box, their current status, and whether they are set to Automatic, Manual, or Disabled. Near the bottom of the list (which is alphabetized), you should see your Web server service (called World Wide Web Publishing Service). If it isn't set to Automatic, highlight the service, and click on Startup to change it. (Note, you can also use this technique to turn off the automatic reboot of your Web server if you ever need to, as well as set options for other IIS-related services, such as your FTP publishing service).

Setting IIS to reboot automatically can save you a lot of trouble. For example, if you are out of town and for some reason (such as a power outage) your server goes down, IIS will kick back on as soon as your machine does. You're up and running with little real oversight or expertise required.

Security

Security is a big issue with the Web, especially when you're running a server. The greatest issues usually arise from increased access to your server and its network. This means that if you make your server available to the whole world (as opposed to protected behind a firewall or on a closed LAN segment), you probably have the greatest risk. Not that somebody from work can't do you in just as nastily as some anonymous Web hacker. Still, the outside world poses the greatest perceived threat for most Web administrators.

There are two sides to look at when considering security—NT security and IIS security—and they're closely tied together. You must have a secure NT system before you can have a secure Web server. A chain is only as strong as its weakest link. That said, you might want to just get started without figuring out the full ramifications of security (maybe you have a pretty trustworthy closed LAN segment). The following section presents some things you'll want to look at.

 These security generalizations are offered as guidelines. They are helpful to understand some of the security issues, but any security policies you set are your own responsibility. If you have a safe LAN segment or intranet, understanding the issues is probably safe enough to get a site up and running. But this is by no means

meant to be a complete and definitive guide to site security. Use these suggestions at your own risk, because giving general security suggestions gives me the willies when I think about liability.

Bottom-Level File System Security

The common rule of thumb says that NT is not secure if you use the FAT (DOS-style) file system. So, if you want to run a Web server, you should look into installing NT with NTFS (NT File System). If you already have NT and it is using the FAT file system, you can convert to NTFS using Microsoft's CONVERT program.

Directory Browsing

In most cases, you want to unequivocally turn off directory browsing. You normally want people to see only the files you have set out for them to see. You don't want them to be able to look at all the files on your hard drive (not only for privacy but for security reasons as well). Off is the default when you set up IIS. Of course, directory browsing doesn't allow surfers to break the server root, but they still have no business randomly searching for files on your site.

Directory-Level Security

You can right-click on any directory and click on Properties to set the permissions (if you are logged on as administrator; otherwise, you might not have access to all directories). From here, you can click on the different tabs to see how the permissions are set and then change them. Generally, you don't need to do this if directory browsing is turned off and you have managed your user accounts wisely.

Managing Users

If you're not yet familiar with the NT administrative tools, it's time to get started. They're available from Start|Program|Administrative Tools (Common). In that group, you'll find the User Manager. If you open it, you'll see a split screen that lets you manage users and groups. If you don't understand those terms, you need to take the time to find out. If you double-click on any user or group, you'll be taken to the property sheet. For example, if you click on a user, you can administer that user's account, perhaps disabling it.

Another thing to do is to highlight either a user or a group on the main User Manager screen and click on the Policies pull-down. You can choose Account, User Rights, and Audit. Here you can set policies, such as locking someone out after so many bad logon attempts, or set up auditing. You might want to set up auditing of file and object access so you can track some of what is happening on your site. This is recorded in the NT Security Log (found in the Event Viewer).

One last recommendation, and maybe this is paranoid: Occasionally check out who your users are and what their permissions are. If you ever find one that you didn't put there and don't understand, it's time to fix your policies and change your passwords (and disable accounts).

One other cool and related tool you might want to play with while managing your site is the TCP/IP netstat command, used at a command prompt. I won't document it here (type in "netstat /?" for documentation), but suffice it to say it is a neat way to check your network configuration and activity, showing connections and statistics.

Log File Notes

You can set IIS to create log files of certain data. You can set these logs so that they grow without bounds. You can also set the logs to reset every day, every week, every month, or when the log reaches a certain size. You might run into problems if you don't set the logs for the proper reset rate. For example, if a log refreshes every day, you can lose a lot of data if you fail to check it. If you make it unlimited, you can easily guess how this can take down your system. If you set a certain megabyte size, I've found that IIS will spew errors once the log file is full (and you must go in to manually delete the log files). This might have been a freak occurrence, but, if you get log file error messages, you might check this out.

Tuning Your Server

Finally, you can tune your server in a number of ways. You can throttle bandwidth, limit connections, turn off auditing and logging if it is becoming a hog, and use auditing and logging to see where the problems are. Most general users need not worry about this aspect. For hardcore users, you have all the tools necessary to analyze and correct problems, getting the most out of your server, depending on your individual needs.

Index

D

P

Q

R

S

W

Z

GET ON THE ROAD TO CERTIFICATION SUCCESS

LEARN IT!

EXAM PREPS are comprehensive and interactive (book and CD) study guides specifically designed to work with our popular *Exam Crams*. Our interactive study system goes one step further than other study guides by providing complete exam simulations that really work, plus thought-provoking case projects so that you can apply what you know.

ISBN: 1-57610-263-7 • $44.99 U.S., $62.99 CAN • Available July 1998

PASS IT!

EXAM CRAMS are 100% focused on what you need to know to pass an exam. Professionals, around the world, rate *Exam Cram* as the #1 exam guide.

"I just finished writing and passing my Networking Essentials exam (70-058). I really couldn't have done it without the aid of the Exam Cram Networking Essentials book. I actually failed my first attempt at this exam about ten days ago, and based on the area where I did poorly, I studied this area in the book. Not only did I pass that part of the test on the second exam, I got 100%!!!! I will definitely be purchasing the whole line of books for my future MSCE exams."

—Ken Campbell, Consultant

ISBN: 1-57610-229-7 • $29.99 U.S., $41.99 CAN • Available July 1998

DO IT!

ON SITE books guide you through real-world, on-the-job planning, deployment, configuration, and troubleshooting challenges. This "in-the-thick-of-it-all" approach helps you move flawlessly through system setup, snafus, hiccups, and flare-ups. You'll find unique editorial features including decision trees, special contents pages, trouble-shooting sections, and design and implementation checklists that will help you solve critical problems.

ISBN: 1-57610-258-0 • $39.99 U.S., $55.99 CAN • Available May 1998

WE OFFER A COMPLETE LINE OF BESTSELLING GUIDES FOR MCSE AND MCSD CERTIFICATION PROFESSIONALS.

Available at Bookstores and Computer Stores Nationwide

Telephone: 800.410.0192 • Fax: 602.483.0193
International Callers: 602.483.0192
Please call: 8-4:00 PM MST
In Canada: 800.268.2222
www.certificationinsider.com

CREATIVE PROFESSIONALS PRESS

Left Brain Meets Right Brain: Creativity Meets Technology

"*3D Studio MAX f/x* is nothing less than the instructional tour de force for using 3D Studio MAX to create completely professional Hollywood-style animation effects."

— *Alex Kiriako*, Assoc. Editor, 3D Artist Magazine

Design and Create	Master Your Tools
Intermediate Designer and Artist	Advanced Designer and Artist

SERIES	MAIN FEATURES	DETAILS	CONTENT FOCUS	AUDIENCE
F/X AND DESIGN Design and Create	The ideal creative professional's practical "show and tell" guide. Focuses on creating impressive special effects and presenting unique design approaches. Provides numerous step-by-step projects that designers, animators, and graphics professionals can really learn from and use. Highly "visual" editorial approach with special tips, techniques and insight from graphics professionals.	8" x 10" format High-quality paper and printing 300 to 400 pages 32 to 96 pages of full color plates CD-ROM $49.99 (U.S.) $69.99 (CAN) CD-ROM features interactive design projects and special effects, professional quality art, animation, and resources.	3D tools, graphics creation and design tools, Web design tools, multimedia tools, animation software: Photoshop, Illustrator, 3D Studio, AutoCAD, Director, Softimage, Lightwave, Painter, QuarkXPress	Animators, graphic artists, 3D professionals, layout and production artists. The ideal books for the working creative professional.
IN DEPTH Master Your Tools	Comprehensive guides for creative power users, professionals, animators, and design experts. Focuses on presenting in-depth techniques to show readers how to expand their skills and master their tools. Jam-packed with "insider" tips and techniques and hands-on projects to help readers achieve real mastery. Ideal complement to the *f/x and Design* series.	7 3/8" x 9 1/4" 600 to 800 pages 16 to 64 pages of full color plates CD-ROM $49.99 to $59.99 (U.S.) $69.99 to $84.99 (CAN) CD-ROM features tools and resources for the "design" professional and power user.	3D tools, graphics creation and design tools, Web design tools, multimedia tools, animation software: Photoshop, Illustrator, 3D Studio, AutoCAD, Director, Softimage, Lightwave, Painter, QuarkXPress	Animators, graphic artists, 3D professionals, layout and production artists. Perfect for the working power user.

Creative Professionals Press offers the graphic designer, Web developer, and desktop publisher the hottest titles in the design industry today! Whether you're a professional working for a design studio or a freelance designer searching for the latest information about design tools, Creative Professionals titles address your design and creative needs. The *f/x and design* and *In Depth* series are highly interactive and project-oriented books that are designed to help the intermediate to advanced user get the most out of their design applications and achieve real mastery.

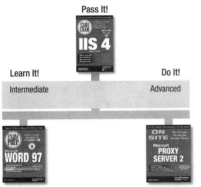